BIG MULES & BRANCHHEADS

BIG MULES & BRANCHHEADS

James E. Folsom and Political Power in Alabama

Carl Grafton and Anne Permaloff

The University of Georgia Press   Athens

Paperback edition, 2008
© 1985 by the University of Georgia Press
Athens, Georgia 30602
www.ugapress.org
All rights reserved
Designed by Kathi L. Dailey
Set in by 10 on 12 Linotron 202 Century Old Style with
Memphis Bold display
Printed digitally in the United States of America

The Library of Congress has cataloged the hardcover
edition of this book as follows:
Library of Congress Cataloging-in-Publication Data

Grafton, Carl.
Big mules & branchheads : James E. Folsom
and political power in Alabama /
Carl Grafton and Anne Permaloff.
xiv, 307 p., [8] p. of plates : ill. ; 24 cm.
ISBN 0-8203-0770-X (alk. paper)

Includes index.
Bibliography: p. [293]-300.
1. Folsom, James Elisha. 2. Governors—Alabama—
Biography. 3. African Americans—Civil rights—Alabama.
4. Alabama—Politics and government—1865–1950.
5. Alabama—Politics and government—1951–
6. Alabama—Race relations.
I. Permaloff, Anne. II. Big mules and Branchheads.
F326.F755 G73   1985
976.1'063'0924 B 19   84-24006

Paperback ISBN-13: 978-0-8203-3188-1
ISBN-10: 0-8203-3188-0

Cover photograph: James E. Folsom in 1962.
Courtesy of Bob Kyle.

To
Jewel Bricker Grafton
Thomas Holloway Grafton
Sophie Czar Permaloff
Allen W. Permaloff

Contents

List of Figures and Tables	ix
Preface	xi
Acknowledgments	xv
1. Origins of the Public Man	1
2. Learning to Win by Losing	14
3. Power in Alabama	38
4. Electoral Success	56
5. Legislative Politics, 1947–1948	77
6. Civil Rights and Remaining First-Term Legislation	109
7. Folsom and Administrative Power: First Term	133
8. Electoral Politics and Civil Rights, 1950–1954	161
9. Second-Term Legislative Relations and Civil Rights	177
10. Folsom and Administrative Power: Second Term	212
11. The 1962 Election and Its Aftermath	226
12. Folsom's Impact and the Web of Power	242
Appendix	265
Notes	269
Bibliography	293
Index	301

Figures and Tables

Figures

1. Distribution of Black Citizens, 1940	2
2. Vote for Folsom, 1942 Democratic Party Primary	34
3. Vote for Sparks, 1942 Democratic Party Primary	35
4. State Highway Funds per Capita	247
5. Public Assistance per Capita	249
6. Expenses per Pupil	251
7. Teacher Salaries	251

Tables

1. House Chairs and Vice Chairs by Regional Base	85
2. Senate Chairs and Vice Chairs by Regional Base	86
3. Malapportionment of the Alabama Senate, 1940	96
4. Adult Blacks Registered to Vote, Alabama versus the South	245

Preface

The 1982 Democratic party primary for governor of Alabama saw former governor George C. Wallace seeking an unprecedented fourth term. Also on the ballot was a legendary figure whose election campaigns in the 1940s and 1950s had helped to launch Wallace's career and whose failure to win the governorship in 1962 brought Wallace to his first gubernatorial term and into the national spotlight. James Elisha Folsom—"Big Jim"—"Kissin' Jim"—the six-foot, eight-inch two-term Alabama governor, had long since been labeled a "perennial candidate," and most people believed that he ran, especially for the governorship, as a reflex action. They would say, "He just can't stand to see an election go by without being in it."

He is blind and still misses not being the center of attention, and running for office attracts reporters in search of colorful remarks good for a corner of the front page. But he also misses election campaigns in which candidates addressed issues that mattered. He does not like television, and he cannot understand a style of campaigning in which candidates are little more than images manufactured by large advertising agencies, appearing before us mimicking warmth, concern, and intelligence, all doled out in thirty-second spots. To him a campaign is a perfect opportunity to go to the branchheads (grassroots) to reeducate the electorate about the need to fight for their rights against the Big Mules (elite) that dominate state government.

He has been working for expanded civil rights for blacks, poor whites, and women throughout most of his career, including his two terms as governor spanning the years 1947–51 and 1955–59. In his last address to the legislature in his first term he bluntly accused the lawmakers of refusing to face the inequity of voting discrimination, reminding them that the Constitution promises equal rights for all—black and white, rich and poor, male and female.

His efforts on behalf of civil rights were not confined to speech making. He actively opposed the 1948 Dixiecrat split in the Democratic party; appointed voting officials who registered blacks; worked for legislative reapportionment on a one-person, one-vote basis; vetoed or refused to sign nearly all of the dozens of segregation laws that poured out of the legislature as it reacted to *Brown* v. *Board of Education* and publicly ridiculed the legislature for passing the laws; gently encouraged the Montgomery bus boycott; and refused to participate in the race baiting that was the leading feature of Alabama and southern politics from 1955 through the mid-1960s. He acted openly in these matters and spoke his mind with a bluntness that would have guaranteed that a lesser politician would never have been elected to statewide office.

Folsom's basic approach to civil rights has remained unchanged throughout his long career. He once summarized his viewpoint with the remark "Women is people too," and then carefully credited Louisiana's Governor Earl Long, whose bizarrely fair-minded "Niggers is people too" he was paraphrasing. Both men were saying as simply as they knew how that all people are equal before the law. For them there was no justification for discrimination against women, blacks, or any other similar group. There was no more to it than that.

Folsom is an interesting and unusual politician. He is an eccentric and a man of principle. He is a three-dimensional, real, living and breathing, flawed, (at once) naive and calculating, funny, sometimes inspiring human being in a time when most government officials appear pale and dull on the two-dimensional surface of a television screen. Almost every Alabamian over the age of thirty seems to possess a collection of "Folsom stories" which he or she delights in telling at any opportunity.

Amusing as these stories are, his life has been much more than a series of humorous anecdotes. He revolutionized the style of political campaigning within the state, going directly to the electorate and educating them about their rights as citizens and government's obligations to them. He served two terms as governor during an extremely turbulent period in the nation's civil rights history. The Dixiecrat split occurred during his first administration, and during his second the South began its reaction against *Brown* and related Supreme Court decisions. Folsom's most famous protégé, George Wallace, broke with his teacher in 1955, ostensibly over his handling of civil rights matters, defeated him when he attempted to win a third term in 1962, and went on to fashion a career which reached all parts of the country. In addition, Folsom (together with other post–World War II governors) presided over an enormous growth in Alabama state government, which, though not as dramatic as his civil rights battles, was no less important.

Another reason for Folsom's importance as a political and historical figure is that he and the civil rights movement represented serious threats to interests that had dominated state government since the late 1800s. Folsom, using one of Governor Bibb Graves's favorite epithets, called these cotton plantation and urban industrial interests "Big Mules," and it was his intention to destroy their power. His efforts to do so, combined with increasingly intense federal civil rights pressure, made the Big Mules retaliate openly, revealing much about the ways political elites function in a democracy. The many pressures impinging on the Big Mules during the period of Folsom's career produced substantial changes in the elite's membership, interests, and ways of exercising power.

This study centers on a man's lifelong passion for politics and the exercise of power. It will be concerned with how Folsom went about trying to get his way, that is, how he sought and exercised power. Individual chapters will concentrate on his election campaigns, his selection of executive branch officials, his participation in the organization of the legislature, his efforts to secure passage of legislative proposals, and his work as an administrator.

An attempt will also be made to evaluate his impact on Alabama. Prior to taking his oath in 1947 at the age of thirty-eight Folsom had never held a state government office of any kind. In addition to being an outsider, the young governor was a raw and abrasive populist and a liberal who not only worked to end voting discrimination and segregation but also advocated sharp increases in spending for health care, education, welfare, and highway construction. Few of these objectives were shared by other state policymakers (especially in his first term), and while he enjoyed greater support among the public, his opinions on government reform and the proper treatment of racial and economic minorities were quite unpopular.

This book is also concerned with the formation of Folsom's personal and political beliefs. It therefore explores his childhood, adolescence, and young adulthood as well as his earliest election campaigns. Included is an investigation of the causes of a deep-seated eccentricity which highlighted the charisma that supported so much of his career, but which finally contributed to his political demise.

When we approached Folsom about this book in the spring of 1973, he promised his "full and complete cooperation" if we would "promise not to do a half-assed job." This is our agreement with Folsom in its entirety. Neither he nor any member of his family has had control over the contents of this book, nor have they attempted to exercise such control. He (and his family) has lived up to his half of the bargain, and we have tried to live up to ours.

Research began in the summer of 1973 and continued intermittently through 1982. We spent hundreds of hours with Folsom and his wife, brothers and sisters, children, and boyhood friends. In addition, we interviewed well over one hundred people associated with Folsom's political career, whether as supporters or opponents. They included governors, cabinet members, legislators, secretaries, newspaper reporters, academics, civil rights leaders, Folsom's subordinates when he was Marshall County CWA director, county electoral supporters, and "men on the street." A number of these individuals were interviewed more than once. Many are identified in the bibliography, while others preferred not to be listed. Since many of the people interviewed are still pursuing careers in or near the edge of politics, the promise of anonymity was sometimes required to conclude a successful interview. We were surprised at the friendly and open nature of our interviews with individuals who had devoted a considerable portion of their careers to opposing Folsom and nearly everything in which he believed. Sam Engelhardt and the late Albert Boutwell were especially notable in this regard.

In addition to interviews, we have searched Folsom's personal and official files, together with the official files of Governors Chauncey Sparks, Gordon Persons, John Patterson, George and Lurleen Wallace, and Albert Brewer and the personal files of others in state government and journalism. Most of these are kept at the Alabama Department of Archives and History, but a few are privately held. They are listed in the bibliography. Newspaper reporting also gave us enormous amounts of information, especially the work of Grover Hall, Jr., Hugh Sparrow, Geoffrey Birt, Rex Thomas, and Bob Ingram.

The pictures that emerge from these sources are usually quite consistent. Whenever our sources disagree and we have been unable to resolve the differences in their accounts, we present the conflicting views and the evidence that supports each position.

Our interview notes and tapes and other documentation will be deposited in the University of Alabama library, and access to them will be permitted at an appropriate date.

Acknowledgments

We thank the many people who aided in the preparation of this volume. James E. Folsom and his family have been extremely helpful both in the time they have given and in permitting us to use the letters and files they have preserved. S. Fleetwood Carnley exhibited special patience and openness in his assistance to us. We also thank the Earhart Foundation of Ann Arbor, Michigan, and the National Endowment for the Humanities (Summer Seminar Fellowship) for their assistance; the many people who consented to be interviewed; the librarians at the University of Alabama at Tuscaloosa (especially Frances Barton, who, with vigor and humor, helped wrestle huge, dusty bound newspapers onto the copying machine); the late Milo Howard and his able Alabama Department of Archives and History staff; the many newspaper reporters whose dedication and accurate work provided so much information; the Birmingham Chamber of Commerce, which provided an office and telephone during interview trips to the Magic City; Debbie Doswell for her typing help; and the late Carol Powell, who provided typing equipment. John J. Boyne's comments on an earlier draft of this manuscript and his encouragement are gratefully acknowledged. We are indebted to the University of Georgia Press staff for the skill and care they devoted to our manuscript.

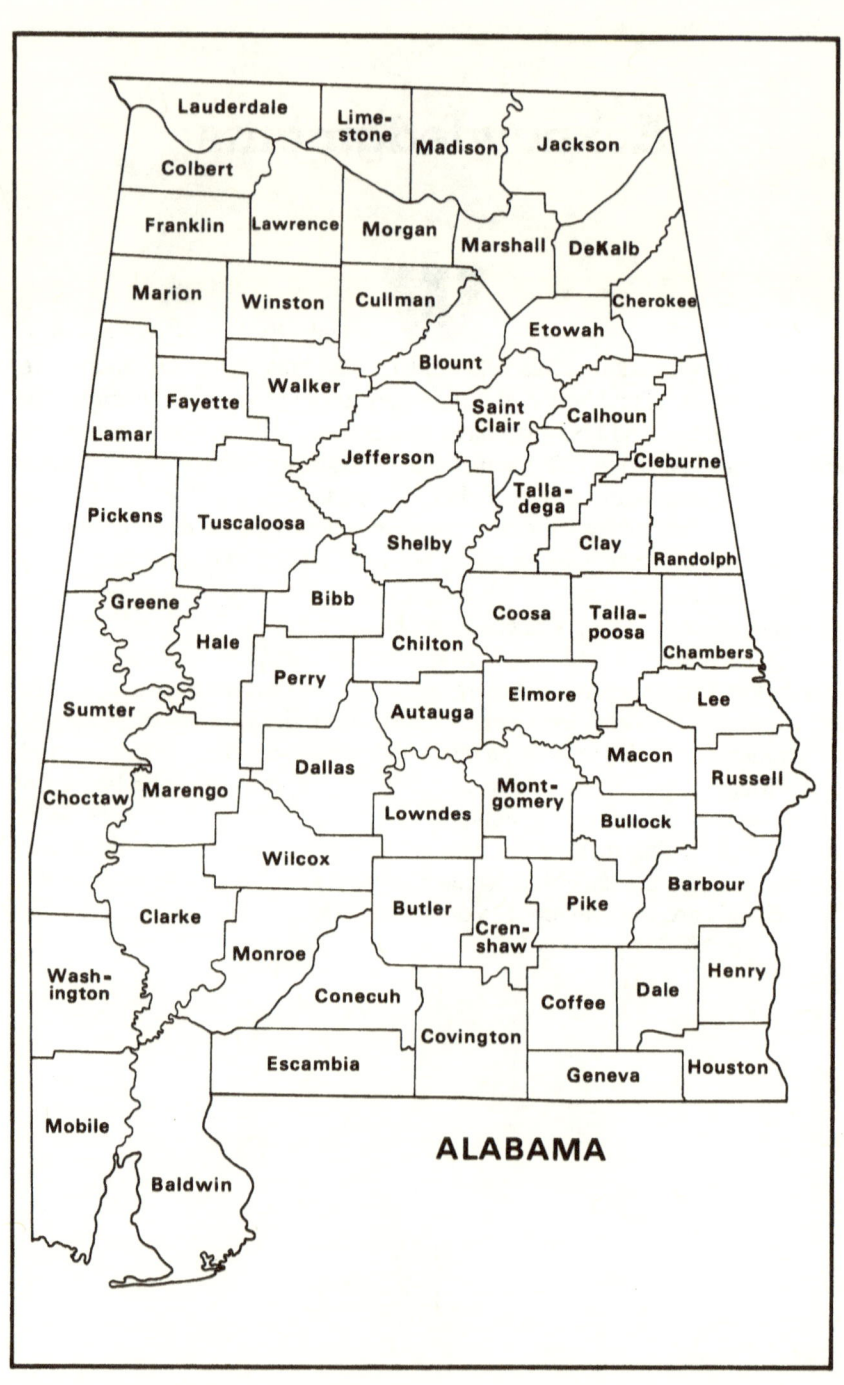

The Old Man laid down some pretty good tracks didn't he?
Andrew Jackson Folsom

CHAPTER 1

Origins of the Public Man

> He was a wire pullin' politician. He never lost an election. Generally, he didn't win by more than just a few votes either. Whatever it took to win. Paw always believed in spendin' just enough money to win and not any more.
>
> James E. Folsom

Many Americans hold an image of Alabama as a place of sprawling cotton plantations and white-pillared antebellum mansions surrounded by hovels—an agricultural state dominated by white landowners and supported by the labor of blacks not far removed from slave status. In reality, Alabama is a state of considerable geographic, economic, cultural, and political diversity. The southeastern section, known as the Wiregrass, has contributed to this diversity.

An area with a comparatively small black population, the Wiregrass borders the Black Belt, a flat band of dark, rich soil running east and west just to the south of Alabama's center. The Black Belt is where the large cotton plantations flourished and where even today the concentration of blacks is greatest. Consisting of fourteen to twenty-three counties (definitions vary), the Black Belt often allied itself politically with four or five southwestern counties (see Figure 1). For a variety of reasons, including poorer soil, Southeast Alabama (the Wiregrass) and North Alabama (the area north of Birmingham) had a different economic base centering on small farms. Birmingham, Alabama's largest industrial center, is located in the state's middle, and Mobile, a major shipping center, is on the Gulf of Mexico in the southwest corner of the state.

In the Wiregrass the Populism of the Texas Alliance found sympathetic ears and strong organizational support. Here too liberal New Deal social and economic policies received overwhelming voter approval. It was in this region that James E. "Big Jim" Folsom was born and raised.

Folsom is as widely misunderstood in Alabama as Alabama is misunderstood throughout the nation. Often he is viewed as a naive and inexperienced, somewhat appealing hayseed whose sudden rise to the pinnacle of state political power was more the result of luck than skill. And his two terms as governor are frequently described only as spoils politics at its

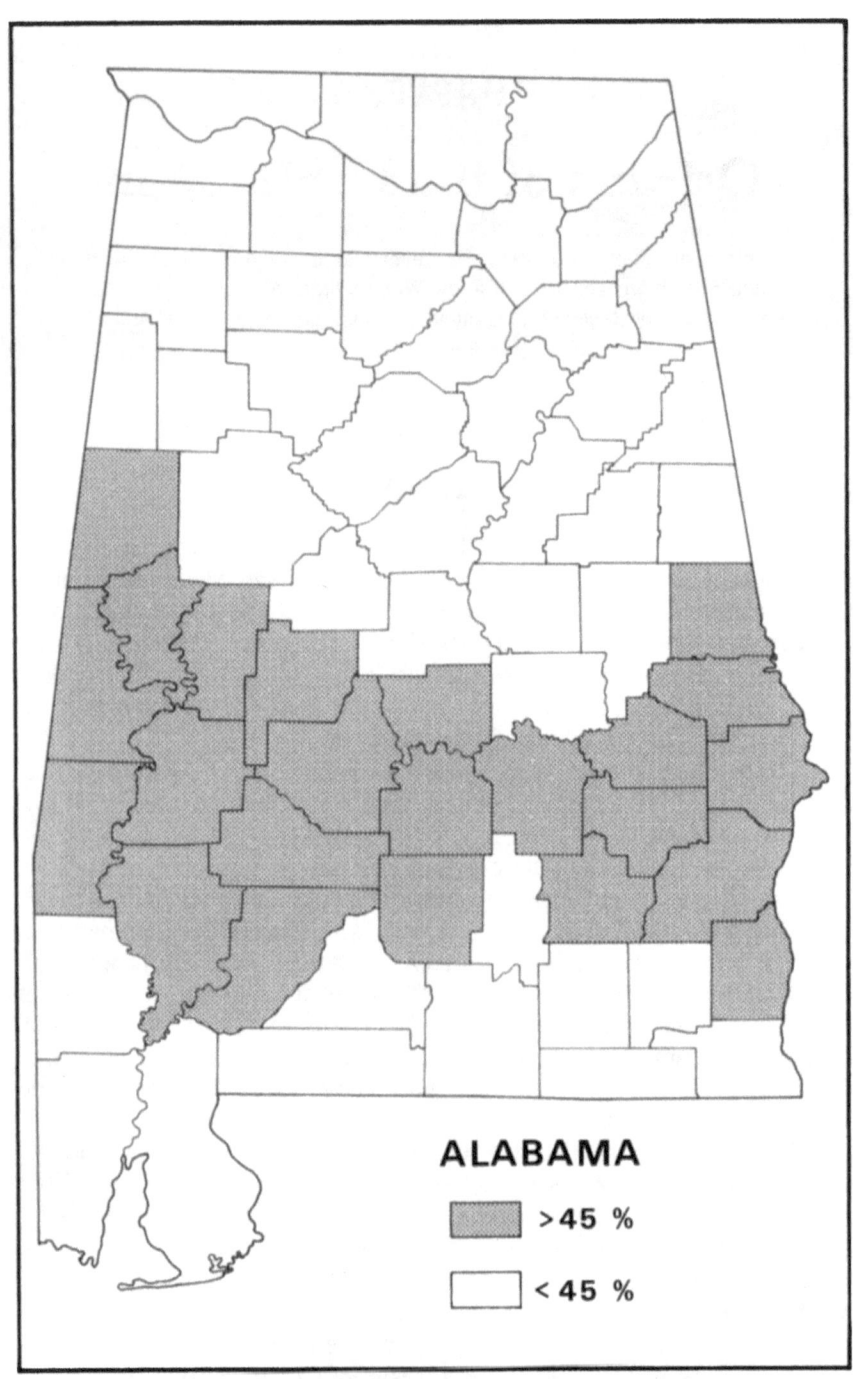

Figure 1. Distribution of Black Citizens, 1940

Source: V. O. Key, Jr., *Southern Politics in State and Nation* (New York: Knopf, 1949), p. 43.

worst. Like most stereotypes, these contain strong elements of truth. Folsom could be very naive. He never held elective office before becoming governor. His personal style was unquestionably rural in its orientation, and he had more than his share of good luck. Furthermore, his administrations were marked by nearly endless scandals. But the stereotypes are also incorrect in many important ways. Folsom was born into a highly political family and married into another. These families reflected various Wiregrass traditions, particularly the populism and racial moderation that later characterized his entire political career. This background plus his habitual reading in politics and history, his experience as a Civil Works Administration county director, and the lessons learned in four unsuccessful election campaigns produced an extraordinarily creative election strategist and a governor whose clearly expressed ideological positions placed him squarely in opposition to the dominant political patterns of the state, which were oriented toward the elite.

The Early Years

James E. Folsom was born in 1908 on the family farm near Elba in Coffee County. Soon after his birth the family moved to Elba, the county seat. There were eight Folsom children. One of his brothers, Alvin, died in early childhood. The three brothers closest to him in age were Robert (Bob), Carl, and Cecil. They were two, four, and six years older than he. His oldest brother, Fred, was sixteen years old when Jim was born. Fred and Jim's older sister Thelma (eighteen years older) helped raise the children; even after they married, they assisted with family finances and served as trusted advisers to the whole clan. Ruby, the baby of the family, was born two years after Jim.

Folsom's father, Joshua Marion Folsom, was a towering, striking looking man with piercing eyes and a thick mustache. He is remembered as a warm, open individual with a lively sense of humor and a keen political instinct. At various times commissioner, deputy sheriff, and tax collector for Coffee County, he was a leader in one of two courthouse rings that contended for power over a series of decades. Joshua Folsom's brother Moses, another ring leader, had served as sheriff until he was murdered in office in 1893.[1]

Joshua Folsom's political ties extended throughout the state. As one of the county's central power brokers, he participated actively in gubernatorial election campaigns, and he carried on a regular correspondence with Alabama congressmen, serving as a go-between, assisting voters with their requests for aid, and transmitting information from Washington to the local county ring.[2] Years later Joshua Folsom's contacts would be very useful to young Jim Folsom as he sought government employment and attempted to enlist for politically important military service during World War II.

Jim Folsom's earliest memories center around his father's political world. He remembers sitting by the fireplace as a young child and listening to his father and his cronies talking politics. "Politics," he says, running the word lovingly over his tongue. "Politics," he repeats, and stares for a time into the distance. "Sometimes I didn't understand what they was talking about, but I sure did enjoy listenin' to that politics."[3] These memories are especially strong because Joshua Folsom took over major responsibility for his son's care when Jim's younger sister, Ruby, contracted a disease which the family believes to have been "whooping cough." Mrs. Folsom had to nurse Ruby through her extended illness and as a result of that effort weakened her own health. So from the ages of four to six, when he was finally old enough to enter school, Jim Folsom spent his days with his father in his father's political world.

Folsom's most vivid early childhood memories are his visits to the county courthouse, riding in the Model T on tax-collecting trips with his father, election campaigns, and the stream of politicians visiting their home. His descriptions of his father are always tied to Coffee County politics, and it is with pride that he calls his father "a wire pullin' politician," a master craftsman capable of manipulating the election machinery of the county to his own advantage.[4]

Joshua Folsom died in 1919 when Jim was only eleven. He died after a fishing trip to Florida, where he drank contaminated moonshine whiskey. Jim was twenty-one before he knew that his father's death was related to alcohol and came to blame governmental restrictions on the sale of alcoholic beverages as the cause.[5] After his father's death Fred Folsom was appointed to finish his father's term as tax collector. A quiet man, Fred preferred working behind the scenes in administrative and organizational tasks to the public demands of a politician's life. After his father's term expired, he turned to other employment and later would return to politics only when his brother Jim was elected.[6]

Upon their father's death the older children helped their mother raise the youngest children. During this time Mrs. Folsom's brother, John Dunnavant, became a major force in Jim's life. Uncle John was a short, stout, happy-go-lucky Irishman. Smart and witty, he made his living from cattle trading, farming, construction, and a variety of other enterprises. He is remembered as both a man of "far-out visions" and "a happy-natured, country philosopher."

Uncle John gave Folsom a sense of the family history and political traditions. A born storyteller, he would recount tales of Jim's Huguenot ancestors persecuted in France and then England for their religious beliefs and of their flight to America in search of personal and religious freedom. He would speak of Grandpa Dunnavant, who had freed his slaves and suffered the wrath of his neighbors and who had opposed the Civil War, only to see his sons fight and die for the Confederacy.[7] Uncle John placed special emphasis on the idea that the Civil War was mainly an economic conflict, a matter of the rich exploiting the poor (both black and white), and he clearly impressed on the boy that the war was a tragic and stupid struggle.[8]

Dunnavant was a Republican who shifted to the Populist party. Folsom's sister Thelma described this action as being "mixed up on the other side of politics," suggesting that Uncle John's political leanings were considered odd in strongly Democratic Coffee County. Uncle John described his trips to far-off Populist conventions and his political beliefs in a romantic, visionary style, as he did his images of the common man and his monied enemies. These tales would later find reinforcement in Folsom's personal and political experiences.

Folsom came to value his uncle's independence in thought and deed, while family members, friends, and other Elba residents saw Dunnavant as a drifter, outside the mainstream of community life. They, however, acknowledged his influence on Jim's beliefs.[9] They also viewed Folsom as resembling his father in political beliefs and style as well as looks. Folsom, on the other hand, frequently compared himself favorably with Uncle John. He viewed his father as "slow and deliberate" and himself as "impulsive." The impulsiveness he proudly attributed to the Dunnavant side of the family: "Go ahead! Get it done! Now! The hell with the consequences. Get it done yesterday. That's where I get my impulsiveness, from the Dunnavant side."[10] And when Folsom described Uncle John's business activities, he could have been describing his own: "He accumulated quite a bit of money, and he'd spend money. Sometimes he'd buy a big tractor and then he'd be broke. Later he'd be back with a fine car driving it through town, and then he'd be broke again. I don't know where he got it from but there it is."[11] Jim Folsom was the embodiment of both Joshua Folsom and John Dunnavant.

Folsom's mother, Eulala Cornelia Dunnavant Folsom, was a deeply religious, unpretentious, unselfish woman who is still remembered in Elba for charitable acts and her concern for the less fortunate. She placed great stress on proper behavior and expected her children to be polite and friendly to others, work hard, do their best, and treat others in a way that assured their dignity and offered them respect. She is widely seen as the "driving force" behind the family.[12]

The Folsom children remembered their parents as stern disciplinarians. Folsom recalled: "Mama ran the house . . . kept the chillun in line 'cause paw was over the county a lot. Papa come home and some of the boys get out of line . . . the older boys. . . . He lined 'em up in the room and just beat the hell out of 'em. . . . he never whupped me but twice 'cause I was the baby. I wasn't old enough to be in the devilment like the others was. . . .

Maw put a finger on me and I was over in the corner, but he never did get me. But Maw would lay that damned thing on me, don't think she wouldn't. The switch. She always had a switch."[13]

The Folsom home was always filled with people. When the father was alive, his political friends were in and out of the house. And the children had their friends and cousins over. Even if no one was home, friends would walk in, sit down, and wait for the family to return.

By all accounts Folsom's early years were relatively comfortable ones.[14] The family was not wealthy, but by the time Jim was born they were doing well and the family was respected in the community. Joshua Folsom had steady employment and the family farm was rented out to sharecroppers. Life became more difficult after Joshua's death. He left only a modest estate; there was some land but little money. The younger children, including Jim, took on odd jobs. The older children helped when they could, but they were starting their own homes. Mrs. Folsom took in boarders periodically, and during World War I, when the family sharecropper was called up for duty, the family worked the farm. They planted, cared for, and harvested their own crop, staying in the sharecropper's cabin and sleeping on the floor.

Friends and neighbors remembered young Jim as outgoing and popular, "nice as can be," "never a superior person." "He always knew people and recognized them. It didn't matter if they are black or white. He recognized them, and if he didn't, he'd ask them who the heck they are."[15]

Jim was not an outstanding student. Indeed, he repeated the fourth grade. His work was average or below average in most subjects, but in history and current events he easily achieved high marks. He had difficulty paying attention to subjects of little interest to him, preferring to read about history and the great political leaders of America's past. Boyhood friends and relatives remembered this reading taking precedence over his schoolwork, and several carried vivid memories of his walking around Elba with a book in his hip pocket.

The College Years

As high school graduation approached, Jim's desire to attend college grew, but financial pressures made it appear impossible. He was graduating in the late 1920s, when the Great Depression was already making itself felt in the rural South, and his mother's financial situation was difficult even with the older children helping her. To make matters worse, Jim did not want to attend just any college; he wanted to go to the University of Alabama, which was then, as now, the best place for politically ambitious young men to begin making contacts. Many of the students were relatively affluent, and fitting in meant having money for social gatherings and fraternity life. But just tuition, books, room, and board seemed beyond the Folsom family means.

Recognizing Jim's great desire to attend college, Mrs. Folsom wanted him to have his dream, but it could only be achieved through sacrifice—hers, the older children's, and Jim's. The older children tried to change Jim's mind, knowing how difficult it would make their mother's already hard life. But Jim was their mother's favorite, and she wanted him to go; so, they worked out a plan. They would scrape together as much money as they could to get Jim started. The older boys and Thelma and her husband Ross Clark would supply any spare money they had. Jim was to hunt for part-time work as soon as he arrived in Tuscaloosa. He was to live frugally, find ways to keep school costs down, and concentrate his efforts on earning good grades. If he ran short of funds, he was to contact Fred, who would coordinate the family's efforts to assist him.[16]

Jim entered the university in the fall of 1927. Mrs. Folsom, taking advantage of one of her husband's political connections, had written a letter to the president of the university asking him to aid her son in his search for a job, and Jim was supposed to contact him immediately upon his arrival in Tuscaloosa. A letter from his mother dated September 16 indicates that he had not done so and that he was not keeping a worried family informed about his activities.

Letter after letter shows that the family finances were tight and that Jim found little work and probably was not searching for it as diligently as he might have. All the family was prodding him from afar, painstakingly explaining all the things he should do, when to do them, and how. (This pattern of advice giving and overseeing his activities is repeated throughout his political life, first by relatives, then by close associates.) Typical of the family's concern is this excerpt from a letter from his mother postmarked September 13, 1927:

> Get your books second hand if you can and get to work. Don't think too much about football unless they will give you lots off your school expenses. Looks like you might get something to do for there is so much to be done. You are not there for a big time. You are there to learn and you should not mind doing any kind of work. . . . W. W. Brandon [former governor] might give you something to do in the afternoons and morning. . . . First tell Mr. Denny [university president] you are there to work and will do anything. I have got you ready and you are there and I don't want any coming home. Wash your own clothes as many of them as you can, and you won't spend so much for laundry. And stay away from town unless you have special business.

On October 3 Jim was still without a job and worrying his mother: "Wonder what your are doing tonight. We have just came from preaching. The preacher preached about Elija's faithfulness. You must be like him, faithful to your savior, to your teacher's studies and everything good. . . . James, if I were you I would work two hours every afternoon. That would give you good exercise, and plenty of time to prepare your lessons. Don't neglect them for anything. Don't go to those dances. They won't get you anywhere. So leave them off."

Several young men from Elba had left for the university at about the same time, and most were having money problems. Lehman Farris had gone a year or two ahead of Folsom. He had his own apartment in Tuscaloosa and ran a hamburger stand. His apartment was almost a flophouse for students and a place where Folsom spent part of his stay. He slept on a cot with his feet hanging over the end, and he helped Farris at the hamburger stand by washing dishes. Throughout this time, Farris remembered, Folsom constantly read "political literature."[17]

Philip J. Hamm, another boyhood friend, was also at the university with Folsom. He remembered this period as a time when he and his friends first began to realize that social and economic distinctions existed and could separate people. "Elba was democratic—everyone was friends—there were no social distinctions. The Dorseys and Rainers and Coopers had money, but there was no social groups. . . . When we went to the university, we began to realize the distinctions. Most who went to the university had money, but there was a group of us who worked." Many students would arrive by train and take a taxi to their living quarters. "But I couldn't take a taxi, first of all, I didn't have the money. I finished buying my books and deferring my fees, I didn't have but five dollars in my pocket, and second, I didn't know how to catch a cab. I'd never seen one before. When the kids would say, 'Let's have a Coke, Phil,' I'd say, 'No I don't care for one.' But I was lyin', 'cause I didn't have five cents to my name."[18] Hamm's account is typical of those of the young men with backgrounds like Folsom's, particularly those from Elba.

Many of these university "outsiders," including Folsom, joined together to work for the election of another university outsider as Student Government Association president. That outsider, Albert Boutwell, was another small-town boy working his way through school and being assisted by an older brother. For him the university experience came after (and during) many odd jobs and a period of travel as a door-to-door pots and pans salesman. Boutwell's election broke the fraternity (and social and economic elite) control of student government, an important symbolic victory for the outsiders. In a transformation to which he never completely adapted, Boutwell later became an important part of the elite's political power structure in state government and one of the ablest opponents of Governor Folsom.[19]

Even though times were difficult financially, Folsom often spent more money than he had, creating even greater problems for his mother. For example, in a letter postmarked October 5, 1927, Mrs. Folsom wrote:

> You have made me so miserable by going ahead and buying that overcoat when I told you not to and you did not tell me you bought the hat charged either. I can't tell you what will be done about the coat. I will pay for this hat when I get something to pay with. . . . Be sure you don't give any more checks for you will be embarrassed and I will too. I'm doing all I can and trying not to spend anything on myself so you will have a better chance than I had and I want you to show your appreciation by doing your best. I spend just as little as possible. You will be thought more of if you help yourself. Have them send your report to me so I can see what your are doing. Don't read books like you did at home.

Thelma was also writing him about his money problems. A March 1928 letter indicates that another check of his had been returned to his mother for payment. And Thelma and Ross wondered what he was doing with the money they had sent. Her letter also indicates that brothers Carl and Bob were without steady work but that Bob was trying to go back into the navy and might be able to help in the next year. In addition, the family still had not seen his grade reports and was worrying about whether the year and their money had been wasted.

Early in 1928 Folsom transferred to Howard College (now Samford University) in Birmingham. He did not tell his family his plans prior to his move, and in early 1928 some of them were still sending their letters to Tuscaloosa. His explanation for the move was that at Howard he had a chance at an athletic scholarship and that Birmingham offered greater opportunity for part-time work. Despite this explanation, the move worried his family, probably because it signified a lack of stability that could spell the end of his college career. Their worries did not lessen when his financial problems continued.

During much of 1928 and 1929 Jim was often completely out of touch with his family. For example, motivated by curiosity, he and another Howard student decided to see the 1928 Democratic and Republican national conventions. So without money and hoping to pick up work in and around the conventions, they rode the freights, going first to Houston. Their Houston adventure ended abruptly on a flatcar in the Houston freight yards. Awakened roughly by a railroad guard, they were given two choices. Either get off the train and go to jail or be put on the next east-bound freight. Choosing the latter option, they made their way to Mobile and then home. Later they did get to the Republican convention in Kansas City. Returning to

Howard in the fall of 1928, Folsom made the basketball team. He also found part-time and temporary jobs in Birmingham, including one at an express company delivering campaign circulars door-to-door for both Herbert Hoover and Al Smith.

Suddenly on March 29, 1929, the Pea River, which flows through Elba, overran its banks and flooded most of the city. The Folsom family home was untouched by the flood, but Folsom and several young college men returned to assist the Red Cross relief effort. He never went back to school.

Drifting

After a few months at home, Folsom hitchhiked to Mobile to sign on with the merchant marine. He relied on friends of his father to help him get on a ship, no easy achievement at that time. His first assignment was as deck boy aboard the S.S. *Quistconck,* where he earned twenty-five dollars per month. The two-and-a-half-month trip took him to Rome, Naples, Palermo, and back to New Orleans. In New Orleans he switched to the Dixie Lines and served as a seaman after lying about his previous experience to win his seaman's license.[20] Shortly thereafter he was hospitalized in New Orleans for surgery on a rupture.

Upon his release from the hospital, Folsom spent one month at home and then returned to New Orleans. From there he shipped out to Liverpool, then Northern Ireland, where he contracted bronchitis, a malady that still incapacitates him periodically. He returned to New Orleans and then shipped out on Coast Line oil tankers, which took him to the East Coast and finally New York City in December 1930.[21]

While waiting for another ship, he went to see the sights and look for temporary work. Eventually he landed a job at the new RKO movie theater as a doorman. His double-breasted uniform overcoat was an endless array of brass buttons from neck to shoe top, making his six-foot, eight-inch frame as much an attraction as the film inside. He used the public speaking techniques learned at Howard to develop a lively patter and attractive style to draw the crowds away from a rival theater. He stayed at the RKO through the Christmas season, when he was fired by the head doorman, who smelled liquor on his breath after a party. He was quickly hired on at the Paramount theater and, except for a short stint as doorman at an Admiral Byrd exhibit, stayed there until he shipped out in the spring.

He wound up in Port Arthur, Texas. From there he hopped a freight train to El Paso and then into Mexico, where his gambling skills made him enough money to stake his way out west, but he rode the freights nevertheless. He made his way to Reno, where he met several prizefighters; then he hitchhiked into the northern California mountains and to Lincoln, California, where he worked as a sparring partner. From there he hitched further north and worked for a railroad, helping to dig out a mountainside for tracks. He then went to San Francisco, where he eventually shipped out to the Far East and such places as Shanghai and the Philippines. The cultures of the Far East particularly impressed him; he found them complex and sophisticated in comparison to their American and European counterparts.[22]

Family letters indicate that he wrote infrequently, but now his mother was less concerned, knowing that he had a place to sleep and enough food to eat. Her letters show she was still taking in boarders and that she had undergone a bout with malaria, a common affliction in semitropical Alabama at that time. Although her concern for his day-to-day welfare was eased, as late as September 8, 1929, she was still wrestling with debts he had amassed while in college. She also began to view his service in the merchant marine as wasted effort. He had little money, no training toward a career, and no prospects for a better job.

While the rest of the family waited for letters, Bob, who made the navy his career, ran into his brother in a variety of strange places. During Jim's New York stay Bob did not know where his brother was, but much to his surprise, he discovered him as he passed the Paramount theater. On another occasion he accidentally spotted a poster advertising a series of prizefights and listing Jim as one of the contestants. The match, which would have been Jim's first, never took place because Jim decided that the risk of facial disfigurement was too great. Bob also found him in San Francisco waiting for a berth on a ship. Jim was standing on the dock as Bob's ship pulled into port. He was hungry, broke, and sleeping in a boxcar. Bob bought him a two-week meal ticket and paid two weeks' rent at the YMCA. He did not give his brother money.

Folsom then drifted and did odd jobs. Weeks later when Bob's ship returned to San Francisco, Jim was waiting for him again. He was hungry and dirty, his clothes were worn out, and his only shoes were full of holes. His fifty-cents-a-week room was full of library books on California and American history and government. Bob again put him in the YMCA for two weeks, bought him another meal ticket, and outfitted him with clothes.[23]

Eventually, Bob talked Jim into returning home to Elba. He even took him down to the train station, bought his ticket, and gave him enough money to live on during the trip. But he made the mistake of not seeing him onto the train. Jim cashed in the ticket and caught a tramp steamer to Panama. From there he got another to Mobile. He worked for free and even had to pay for his own meals.[24] Finally, after more than fourteen months of logged sea duty and many other weeks of drifting, Jim Folsom was home.[25]

Return to Elba

During the early 1930s many young Elba residents were going home. Like Jim, some had left the area in search of work. Others never had a chance to work; they left high school or college with little hope of employment. Folsom began to socialize with a group of unmarried and unemployed men about his age. They made home brew, went to dances, and held parties together. The men were joined by a number of young women with whom they had attended high school. Several had been, or were, schoolteachers with little money. One of the former teachers was Sarah Carnley, who would become Folsom's first wife. Sarah was the daughter of Judge J. A. Carnley, Coffee County's probate judge and a major political rival of the Folsom family and its political ring.

After graduation from high school Sarah attended Judson College, a small liberal arts college for women. She then taught school in Columbiana, where, among other duties, she coached the girls' basketball team. In February 1931 Sarah suffered serious facial disfigurement in an automobile crash following an out-of-town game. The car, driven by the mother of one of the team members, went off the road and hit an obstacle with such force that Sarah was thrown through the windshield. The impact caused severe cuts under her eyes and across her nose and almost severed her eyelids from her face. The stitches required to close her wounds and repair her eyelids left very noticeable scars.

After the accident she returned to Elba. At first she found it difficult to meet and be with people, and so for several months she stayed at home with her parents and her younger brother, Fleetwood. During this time her already close ties to her father were strengthened as she spent hours talking with him.[26] As time passed and her confidence increased, Sarah joined her old friends. Folsom recalled that after a while, he and Sarah "jus' got goin'" with one another."

At first Jim and Sarah would not meet at the Carnley house, for they knew that Judge Carnley was not fond of the Folsom clan. According to Fleetwood Carnley:

> My father didn't like the idea of Sarah going with Jim Folsom. My father was rather an opinionated person—he was always active in politics, sometimes against Jim's father—they were bitter political enemies. . . .
>
> My father . . . graduated from the University of Alabama Law School, and then he came back to Elba and started the practice of law. . . . He didn't get into trouble until he ran for a term in the legislature. The first time that he ran . . . his opponent . . . defeated him, and my father felt that he had stolen it, and he protested to the legislature and was seated. . . .
>
> The Folsoms, Rainers, the Brooks, they were a well greased and oiled ma-

chine, and they didn't like a little maverick upstart like my father comin' in and winnin' like this. . . .

In 1922 my father decided that he would run for probate judge. My father ran and was elected. At the time he ran, there were several attempts made on his life. When he was traveling back from Troy, he was shot at. There were assassins hired to kill him. There was a bitterness attached to all this. His automobile was vandalized. . . .

My father just didn't want his daughter to go with Jim Folsom.[27]

Sarah and Fleetwood finally brought Jim to the house one day. The judge happened to be reading a book about one of his heroes, Andrew Jackson, who was also one of Jim's heroes. When Jim began to speak to the judge about Jackson, Fleetwood believes, his father began to assess Folsom as a person, not as a Folsom. As Jim courted Sarah, he came to know the judge and spent many hours in discussions with him.

Judge Carnley stimulated Folsom's political thinking and later greatly aided him in political campaigns. The two men were greatly different in personal style: The judge was deeply religious, a super dry, and led a clean life and expected everyone else to do the same. In political beliefs, however, Judge Carnley's ideas reinforced Folsom's. Carnley had run for governor in 1930 on an anti–Big Mule campaign with the big power companies, the big banks, and the railroads as his prime targets. The average worker and farmer were the voters toward whom he directed his political messages.[28] Folsom would later seek a similar constituency by using similar themes.

The personal styles and political philosophies of Joshua Folsom, John Dunnavant, and J. A. Carnley had a profound impact on Jim Folsom. The politics of each was set within the framework of the Wiregrass economy and its political traditions. These forces combined with Folsom's personal experiences to influence his entire political career.

CHAPTER 2

Learning to Win by Losing

The old order is dying and the voters are ready for a change.
James E. Folsom

Over the years Alabama has produced a remarkably varied group of election winners: the cerebral civil libertarian Senator (later Supreme Court Justice) Hugo Black; wild, raging Senator Cotton Tom Heflin; respected liberals Governor Bibb Graves and Senators Lister Hill and John Sparkman; the brilliant reactionary Governor Frank Dixon; and George Wallace, who has held the governorship longer than anyone in the state's history. The campaigns waged by these individuals were as diverse as the men themselves, but even amid such rich variety, James Folsom's two successful gubernatorial bids in 1946 and 1954 stand out for their novelty and creativity. He won in 1946 campaigning on a shoestring, opposed by virtually every newspaper and public officeholder in the state, running against two experienced and well-financed politicians. In 1954, four years after a tumultuous first term which few believed would be followed by a second, he defeated seven opponents without a runoff while he simultaneously brought to power a legislative slate that gave him a working majority in both the House and Senate.[1] These amazing victories were preceded by the four electoral defeats that he suffered from 1933 to 1942. In those races he developed a network of contacts, learned the value of careful planning, and became progressively more sophisticated in his tactics. Nearly all the elements of the 1946 and 1954 races could be seen developing in those early years.

South Alabama Campaigns

In 1933, at the age of twenty-four, Folsom ran as a wet for a place in the state convention that was to determine Alabama's stand on Prohibition. His motives for running, and for running as a wet were mixed, as they always would be. First, he was "running to get acquainted," to publicize his name with an eye toward future election races.[2] Even as a young man he was quite ambitious. Folsom's brothers, sisters, and boyhood friends differed somewhat in their estimate of when he first thought seriously about running for high office, but they agreed that by the time he had reached college he intended to seek a major electoral position. Although some placed his firm commitment to run for office much earlier, the letters written to him when he was attending college suggest that his goals were not firmly established even then.

He ran as a wet partly because of the manner of his father's death. Folsom remembered: "I didn't know it at the time, but his death really hurt me and influenced me too—I didn't know it was poison whiskey that killed him until I was 21 years old, and when I found it out I was determined to do something about it, and the first office I ever run for was the campaign for the repeal of the Prohibition amendment."[3] It is also more than likely that he ran as a wet because, having developed a liking for crude homemade wines, he wanted higher quality and more potent libations made easily available.[4] Finally, he saw the Prohibition question as a matter of an individual's right to choose between drink and abstinence, a matter of personal freedom and states' rights.[5]

The scant newspaper coverage and small, routine advertisements suggest that it was an unremarkable contest. Elba residents later remembered nothing about it, and Folsom himself had little to say on the subject except that he traveled throughout the county talking to small groups about the evils of Prohibition and the need to provide Alabamians a free choice. Ironically, his opponent, a farmer named Charles Dozier, was supported by Folsom's future father-in-law.[6] Folsom was defeated by sixty-two votes. Someone less optimistic might have been discouraged by such an outcome, especially since Coffee County voted for a state at-large candidate who was a wet.[7]

A short time after his defeat, using his family's political contacts and by lying about his experience in an interview, Folsom received an appointment in North Alabama as head of the Marshall County Civil Works Administration (CWA) relief program. Soon Sarah Carnley, who had become a Coffee County social worker, also moved north, taking a similar job in Winston County. She boarded at the home of the Frank M. Johnsons, friends of her father. Johnson's son, Frank, Jr., periodically drove her around the county on her rounds. He would become the famous Judge Johnson who as a federal district judge in Montgomery issued major desegregation decisions against Alabama officials. While in North Alabama, Sarah also attended Montevallo College for graduate work. She and Folsom continued to see each other often.

Folsom's job in Guntersville placed him in charge of one of three countywide relief efforts. He worked with a staff of about ten, most of whom he had appointed. Included in the group was an idealistic, intense liberal named O. H. Finney, who served as his office manager and who was responsible for any order and structure that existed in Folsom's office.[8]

Folsom came to his job with an intense desire to help people. His own financial problems and his difficulty finding work had already convinced him that it was the system and its leaders that were faulty, not the average citizen. His experiences in Marshall County reinforced those beliefs as he witnessed the agonies of good, hardworking farmers and businessmen without food to feed their families and without the resources to make any type of living after their farms and businesses failed. What he saw confirmed the populist ideas he had absorbed in his reading and in discussions with John Dunnavant and Judge Carnley. The experience not only reinforced anti–big business sentiments (especially concerning railroads, electric utilities, and large banks) but also helped instill a belief that bureaucratic rules and regulations were frequently the biggest obstacles to the improvement of people's lives. He knew that government had money and other resources and that he was a government representative in an area where assistance was badly needed. He saw it as his duty to get that money and help to the people, regulations or no regulations, and he believed that this aid should be given with dignity because the recipients had earned it through hard work. This view would later lead him as governor to change the name of the Department of Welfare to the Department of Pensions and Security.

By all accounts, he did a superb job as CWA director. He and his staff found or made jobs for hundreds, obtained seed and fertilizer for countless farmers, paid doctor bills, and bought groceries.[9] By December 14, 1933, approximately one month after he had taken office, approximately 500 men were working under his auspices, primarily on road and bridge construction. His employment quota for that period was 1,072, and he quickly reached it. His November 1933 through May 1934 budget was reported as $185,000, not including county and city funds.[10]

Sometimes Folsom purchased groceries with his own money and delivered them personally, telling grateful recipients that the food had been paid for with government funds. He solved every problem he confronted with an application of direct effort. He did not use or possess knowledge of bureaucratic rules and procedures, nor did he apply administrative expertise in any other form. He gave problems his personal attention and wrestled them to the ground. And it worked. "He didn't know what he was doing," said O. H. Finney, "and he was a harum-scarum person, a harum-*scarum* person." At one point he hired more people than had been authorized by his superiors, and this action generated an angry letter from Montgomery. Folsom replied tersely, informing his superiors that people were starving in Marshall County. That was the beginning and the end of his explanation.[11]

Mules, which provided the motive power for plows, were in increasingly short supply, for as their mules died, impoverished farmers were unable to afford replacements. Someone in the nether regions of the federal government, having heard about the problem, sent a number of oxen, or "steers," as they were called in the newspapers, to be distributed free among farmers who lacked mules. Oxen were sent instead of mules because they were less expensive.[12] A few were tried on an experimental basis, but there were difficulties. First, oxen and mules are shaped differently; the straps by which mules were connected to the plow did not fit the oxen. After jerry-rigged connections were prepared, a second difficulty arose. The farmers did not know how to make the beasts move, and once the oxen had decided more or less on their own to move, the farmers did not know how to stop them. Finally, Marshall County terrain is extremely hilly and rocky, and the ungainly beasts tended to fall.[13] According to his staff, the disgusted Folsom, with characteristic disregard for rules, placed the oxen in a corral, purchased two to three hundred mules and brought them back to Marshall County by train, and shipped the oxen to district administrators. He took all these actions without authorization.[14]

Folsom's Marshall County days did not earn him the approval of his superiors, but did produce some important rewards. First, his populist ideas flowered, now based on personal observation and not just legends and historical accounts. Second, a loyal and dedicated staff, especially O. H. Finney, who would share future political wars and governmental responsibilities with him, had developed personal commitments to him as their leader. Third, he formed a political power base outside South Alabama. Those whom he had aided and treated with real concern for their personal dignity felt gratitude, and that gratitude translated into support that would help him to electoral victories.

His political connections and his support base in Marshall County probably made it awkward for his superiors to fire him. In 1934 he was eased out when the Marshall County CWA office was closed in a reorganization.[15] According to the *Sand Mountain Banner*, this change resulted in the removal of many needy people from relief rolls.[16]

The next year Folsom traveled to Washington without any prospects of a job. At Works Progress Administration (WPA) headquarters he told administrators of his "experience on the ground" as county administrator and was hired immediately. He would remain in Washington for six months.

He became a statistical clerk in the office of the head of the Project Control Division. The office made major decisions on placing work projects, which made it an excellent location for meeting and helping political influentials, especially congressmen seeking aid for their districts. Folsom also made it a point to move around Washington introducing himself to fellow

Alabamians both in the executive departments and in Congress. One person he came to know quite well was Frank Boykin, a newly elected Alabama congressman. Boykin was also trying to find his way around Washington, and he discovered in Folsom a useful source of information especially concerning potential work projects for his district.

During this time in Washington, Folsom lived at the YMCA. One of the Washington-area universities operated a night law school at the Y, and, while not formally enrolled, he sat in on many of the lectures. He also took a public speaking course at George Washington University.

After about six months, he lost his job as the result of another reorganization. So, early in 1936 he returned to Elba and ran for Congress. He portrays the decision to run as a rather simple one: "I got fired in Washington, came down to Alabama and me and my brother [Carl] got enough to qualify. . . . Hell, I was as damn good as anybody else. I could run just as good as anybody could. And another thing. I was already in welfare work. I was always for the old age pension—old age movements were at work—spread to Alabama. Lots of People here [Elba] pushed me to run. Me and my brother talked that over—went up to Troy and borrowed the qualifying fee. . . . Hell, I never did have anything. I haven't got it now."[17] To pay the two-hundred-dollar qualifying fee and to cover initial campaign expenses, Carl cosigned over four hundred dollars in loans, for he, not Jim, had a job that would make the loans possible. (Six years later, a friend cosigned another note to raise the filing fee for the governor's race, even though Folsom's insurance business was flourishing. He may have been temporarily short of funds or he may have been testing his friend's sincerity.)

Folsom sought to displace the powerful chairman of the House Banking and Currency Committee, New Deal Congressman Henry B. Steagall. While the *Elba Clipper,* Folsom's hometown newspaper, described "Long Jim's" candidacy as a "bombshell on the camp of the opposition," the venerable lawmaker was not deeply concerned.[18] In addition to enjoying all the advantages of an incumbent who was chairman of one of the most important committees in Congress, he was extraordinarily popular throughout his district. One Coffee County resident told the authors that she was a teenager before she realized that "Uncle Henry," as he was known by many, was not really her uncle by marriage or blood.[19] Uncle Henry was unbeatable.

Why did Folsom select such an awesome opponent? He was, once again, running to get acquainted. Covering a much wider geographical area (nine counties) than his first race, this campaign would receive the attention of the states major political newspaper, the *Montgomery Advertiser.* Also, he wanted the experience of conducting a relatively large-scale campaign.[20] Finally, considering Steagall's relatively advanced age and a serious illness that had plagued him for well over a year, there was a possibility that he would die between the filing deadline and the election, thus giving Folsom a strong chance.[21] When Folsom informed a friend that he was filing against Steagall, his friend said, "You ought to have better sense than that." Folsom retorted, revealing a cold-blooded streak that occasionally surfaced, "If that ole man falls dead, I'd win."[22]

Some Coffee County residents opposed Steagall out of a populist-bred feeling that he was too close to bankers (he was largely responsible for legislation creating the Federal Deposit Insurance Corporation), but Folsom had few real objections to the congressman.[23] He later said that he ran mainly because of personal ambition. This should not be interpreted to mean that Folsom did not take the campaign seriously. His state of mind during one part of the 1936 race is indicated by this letter to local campaign managers: "Please disregard any attempt of any of our half dozen Elba opponents to belittle our campaign. They are either jealous, fit subjects of the insane asylum; or they have sold their birthright for a mess of pottage. Such tactics are further proof that the old order is dying and the voters are ready for a change. Work harder as we have something to work for."[24]

The Folsom campaign attacked Steagall from the left. The Townsend Plan, which would have provided generous financial assistance to the aged, and the Frazier-Lemke Farm Refinancing Plan, which sought to lower interest rates on farm loans, were the centerpieces of a platform that also included federal aid to education, paved farm-to-market roads, improved flood control, expanded farm relief, easier rural credit, and accelerated rural electrification, a standard set of programs for a populist in the mid-1930s. Huey Long had achieved wide popularity promoting similar ideas, and while the Townsend movement was beginning to disintegrate, it was still large and influential, especially in the rural South. A week after Folsom announced his candidacy a Townsend Club numbering 114 members was organized in Elba at a courthouse meeting. The group listened to addresses by organizers from Montgomery and San Francisco who urged the fledgling Townsendites to support Folsom, "the Tall Sycamore."[25] As of April 6, 1936, there were thirteen Townsend Clubs in the Third Congressional District, and by the end of April there were seventeen.[26]

Folsom campaign files indicate a strong symbiotic relationship between Folsom and the Townsendites. As we have seen, Folsom grew up in an atmosphere redolent with populist ideas, and university life reinforced his populist outlook by providing him with sympathetic and stimulating professors and a large supply of books. College also sparked a note of jealousy as he compared the differences between the elegant existence of students from wealthy homes with the scrape-to-make-ends-meet subsistence of those like himself. His populist orientation was reinforced still more by his talks with Judge Carnley and his work in Marshall County.

Folsom's campaign treasury was far short of the money that would have been required to defeat Henry B. Steagall. His brother Carl provided the largest amounts, and O. H. Finney the second largest ($100 from a loan). The expenses listed with the Alabama secretary of state totaled only $685.43, although this figure is probably low. Money problems were countered to some degree by a combination of energy and political sophistication. Folsom himself supplied much of the energy as he drove the bumpy, unpaved roads, knocking on doors, sometimes panhandling cornbread and buttermilk, holding small rallies, and attending church meetings. But Carl Folsom also did a great deal of traveling, and he wrote hundreds of letters and served as office manager. Carl was an excellent source of contacts throughout the district. Having worked for the railroads, the state, and various business concerns in the late 1920s and 1930s and possessing an agreeable personality, Carl had many friends beyond the confines of Coffee County. In many ways like his father, he had a humor and an outgoing nature that helped him quickly fit into any community or group he entered. Folsom's sister Thelma Clark, Coffee County Tax Collector J. M. Garrett, Philip Hamm, and Eris Paul also devoted much time and energy to the effort.[27]

O. H. Finney worked on the campaign from Albertville in North Alabama. He typed hundreds of letters to potential voters, working at home in the evening with occasional help from other former CWA personnel. Letters from Finney to Folsom give us insight into Folsom's organizational and management tendencies that persisted throughout his career. There is, for example, this undated letter from Finney to Folsom in the 1936 campaign files (saved by Carl Folsom and preserved by Thelma Clark):

> I am sending with this the list of Bullock Co. voters. I will be out of stationery by the time I get through with Lee County and Sarah said that the rest of the letters were to be put on union stationery and to send her the lists and she would finish up. I can't have union stationery made up here.
>
> I will mail the remainder of Lee County letters the last of next week. Do you want me to send all of the lists that I have been writing?
>
> About the clauses—I have only been writing just what you told me to. I admit that the letters have been poorly constructed but I was trying to follow through with your instructions as much as possible. Everything that we used was used by Lister Hill and Frank Dixon. The clause that you made reference to so much was one of Hill's favorite ones. You see you send me a form and then when I write say 500 or 1,000 letters you come back and say that it won't do when I have already quit using that form and etc. I really can't understand you. The last form that you sent me from Auburn is terrible. Surely you wouldn't want it to go out like that. I changed it around a little. Vivian has been helping me some and she made a few suggestions too. See if you like the form enclosed and if not please let me know immediately before I finish up these 4 or 5 hundred letters from Lee County.

I hope you are not too over-confident. Of course, James we all expect you to be in the run-off without fail but you must remember the vote that you get in the first primary will determine largely the vote you receive in the second primary. I hope that you don't get too "cocky".

Now James remember this please. The Campaign is only four weeks more. The election officers will be elected around the 20th I imagine. You are going to be more busy than ever speaking and etc. Last minute letters of several thousand cannot be turned out in the last few days without a great many people working. It takes a week for me working every night to turn out 400 or 500. If you plan any last minute letters please be thinking about them now if you expect me to do them.

The third and fifth paragraphs of this letter are particularly important. They reveal a Folsom who can change his mind often and a Folsom who has not been personally concerned with details of implementation but notices them after they have been attended to by others and then responds to mistakes. In addition, the letter has the same stern instructional tone of many of those written to young Jim by his family in 1928–29. Once again, someone else is reminding him what to do, when, and how. Those close to Folsom adopted this role over and over again, but the years gradually stripped away people willing to undertake this arduous task.

The 1936 campaign marked the first time that the Folsom-Rainer and Carnley rings backed the same candidate. Judge Carnley's support was based on two factors. First, he had discovered many philosophical similarities between himself and Jim during their talks. Second, he and Sarah were very close. She could make the somber "Bull Dog" smile, and she made him recognize the positive side of Jim Folsom.

Judge Carnley wrote letter after letter to his friends and political supporters. He wrote to public officials in the district, and he authored long guest editorials in local newspapers. The judge's letters and editorials stressed Folsom's background in one of the "pioneer families of Coffee County"; his "sterling character and ability"; his platform; and his rural yeoman and nonpolitical beginnings.[28] In a speech on the Elba courthouse steps Judge Carnley attacked Steagall as having spent his entire career in Congress working on behalf of banking interests. "What we need," he declared, "is a man who will represent us and not Wall Street."[29]

Carnley and Folsom shared some election campaign characteristics. In his pursuits of public office (the state legislature and the governorship, among others) Carnley frequently seemed to ignore opponents, preferring to concentrate on long, complex analyses of such matters as the abuse of corporate power and the faults of Alabama's regressive tax system.[30] Folsom shared the judge's penchant for detailed, ideologically charged explanations of and prescriptions for public policy. Both men saw campaigns as opportunities for educating the electorate; they tried to sensitize working people to their victimization at the hands of the Big Mules—the electric utilities, steel companies, and plantation owners—who they believed dominated state government. The major difference between Folsom and Carnley was stylistic. Carnley favored a somewhat heavy, pedagogical approach, which Folsom seemed to emulate in his early campaigns but later abandoned. Folsom's handwritten notes for those early stump speeches and a small number of radio talks (approximately five) are very stiff and formal.

This campaign featured more than just hard work; it operated at a level of sophistication not remembered even by Folsom, Thelma Clark, Hamm, or Eris Paul. They conducted a great deal of research. At Folsom's request, staff members at the national office of the Brotherhood of Railroad Trainmen compiled and analyzed Steagall's voting record. Other research was performed for Folsom by people in Washington, D.C., whom he had met during his short employment there. The following items found in the files illustrate the kind of information being gathered: copies of legislation that Steagall originated or cosponsored; data on Steagall's income and expense allowances (for comparison with Townsend Plan pensions, which the congressman had voted against); copies of newspaper columns on Steagall; various states' old-age assistance laws; pamphlets for various interest groups, especially those representing farmers and Townsendites; materials on the Frazier-Lempke Bill; newspaper articles that could be worked into speeches; and lists of voters categorized by groups, such as city and county officials, veterans, women, doctors, undertakers, fertilizer dealers, farmers, farm co-op managers, cotton buyers, "traveling men," county agents, home agents, insurance men, Democratic party executive committee members in each county, election officials, absentee voters, and bankers.

Little of this information went unused. Letters were sent to each voter in the above categories from whoever had the best chance of reaching them. Folsom, using the letterhead stationery of the Emergency Aid Life Association, of which he was part owner, wrote a letter which began, "As one insurance man to another . . ." Sarah wrote to women, Judge Carnley to judges, the Coffee County tax collector to tax collectors, and so forth. O. H. Finney arranged for O. L. West, president of Local 2093 (North Alabama) of the United Textile Workers to write letters (which Finney typed on the union's letterhead stationery) to South Alabama workers which said in part: "[Folsom] was here during our battle last summer a year ago and worked most of our men on relief work during the strike. Mr. Folsom was sympathetic and helped us in our battle in every way that he could."[31]

Compared to Steagall, Folsom had relatively few courthouse and interest group endorsements, but Folsom, Rainer, and Carnley family connections constituted an impressive network. Folsom had people in virtually every town to whom he could write a short note asking them to arrange for a rally on a certain time and date.

Letters flowed into as well as out of the Folsom campaign headquarters. Many offered moral support, optimistic estimates of conditions in their part of the district, or reports on their activities. Others asked for money to spend on Folsom's behalf, and sometimes a little, averaging three dollars, was sent. A considerable number of letters promised support in return for favors, such as employment for a son. One came from a hospitalized man asking for "a little help to buy my medicine," and another from a woman who asked for ten dollars to assist her mother who was about to enter a hospital. One wanted money ("Hon. H. B. Steagall paid $5.00") to buy song books for a Sacred Harp singing group in Ozark. And some wanted Folsom to pay their poll tax so they could vote for him.

Folsom's challenge to Steagall came at a particularly difficult time for the infirm congressman, and early in the year, when Folsom was still testing the electoral waters but before he had filed for the primary, he was offered a job in Washington paying three hundred dollars per month in exchange for his promise not to run.[32] The offer was extended indirectly via Congressman Frank Boykin of Mobile. The reason for Boykin's involvement was made clear in a letter to Folsom from Ernie W. Wagar of Alexandria, Virginia, dated March 2, 1936: "Please do not ruin your future by trying politics, your age will not permit it, those that are telling you will make you feel foolish afterwards, it not only will hurt you but the party opposing you may greatly interfere with the future of your wonderful friend, Frank W. Boykin. . . . Your opponent may have the wrong idea and it would be very easy for him to interfere in Congressman Boykin's district on account of you."[33] It would have been easy for Steagall to conclude that Boykin had encouraged Folsom, since the conservative Mobile congressman so often voted against Steagall on the House floor.[34]

When the job offer was rejected, Boykin apparently called with a better one, and he simultaneously threatened the jobs of J. Ross Clark, Folsom's brother-in-law, and his brother Fred, both of whom were employed by the Alabama Seed Loan program.[35] One telegram from Boykin to Folsom dated February 28, 1936, reads: "Mr. Crowley asked me to have you report at once [to Washington, D.C.] for position had fine conference and everything made for love come on back as we miss you advise regards."[36] "Everything is made for love" was Boykin's all-purpose life slogan. Another telegram quoted in a Folsom press release apparently read:

> Hon. Gaston Scott, Montgomery, Alabama. Have just heard that James Folsom of Elba intended to file against Congressman Henry Steagall tomorrow. We have gotten James a fine position of Three Hundred Dollars a month, good

permanent position. I have just talked to Folsom at Elba and told him I thought he was making a mistake and I know he is. Folsom's brother lives in Montgomery and is the Seed Loan Man. Get a hold of him tonight and have him stop James and send him on back here to get this good position. If you cannot go down there, telephone James. This needs fast action and will be helpful to both Steagall and Folsom. Please advise results. Regards, Frank W. Boykin, M.C.[37]

It was also suggested to Folsom that Steagall would be named to a federal judgeship before the 1938 primary; if Folsom pulled out in 1936, it was said, Steagall would support him in 1938.[38]

Steagall campaigned as vigorously as his precarious health would permit and advertised widely. His newspaper ads emphasized three points: his position in Congress; his achievements (which were considerable); and his consistent support for and access to President Roosevelt.[39] Subtly in his ads and more openly in personal appearances, the congressman isolated Folsom on the far left, suggesting gently that the Townsend Plan and the other planks in the Folsom platform were not to be taken seriously. Steagall also stressed Folsom's youth and the fact that the young man was not a lawyer.[40]

Something about the mammoth, handsome young man must have appealed to the voters because he polled 38 percent in the district as a whole and in Coffee County defeated Steagall 1,983 to 1,216, a respectable showing against such an opponent.

On Christmas Day, 1936, Jim Folsom and Sarah Carnley were married at Judge Carnley's home. Soon Folsom and his family began to prepare for a rematch with the venerable congressman in 1938. He also turned his attentions to making a living. Ross Clark, together with relatives and a few close friends, had organized the Emergency Aid Insurance Company, which specialized in burial insurance. Folsom set to work as agent for the new organization. His sales trips expanded his personal contacts throughout the Wiregrass. At that time he and Sarah lived with the Carnley family, allowing him to continue his long political discussions with the judge.

The 1938 campaign was largely a repeat of the 1936 race: the same people were active (with Sarah's role even larger); the two Coffee County courthouse rings gave their support; and Folsom campaigned on the same platform. A handwritten draft of his 1938 announcement of his candidacy reveals the same stiffness that characterized his 1936 speeches and newspaper advertisements:

> Every man is said to have his peculiar ambition. I can say for one, that I have none so great as that of being truly esteemed by my fellow man, by rendering my self worthy of that esteem. How far I shall succeed in gratifying that ambition is yet to be developed. I am young only twenty nine. I was born and have ever remained in the most humble walk of life. [*crossed out*: I have no wealthy friends or great newspapers to recommend me.] My case is thrown exclusively

upon the voters who believe in democratic government and not perpetual officeholders; and if elected they will have conferred a favor upon me for which I shall be unremitting in my labors to compensate.[41]

The 1938 campaign had the same high energy level that characterized the 1936 race, and it was run with the same careful attention to detail. The campaign files contain checklists for newspaper advertisement placement, motorcade scheduling, signs for motorcades, sending letters to various categories of voters, and paying bills for the telephone, rent, radio time, and newspaper space. Despite these efforts, Steagall defeated Folsom by an even greater margin in 1938 than he had in 1936.

Uniting the White Counties

After the 1938 defeat, Ross Clark asked Folsom to become the insurance company's North Alabama representative. So in 1938 he moved to Cullman, the county seat of Cullman County, in the center of the populist north and adjoining Marshall County, where he had served as CWA director.

To comprehend the significance of Folsom's move to North Alabama, one must understand the political similarity of the northern and southeastern counties and the importance of localism in Alabama statewide elections. The Wiregrass was characterized by small farms, relatively few blacks, and strong populist traditions. A similar tradition, described below by Virginia Van der Veer Hamilton, was even more intensely defined in North Alabama.

> Although they owned few slaves, if any, the overwhelming majority of these yeomen fought for the Confederacy. Yet Alabamians, accustomed to thinking of Confederate loyalty in their state as monolithic, are sometimes surprised to discover forebears who donned the Confederate gray only reluctantly, deserted the Southern cause, or even served in the Union Army.
>
> Glancing back at the political heritage of their ancestors, folk historians might well be skeptical of the old saw that Grandpa always voted the straight Democratic ticket. . . . During the 1890s plain citizens erupted in angry revolt against the Democratic leadership and would have seated a party rebel in the governor's chair had their votes been fairly counted. To envision all the ancestors as stubborn conservatives is also risky. The odds are strong that many of one's forebears . . . took part in turbulent movements such as the Grange, the Farmers' Alliance, or a brand of Populism known as "Jeffersonian Democrats," and in their day were considered radicals.[42]

When he moved to Cullman, Folsom was fully aware of the electoral potential inherent in having two homes bracketing the state's conservative midsection.[43] On first acquaintance, Folsom does not convey the impression of someone temperamentally suited for such long-range thoughts. Over the years he had found it profitable to project an image of bucolic naiveté laced with nonstop political sermons, history lessons, and humor, which lulled opponents into a false sense of security. Although his unique image worked for him, it caused endless vexation and torment among his supporters, who were never sure where naiveté ended and calculation began. Nor did most of them understand the personal importance to him of the sermons and history. Worst of all, perhaps, they never knew when the humor that served him so well would shade off into uncontrollable fits of self-destructive zaniness. But he was at times capable of brilliant long-range planning, and at the beginning of his career his opponents did not appreciate this ability until it was too late.

The importance of localism, or "friends and neighbors politics," in Alabama during this era was carefully analyzed by V. O. Key.[44] Localism means that voters have a strong tendency to vote for statewide candidates from or near their own counties. Localism is an important factor in most states, but it was especially so in Alabama because, aside from north-central-south sectionalism, there were no parties, no equivalents of the Long or Byrd machines of Louisiana and Virginia, and no significant urban-rural conflict. While county rings sometimes lasted for decades, groupings at the state level were bound to the fortunes of a particular candidate, and when he went, they disappeared with him. Turnover of officeholders was ordinarily very rapid. One reason for this was the constitutional stipulation that the governor and all other major statewide officeholders could not succeed themselves. This made it difficult for an individual to build a cohesive organization because he lacked the ability to maintain the steady stream of patronage required to hold a membership. Officeholders came and went with dizzying speed. No sooner had voters accustomed themselves to a governor than he vanished and left them with the task of selecting his replacement from a group consisting mainly of strangers.

It must be emphasized that this portrait of Alabama politics as chaotic and foundationless is a characterization of visible electoral politics—the stuff of newspaper stories and candidates' speeches. The next chapter explores the possibility that, at a deeper, more fundamental level, Alabama politics had a stable and orderly structure.

In his move to Cullman Folsom established a second home, but he was already well known there for his flamboyant and effective relief work. Between 1938 and 1942, when he first ran for governor, he traveled throughout North Alabama, greatly adding to the company's expansion. Eventually, he organized ten district offices in the region and supervised their activities. Many of his friends attributed much of this success to Sarah's skills. They saw the basic growth in the business as due to Folsom's salesmanship but contended that if he alone had maintained the office, the business would have quickly disintegrated. Nevertheless, his fame spread further with his energetic insurance selling. Who could forget and who could resist this gigantic, earnest salesman? His two homes, in locations to which he was perfectly suited ideologically, formed a solid foundation for a gubernatorial campaign.

The First Gubernatorial Race

The 1942 Democratic gubernatorial primary seemed to be in the bag for the widely loved and respected liberal Bibb Graves, the "Little Colonel." He would be serving an unprecedented third term. For once, a majority of Alabama voters knew a gubernatorial candidate and liked him. His only serious opponent was the bland conservative Chauncey Sparks, dubbed the "Bourbon from Barbour" by some newspapers. The situation was explained by a long-time Cullman politician, Judge Kenneth Griffith, who claimed responsibility for Folsom's running.

> I wasn't going to have too much to do with Graves, but I had friends who were Graves lieutenants with whom I had been in school. They told me that the Little Colonel was a sick, a very sick man. And it developed that the only opposition was Sparks. I had managed Sparks's campaign in this area when Dixon [Alabama governor, 1939–43] beat him. But I wasn't going to work with Sparks this time because he had sold out; Sparks didn't confer with his people and just failed to run it off [the 1938 Democratic party primary]. I had already set up the machinery to fight the runoff against Dixon. I couldn't explain it to my friends. I evaluated the possibility of Graves dying, which would leave Sparks home free. I called Folsom over to my office three of four days before the midnight March 1 filing deadline. I talked him into running. If something happened to Graves . . . [45]

Folsom's version of this story has a slightly different emphasis. Asked if he would have run in 1942 without Griffith's encouragement, Folsom responded:

> Oh, certainly I would have. I just had it in the back of my head. All of us was meetin' in the men's clothing store . . . that's where all the young fellas met and it was a week before the deadline and Sparks had got over there in Blount County and he had said, "I'm going to be for old age pensions up to $30 a month." Well, I knew damned well he wasn't going to be for a dollar a month according to his record, and I knew Bibb Graves would go along with the New Deal pushin' Social Security. . . . I had run on the platform of the Townsend Plan limited to $50 a month. . . .
> I knew Kenneth's daddy, but I'd never been around him very much. . . . I

was preachin' just like I was preachin' out on the stump, and I said, "By gosh, if he comes out and says he's for any kind of old age pension I know he's a liar," and I just kept raisin' hell about it and I just hinted around that if there was no one from North Alabama runnin', Sparks was just up here tryin' to split up Bibb Graves's vote on the old age pension issue, why I'm going to qualify myself because I've got a good record on that runnin' for Congress and old Kenneth heard me and the next time I heard from him was about five days before the election deadline.

He called me up at my office—he was about half in the bottle—and that's really the first time it was openly discussed that I was going to run. He said, "You run for Congress down there in South Alabama and you're peddlin' insurance all over North Alabama. Why don't you run for governor?" I told him if there was no one else to run from North Alabama I'd be in there to protect Bibb Graves. That was a political strategy. I wasn't there to protect Bibb Graves—I was in there to get elected and to get my name before the people. . . .

When he called me up there we had a few drinks—it was Pogue's Old Time Delux. I never did see that bourbon before, and I went over to—we had about two drinks apiece left—I says, "Let me go yander and get another pint—we'll talk some more." That gave me the courage and got him committed.

The next mornin' I was over to Kenneth's house, and I was sober then. I knocked on the door and said, "Kenneth, did you mean that? Will you go over to the bank, and go in on a note with me?" And he said he would and we went over to the bank to borrow the $125 it took to qualify.[46]

Folsom said that he was also stimulated to run by what he believed to be Sparks's close relationship to Governor Frank Dixon. Dixon was associated with a large burial insurance company located in Birmingham which, according to Folsom, was disturbed by the growth of small independent companies. He believed that this large company, with the help of the governor, had convinced the state insurance commissioner to create new regulations increasing the cash reserve requirements for insurance companies. Those regulations had been so injurious to small companies that in the preceding year five had been forced out of business and Folsom and his associates had suffered a large financial setback. "By God, I was handicapped as hell, and I was determined to do something to cut those sons of bitches' nuts out and the best way I knew to do it was to cut the Sparks vote up here in North Alabama."[47]

Folsom held a press conference to announce that he was running. Those present made little effort to mask their boredom, for they knew that he did not have a chance. Graves died a few days after the filing deadline.

Griffith was interested in Folsom over other possible candidates only because he believed that Folsom would be a prime vote getter. He was a reactionary who was completely disdainful of Folsom's populism. "You can't have one man one vote in a democracy," he said.[48] His sole objective in 1942 and again in 1946 was to place a North Alabamian in the governor's chair. He would have been happier with someone more conservative, but this was the least of his concerns, and he did not take Folsom's never-ending populist tirades seriously.

William Bradford Huie, who in 1942 owned the *Cullman Banner*, also regarded Folsom as little more than a pawn. Huie, part of the courthouse ring that dominated Cullman County in that period, wrote:

> We . . . belonged to the statewide Graves Gang, also known as the Pie-Eaters. The "Little Colonel's" slogan was THOSE WHO HELP BAKE THE PIE SHALL EAT IT. We helped him bake—and helped him eat.
>
> Then—the Act of God. After the deadline for qualifying, Colonel Graves died—and left the Pie-Eaters without a candidate. We couldn't win. And while there is wisdom which holds "if you can't beat 'em join 'em," we could espy no profit in joining our opponents. They'd sell the paroles and contracts, collect the liquor kickbacks, wallow in insurance premiums. So we could only groom somebody for a race four years later.
>
> It costs fifty dollars to enter the Democratic primary in Alabama; and usually there are, in addition to the serious candidates, six or eight citizens who "run" for the fun of it. One of these funsters in 1942 was Big Jim Folsom; and in our extremity we noted that he not only was a hometown boy but an upstanding young man.
>
> Big Un was indeed upstanding. Wearing a size 16 shoe—on Sundays—and an 18 collar, he stood a foot taller than most of his fellows. . . .
>
> Big Un was thirty-four. Born in a log cabin. Had grubbed in red clay. Familiar with the south end of a northbound mule. Raised on cawn pone and turnip greens. He was an Elk, could sign his own name. He'd make a great governor.[49]

In a personal interview, Huie retracted his vivid but inaccurate portrait of Folsom as an illiterate bumpkin.[50] And, unbeknownst to Huie, Kenneth Griffith, a young Pie-Eater, had arranged with Folsom to run him for office well before he could have been "summoned" by senior ring members. Griffith, in an interview, refuted this part of Huie's article point by point and described the disdain with which a senior ring member, his father Quill Griffith, regarded Folsom. Quill Griffith viewed Folsom as uncontrollable and dangerous, and there is considerable doubt whether he or any other senior ring members recognized Folsom's vote-getting potential prior to the 1942 primary.

Four other men were also in the gubernatorial race. Three were, to borrow Huie's phrase, funsters. One of them, Henry J. Carwile, "the man from the mountains," traveled about in a red-white-and-blue Model T promulgating his timeless slogan: "Save the perishing and care for the dying."[51] The other two ran somewhat more conventional campaigns calling for increased old age pensions and improved schools. A *Montgomery Advertiser* editorial commented with characteristic wit that "they appear to find the campaign an outlet for their love of vaudeville."[52] Another candidate, however, entered with more realistic and serious intent. Chris Sherlock had served as Governor Dixon's highway director, a position that demands high levels of administrative competence and political awareness and that permits its occupant to make lasting personal contacts in every county. Sherlock campaigned aggressively, predicting that Graves would die in office but that in the meantime the "very weak, sick old man" would "be controlled by a bunch of sycophants."[53] When Graves died, most of his supporters remembered that remark and, sensing the inevitable, shifted to Sparks, leaving Sherlock in a weak position.

Folsom's 1942 campaign was his biggest to that point, but it was nevertheless a scanty affair for a statewide race. He began with a rally in Fort Payne, a small town in DeKalb County. A local band was hired, and after it was paid, the campaign chest stood empty.[54] After that, John Steifelmeyer, a Cullman resident whom Folsom had met in a poker game, would, with little or no advance publicity, drive slowly through a town in a sound truck announcing the impending arrival of "the next governor" at the courthouse or town square; then he would go there, continue to build a crowd with his announcements, distribute literature, introduce the candidate, and move on to the next town as Folsom began to talk.[55] Funds were very short. Folsom had a growing business, but he also had a growing family, and he was unable to put much money into the race. Sometimes there was not enough to buy meals or gasoline, and they were obliged to ask for free hamburgers and fuel, always promising to repay the generous merchants. As he had in his congressional races, Folsom attempted to compensate for his slender finances with energetic campaigning. "He was a demon for work," said one of his handful of aides. "He'd work your butt off from six in the morning 'till twelve at night."[56]

Surprisingly, the Sherlock campaign became a major funding source for the impoverished Folsom campaign. Folsom explained the strategy behind this unusual turn of events: "They didn't want Sparks to win without a runoff. The people who was financin' Sherlock saw that he didn't have a chance so they turned to me as a last resort. . . . They gave me enough money to keep on the road. . . . John Steifelmeyer would set up a loudspeaker on a street corner, we'd come to make a speech and go on to the next town and make another and not even advertise in advance. But the next time [1946] I done it different."[57] Folsom went on to explain that in one county a supporter had, on his own, mailed circulars announcing one of his speeches to every address in the county. Folsom unexpectedly carried the county, and he credited the mailing for his victory. In 1946 he adopted a modified version of this simple and economical technique, with highly positive results.

Before Folsom, the standard campaign approach was somewhat different. When a candidate arrived in a town, he would go directly to the courthouse, where he would confer with the "courthouse crowd" and try to win their support. Then, if he had time, he might stroll out onto the courthouse steps, make a perfunctory speech, and shake a few hands, before moving on to the next county seat. Older Alabamians remember some gubernatorial candidates whose only direct contact with the voters was a wave and a smile as their cars drove away from the courthouse. As election day approached, large newspaper advertisements would appear, and if his war chest were especially flush, a candidate might make a number of radio broadcasts. This classic insider's approach, however, required friends at the courthouse and large sums of money. Folsom had little money and few courthouse allies; the courthouse crowd was not interested in funsters. Necessity forced him on the road, where he made speeches to small groups at any street corner. In so doing he developed a campaign style new to Alabama; it proved to be so much more effective than the old one that by 1950 it had been adopted by all candidates.

Stump speaking came easily to a successful insurance salesman. Quiet meetings with a county's Big Mules would not have fit his theatrical temperament, nor would that campaign style have been consistent with his belief that electioneering should be an educational process. And Folsom knew from his reading that like-minded candidates in other states had become governor by going directly to the electorate. For example, Mississippi's James K. Vardaman had campaigned for governor in 1903 traveling between rallies on an eight-wheeled lumber wagon drawn by eight white oxen. A skilled showman, Vardaman was able to identify himself with poor landless whites and small farmers.[58] By 1942 Folsom had begun to develop the skill of compressing complex ideas into biting epigrams and amusing, homey anecdotes. Even when he felt obliged to lecture an audience, he began to adopt his father's style of making a serious point with a well-timed joke.

Folsom's campaign style also resembled that of Sidney J. Catts, a former Alabama Baptist preacher who won the Florida governorship in 1916. Both campaigned under severe financial restraints that forced them to rely heavily on public rallies and collections taken up afterward. Like Folsom, Catts, who stood six feet tall and weighed two hundred pounds, took advantage of his imposing physical presence. And he was an extremely entertaining speaker who used humor with great skill. While Vardaman and Catts held generally populist views, they were intensely racist and anti-Catholic, respectively.[59] Folsom, on the other hand, avoided racial and religious slurs and throughout his career confined negative campaigning almost entirely to criticism of the Big Mules.

When his finances permitted, Folsom used a string band to warm up the crowds at his rallies. This practice was also part of southern campaign tradition. In 1922 agrarian socialist Jack Walton campaigned for the Oklahoma governorship using a string band, and in 1938 flour salesman W. Lee "Pass the Biscuits, Pappy" O'Daniel won the Texas governorship with the assistance of his Light Crust Doughboys, a radio string band. Folsom's generally amiable approach was probably closer to O'Daniel's than to that of any other southern campaigner.

Finally, Folsom knew and emulated Huey Long's electioneering style. He consciously modeled some of his policy positions after Long's, especially in his races against Congressman Steagall, but it would appear that Folsom ultimately became the more colorful campaigner. Long relied mainly on his considerable speaking abilities and the intensity of his personality. They also shared a penchant for outrageous actions off the stump that defined their personalities and perspectives for the voters as clearly as their formal speeches.[60]

An important part of any election campaign is a candidate's public image. For many years, in what seemed a tradition in Alabama politics, gubernatorial candidates were known by such monikers as the "Little Colonel" or "Plain Bill" Brandon. And years later George Wallace gained considerable mileage with his "Fighting Judge" appellation. During the 1936 campaign Folsom had been labeled "Long Jim" by the Wiregrass newspapers, and even earlier at the University of Alabama he had been known as "Rat Legs" and "Shorty." In 1942 there seemed to be a competition to attach a fitting title to him. Jack Huie, in a *Cullman Banner* editorial, referred to him as "the tall cedar from the Tennessee Valley" and incidentally predicted that he would "scourge the money-changers from our temples and give substance to the dreams of Franklin Delano Roosevelt."[61] Fred Taylor, an anti-Folsom Birmingham columnist, referred to the candidate as the "Tall Sycamore from Cullman County," but seeing this phrase begin to catch on, he began using "Tall Sapling."[62] A campaign circular referred to him as "Fighting Jim" and another anti-Folsom columnist, Atticus Mullin, called him "Long Jim," but neither name stuck.[63] Kenneth Griffith favored "Big Jim" as simple and descriptive, and this is the label that has been used ever since except for a brief period some years later when, for good reason, the press called him "Kissin' Jim." Griffith was also responsible for the big white hat that was a Folsom trademark for many years.[64] A big white hat perched atop Folsom's six-foot-eight-inch frame would seem to be gilding the lily, but in fact it gave him an even more imposing presence, and he enjoyed waving it at cheering crowds.

The message Folsom took to the voters in 1942 was vintage Bibb Graves–New Deal rhetoric. Updated and pushed a bit to the left, it was targeted at the aged, young parents worried about abysmal public schools, factory workers, small farmers, and the disaffected in general. Almost completely absent was the radical challenge to the status quo that would appear in 1946. His thirteen-point platform featured "old age pensions for every person over 65 years of age—no strings attached; better pay for schoolteachers and the placing of schoolteachers on the same basis as other state employees; removing the sales tax from the laborer's bread and meat and letting the big mules carry their share of this tax; so amending the Workmen's Compensation laws in such manner as will insure all men and women covered by Workmen's Insurance, this assistance when needed from any cause; expanding the road and bridge system of the state to the point where every populated area will be easily accessible."[65]

As the campaign moved along, Sparks tried to project an image of being all things to all people. Before Graves's death, Sparks had moved so far to the right in an effort to attract conservatives that even the ultraconservative Atticus Mullin had characterized him as a "reactionary bourbon."[66] After Graves died, however, former Graves leaders tried to extend Sparks's left wing by portraying him as the true liberal in the race, and his huge newspaper advertisements were virtually devoid of information about his policy views.[67] Chris Sherlock, who earlier had been trying to attract conservatives, attempted to bill himself as a New Deal liberal while simultaneously attacking Sparks as a heartless enemy of veterans, rural electrification, farmers, and the aged. Toward the end, Sherlock desperately accused Sparks of religious prejudice and World War I draft dodging.[68]

Most newspapers, including the Black Belt–oriented *Montgomery Advertiser*, favored Sparks. The *Advertiser* accorded approximately ten times more space to Sparks than to the other candidates combined, and the tiny, badly placed stories about Sherlock and Folsom were devoted entirely to their problems and drawbacks.

Few were surprised when Sparks won a majority, giving him the Democratic party nomination without a runoff, but Folsom came in second with 26 percent and that was unexpected. The county-by-county results are shown in Figures 2 and 3; they illustrate some of the points made earlier about the importance of localism and north-central-south sectionalism in statewide elections. As Figure 2 shows, Folsom's greatest strength came from his adopted North Alabama home and Coffee County (his original home) and its southern neighbor Geneva. His relatively weak showing in other counties

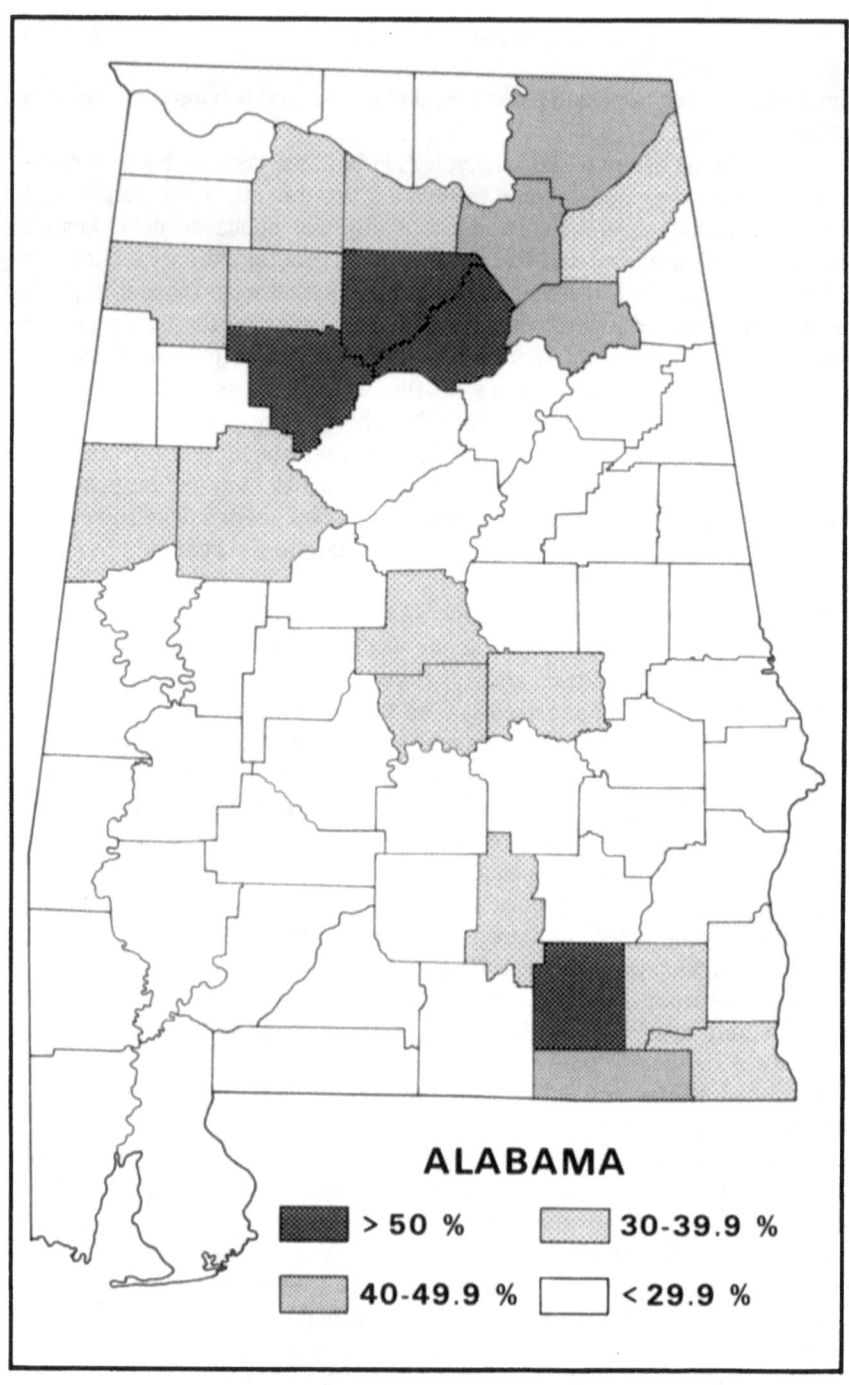

Figure 2. Vote for Folsom, 1942 Democratic Party Primary

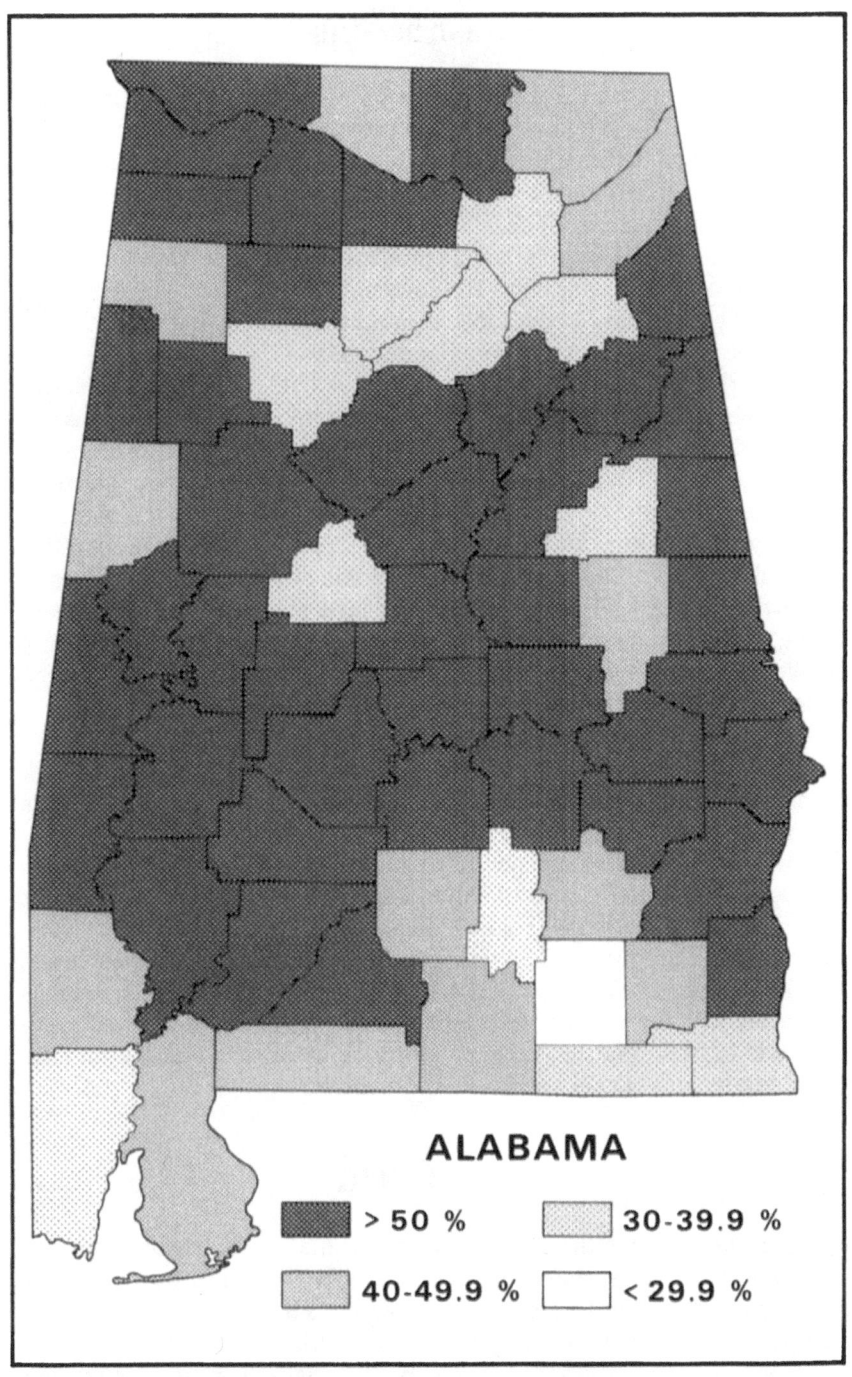

Figure 3. Vote for Sparks, 1942 Democratic Party Primary

neighboring Coffee was due to the proximity of Sparks's home county, Barbour (see Figure 3). Sherlock exhibited similar strength in and around his home county, Mobile. Sparks was able to take the Black Belt because, despite his campaign attempts to straddle the fence, he was far more conservative than Folsom or Sherlock.

Folsom's 1942 race established a pattern that would be repeated in his 1946, 1954, and 1962 campaigns for governor. His greatest support would continue to come from North Alabama and the Wiregrass of the southeast. Those basically white counties were largely rural in composition. The farmers and workers in those regions responded positively to Folsom's populist–New Deal economic appeals. Because of those same economic positions and his racial moderation, his greatest opposition consistently came from the Black Belt counties. While these counties had the highest black populations and Folsom attracted black voter support, legal and illegal restraints on black registration and voting made these counties white conservative strongholds. While black registration increased in the 1950s and early 1960s, the numbers of black voters remained relatively low throughout Folsom's political career. Mobile and Jefferson counties were also areas of opposition, but the level of their opposition would fluctuate as urbanization and industrialization changed the structure of their electorates.

According to the conventional wisdom in Alabama, the candidate who took second place in one gubernatorial race would win the next, and in fact this pattern held quite often. Since a governor could not succeed himself, candidates were not obliged to run against an incumbent; the preceding election's second-place candidate usually held an advantage because of his superior name recognition. But when Folsom took second, the conventional wisdom was generally discounted. Most political experts, after shaking their heads over the vagaries of the electoral process, promptly forgot Big Jim. He was an outsider with few courthouse ring connections, he was from North Alabama, and he was appealing directly to a type of voter considered of little importance in a traditional statewide election campaign.

Toward 1946

Big Jim pushed through the surprised crowd at the Sparks celebration party at the Jefferson Davis Hotel in Montgomery, walked directly to the bar where he reached past the bartender, pulled out a bottle of bourbon, filled a large tumbler, drained it without stopping, and then slammed it back on the bar upside-down and surveyed the staring faces with a grim, confident smile.[69] He was certain that he was well on his way to developing a set of strategies which would bring victory in 1946: a progressive platform expressed simply and dramatically; direct appeals to the electorate rather than courthouse rings; use of obvious but nonetheless powerful symbols, such as a white hat; use of rural-oriented theatrical devices, such as string bands (barely applied in 1942); reliance on humor and parables (just beginning in 1942); few direct attacks on opponents; and use of mail circulars to announce rallies (used only once in 1942).

The direct assault on the foundations of establishment power, which would become the centerpiece of his 1946 campaign, was not a significant part of his 1942 effort. His 1942 speeches contained a few sarcastic barbs aimed at the Big Mules, but nothing really basic. The Folsom style was still evolving.

CHAPTER 3

Power in Alabama

If we have anything at all, it is only by enterprise and continued effort that we hold what we have.

J. Bruce Henderson

Big Jim Folsom believed that Alabama state government was controlled by a power elite, a small number of the wealthiest corporate and agricultural leaders who made all key decisions which were then executed by government officials. In his 1946 speeches he promised to rid the state of its self-appointed royalty; more precisely, he promised average people the political tools to accomplish that mission—the right to vote and legislative representation on the basis of one person, one vote.

Students of Alabama politics have emphasized the fluid, fragmented, "friends and neighbors" quality of the process by which political leaders, and especially governors, gain power.[1] Personalities come and go, and factions typically last only a decade or less. Underlying the near chaos of the electoral process, however, are hints that an informal coalition of big agriculture and big business, the Big Mules, exerts considerable, but usually unspecified, influence over gubernatorial and legislative elections and governmental policymaking.[2]

To understand the 1946 election campaign, the opposition's reaction to Folsom's victory, and the remainder of Folsom's career it is necessary to ask, who really governs the state of Alabama?[3] And to answer that question fully requires some knowledge of events that occurred as far back as the period following the Civil War. Elites in democracies tend to remain unobtrusive. Sometimes they seem able to influence events almost invisibly, by the sheer fact of their existence. Thus it can be difficult to detect their existence, much less understand their impact on events. However, an elite can be observed when it is first taking power and when its existence is threatened. After the Civil War an elite took, or retook, power in Alabama, and it suffered heavy attacks several times thereafter. Those events reveal a great deal about the structure and power of that elite and its potential weaknesses as well.

Folsom, together with many of his allies and opponents, understood that the post–Civil War years created roles that they were still playing. It is impossible to know these people without understanding their sense of the past. The appendix provides a more detailed discussion of theoretical issues associated with studying the distribution of political power in a community or state.[4]

Elite Politics in Alabama

The South was ruined by the Civil War; socially, economically, and politically the damage was awesome. There is disagreement, however, as to the extent of the harm done to the economic and political leadership, especially to the plantation owners.

Some historians argue that the postwar situation was entirely new and constituted a new political order.[5] They argue that at least a majority of the plantations in the 1880s and 1890s had new owners because antebellum planting families had difficulty maintaining their properties. Their lands were acquired by bankers and merchants (often northerners) who took advantage of the economic situation to buy out antebellum families, often after having caused their financial difficulties in the first place.[6] The fall in land prices and the breakup of large landholdings in tax forfeitures facilitated the changeover.[7]

Another version of these events is arrived at by analyses of land-ownership records. Studies of Alabama's Black Belt show that elite planters (the top 8 percent of landowners) exhibited a stability of land ownership from 1850 to 1870 that was little affected by the war.[8] At first glance, landownership records appear to support the view that large numbers of planters were wiped out by the war. In five Black Belt counties, of 236 elite planters present in 1860, only 101 (43 percent) remained as the largest landowners by 1870. However, only 47 percent of elite planters had remained as major landholders in the same counties from 1850 to 1860, suggesting that the war alone was not the cause of the dissolution of more than half of the Black Belt elite planter class. A large proportion of landowners remained in the elite category through the war and Reconstruction, as compared to the preceding decade. Moreover, although the absolute value of their properties dropped precipitously, the relative value of their holdings (percentage of total land values in a county) increased during this period. By contrast, in the period 1850–60 the elite landowners' share of land value actually declined.[9] Changes in status among elite families in this period seem to have depended more on family structure and the original size of landholdings than on the war.

Wealth was very unequally distributed in Alabama Black Belt counties in this period. In 1870 Marengo County, which was quite typical, 63 percent of the land value was owned by 10 percent of the population (compared to 57 percent in 1850). The next 10 percent of the population accounted for an additional 17 percent of the land value in 1870. The bottom 70 percent of the population owned only 12 percent of the land value.[10] Thus it is fair to characterize the major landowners as an economic elite. Whether they were also a political elite remains to be seen.

Although many believe that most of the newcomers to this economic elite in 1870 were predatory northern businessmen who invaded the postwar South to buy huge tracts of land at bedrock prices, census figures indicate that fewer than 5 percent of the elite planters were northerners. Nor were many of the newcomers "social climbers" from within a given county; most were wealthy southerners from other counties or states.[11]

To some degree the bankers and merchants were able to threaten the planters' economic hegemony. The weakest point in the economy (and therefore the planters' weakest point) was capital, which was in critically short supply.[12] With capital very scarce and slavery eliminated, a new relationship between owners and workers had to evolve. The crop lien system represented a grim, insalubrious solution.

The most important sources of capital were the "furnishing merchants," with their northern business contacts, and the largest planters. The merchants and planters "furnished" supplies on credit to small landowning farmers or tenants with the forthcoming crop as security.[13] These merchants and planters, who sometimes paid annual interest rates of 18 percent or more to northern banks, commonly charged 100 percent to their customers.[14] Such usurious rates were arrived at through a combination of exorbitant base rates plus a surcharge for merchandise sold on credit. The farmer could seek lower prices elsewhere only if he had cash, for no merchant would extend credit to someone who could not provide equity.

Planters also used tenant systems under which they charged rent or received a fixed share of the crop in exchange for use of their land.[15] Rent and sharecropping rates were fixed and not subject to the gross manipulation possible under corp lien arrangements, which made the lien a more efficient tool for squeezing every last bit of profit from customers.[16]

The new system brought a great increase in merchant wealth. By 1870 a substantial number of merchants were moving rapidly into elite status. For example, in Marengo County, Alabama, "the total value of the land owned by all residents of the county declined by 61 percent between 1860 and 1870, the total landholdings of the planter elite declined by 53 percent, but the total value of real estate owned by county merchants actually increased by 24 percent."[17]

The legal basis for the crop lien system was a state statute passed in 1866 which permitted any person to own a lien on a crop.[18] No more than two years later the planters began to realize some of the consequences of this law. The planter-oriented *Columbus Enquirer, Montgomery Daily Advertiser,* and *Mobile Daily Register* recognized that the merchants were a substantial threat to planter economic dominance, and they called first for planters to organize politically and then for the passage of antimerchant legislation.[19] The requisite legislation followed quickly in 1871. Essentially, it made liens held by landlords superior to all other liens, giving the landlords a strong advantage over the merchants. Soon large numbers of merchants moved out of the Black Belt into white counties, where the small independent farm base offered no planter competition for liens.[20]

An economic elite consisting of a small number of wealthy planters survived the war, and though still in a weakened condition, it fought off a threat to its existence through action in the state legislature. It would be incorrect to conclude from this single event that the planters were a political elite either in their own counties or in state government, but a move of such agility and strength could only be accomplished by a superbly organized group with enormous political resources.

The constitution of 1868 gave the Radical Republicans control of Alabama state government. In the election of 1874 the Democratic party, under the leadership of George Smith Houston, "The Old Bald Eagle of the Mountain," of North Alabama, wrestled control of all three branches of state government from the Radicals, who maintained control only of local governments in the Black Belt.[21] The Democratic party campaign had been dominated by one issue, that of white supremacy. *Montgomery Daily Advertiser* editorials highlighted the situation.

> *Are you a negro in principle or are you a white man?* Put this question to every candidate and compel him to answer it.[22]

> The one great question to be decided in November is: shall Alabama be ruled by the white race or ruined by the black.[23]

> South Alabamians! Now or never is the time to fling off chain and handcuff rule. . . . Shoulder to shoulder, white men! Beat back the mongrel foe![24]

> South Alabama raises her manacled hands in mute appeal to the mountain counties. The chains on the wrists of her sons and the midnight shrieks of her women sound continually in their ears. She lifts up her eyes, being tormented, and begs piteously for relief from bondage. Is there a white man in North Alabama so lost to all his finer feelings of human nature as to slight her appeal?[25]

The highest priority for the newly elected Democrats was a constitutional convention to rewrite the constitution of 1868. That document required that a referendum be held that would simultaneously decide whether a convention should be held and, if so, who the delegates would be. The referendum campaign can be summarized in the epithets used by both sides: Republicans called Democrats "Bourbons," referring to their domination by the wealthy, and Democrats called Republicans "Jacobians" and "niggers," focusing on their egalitarian orientation.[26] The vote in August 1875 was 77,763 to 59,928 in favor of the convention. The delegates consisted of eighty Democrats, twelve Republicans, and seven Independents. With blacks voting in great numbers, most of the Republican and Independent delegates came from the Black Belt.[27]

Malcolm C. McMillan describes the convention as dominated by "a conservative agrarian-minded policy, which showed a distrust of Republican interest in Alabama's railroads, mining and industrial resources."[28] Probably the most important convention action was a reduction in the representation of Republican Black Belt counties and an increase in the representation of some Democratic counties.[29] No attempt was made to restrict suffrage, because of the danger of federal intervention.[30] The convention delegates and later the voters approved the document overwhelmingly.[31]

Passage of the 1875 constitution was followed by a rapid increase in the power of Black Belt plantation owners and other wealthy individuals. At first, they were obliged to rely on north and southeast counties for support because their own counties were still controlled by Republicans and blacks.[32] As soon as they regained control (with the assistance of Democrats at the state level), however, they utilized the blacks, manipulating their votes to defeat the white counties in statewide elections.[33]

The systematic election fraud that was the main ingredient of Black Belt electoral victories in the 1870s and 1880s was accelerated by changes in the election laws passed in 1879. One law required that the ballot be an entirely blank piece of white paper, making voting difficult for the largely illiterate blacks and poor whites. Another law eliminated the need for correspondence between a voter's ballot number and poll number.[34] Advocates of these laws argued that they protected voters' privacy. The Alabama legislature had indeed achieved the ultimate in secret ballots; the editor of the *Huntsville Advocate* observed that "some ballots that are cast are so secret they are never heard of again."[35] A North Alabama attempt to rescind these laws in 1881 was defeated by Black Belt legislators.[36]

The audacity of Black Belt fraud was reflected in the 1880 election, in which Republicans received a total of seventy-nine votes in the Black Belt counties of Dallas, Perry, and Marengo, all three of which contained black Republican majorities.[37] The *Montgomery Advertiser* made little attempt to hide its sympathies in this matter when it boasted: "The enfranchisement of the colored race whatever may have been the motives of the dominant party when accomplishing it, has resulted well for all our people."[38] Former governor William C. Oates was even clearer: "The negroes were enfranchised and they went right on and crowded to the polls, and they were in the hands of carpetbaggers and scalawags, and being led by them, brought governmental evils almost untold, and there were but two ways to correct it. One of these was to take shotguns and go to the polls and disperse them. . . . The other way was to cheat them. I was an advocate of the latter because it didn't take life."[39] Oates neglected to mention that cheating the blacks had the added advantage of providing the Black Belt with thousands of votes that could be used against the white counties.

As they consolidated their power in the last decade of the century, Black Belt leaders found themselves faced with two problems: rapidly growing Populist strength and the development of industrial centers in Birmingham and Mobile. Both of these problems represented deadly threats to their power, and their responses were revealing.

Populism was a complex, multifaceted movement born out of rural economic hardship caused by restrictive national monetary policies, the crop lien system, monopolistic railroad shipping rates, and overproduction. Postbellum monetary policy could hardly have been more damaging to farmers. The government had left the gold standard during the war with the issuance of greenbacks, and after the war the money supply was frozen as part of a gradual return to economic orthodoxy. A constant money supply in a country with a rapidly growing population meant that there was a diminishing money supply relative to population. This forced prices down. So a debtor was obliged to repay his loan in more valuable, more-difficult-to-earn dollars. In addition, interest rates were forced up, making it more difficult to borrow money. The crop lien system and high railroad rates together with a return to the gold standard amounted to a de facto expansion of slavery, trapping many whites as well as blacks.[40] Crop overproduction further hurt farmers, large as well as small. The populist response to these economic forces directly threatened the Black Belt planters.

The Populist movement started in Lampasas County, Texas, in 1877 with the creation of the Knights of Reliance, a group of farmers whose purpose was to organize against "the day that is rapidly approaching when the balance of labor's products become concentrated into the hands of a few, there to constitute a power that would enslave posterity."[41] The group's name changed several times thereafter, but it was most commonly known as the Texas Alliance. At first, its objectives were vague, but by 1883 it had narrowed its focus to the problem of agricultural credit.[42] Quickly, cooperatives were created that could buy crops and sell supplies at reasonable prices.[43]

The rapid growth of the Texas Alliance had been facilitated by a band of traveling lecturers, several of whom came to Alabama, where, often working under dangerous circumstances, they managed to organize nearly every county within three years.[44] Cooperatives were established, and in some counties they became commercially successful, selling supplies to farmers at far lower prices than those charged by merchants.[45]

Alliance efforts of the late 1880s were devoted almost exclusively to the cooperative movement, but this strategy was too narrow to handle the broad spectrum of problems that farmers faced. Many farmers were so far in debt to furnishing merchants that they were unable to take advantage of the cooperatives. In addition, many cooperatives were barely surviving because of credit shortages and strong opposition from banks, railroads, suppliers, and various government entities. Finally, the cooperatives had no effect on those federal government monetary policies that worked against small farmers.[46]

By 1890 the Alliance had moved into full-scale political action. Attacks on the political positions of the elite were combined with efforts to change railroad regulations, alter crop lien laws, and the like. The election of Alliance members to statewide and legislative office became a central method by which such goals were to be achieved.

The Alliance candidate for the Democratic gubernatorial nomination in 1890 was a highly successful farmer, State Agriculture Commissioner Reuben Kolb.[47] One of his four opponents was Thomas Goode Jones, former speaker of the Alabama House of Representatives and a prominent lawyer for the Louisville and Nashville Railroad Company (L&N) who had the support of the *Montgomery Advertiser*, a signal of how the Black Belt would handle the state's rapidly growing industrial presence.[48] Even with the convention packed by the Democratic party regulars, Kolb polled 29 votes short of the 264 necessary to win.[49] After thirty ballots, which produced only small changes in the first count, the issue was settled in an all-night meeting attended by the other candidates. These men and their powerful supporters led two growing Democratic party factions: the ultraconservative major industrialists and another group of businessmen who tended to operate somewhat smaller concerns and who in a few years would constitute the core of the party's Progressive wing. These future antagonists were united in their desire to stop Kolb, and they chose Jones.[50] Apparently, few if any Black Belt representatives were present; nearly everyone at the meeting represented the growing industrial interests. Although Jones won the nomination and, of course, the election, Kolbites captured a near majority of seats and several leadership positions in the state legislature.[51]

Two years later Kolb tried again, but the convention was carefully rigged against him.[52] Kolb then bolted the party and created the "simon-pure Jeffersonian Democrats."[53] Not surprisingly, the Kolb platform had election reform as its first priority, followed by improved schools and roads, tax reform featuring a graduated income tax, elimination of the convict lease system, miscellaneous legislation to improve the condition of small farmers and industrial workers, and equal political rights for blacks. Jones's campaign was an encyclopedia of racial scare tactics.[54]

Kolb lost in what has been well documented as one of the most dishonest elections in the nation's history. Even Black Belt newspapers admitted this, and a congressional investigation discovered thousands of dead, nonexistent, and nonresident blacks who had turned in overwhelming majorities for Jones in Black Belt counties.[55] Congressional investigators were sometimes rhapsodic in their descriptions of the imaginativeness and variety of techniques used to coerce voters, steal ballot boxes, and misplace inconveniently marked ballots; they hated what was done, but they had to admire first-rate thievery. Despite Kolb's loss, the Jeffersonian Democrats succeeded in electing considerable numbers of state legislators and hundreds of local officials.

The effects of electoral corruption, a topic of widespread newspaper coverage by 1892, soon spread throughout the political system. In a public speech in Mobile the speaker of the Alabama House of Representatives said that Negro suffrage had forced whites "to crimes of larceny and perjury and had corrupted the jury, the judge, the solicitor, and others."[56] With a growing public uproar over fraudulent elections and with North Alabama counties poised to use the same tactics, Black Belt leaders realized that the manipulation of black votes in their counties had to cease. But they faced the growing Populist threat, and they needed an electoral "edge" to deal with it. They concluded that the answer was to limit voting rights to those who possessed "virtue and intelligence," a phrase taken from a suffrage limitation plank in the 1892 Alabama Democratic party platform.[57] A constitutional convention was not the answer, because there was too much danger that it would be taken over by Populists. These considerations, plus the fact that other southern states had moved successfully to disfranchise blacks through the poll tax and property, educational, and other qualifications, led to the passage of the Sayre election law in 1893.[58] This law provided for extremely complex registration and election procedures which, by their very complexity, kept tens of thousands of illiterate blacks and North and Southeast Alabama whites from voting.[59] Effective as it was, though, the Sayre Act was by no means the end of the Black Belt–engineered restructuring of Alabama government.

Kolb made another attempt at the governorship in 1894, but he lost by a wider margin than he had two years before.[60] Although ballot stuffing was again a factor, Kolb's greatest problem seemed to have been a lower voter turnout in the white counties, signaling a decline in Populist strength and perhaps the first effects of the Sayre election law. Populist representation in the state legislature also declined, and those who remained were ineffective and disunited.[61] Populism was also beginning to unravel nationally.[62]

The Black Belt planters must be classed among the most brilliant political strategists in this nation's history.[63] After the Civil War, in danger of being edged off the political map, they defeated the merchants with one deadly stroke in the state legislature. Then they helped to execute the Democratic party takeover of state government and the drafting and approval of the 1875 constitution. With the assistance of the state Democratic party officials they took control of their own counties, and then, using massive vote fraud, they quickly became a powerful force in state government. In 1879 they secured passage of election laws that facilitated their all-important election thefts. The Populist revolt could have destroyed less imaginative and more easily embarrassed opponents, but the planters unabashedly extended election dishonesty to new lengths, and when they realized that this could not be continued indefinitely, they made their first move toward restricting the electorate.

Just as the Black Belt elite was overcoming the Populist challenge, a new political force, fed by the Industrial Revolution, had begun to gain strength with startling speed. The planters had been forced to take on the merchants because the merchants had operated in their counties. The Populists had been destroyed because they were a threat and because they were sufficiently weak to make their elimination convenient. The industrialists, however, were located mainly in the north, where they did not represent the immediate threat that the merchants had; moreover, they were a powerful new force that could never be defeated in direct combat—the future was on their side. In the battle against the Populists, the Black Belt and the industrialists had formed an alliance, but whether it would hold once the Populists had disappeared was another question.

The transformation of farmland into the city of Birmingham was begun by railroad companies and speculators in 1871. The attraction was not the land but what lay under and around it—a mixture of coal, limestone, and iron ore perfect for pig iron and steel making.[64] In addition to mineral resources, Birmingham industrialists had access to some of the nation's cheapest laborers—prisoners enslaved by the convict lease system and blacks. Soon Birmingham was producing pig iron so inexpensively that it was underselling the English product in England, and less than thirty years after surveyors first began laying out city streets, Birmingham was producing 75 percent of the country's pig iron exports. By 1900 Birmingham's population was already larger than Montgomery's and on the verge of outstripping Mobile's.

At the same time other North Alabama industrial centers, such as Gadsden, were developing at a similarly rapid pace.

Many people, especially those residing in the growing industrial centers, agreed that the 1875 constitution was hopelessly archaic. Local tax limits contained in the document inhibited the development of schools, city and county streets, fire departments, and many other basic elements of progressive city government. It forbade the state from building or improving roads, delegating that task to the counties, which in turn were debilitated by tax limits. The constitution permitted monstrous criminal justice abuses, such as the convict lease system, which condemned prisoners to work in the mines under conditions that produced shocking death rates. For these and similar reasons a considerable number of humanitarian and good government groups favored constitutional revision.[65] Others were interested in changes in the political process: some wanted primaries statewide; many, fatigued by the almost never-ending election campaigns that resulted from two-year legislative and gubernatorial terms, wanted them extended to four years; and considerable numbers, not just those in the Black Belt, favored increased suffrage restriction. Most groups dissatisfied with the constitution decided that the amending process was unsatisfactory and determined that a constitutional convention was the only answer.[66]

In 1900 the Black Belt elite and other convention advocates succeeded in passing an enabling act for a convention referendum. Various referendum campaign committees were then formed, such as the one headed by the president of the Alabama Railroad Commission which settled on the slogan "white supremacy, suffrage reform, and purity in elections."[67] Despite Populist and Republican opposition, the convention was approved by the voters by an almost two-to-one margin. Geographically the major opposition came from northern and southern white counties, a pattern which was to repeat itself in Folsom's gubernatorial campaigns more than forty years later.

The 1901 constitutional convention spotlighted the social, economic, and political changes that had occurred in the last decade of the nineteenth century. In a manner that highlights these changes, Sheldon Hackney categorizes the convention delegates as Bosses, Planters, Agrarians, and Progressives. The Bosses, coming mainly from the Black Belt, Birmingham, and Mobile, represented a political alliance. The Boss delegates' backgrounds, voting records, and statements during the convention, suggest their outlook: "Generally, [they] voted for lower tax rates and lower levels of government spending; they strongly opposed any stricter regulation of railroads or any change in the system of leasing county convicts to corporations operating outside the county; and they consistently objected to changes that might upset the established system of winning and holding office. With a few exceptions, they usually voted against any change, the chief exception being the change to a more restricted electorate."[68] The Bosses dominated the convention, even though there were only 60 Bosses out of a total of 155 delegates. The president of the convention was John B. Knox, a leading railroad lawyer. Committee chairmanship appointments were confined to Bosses, with the appointment of T. W. Coleman, a former slaveholder, as chairman of the Committee on Suffrage and Elections being typical.[69]

One of the major issues of this period was the degree to which government should regulate large corporations in general and the railroads in particular. Since smaller plantation owners used rail transport and the services and products of other large businesses, it is natural to expect that at least some of them would find themselves out of sympathy with the Bosses on those issues. This was in fact the case, and it accounts for Hackney's Planter category, which included 37 delegates. The Planters favored greater governmental protection against big business, as did small businessmen throughout the state. Aside from business regulation, though, the Planters distrusted state government and wanted its powers severely limited. In this and in their attitude toward suffrage restriction, the Planters and Bosses usually agreed.[70]

The Agrarians were a motley lot consisting of 13 Democrats, the 6 Republicans at the convention, and 6 of the 7 Populists there. They came predominantly from North and Southeast Alabama. The Agrarians differed with the majority on further suffrage restriction, which, like the Sayre Act, would disfranchise poor whites as well as blacks. They were also in the minority in favoring limits on the powers of local government officials and a reform of the convict leasing system. However, The Agrarians voted with the Bosses surprisingly often. According to Hackney, "The Agrarians were not interested in railroad reform; instead they steadfastly advocated lower limits on taxation, debt, and spending. Ignoring the realities of a modern industrial state, they remained chained to their preference for a small passive referee state."[71]

The Progressives, numbering 32, were primarily small businessmen. "Their mixture of votes was a compound of humanitarianism, concern for clean government, a felt need for government regulation of powerful concentrations of wealth and a desire for increased public services. That the Progressives knew the cost of progress and were willing to pay it was reflected in their distinctive advocacy of higher debt, taxation and spending levels. They also wanted the state government to step in and regulate railroad rates so that some of the profits of progress would stay at home rather than flowing into the coffers of Northern corporations."[72] They also sought reform of the convict lease system, antilynching laws, and more open access to political officeholding.

The Progressives had had their first important victory in 1896 with the election of Governor Joe Johnston. The Progressive governor partially succeeded in making the property tax less regressive and in bringing about modest educational reforms, but he failed in most of his other reform efforts.[73]

Neither in Johnston's administration nor in the 1901 convention were the Progressives able to build a solid winning coalition. The 1901 document was written by the Bosses. Legislative apportionment favored the Black Belt and would come to favor it even more as the years brought further urbanization. The 1901 apportionment would remain unchanged until the 1960s, despite the constitution's provision for reapportionment every decade.[74] The convict leasing system was unchanged by the convention. The 1875 constitutional limitations on taxing, which crippled the school system, were carried on in the 1901 constitution. Black Belt interests by and large opposed change in this area because counties received state money according to the number of school-age children in each county. Since the Black Belt counties had the largest black populations and spent most of the money on white schools, they were satisfied with the status quo, while counties that distributed money equally among all their schools experienced severe problems. The new document also contained severe limits on road construction. Finally, new suffrage restrictions were added, such as "lengthy residency requirements, a $1.50 cumulative poll tax, and a literacy or property test with temporary exemptions for ex-soldiers, the descendants of ex-soldiers, and men of 'good character.'"[75] These changes succeeded in eliminating tens of thousands of voters. More whites than blacks were disfranchised, and these North and South Alabamians were precisely the whites the Bosses wanted eliminated.[76]

The proceedings in 1901 reveal the solidification and victory of one coalition (the Bosses), the potential for the creation of a second one (Progressives and Planters), and the decline of the Agrarians (that is, the Populists). The Agrarians had been the major opponents of the Bosses in the preceding decade, but they never succeeded in gaining power because they were poorly organized and too narrow in focus. They failed to draw support from two critical groups dissatisfied with Boss-dominated government: small businessmen and planters. Despite their unhappiness with the Bosses, these groups were a long way from favoring drastic reform.

It is tempting to describe Alabama politics after 1901 as a bifactional system featuring Bosses versus Progressives. While it is true that there were important points of disagreement between the two groups, there are at least two faults with this view. First, both in social origins and governmental policies they were quite similar. On many important issues, such as black disfranchisement, segregation, and labor unions, the Bosses and Progressives were as one.[77] Second, only three governors before 1946 could be called Progressives: Braxton Bragg Comer, Thomas E. Kilby, and Bibb Graves. Despite the fact that they brought about substantial reforms in public education, prisons, welfare, and the like, they did not touch the central structures of power in the state.

Thus it is fair to say that Alabama state government was dominated by the Bosses through most of the first half of this century. Folsom's 1946 election did not represent a Progressive victory, since he was more populist than Progressive. The Progressives occasionally invaded the governing power of the Bosses on those occasions when they disagreed with special severity with what the Bosses were doing and when they could field a particularly attractive gubernatorial candidate.

Until the post–World War II period only one set of events disturbed Boss hegemony: a populist or neopopulist resurgence featuring the Ku Klux Klan and Senator J. Thomas Heflin and the election of Bibb Graves as governor (1927–31 and 1935–39). These events were closely related, but there were important differences between them.

The 1926 election was probably the Klan's high-water mark in Alabama. Bibb Graves, relying almost exclusively on Klan support, defeated the Boss candidate Charles S. McDowell, Jr.[78] The virtually unknown Klan candidate for the Senate, Hugo Black, defeated three of the leading politicians in the state, and the KKK was given credit for electing the attorney general, several congressmen, and numerous state and county officials.[79] At this time the Klan was not exclusively a race-oriented organization; in their campaigns both Black and Graves emphasized their support and sympathy for the common man.

The Klan went into the legislature determined to enact Graves's Progressive program and a "press-muzzling bill," which would have changed the libel laws to mute press criticism of the Klan. The Bosses fought back in the 1927 legislative session with an antimask bill and a change in the laws regulating primaries.[80] What the *Montgomery Advertiser* called the "bedsheet bloc" held a slight majority in both houses, but the Boss legislators possessed many years of legislative experience. The press-muzzling bill was defeated, and in a compromise measure flogging was raised from a misdemeanor to a felony and the antimasking legislation dropped. The Bosses' primary bill was defeated by a slim margin. The Graves program was passed, with some compromises: the convict leasing system was abolished, the corporation franchise tax was doubled, a small gross business tax was placed on public utilities, highway construction was accelerated, education was expanded, and hospitals for the retarded were constructed.[81] Voting on these issues broke down into Black Belt versus North Alabama.[82]

Senator J. Thomas Heflin was the most prominent KKK leader of this period. He was anti-Catholic and an extreme racist, even by the standards of the time. Those attitudes were only mildly disturbing to the Bosses, who viewed him as an eccentric nuisance.[83] He became more than a nuisance in 1928, however, when he attacked Senator Joseph Robinson of Arkansas, who, though an Al Smith opponent, had defended the virtues of religious toleration. Heflin attacked Robinson in a bitter tirade, warning that if the Arkansan ever came to Alabama, he would be tarred and feathered. This outburst represented a danger signal to the Bosses, who had no affection for Smith but who feared any breach of party regularity.[84] The one-party system was an important component of their power base; it had not been many years since they had crushed the Republicans and Populists. Heflin went even further when he announced that he would campaign against Smith. Finally, he stated publicly that he would vote against Smith.[85]

Smith defeated Hoover in Alabama by a vote of 127,796 to 120,725, with the Black Belt supporting Smith and North Alabama voting for Hoover. The Bosses feared that this pattern represented the beginning of a bolt, with Heflin taking his hill-country supporters out of the Democratic party.[86] After a great deal of nearly public debate, Heflin was expelled from the Democratic primary and thus was kept from winning reelection to the Senate.[87]

Heflin's expulsion and a well-orchestrated newspaper attack on the Klan (which won Grover Hall, editor of the *Montgomery Advertiser*, a Pulitzer Prize) were accompanied by a precipitous decline in KKK membership.[88] This was not a simple cause-and-effect relationship; Klan membership was declining throughout the South for many reasons. These events show, however, that the Bosses were able to respond decisively and effectively to threats to their power.

Bibb Graves was much less of a problem. Though he had heavy Klan support at first, he relied on it less as his personal rapport with the voters grew, and though the Bosses opposed Graves and his programs, he was someone they could deal with. Graves was no threat to the Bosses.[89]

The Bosses moved uncomfortably through the 1930s, losing money in the Depression, suffering through a second Graves term, and increasingly irritated by the New Deal, but their power was secure. They ended the decade and began the next with the administrations of conservative governors Frank Dixon (1939–42) and Chauncey Sparks (1943–46). The Bosses had every reason to believe that one of their two candidates, Agriculture and Industries Commissioner Joe Poole or Lieutenant Governor Handy Ellis, would win in 1946.[90]

Every elite develops and promulgates a set of myths or a package of beliefs that justifies their conception of the status quo. Elite myths are rarely produced from whole cloth; instead, they are drawn from existing values. That is what makes them so effective. The core idea in the Alabama leaders' system of social and political beliefs was probably Social Darwinism. W. J. Cash traces its popularity to the antebellum South's proximity to the frontier. *Gone with the Wind* imagery notwithstanding, the prewar South possessed nothing remotely resembling a fully developed aristocracy.[91] Instead, the South constituted a large portion of the American frontier, and its people were competitive and individualistic. The plantations perpetuated frontier conditions, and the crop lien system further reinforced competitiveness.[92] Alabama leaders felt obliged to soften the harshness of competition with frequent references to Christian charity and kindness to one's inferiors. For example, in his opening address to the 1901 constitutional convention John B. Knox said: "When it comes . . . to dealing with the negro, in domestic service, or in a business way, the Southerner is infinitely more indulgent to him than his Northern compatriot."[93] The treatment accorded predominantly black employees and prisoners in Alabama coal mines and steel plants suggests a harsher reality.[94]

Closely related to the notion of life as a competitive struggle in which those who win are the best was the idea that the best should and do rule. The elite myth held that human talent was hereditary; politicians and writers frequently referred to bloodlines, often in a Social Darwinian context. This theme merged easily into the idea that there existed a fixed, natural hierarchy with blacks at the bottom. Knox expressed this point in his constitutional convention address: "There is a difference . . . between the uneducated white man and the ignorant negro. There is in the white man an inherited capacity for government, which is wholly wanting in the negro."[95] Twenty-seven years earlier the *Montgomery Advertiser* editorialized: "The chief end and aim of this convention [of 1875] . . . is to guard the honor of the white race and secure 'the blue blood of the Caucasian,' against threatened pollution."[96]

Elite beliefs emphasized the naturalness and stability of this hierarchy. Blacks and poor whites, according to this view, were satisfied with their lot in life, and any complaints on their part were invariably instigated by foreign (Yankee) influences. As Knox stated, "The Southern man knows the negro, and the negro knows him. The only conflict which has, or is ever likely to arise, springs from the effort of ill-advised friends in the North to confer upon him, without previous training or preparation, places of power and responsibility, for which he is wholly unfitted, either by capacity or experience."[97] Populist lecturers from out of state fit neatly into "outside agitator" stereotypes, making them easy targets. The *Montgomery Advertiser* went so far as to accuse the Alliance of making "communistic utterances."[98] In later years, "progressives" admitted that perhaps some blacks disliked segregation and disfranchisement and that their feelings did not necessarily originate in northern propaganda, but they insisted that the South had to deal with its problems in its own way without outside interference from freedom riders and federal troops.

Despite the fact that the elite myth justified elite economic and political dominance, it also included democratic governance; the best ruled, but they were selected by the people, or at least propertied, literate white people, and of course these selections were confined to the Democratic party.

When Folsom won the governor's chair in 1946, the elite myth had been slowly crumbling for some fifteen years, but it still enjoyed remarkable vigor among Alabama's Big Mules. During Folsom's career three men gave expression to these ideas with special clarity: Governor Frank Dixon, a self-styled Birmingham Brahmin; the icy State Senator J. Bruce Henderson, a planter from the Black Belt county of Wilcox; and Gessner McCorvey, the blustery Mobile County lawyer and chairman of the state Democratic party executive committee.

Dixon, Henderson, and McCorvey believed that the best should rule and that they were the best. Here is Henderson addressing a Montgomery civic club:

> Because of something you have in leadership, integrity, initiative, energy, ability, enterprise and other qualities of the spirit, you stand out preeminent among your fellow men. You belong to the 4.23% of the people of this nation who enjoy incomes above $6,000.00 a year. You belong to the 4.23% of the people who pay 51% of the income taxes. You build the churches. You handle the charity campaigns. You pave the streets. . . . You are the presidents and executive officers, and you hold the high commissions. Some folks even call you the "Got Rocks" [referring to one of Folsom's favorite epithets]. I now accuse you of having some of the "Rocks." And what is more I charge that if you didn't have the "Rocks" you would get the "Rocks." You are not only respected because you have the ability to get the "Rocks" but because of your character, your leadership, your vision. . . . None of us have so many rocks but that if we rested our oars we would go down stream. If we have anything at all, it is only by enterprise and continued effort that we hold what we have. . . .
> . . . I have an idea that if you could keep things just like they are you would like to stick to your own knitting and let politics and government alone. . . .
> But what about the other 96%. They cast the votes. If you, on whom they depend for leadership in business, in church, in civic and social affairs desert them in politics, and if you are so absorbed in your business that you surrender to be organized by the renegade politicians, by the demagogues, the socialistic and the communistic thinkers, you can be sure that they will continue to take a larger and larger percentage of what you earn.[99]

As Henderson explained in a letter to *Montgomery Advertiser* publisher R. F. Hudson, his ideal was Virginia. "In Virginia and a few other states big business stands like a stone wall behind such men as Byrd and maintains an atmosphere which develops state political leaders—like Byrd—who are statesmen." In the same letter he suggested convening Alabama's major corporate leaders and landowners for the purpose of unifying their efforts in support of a single gubernatorial candidate.[100]

Many Alabama leaders of this period were prolific letter writers, and the messages they sent one another resemble deliberations of a corporate board of directors, its members possessing somewhat dissimilar perspectives but agreeing unanimously on major policies. One such point of agreement was the need for a restricted electorate. With Folsom in office and having a strong voice in the appointment of voting registrars, correspondence between Dixon, Henderson, and McCorvey showed the depth of this agreement. For example, McCorvey wrote the following to Dixon in 1947:

> You were worried particularly about North Alabama. Of course, in North Alabama they have a comparatively few number of negroes. What I was particularly interested in was Mobile, Jefferson, and Montgomery counties, and I believe we are going to get the situation down here handled all right, although Folsom's appointee is going to be absolutely all wrong. . . . I realize that up in North Alabama the wrong sort of Board of Registrars will register a lot of white people who have no business being registered, but, after all, we are not going to be able to do much in the way of preventing the registration of white citizens even though they are of a type which has no business voting.[101]

They also saw the poll tax as a way to eliminate bad elements from the electorate. In a 1945 letter to the members of the Alabama legislature McCorvey wrote:

> I think the poll tax, with its cumulative feature should be maintained in full force and effect. It is a lawful and legitimate method of getting rid of a very large number of people who would not cast an intelligent ballot even if they were given the right to vote. . . . I feel that it is as little as those of us who live in other sections of the state can do for that splendid group of Alabamians living in the Black Belt, to aid them in retaining control of their respective counties and prevent an ignorant and irresponsible group from taking charge. I had occasion to read the list of the signers of the Alabama Constitution of 1901 and I was struck with the high type of citizens, now for the most part passed to their reward, who drafted that Constitution. I do not think that we have a right to undo the work of that great group [who] had only in mind [the best] for their state and the determination to see to it that no radical and irresponsible group could take charge of our State Government or of any of our County Governments.[102]

Dixon, Henderson, and McCorvey hated integration with an intensity that is only partly reflected in the above quotations. For example, Henderson in a 1959 Camden Presbyterian Church document wrote: "Can a minority of agitators of two races, mix youth and sexes—without suffering a God-forbidden plunge into immorality when the established differential, in taking life is 5 to 1, when in rape it is 8 to 1, and when in the spreading of venereal diseases it is 18 to 1? Certainly integration will lower the degree of morality of the race with the older civilization."[103]

Governor Dixon had moments of self-doubt concerning his racial beliefs, but they passed quickly.

> We are behind the times, I admit. The Huns have wrecked the theories of the master race with which we were so contented so long. Derbies are now being worn by Jackasses and silk purses being made out of sow's ears. Bloodlines are out. The progeny of a cornfield ape blackened with the successive suns of Africa and Alabama, mated with a swamp ape from the Louisiana rice fields has developed promise as great as the sons of the great American families such as the Adams clan of New England. Henry Wallace is right—anthropology so teaches. But I buy dogs of a certain breed to fight, and I know that the sons of Man-O'-War are going to win races against all comers. The man who is close to the land—who follows bloodlines, knows the doctrines in which in my very human weakness, I prefer to keep my faith.[104]

As we show in the appendix, descriptions of decision making concerning political conflict of the sort presented in this chapter tend to lead to findings that power in a community, state, or nation is highly fragmented. But Alabama's history from 1870 to 1946 suggests the opposite conclusion. The 1901 constitution established an elite alliance composed of the state's two major economic estates, big agriculture and big business. Black Belt domination of the legislature facilitated the Birmingham–Mobile–Black Belt coalition's control over state government, and the elite's financial resources insured that its gubernatorial candidates enjoyed well-funded, but not always successful, campaigns. The shared philosophical views of its outspoken leaders gave the moral justification for their position and actions to preserve it. Folsom's belief that the Big Mules—the Got Rocks—dominated state government was well founded. In 1946 he embarked on a collision course with their immense power.

CHAPTER 4

Electoral Success

James E. Folsom . . . has put a hex on some Alabamians, and it's bad.
John Temple Graves

In March 1943 Folsom volunteered for the armed services, but he was denied entry because of his height. He was appalled at this turn of events, since success for a young man in the next election would require a military tour, preferably abroad in combat. One month later, after a vigorous application of political pressure, he was admitted into the army. After six months he was released because his size made him too difficult to outfit. He then joined the merchant marine as a chief petty officer. This was a better place for him than the army. Service aboard a troop ship was sufficiently life threatening for campaign purposes, and he was experienced in this work, having served on many voyages in the merchant marine during 1929–31.

With a postcard sent from Florence, Italy, while he was still in the merchant marine, he filed for the 1944 Democratic party primary in which delegates to the national convention would be selected. Typically, convention delegates were governors, senators, and wealthy contributors, but even though he was still at sea and did virtually no advertising, Folsom received over one hundred thousand votes and was elected a delegate-at-large. For Folsom this race was both a test of his popularity and another device to keep his name before the public; the huge vote he received meant that he had been highly successful on both counts.[1]

Tragically, soon after the primary his wife, Sarah, died from complications associated with a pregnancy. During the first year of their marriage she had experienced a very difficult pregnancy, and that first baby had been lost. Their children, Rachael and Melissa, were born after two more complication-ridden pregnancies, and after Melissa's birth the Folsoms had been warned that another pregnancy would be dangerous to Mrs. Folsom's health.

In 1944 she became pregnant again. Approximately two weeks prior to her death, Sarah and Jim Folsom journeyed to Elba, where Sarah and her brother Fleetwood held an anniversary party for their parents. During that visit she told her brother that she was not feeling well but not to say anything to the family. Two weeks later, Fleetwood took a phone call for his parents from Folsom, who told him that Sarah had just been hospitalized from a stroke, which caused partial paralysis, and that the doctors had had to take the baby. Shortly thereafter, blood poisoning set in and she died. That was in July 1944.[2] Upon Sarah's death he was released from the service to return home to his daughters.

Folsom's mother moved from Elba to Cullman to take over the house and raise the girls, but at her age the strain of such activity proved too great and she suffered a mild stroke. She returned to Elba, and Folsom's younger sister, Ruby Folsom Ellis, and her family then moved to Cullman to look after Jim and the girls. Ruby continued to care for the children after Folsom's inauguration in 1947, when she became Alabama's First Lady.[3]

Everyone who knew Jim and Sarah Folsom described Sarah's death as having a catastrophic impact on his life. One friend said: "When she died, he went into shock. He had a lot of respect for her ability. She and the judge had connections. Gradually, there was an increase in the booze and cards." Another friend recalled: "What hurt Folsom was the death of his wife. She was a very strong-willed individual who kept him in line. He really went ape after that."[4] Friends said that she quieted him not so much by what she did overtly as by the example of her modesty and intelligence. Many people close to him observed that his drinking (generally described as heavy, but never a problem) increased dramatically and began to include periodic binges.

After his mother's return to Elba the strong people in the family who, to some extent, could moderate his behavior and had something of Sarah's stabilizing influence—his mother and sister Thelma, Ross Clark, Judge Carnley, and his brothers—were hundreds of miles away. Fred was in Elba, and Robert and Carl (the brother Jim viewed as most like their father) were in the service. Many who would join his 1946 campaign were themselves heavy-drinking "Good Ole Boys" who reinforced Folsom's worst tendencies. There was much camaraderie, story telling, card playing, and partying, but there is little indication of the strong emotional support that could check his excesses.

Hoping attention to politics would ease his grief, friends urged him to attend the national convention. His performance at the convention sparked great controversy during the 1946 campaign. His opponents claimed that he had supported the hated left-leaning Henry A. Wallace for vice president over the popular Alabama Senator John H. Bankhead. This did not occur, however. The *Montgomery Advertiser,* always opposed to Folsom, reported accurately that he supported Bankhead until Bankhead withdrew in favor of Harry S. Truman.[5] At that point Folsom alone in the Alabama delegation voted for Henry Wallace. William D. Murray quoted Folsom as saying that he preferred Wallace to Truman because of "personal convictions."[6] In an interview Folsom maintained that he had little personal feeling for Wallace, but that the Congress of Industrial Organizations (CIO) had supported his 1942 gubernatorial bid, and so he felt obliged to return the favor by supporting Wallace. He further maintained that he had been unaware that Bankhead wanted the delegation to support Truman. "I didn't get the word," he said, very unconvincingly.

Although it is clear that Folsom carefully waited until Bankhead's withdrawal before shifting to Wallace, he could not have selected a more unpopular candidate to support. Wallace was the perfect image of the liberal Yankee intellectual whom conservative southerners love to hate. Folsom's action, a mixture of political calculation, ideological consistency, and wild abandon, was typical of many that would follow. Another indication of Folsom's unique approach to Alabama politics came on the train ride back from Chicago immediately after the convention. Alabama Democratic party leaders overheard a startling conversation between Folsom and a black Pullman porter named E. D. Nixon. The fact that Folsom was having a serious conversation with a black Pullman porter was itself unusual, but when Folsom declared, "Let me tell you, the day is going to come when we will recognize the Negro," he was jeered and ridiculed by his fellow delegates.[7] Later, during Folsom's second term as governor, Nixon organized the Montgomery bus boycott, one of the most important chapters in southern civil rights history.

After the convention Folsom returned to his insurance work. A year later he and his family were again hit by tragedy when Carl Folsom was killed on July 25, 1945, in Luzon, the victim of a military vehicle accident and, according to Folsom, of his ambition and politics.[8] Carl had spent most of the war coordinating military freight shipments in Mobile. Near the end of the war he had written Congressman Frank Boykin asking for a promotion in rank. Boykin's office sent the letter through channels, and a short time later Carl was suddenly transferred to the Philippines. The transfer may not have been instigated by Boykin but instead may have been the military's way of discouraging others from seeking promotion through their political connections. Carl had not only been important in Folsom's early campaigns but was to have had a central role in future races. Their plans called for Carl to be his "main campaign leader" after the war. To Folsom, Carl was a "wire-pulling political officer. . . . He was the best politician—better than I was. Best at working under the table and getting things done."[9]

Folsom had barely recovered from the shock of Sarah's death, and Carl's drove him further toward alcoholism. But he continued to work, and his North Alabama business thrived. Meanwhile, his insurance sales trips had a second purpose: he was quietly but systematically making political contacts wherever he went. The stealth with which he went about this work can be gauged from this comment by the *Montgomery Advertiser*'s lead political columnist Atticus Mullin on January 2, 1946: "No well posted political observer believes that Jim Folsom will run for governor. It is true that Jim has personal strength, but he has no statewide organization, and such an organization takes time and money."

Not long before Mullin wrote Folsom's premature political obituary for the governor's race, musicians in North Alabama were answering nondescript newspaper advertisements asking for people who could play "string music," what today would be called "country and western." The call was for accordion, fiddle, banjo, and guitar players. A string band called the Strawberry Pickers was formed to play as part of Folsom's campaign. At first, members of the new band were not even told what office he was pursuing.[10] The Strawberry Pickers was a good name; it carried the country imagery that Folsom wanted, and it contained a little play on words typical of the Folsom style.

The 1946 Campaign

Campaigning began in January, months earlier than normal, in the smallest towns. The conventional wisdom was that it was a waste of time to start a campaign that early because by voting day in May people who had heard a speech four months before would have long forgotten it. Folsom's logic was that people in rural areas had few sources of entertainment and little to do in January and February; so they would welcome a good string band (and the Strawberry Pickers, who, when his schedule permitted, included Hank Williams, were first-rate) even if it were accompanied by a politician. And, as it turned out, Folsom was as entertaining as his band. As the months clicked by, the group slowly spiraled in from the small towns to larger ones, where entertainment was more plentiful, life quicker, and memories shorter, and fewer people were busy with spring planting. The state's major urban centers were saved until the end. Part of the basic strategy, an extension of what had been done in 1942, called for mailings of circulars announcing Folsom's rallies to build up the crowds.

Folsom, the Strawberry Pickers, John Stiefelmeyer, and a few others started on a cold, cloudy morning in friendly territory—North Alabama. They began with less than two hundred dollars in expense money. By the end of their first day food and hotel expenses had drained most of their cash. The next day they were forced to pass the hat, or, more accurately, a bucket. Hobart Key, one of the band members, recalled: "When Jim came out with that bucket on the second day I was shakin' in my shoes—I didn't know whether it was goin' over or not. But the first haul was twenty-seven dollars and some odd cents."[11] The second rally on the same day netted over forty dollars. Roland Johnson, another Strawberry Picker, remembered: "When Jim counted the money on our first day of passing the bucket it came to more than one hundred dollars and Jim said, 'Boys, I'm gonna be the next governor of the state.' We figured that one hundred dollars a day would keep us on the road."[12]

This was the high point of Folsom's life. When he described it in later years, he relived it. He repeated the speeches as though he were back on a makeshift platform, on a tree stump, on the back of a pickup truck, in a high school auditorium, or on courthouse steps. "You see this corn shuck mop? You know what I'm goin' to do? I'm going to take that mop and scour out the kitchen and open up the windows and let a green breeze out of the north—called it a green breeze—a green breeze out of the north and you'll have the freshest, sweetest smell that you've seen in that Old Alabama capitol since it was built. Or somethin' like that. Now while the boys strike up a tune of 'Down Yonder in the Governor's Chair' . . . we'll pass the bucket."[13] His audiences were made up of tough, taciturn farmers in baggy bib overalls, jackets, muddy workshoes, and weather-beaten felt snap-brim hats, and he spoke in language they could understand.

> I'd say, "Turnip greens. I remember my mama she would be cookin' turnip greens and I'd see her hittin' those turnip greens on her hand, put 'em in water. . . . Turnip greens! Black eyed peas! I remember my mama cookin' those turnip greens. Folks, I didn't know what she was hittin' those turnip greens on her hand for till I was 19 years old and I was in Atlanta, Georgia, right across from the Langley Hotel where the Alabama football team was staying and we was eatin' turnip greens—the first storebought turnip greens I ever ate in my life, and I got into the turnip greens and tastin' sand, and right then I knew what ma was hittin' those turnip greens on her hand for. Cornbread! Ham! Put that all in together. You see this corn shuck mop? You know what I'm goin' to do? . . .
>
> Black eyed peas, cornbread, turnip greens, throw them in that black iron pot. They talkin' about these fancy cookin' pots advertisin' as the greatest in the world—they keep the vitamins and they'll do this—but mama's old black iron pot didn't do so bad."[14]

These accounts illustrate several important Folsom campaign tactics. Many have observed that he seldom read a formal speech word for word but instead used it as a foundation for extemporaneous remarks, often straying far from the written word. Those who conclude from this that everything he said publicly was extemporaneous are mistaken. Folsom developed campaign set pieces (not entire speeches), just as many stand-up comedians string together jokes to build routines. He often started with a memory or an observation (his mother hitting turnip greens on her hand) which he would then gradually build into an organized piece in speech after speech, changing a word here, adding a sentence there until it elicited the kind of response he intended. It would then be used repeatedly in that perfect form. These routines served as building blocks for speeches, and they could be moved around and used or not used as each audience and the time available required.[15]

He used symbols masterfully. In interviews he emphasized his use of the word "green" in the phrase "green breeze out of the north." He used the word not because of any literal meaning it held but because it added something to the phrase "breeze out of the north" and because it reinforced the next part of the sentence, which concerned the fresh, sweet-smelling capitol. Turnip greens have nothing to do with politics, but his dissertation on that subject established him as one of the crowd, a candidate for the state's highest office who actually knew what their lives were like because he had lived the same life. Folsom's reference to the sand in restaurant greens contained quiet suggestions that he and his backcountry listeners were united against an alien and somewhat grimy outside world. This is a typical populist theme, but rarely is it conveyed with such subtlety and warmth.

Effective as they were, none of his many symbolic devices compared with the corn shuck mop and the suds bucket. The corn shuck mop again established him as part of the society of common men, and the analogy between cleaning a house (he used rich detail to carry his listeners with him into his home) and cleaning the capitol was very powerful. It was also completely meaningless when applied to the complexities of governing a state, but symbols need have little relationship to reality to be effective. The suds bucket that he passed among the crowd was his premier device. It carried the suds (money) which would enable Big Jim to clear out the capitol (with the mop) the way the people wanted it done. Folsom drew the suds bucket strategy from his reading about Huey Long and W. Lee O'Daniel, both of whom passed buckets. O'Daniel, a flour salesman, had written on his buckets, "Flour and not pork." Folsom's carried the inscription, "Suds for Scrubbin."

Collections from the suds bucket represented a major source of funding for the campaign when money was in critically short supply. There can be little doubt that had the suds bucket failed, Folsom would have abandoned the campaign or lost.[16] The bucket saved him on several occasions. He was sometimes so low on funds that impromptu rallies had to be held just so that the bucket could be passed. Occasionally, he and his campaign team reached that point because they stayed in the best hotels and ate the finest food their budget would tolerate—shades of things to come.

The suds bucket was also a psychological ploy. When a person made his contribution, even if it was only a nickel or a dime, he had made a commitment to the Folsom movement and this commitment was as important as the money collected. Folsom tells of the time when Steifelmeyer was passing the bucket and he ignored an elderly black man. The man called him back. "'Come here, boss,' he said, and reached down into his dog-eared pocketbook, got a dime out, put it in there and said, 'Boss, I wants to jin up with y'all.' Couldn't even vote y'know. That was during the disenfranchisement."[17] Experience brought increasing sophistication in the use of the bucket. While it passed through the audience, he would emphasize that no one was allowed to contribute more than two dollars apiece. "That would make them put in five dollars just to show that they could do it."[18]

Folsom refused to play on racial fears in this or any other election campaign. In 1946 issues of segregation and black voting rights were not as important in Alabama as they were in other southern states, but, nevertheless, they frequently bubbled to the surface. Folsom said: "Gene Talmadge, Herman Talmadge's daddy, . . . got elected in 1946. I got elected cookin' turnip greens and he got elected on the race issue. That was his personal preservation, and I never did use it. The same time right in adjoining states—the same background—ethnic background. . . . He got elected just raisin' hell about the race question. Negro, Negro, Negro, Negro, and I never mentioned the thing. And I shook hands with the Negro."[19]

By shaking hands with "the Negro" he was committing an astounding breach of southern mores: he was treating blacks as men, not boys. Sometimes during campaigns, and also as governor, he would get out of a car, march past white dignitaries, and shake hands first with black laborers watching on the fringes of the crowd.[20] With all his tricks and artifices, amid a cool and rational drive for the power that he ached for, he insisted on using the campaign to "agitate for liberty."

The platform that he outlined in his speeches was ambitious. He advocated free textbooks through high school, more schools, a nine-month school term, increased salaries for teachers, increased Workmen's Compensation, increased unemployment insurance, compensation for occupational diseases, such as black lung, paved farm-to-market roads, a fifty-dollar monthly minimum pension to every person over sixty-five years of age (more than double the average at that time), repeal of the poll tax, and reapportionment of the state legislature on the basis of one man, one vote via a constitutional convention. He also stood in opposition to the Boswell Amendment, a proposed addition to the state constitution designed to circumvent Supreme Court voting rights decisions. To some contemporary eyes Folsom's platform may appear modest, even conservative, but in Alabama in 1946 it was radical. If enacted, it would have fundamentally changed the status quo. Alabama's political elite regarded a malapportioned legislature and disfranchisement of blacks and poor whites as crucial to their defense of power and privilege, and they were opposed to most of his other programs as well.

Commissioner of Agriculture and Industries Joe Poole, a colorless Black Belt plantation owner and the candidate of the most conservative Bosses, was one of Folsom's two major opponents. One newspaper reporter described him as a man of narrow vision whose main interest was in subduing blacks and poor whites. "He knew how to plow cotton and cuss niggers and little else," the reporter said.[21] The wealthy and powerful Alabama Farm Bureau Federation was the largest single group behind Poole's candidacy. He was also supported by large segments of the Agricultural Extension Service (which was supposed to be nonpolitical, but which rarely sat out any election of consequence), Alabama Power Company, and U.S. Steel Corporation.[22] Unaccountably, prohibition formed the centerpiece of Poole's campaign. He started with a flourish, attacking the other leading candidate, Lieutenant Governor Handy Ellis, a former dry, as the "pride and joy of the honky-tonk and gambling fraternity."[23] Many of Poole's conservative supporters sympathized with his desire to end the bane of liquor, but the state was heavily dependent on revenues from alcoholic beverage sales and their termination would mean that new sources would have to be found, a prospect few wanted. As Poole recognized the consequences of his stand, he softened it, claiming, "I am neither extremely dry, nor am I really wet."[24] Poole's campaign continued at this level and never recovered. Ellis took advantage of Poole's awkward retreat, saying, "Joe began to crawfish out—a crawfish, you know, always moves backwards."[25]

Handy Ellis, known in some circles as "Mule Skinner Ellis," a cigar-chomping, square-jawed veteran officeholder, was almost a caricature of a career politician. A highly experienced lawyer and a competent parliamentarian who had actively supported Graves in the Alabama Senate and during campaigns, he was the candidate of Progressives and a considerable number of Bosses who believed that Poole's inadequacies as a campaigner would keep him from winning. Employing classic Progressive rhetoric, Ellis attacked Poole as a Big Mule–Frank Dixon puppet.[26]

Ellis and Poole stressed many of the same pocketbook issues as Folsom. They called for more roads, better teachers' salaries, and the like. They rarely spoke in specific terms, however. Folsom's stands on such issues were more ambitious in the numbers of persons who would be affected, the amounts of money that would have to be spent, and the geographical scope of the programs. In addition, only Folsom spoke about civil rights issues, especially the need for legislative reapportionment, poll tax abolition, and open voter-registration procedures.

Two other candidates, Elbert Boozer, a conservative, and Gordon Persons, a moderate, were able campaigners, but they lacked the resources necessary to win. They were never serious contenders.

Ellis, Poole, and the press ignored Folsom and his platform until far into the campaign. There seemed no reason to take him seriously. In its early months his campaign appeared to be a shambles. Grover Hall, Jr., attended one rally when by accident the mailings announcing the rally had not been delivered. The audience was small and unresponsive, and Folsom's performance was weak.[27] Even as late as March, Hall found that little had changed in the rallies, but he had, for reasons not made clear, begun to doubt his perceptions. Barnard suggests that Hall was unaccustomed to judging reactions of laconic country people and that local newspaper editors were alerting him to the fact that Folsom was stronger than he appeared.[28]

Reporters seeking evidence of Folsom's progress in the size and tightness of his organization also underestimated his progress. In his speeches Folsom flayed his opponents for maintaining headquarters in Montgomery, "where they gather in little cliques and clans to huddle up in rooms, plot and plan more double talk. My headquarters are on the political stump and I have no managers, being responsible to the people and the people alone."[29] There was considerable truth in his description of his own organization. Gould Beech, editor of the populist *Southern Farmer*, was attracted to Folsom early in 1946; he called the Folsom office in Cullman, where he spoke to O. H. Finney, one of Folsom's key aides. Beech asked to speak to the campaign manager, and Finney responded that there was no such person but that he was the office manager and he would be happy to help. Beech volunteered to run Folsom's ads at no charge in his newspaper, and he asked Finney to send campaign materials that he could reproduce and print. Finney replied that he had none, but anything that Beech cared to print would be fine. On one occasion Beech attempted to contact Folsom headquarters in the state's second largest city, Mobile. The long-distance operator had no listing, but her supervisor happened to know that Folsom supporters often congregated in a particular barber shop, which in fact turned out to be the official headquarters. Similarly, it often happened that after a rally someone would pull Folsom aside and tell him that he had a sum of money to invest in newspaper ads and he would ask what Folsom wanted printed. Folsom would drape his arm over the person's shoulders and say, "You know the local situation better than I do. Whatever you put in is all right with me."[30]

The organizational looseness suggested by these examples was partly the result of calculation. Folsom reasoned that people worked hardest for a campaign when they held the hope that their efforts would be rewarded by a high governmental office. It followed from this that one's future situation could be estimated by one's position in the campaign machine, and if this machine were hierarchical (campaign manager, district manager, and so forth), only those few near the top would work diligently. No hierarchy meant that more people could be motivated to put greater effort into the campaign.[31] The loose structure also fit Folsom's personality. There has probably never been a major political figure in this country less inclined toward neat organizational charts and careful supervision of subordinates than Folsom.

The Folsom "organization" was assembled over a period of years in a casual, almost haphazard manner. It would probably be fair to say, however, that William (Bill) Drinkard, a Cullman mortician and businessman and vigorous bow hunter, was the campaign manager and central fund-raiser in both 1946 and 1954. Drinkard handled mailouts, dealt with printers, coordinated rally schedules, and performed many other critical functions. He was one of the first financially comfortable (but not wealthy) individuals to support Folsom.[32]

Ward McFarland of Tuscaloosa, one of Folsom's leading central and southwestern supporters, met him at the University of Alabama when they were both students there. It would be difficult to exaggerate the political importance of "The University," as it is often called in Alabama. Informal groupings among both undergraduates and law students often last for decades of governmental service. McFarland was a Graves Pie-Eater who turned to Folsom in desperation in 1942. By then he was an attorney, and few others of his stature were willing to work for Folsom in that part of the state.[33] In both 1942 and 1946 McFarland's major responsibility was the creation of campaign committees in the western counties from Tuscaloosa south to Mobile. These committees consisted largely of people he had met at the university and through his law practice. McFarland was the kind of person Folsom had in mind when he opted for a loosely knit campaign organization. McFarland had little or no interest in Folsom's desire to break Big Mule power. His main concern, like that of many others drawn to political campaigns, was the development of personal contacts from which he could profit in later business ventures.

Folsom met his driver Bill Lyerly at an American Legion conference in January 1946.

> He don't drink and he don't smoke, and there's a lot of stuff in politics—he's pretty strict—straight laced. The first time I run into Bill he was a high point man back from World War II—he had priorities—had him an automobile—and I was jus' enjoyin' myself with some old friends who had helped me in '42 and we was a-drinkin' and enjoyin' ourselves and just havin' a ballgame. And I met Lyerly. And he said, "I've got this brand new Ford automobile. When you get ready to run you let me know and I'll be there with you." Why, hell, I thought it was jus' a bunch of god damned malarky. I didn't pay no attention to him. And I got down to Prattville, and I was speakin' to 'em. And there was a big crowd

and he came up to me a-smilin' and a big handshake, and he said, "You remember me?" and I said, "Oh, yeah, you're that boy from Montgomery. I thought you was going to bring that automobile." He says, "It's right out there. Brand new. All you've got to do is sit in the back seat. I've got the gasoline. We'll ride." And he had a back seat back there. And I could lay down back there and prop up my foot and I would sleep between speeches.[34]

Like McFarland, Lyerly was essentially nonideological, but Lyerly was not nearly as ambitious; he developed a personal loyalty to Folsom. His was an honest, straightforward attachment.

The ultraconservative state Representative Ira Thompson was another early Folsom supporter, despite his close ties to the KKK. Folsom defended his association with Thompson. "I inherited the old Bibb Graves followin' and Ira Thompson was part of it. I remembered the trouble he got in when the *Advertiser* exposed him as a Kluxer, but the Kluxer business was dead, and I wanted Thompson on my side. . . . Now, I'm anti-Klux, but the Klux business was used for political purposes. My folks were agin it from the word go. Always have been."[35]

As the campaign developed, it was joined by Gould Beech. A brilliant young journalist who had held editorial positions with the *Birmingham News* and *Montgomery Advertiser* before assuming editorship of the *Southern Farmer,* he had also done free-lance speech writing for several legislative candidates and for Handy Ellis early in 1946. Beech's multifarious past belied his strongly held populist-liberal beliefs. Before enlisting in the Folsom cause Beech quizzed him on the sincerity of his populist ideas. Folsom satisfied the writer with a recitation, delivered while lying on a hotel bed wearing combat boots with no socks, of how his grandfather and uncles had opposed Alabama's entry into the Civil War. In Beech, Folsom had a writer who could fit his simple, straightforward style of speaking.

O. H. Finney was a bulwark of order in the 1946 campaign as he had been when serving as Folsom's administrative assistant in Marshall County and aide in the congressional race. Anyone as disordered as Folsom who attempts something that involves administrative complexity needs someone who is intelligent, hardworking, and (above all) systematic. Finney fit all those requirements. Like Beech, he was a populist and had a strong personal loyalty to Folsom.

These men were typical of the untypical nature of the Folsom camp. Surely few political candidates have ever had as fluid and heterogeneous a campaign organization as the one that came together around Folsom in 1946.

In the midst of the campaign on April 18, 1946, Folsom's mother suddenly died. Folsom had not fully recovered from the deaths of his wife and brother, and he was jolted by this third loss, but after a few days of mourning he plunged back into the campaign.

The campaign, with its three to five rallies a day, quickly developed into a routine. Strawberry Picker Hobart Key remembered it well. "We would start playing 15 minutes before the scheduled beginning of the speech. You could hear the music all over town. Folsom would hit the edge of town with Bill Lyerly about five minutes before his time and wait until he heard his cue and then they would drive in on cue. At first we couldn't get a local person to introduce him, so a member of the band would. Then we kept it up to avoid irritating local factions. Also, the propaganda was that we didn't have a chance because none of the local people wanted to get involved, and this helped our image."[36]

When Folsom arrived at a rally, he did not always begin speaking immediately. The *Montgomery Advertiser* gave this colorful description of Folsom's warmup. "It has been his common practice upon arriving at a speaking location to announce that he is tired and will have to rest. Whereupon he removes his brogans, and, taking care to show that he wears no socks, extends himself on the bare ground. In due time the giant stirs, sits upright, studiously brushes the dirt from his toes, puts on his shoes and gets up for business. With a hearty handshake for every man, woman, and child in sight he is ready for his speech which consists largely of praise for pretty women, thoughts of the old mule who was dear to him, and reminiscences of how his mother used to fix turnip greens."[37] Asked about his practice of removing his shoes in public, Folsom responded tersely: "Got big feet. Shoes hurt. Can't think when my feet hurt, so I took off the shoes. Helps my thinkin' to be able to wiggle my toes."[38]

Folsom's rallies developed into an art form. The *Tuscaloosa News* carried this report of Folsom's visit to that town. "Snappy fiddling tunes that would make grandma take on hepcat ways, mixed with lonesome numbers that moaned of trouble between a gal and her man attracted a crowd of some 400 Tuscaloosa Countians Saturday morning to hear J. E. (Big Jim) Folsom. . . . It looked like an ancient Fourth of July celebration observing the termination of a community logrolling, lacking only a plate of turnip greens, side meat, and a snort of apple cider to complete the picture. . . . One man parked a truck full of cows in front of the courthouse steps where Big Jim spoke and stayed through the speaking. The cows didn't even switch their tails."[39]

As the campaign developed, new set pieces were added. "Roland," Folsom would command a band member, "hold up that foot." Roland Johnson would then exhibit a muck-encrusted shoe from a rain-soaked mud road. "There ain't gonna be no more mud on that boy's foot when we come back," Folsom would intone.[40] Road construction was a major issue in 1946. Few rural roads were paved, and many roads connecting even county seats were either unpaved or a complete ruin, but while Poole and Ellis were dully proclaiming that they would construct new roads in an efficient, businesslike manner, Folsom was making the point with Roland Johnson's foot.

As the weeks went by, his speeches became ever more fluid, mixing folk history, blunt position statements, and self-destructive ad-libs. He chose conservative Montgomery as a good place to proclaim his opposition to the Boswell Amendment.[41] At the same rally he spoke against the Marshall Plan in general and aid to England in particular. At the time the Marshall Plan, which gave assistance to war-torn Europe, was enjoying extraordinarily widespread bipartisan support throughout the country. Here he was following his father-in-law's example of using an election speech to educate the populace to his viewpoint.

Some of his ad-libs would have ruined a normal candidate. On one hot day in Talladega he commented in his speech that his performance would be improved by a cold beer. Later he found that the county was having a wet-dry referendum. Even though the county went dry, Folsom led the ticket. The lesson he drew from that experience was that "it didn't matter what you say so long as you tell the truth and you are sincere."[42]

He seemed to enjoy taunting conservative whites in the Black Belt during his infrequent rallies there, knowing that he would receive few of their votes no matter what he said. He would sometimes look around the audience and observe that he saw a lot of people they called "black" who were nearly as white as he was, and "I want you to know that the sun didn't bleach 'em."[43] Similar lines were used in Black Belt counties throughout his career. According to a reporter, in his 1962 gubernatorial campaign, at the height of the most intense racial turmoil of the century, he surveyed a Black Belt audience, noted the presence of many light-skinned Negroes, and commented that, despite Black Belt lawmakers' opposition to integration, "There's a whole lot of integratin' goin' on at night."[44]

After he had finished a speech, Folsom would work his way through the crowd, kissing women on the forehead and engaging people in quick, friendly conversations. An especially tall individual would be greeted with, "Hi, big 'un!" To others he would say, "What's your name, boy?" One of his campaign workers overheard people say in awe, "He was interested in what my name was." As he moved slowly along, people would reach out and gently touch the edge of his jacket or his shoulder. By the time he had finished, strangers believed that they knew him personally. He generated an affection and loyalty unlike anything seen in Alabama before or since.[45]

Folsom loved people or, more precisely, he loved being loved. This often made it difficult for schedule-conscious aides to pull him away from crowds. On one occasion Bill Lyerly managed to get him to the car, where he briefly left Folsom to the business of accepting large contributions (averaging between twenty and fifty dollars) that people did not want to place anonymously in the suds bucket. Upon his return Lyerly discovered that Folsom had disappeared. After several inquiries, Lyerly, grumbling to himself about how anyone could manage to lose a six-foot-eight-inch candidate, tracked him to a grocery store and found him juggling oranges and telling stories, to the delight of surrounding admirers.

Adherence to a schedule was made even more difficult by Folsom's habit of stopping for catnaps and meals on the road. Between rallies he would abruptly command Lyerly to stop, whereupon he would fall asleep in the back seat and awake a few minutes later completely alert. This ability helped him maintain the grueling schedule of three to five rallies per day week after week. Lyerly put nearly thirty thousand miles on his car and wore out two sets of tires. His trips were often interrupted by more or less random snack stops at the homes of complete strangers along Alabama's back roads—a habit he had developed in 1936 and 1938. Folsom would arrive unannounced at a house and ask for something to eat, preferably cornbread and buttermilk, which he would wolf down on the front porch. Those visits were often accompanied by promises of road paving, which by all accounts he remembered and acted on as governor. During one such stop he noticed a housewife struggling with wet laundry on a line while a car sped past on a dry dirt road, enveloping the laundry in clouds of red dust. Folsom turned to Lyerly and said sadly and quietly, "No one ought to have to live like that."[46]

During the campaign Folsom met his second wife, Jamelle Moore, a beautiful brunette southern belle. Here is Folsom's description of how they met.

> I was campaignin' and I was happy go lucky and enjoyin' the campaign—just immensely enjoyin' it—it was proof that I was winnin'. I was just radiating a winner. Naturally, when I saw a good looking girl and so on and so forth. I wasn't married. I spoke at Berry. That was my last speech of the day before I spoke at the county seat that night. And Berry was covered up with people, and I was shaking hands with people waiting until the band got through playin'. . . . And that particular day I was concentratin' on shakin' hands and I went into a little country store and there was my wife standin' there with some sales ladies and so forth, they was on the inside lookin' out. And I asked her name and told her when the speech was over I wanted to buy her a cold drink. And I bought her a cold drink and walked home with her and made a date with her and had one of the band boys pick her up and carry her over and brought her back. And that's the way it happened. She was attractive to me. I believe in marryin' somebody who's attractive to ya, instead of marryin' for influence or this, that, and the other. I wanted a female that's attractive so you'll have attractive chillun'.[47]

When she first met Folsom during the 1946 campaign, Jamelle Moore was a teenager. She and her friends knew nothing about Folsom, but since his coming to her hometown carried with it a carnival air, they went to the town square. They congregated in the drugstore near the square drinking soda pop, and as he began speaking, they went outside to hear him. As they stepped out of the store, she remembered, Folsom fixed his eyes on her and said, "If this town can produce such pretty girls as that, it must be a fine place." Mrs. Folsom says today, "Of course, I was pleased."[48]

When Folsom finished his speech, he pushed his way through the crowd and asked her to attend a rally in a nearby town that evening. She had seen pictures of him with his two daughters and assumed that he was married. When she told Folsom this, he explained that he was a widower and that he would not have asked her out if he had been married. She agreed to accompany him if she could get her parents' permission. Jamelle's father was a strong Folsom supporter and had brought his wife to the rally. Jamelle and Folsom walked over to her parents to obtain their approval for a date. Her father quickly assented, but her mother protested until her father abruptly growled, "If I say she can go, she can go."[49]

Later that evening one of Folsom's aides escorted Jamelle to the neighboring town. The rally there was held in the courthouse, and it was packed. After the rally, Folsom took her to a party. She remembered that there were dozens of beautiful girls there who surrounded Folsom crying, "Kiss me, Big Jim, kiss me!" She thought, "How can I compete with them?" She was asked if she wanted a drink, but she had never had alcohol in any form. She said, "In the town in which I grew up, there were always three or four families who had a bottle hidden under the kitchen sink, and everyone knew who they were," but her parents were not in that small group. She requested and received a milkshake.[50] That was the beginning of their two-year courtship.

In Birmingham a young legislative candidate just back from World War II and, in his words, "full of vim and vigor ready to reform the damned world and do away with corruption and waste in government" had just finished a grueling race for an Alabama House seat. "When my wife and I were ready to vote after a hell of a campaign (I would melt down three shirts a day and my wife spent hours a day on the telephone), we went to the polling place, a country grocery store on the north side. We got in there and my wife said, 'Wait a minute. Who are we going to vote for for governor?' I said, 'I believe what Ellis said about Poole being a crook and vice versa. I don't know Folsom. Some people say he's a clown, but underneath I think he may have the ability to be governor.' She said, 'Me too.'"[51] Many others thought the same thing.

Folsom won the May 7 primary with 104,152 votes, 28.5 percent of the total, far short of a majority but nevertheless an amazing victory. Again, his greatest strength came from the rural North Alabama—Wiregrass coalition, and his greatest opposition from the Black Belt. In its postelection analysis the press determined that he had won largely because of his personal charm combined with voter ignorance of his true nature.

Joe Poole's defeat was widely attributed to his lack of personal appeal and a bungled campaign. As we shall see in a later chapter, however, it was an early event in what was to be a decline in the political fortunes of Black Belt leaders caused by basic changes in Alabama's social and economic structure.

Newspaper editors agreed that once voters had cleared their heads, Ellis, who ran a close second with 24.2 percent of the vote, would win the runoff. Ellis quickly adopted this theme, saying that the people had had their "small fun in the first primary," but that the time had passed "for clowning and hippodroming and putting on a medicine show. It is time now, and high time to get down to business—serious business . . . to turn back the most serious threat that has faced us since reconstruction days."[52] Ellis's characterization of Folsom as being a "serious threat" to the status quo was probably more a matter of campaign rhetoric than a careful evaluation of Folsom's actual potential. At this point Folsom was viewed by most Big Mules and their minions as a talented vote getter and an irritant, but hardly a "threat."[53]

At first glance, Ellis's position after May 7 appeared fairly sound. He was only 4.3 percentage points behind Folsom and a logical argument could be made that Folsom would receive few votes from the relatively conservative Poole, Boozer, and Persons camps. A few days after the primary Poole and Boozer threw their support to Folsom, but Persons, together with most other political influentials in the state, favored Ellis, and there was no guarantee that Poole and Boozer supporters would follow the suggestions of their leaders and vote for Folsom rather than Ellis, with whom they were in much greater ideological sympathy.[54] Still, Ellis, whose career had by and large been one of progressive moderation, must have felt some desperation, for he turned to a nasty mixture of red-baiting and racism. He also called attention to organized labor's active support of Folsom through the Congress of Industrial Organization's Political Action Committee. He referred to Folsom as a "naive and inexperienced young opportunist" who was serving as a CIO "puppet." Ellis charged that if the CIO "seizes the sole power, it will wreak all other unions in our state, destroy our traditions, and disrupt our fine and wholesome race relations by breaking down our segregation laws."[55]

Newspapers that supported Ellis also gave prominent attention to CIO-PAC's endorsement of Folsom. The editor of the *Dothan Eagle* wrote an editorial reprinted in the *Huntsville Times* that linked Folsom and the CIO and accused the CIO of being controlled by "the Communist fringe."[56]

Big Mule fears of CIO victories in Alabama gubernatorial, congressional, and state legislative races were fueled by wire service and *New York Times* coverage of CIO-PAC's national campaign, complete with accounts of multimillion-dollar war chests being used against conservative candidates.

Folsom responded with his deadliest weapon, wit. He told a Montgomery crowd: "Before May 7 all you heard was that Folsom was a nice country boy—with no organization, no machines, no corporations, no state politicians—just a country boy out in a sea of humanity trying to get himself a few votes. But since May 7, Big Jim is a bi-ig, ba-ad booger!"[57] Later he would recall this critical period:

> Right up to that time they had ignored me. But in the runoff I was a Henry Wallace communist. Oh, I was just everything, really bad. They really pictured me sinister. I remember this rally in Montgomery and it was just slam runnin' over, and, of course, they had to lock the doors and there were just as many outside. . . . And I cited way back in the history of the family: "There's one thing between me and Pa. He run all his life and never was beat, and I've run all my life and never was elected, and I'm tellin' you I wants on the payroll!" That just tore the house down. . . . And I told them another joke. I had old Army shoes. They didn't have these king size then and I had to order my shoes and I didn't have anything except the Army shoes had the size stamped on the side. . . . And I told this story: "They tellin' a big ole political lie on me. They tellin' it on salt water down on the Gulf. They tellin' it in the Piney Woods. They tellin' it around the state capitol. They tellin' it through the mountains. What they tellin' on me? I want Y'all to help me beat it down. Its a big ole political lie." And they'd say, "What in the world are they tellin' on Big Jim now?" "They tellin' that I wear a size 16 shoe, and it ain't so folks I just wear a 15 ½."[58]

At this point he would elevate his monstrous hoof into the air and point with delight at a "15 ½" stenciled on the instep. The laughter was deafening.

Once again, Folsom had more than comedy in mind when he used the combat boot routine. He was able to say things clearly and directly, but he preferred symbols and parables. While people laughed at the "15 ½," an important message was being imprinted on their minds: his footwear was no ordinary boot; it was a U.S. Army combat boot, which meant that Folsom was a veteran, "the only war veteran in the governor's race," as the idea was less subtly expressed in an infrequently run newspaper advertisement.

Folsom possessed his own sense of taste and propriety. He did not care for the flag waving so popular among World War II veteran political candidates in 1946. It was crude and obvious and unseemly. The size 15 ½ boot was in a peculiar way graceful and smooth. He dealt with religion in the same manner. In the course of some of his speeches he would mention that his pastor had approached him about becoming a deacon. "I'm not the best caliber person for that job," Folsom would say, describing his response. "I'm sure you know that I take a nip now and then and sometimes my language is not the best." According to Folsom, the preacher responded, "That's alright, Jim. We want someone to represent the rougher element of the church." This was Jim Folsom's way of telling the voters that he was a

Baptist. He was sensitive about overusing religious symbolism in his campaign.

As the days went by, Folsom's performances became ever sharper, new set pieces were developed, now with Gould Beech's expert assistance, and audiences became more responsive. People at Folsom rallies laughed, applauded, and danced. Even Ellis loyalists and hardened newspaper men found themselves reacting in spite of themselves.

Handy Ellis tried in vain to project a "man of the people" image by having himself photographed behind a plow mule. But the rigging was wrong. Folsom spotted the mistake, had the picture enlarged, and exhibited it at rural rallies while lecturing audiences on the proper way to hitch a mule: "If you don't do this right he's going to fill up his stomach with air." His audiences knew how to hitch a mule, and they knew that he knew and that Ellis was nothing but another city slicker trying to fool them.[59] Folsom's folksy style was reinforced by photos in *Life* magazine a few days before the runoff showing him in his bathtub and eating dinner barefoot.

The *Birmingham Post*'s brilliant conservative columnist, John Temple Graves, could hardly stand the sight of the hapless Ellis sliding toward defeat. In a fit of frustration he wrote:

> James E. Folsom, the Cullman insurance man, has put a hex on some Alabamians, and it's bad. . . . The big part of his following is among our farmers. And you can only understand how they would be voting for the very man they should oppose [because of his ties to labor unions] by saying he has them hypnotized.
>
> The hypnotic word is simple, and easy to say. It is "fokes." Folsom just stands up before our fine farm people and says, "fokes." Then he says it again—"fokes." And then he says it a few more times—"fokes"—and you begin to feel all warm and happy and careless. You stop noticing what he is saying, you overlook the promises that can't be kept. . . .
>
> Fokes—fokes—fokes! But he isn't our folks.[60]

Folsom responded to attacks with more than humor. He counterattacked with a combination of tartness and humanity. "They can't stop us by trying to divide race and race, class and class, or religion and religion. We've just finished fighting a war against hatred and violence. We're starting a good neighbor policy right here in Alabama. . . . They are satisfied with things as they are. They are satisfied for Alabama to be way down at the bottom among the 48 states. They are satisfied for Alabama people to make less."[61]

During this period Folsom delivered a classic speech, as effective as any in his career. It dealt with state liquor stores. During World War II liquor was rationed because alcohol was needed by the chemical industry. On those rare occasions when a shipment of decent liquor reached Alabama only a favored few got it. What was mainly sold to the state stores was "Spot

Bottle" whiskey, really awful stuff purchased by the Alcoholic Beverages Control Board in bulk and bottled within the state (less than a month from still to sale). The bottles bore a large black spot on the label. Another brand was called "Torpedo Juice." Folsom used this situation to make a point about power and privilege: "You go to a liquor store and stand in line for two hours in the hot sun, and you know what's wrong in Montgomery. And you get to the counter and there's nothing left but rot-gut whiskey, and you know what's wrong in Montgomery. And when you get home and you drink it and wake up the next morning, you *sure* know what's wrong in Montgomery."[62]

Every city has a group of families who have lived there for several generations, who own considerable amounts of property, and who represent the pinnacle of high society. In some places they are called the "country club set," but in Montgomery they are called "Old Montgomery." One such Montgomery family held a conference each night before an election at the once-grand mansion of the family's matriarch in the Cloverdale District. This elegant lady was very weak physically, and so they met in her bedroom; she was propped up with pillows as though she were on a throne. It was almost a ritual—everyone had his place to sit. The decision for governor in the first 1946 primary had been easy—they voted for the distinguished looking, steel-gray haired *gentleman,* Gordon Persons. Persons lost, and the runoff left Ellis and Folsom. So they met again, and the grandmother said, "Ellis is the candidate of the *Advertiser* and the *Advertiser* is always pro-whiskey." Usually, that would have been sufficient and the discussion would have ended without it even having to be said that the family would vote for Ellis's opponent. But this time one of her sons spoke up and said, "I could tolerate a crook, but I just can't vote for a clown." The venerable old lady thought and paused several seconds before replying: "We vote for Ellis."[63]

Folsom defeated Ellis by 195,000 to 140,000 votes. His strategy of appealing to the largely white counties of the north and south had finally paid off in a victory. His election, together with the election of more than 100 new legislators out of a total of 140 in both houses, was widely interpreted as a "revolt of the 'outs' against the 'ins.'"[64] Governor Frank Dixon's feelings about the election, contained in a letter written to a friend, were widely shared: "[Folsom's] nearest opponent was an old-time politician, surrounded in large part by the sorriest element of the old line political forces in the state. The other candidates pretty well succeeded in tearing Ellis, the old-time politician, to pieces in the first primary. . . . [Folsom's] greatest vote came from rural people, to whom the P.A.C. threat apparently means very little."[65]

Most analysts agreed that the election result could not be explained by CIO-PAC power because Folsom's victory margin had been far too large and many CIO-PAC candidates had been defeated even in industrial counties.[66]

One clue to the outcome could be found in the makeup of Folsom's most active supporters. Bill Lyerly and Hobart Key were typical of many who were attracted to the Folsom campaign. They were young veterans who, after defeating the greatest war machines ever created, returned home with vastly expanded feelings of what could be accomplished. These World War II veterans seemed to share not an ideology or a single program but rather a desire for change, and this was reflected in the results of many primaries and general elections throughout the country in 1946 and 1948.[67] Campaigns aimed against the status quo worked against conservatives in some places and against liberals elsewhere. Hobart Key said: "In 1946 World War II was just over. War experiences encouraged dissatisfaction with the status quo. Vets saw what things were like elsewhere and what could be accomplished with determination. Before we went we didn't realize where taxpayers' money was going. When we got back we didn't have anything to come back to—no money, no jobs, nothin'."[68] Returning Alabama veterans faced a stark choice between, on one side, four Big Mule candidates who seemed more closely tied to 1901 than 1946, men who seemed completely removed from their daily world and who often spoke in gloomy tones about the future and, on the other side, Big Jim, a fellow veteran, for whom all men were equal and everything was possible.

And there was his charm. He possessed, at least as seen from a distance, a little boy's charm. Up close he was liked by men and attractive to women, without that attraction being threatening to men. He did not use his awesome frame to intimidate—there were no loud, mean-spirited harangues; he was low keyed and funny. He seldom preached political sermons, and those few he delivered carried a positive, constructive tone—not hell fire but salvation. And he was charismatic. His charisma partly derived from his size—breadth as well as height. When that bearlike figure lurched into view, the effect was startling and disquieting. Part of the magnetism derived from his single-minded devotion to politics—ideological politics—politics with goals. He was far more interested in where people stood on the *issues* (one of his favorite words) than in who was likely to win or lose. At its core, politics, in his view, was not a game; it was, despite the jokes and humor, a deadly serious, centuries-old struggle of working people versus kings, slaveholders, or corporate elites. Nothing else really mattered. This single-minded passion compelled one to pay attention to him. At the same time, it served as an impenetrable barrier, keeping everyone at a distance. When his mind was not occupied with kings and slaveholders, politics was a relaxation for him.

Folsom's 1946 victory was a vivid demonstration that county rings could be circumvented by direct appeals to voters combined with the organization of ad hoc county and city groups. No more would candidates be able to win merely by collecting the endorsements of politicians in courthouse meetings. With one exception, the 1978 campaign of Forrest (Fob) James, all successful gubernatorial candidates after 1946 would emulate Folsom's campaign approach in whole or in part.

When Folsom won, it was widely assumed that his ambitious platform had been little more than a tool for achieving electoral victory. The Big Mules reacted with simple horror. How could such a bumpkin have stumbled into the governor's chair? Chauncey Sparks was one of the first to understand that there might be more to him—that he might be a serious-minded reformer—and in letters he warned others.

CHAPTER 5

Legislative Politics, 1947–1948

> If I would dance to their tune, you'd see big fine editorials about what a great governor "Big Jim" is. But I'm not dancin' to their tune—I'm dancin to *your* tune.
>
> James E. Folsom

A superficial reading of the Alabama Constitution would suggest that the governor's major responsibilities are confined to administration, that is, to the efficient implementation of policies formulated by the legislature. This is in fact a major gubernatorial responsibility, but the governor has over the years become "chief legislator" as well. The role of chief legislator is largely customary, but that does not make it any less real or important. These two roles are closely related, and it is somewhat artificial to cover them in separate chapters, but failure to do so would result in great confusion because of the complexity and scope of legislative and administrative operations.

The Alabama state politics of Folsom's era (and to a large extent of today) was a one-party multifaction system. The major contests were in the Democratic party with the most intense competition being in the governor's race during the Democratic primary. With many candidates in this race, the hopefuls ran on elaborate platforms to distinguish themselves from the herd, and they campaigned independent of the legislative candidates, each of whom ran on his own locally oriented platform. Coordination of legislative and gubernatorial candidate positions or organizations was rare.

When elected, the gubernatorial candidate turned his personal platform into his legislative program. This was the situation that Hallie Farmer sketched for the 1930s and 1940s and Coleman Ransone described for the 1950s:

> Members of the legislature are elected on a personal platform, which usually has little relevance to the governor's avowed program. . . . There can be no successful appeal to party responsibility or regularity. The governor must painfully build up his own factional group within the legislature to achieve and maintain sufficient strength to have the major part of his program enacted into law. The construction of this factional machine is a time-consuming process involving a great many personal interviews and not inconsiderable patronage. Hence,

the southern governor may have some grounds for feeling that the legislative aspect of his functions should be given more importance than is assigned to it by his counterparts elsewhere in the nation. Most southern governors seem to feel that the electorate tends to judge them primarily on their ability to secure passage of a major part of their program.[1]

Ransone identified several methods of influencing the legislature in a one-party state. They included presession caucuses with party leadership or factional groups to establish communication channels and select legislative leadership, messages to the legislature, and individual or group conferences with legislators throughout the session. Failure to build a workable coalition using these tools meant that the governor would have to use veto threats, patronage, appeals to the public for support (accomplished by media appeals and, if necessary, the special session), and, if all else failed, the veto.

The 1901 constitution established a 105-member House of Representatives. The four most populous counties at that time (Jefferson, which included Birmingham, at 140,420; Montgomery at 72,047; Mobile at 62,740; and Dallas at 54,667) received 7, 4, 3, and 3 House seats, respectively. Twenty-six counties ranging in population from 25,162 to 43,702 in population received 2 seats apiece. Fifteen of these counties were in the Black Belt. The Black Belt and Jefferson County working coalition would control half the House votes.

The Senate was apportioned among 35 districts; the 12 most populous counties became single-member districts. As in the House, the Black Belt together with Jefferson County could control half the votes.

Changes in the constitution could be made only by constitutional amendment requiring both legislative action (three-fifths vote in each house) and a popular vote. Initiative and referendum were unavailable as a mechanism for voter action.

In the first legislative session in 1947 Folsom learned about the realities of dealing with this Boss-dominated legislature, as progressive governors had before him. In 1948 the Boss-dominated legislature learned about the reality of dealing with a governor unlike any the state had ever seen. Many of their old techniques for influencing the governor failed; new means of control had to be developed.

Two important events closely followed the 1946 primary: the campaign for Senator John Bankhead's position following his death late in May and the struggle over a voting disfranchisement measure known as the Boswell Amendment. As the new titular head of the Democratic party, Governor-elect Folsom played a role in both fights. His actions sent signals to his opponents that for him politics was not a game but a serious matter and that his campaign pronouncements were more than rhetoric.

The Senate Campaign

Bankhead's seat was pursued by Congressman John Sparkman, Congressman Frank Boykin, and former state senator James Simpson. Sparkman, a North Alabama tenant farmer's son, had worked his way through college, served five terms in Congress, and in 1946 was majority whip. Mobile's Frank Boykin, also a five-term congressman, was a cartoonist's image of a jowly hack politician come to life. He has been described as being more interested in building his personal fortune than in carrying out his congressional responsibilities. James Simpson, from Jefferson County, had been defeated two years earlier in his bid for the other Senate seat won by Lister Hill. He was the Frank Dixon–Big Mule candidate. Sparkman and Boykin openly courted Folsom and even Simpson attempted to take oblique advantage of the governor-elect's popularity by trying to market himself as the "true 'liberal statesman' in the race."[2] Senator Hill (a moderate), most major newspapers, and Folsom all endorsed Sparkman. Folsom pretended to agonize over the choice to spare Boykin's feelings, but Sparkman represented one of Folsom's two adopted homes, he was much closer to Folsom ideologically than was either of the other candidates, and Folsom suspected Boykin of being partially to blame for his brother Carl's death.[3] Folsom says today that there was never any doubt as to whom he would support. Despite Boykin's last-minute claim that Bankhead had endorsed him on his deathbed, Sparkman won overwhelmingly and went on to build a distinguished career in the Senate.[4]

Despite the fact that Sparkman, Hill, and Folsom had similar bases of voter support and each focused on a combination of populist–New Deal positions, particularly in relation to economic issues, they would never coordinate their campaign activities. Nor would the three come to work together in the state political arena. (Hill and Sparkman would work together closely in the Senate.) All three drew a great deal of support from black voters and lower socioeconomic groupings of whites. Analysis shows that Sparkman and Hill were able to gain greater support from upper-middle-class and upper-class whites.[5]

The Boswell Amendment

In a one-party state such as Alabama, the primary was far more important than the general election, since winning the majority party primary almost automatically meant general election victory. Alabama, like so many southern states, had allowed the Democratic party to operate under the so-called white primary system. Under this arrangement the party was deemed a private organization with the right to determine its own membership and regulate its own activities. The primary was viewed as a party activity and therefore outside state control. The party could limit voting in the primary to party members, and, of course, the definition of membership was left to the party. Carefully drafted membership rules, tied to past patterns of Populist or Republican voting, allowed the exclusion of blacks and many poor whites. In 1944 the Supreme Court extended the Fifteenth Amendment to political parties and struck down the white primary.[6]

Fearing that large numbers of blacks and North Alabama whites would register to vote, the Alabama legislature responded with the Boswell Amendment to the state constitution. The amendment had its origins in letters between State Democratic Executive Committee Chairman Gessner McCorvey and former governor Frank Dixon.[7] It gave local voting officials enough discretion to permit them to deny registration to those they viewed as unfit. A new applicant would be required to "read and write, understand and explain any article of the Constitution of the United States." The content of each test and the judgment as to whether an applicant met those requirements were to be made by local voting officials, whose decisions were not expected to be objective.

As a constitutional amendment, the Boswell Amendment had to be voted on in a statewide referendum. Dixon, McCorvey, and a distinguished group of Big Mule political leaders, including Wilcox County Senator J. Bruce Henderson and his predecessor J. Miller Bonner, Joe Poole, Governor Chauncey Sparks, and Horace Wilkinson, a well-known segregationist, led the campaign for ratification. The advocates of the Boswell Amendment employed blunt, often brutal language to defend their proposal, although it was almost diplomatic compared with what was to come in later years. In a September 1946 open letter addressed to the "Voters of Alabama," McCorvey made it clear that the issue was white supremacy: "We have done in the past, and we intend to do in the future, everything that can legally be done to preserve white supremacy in our State."[8]

Chief opponents of the amendment included progressive Richard Rives (a close associate of Bibb Graves), Senator Hill, Senator-nominate Sparkman, Folsom, labor unions, and, foreshadowing future splits among Big Mules on racial matters, most of the state's major newspapers. J. A. Carnley actively opposed the amendment, and he encouraged Folsom to make a strong public stand against it.[9] Folsom and the others, however, attempted to approach the issue obliquely by focusing on technical problems associated with the measure. As Barnard notes, "It took no small measure of political courage" for them to take even this "dissembling stand."[10] Earlier, in the primary,

Folsom had also made his opposition to the Boswell Amendment a small part of his campaign. Gessner McCorvey tried to paint amendment opponents as consisting mainly of meddling northerners, Communists, and Republicans. On the same day they elected Folsom governor, the voters approved the Boswell Amendment by 89,000 to 76,000 votes.

A Beginning

The inauguration party was effervescent, exhilarating, and tumultuous. "Three thousand people jammed Hanger Six at Maxwell Field for the dance that ended the day's festivities. It was an amazing, stirring sight. It was democracy at play. From every strata of life people had come. Girls jitterbugged in slacks next to dignified matrons in ultra formal gowns. Leather lumberjacks rubbed against the broadcloth of tails and tuxedos. The fragrance of dime store cologne mingled with the kind you buy by dram and number."[11] At midnight, the moment he officially became governor, Big Jim was jitterbugging.

Earlier that day, resplendent in tails, he had taken his oath of office from the Jefferson Davis Bible open at the Sermon on the Mount. His inaugural address was a mixture of personal reminiscence, populist ideology, and proposals taken from his campaign platform.

> I believe in the kind of democracy that touches the home of the average man. The kind of democracy that goes back to the branchheads and the bush arbor gathering places. Now that's the kind of democracy that gives the average man and woman more to say about the way our government is run. It means we want to get rid of wornout restrictions on voting. . . .
> It is the kind of democracy that says every section of the State shall have a fair representation in our government.
> Another thing that needs to be done to make Alabama more democratic is to open the way for women to have a full share in our government. . . .
> There are those who are frightened by real democracy. They have always worked to trim it down a little here and trim it down a little there. They want to keep power in the hands of a few.
> I am not afraid of too much democracy. I am afraid of what happens to people when they have too little democracy.[12]

His exciting address belied his inept efforts to organize the legislature. The lieutenant governor presides over the Senate, and in practice he can be extremely influential. In most cases, the lieutenant governor names all Senate committee members and chairmen. By custom these selections are made in consultation with the new governor. By tradition, the governor's choice for president pro tempore is also accepted, with this officer normally designated as the governor's floor leader in the Senate.

The presiding officer of the House is the speaker. Formally, the speaker is elected by a simple majority of House members, but in practice his selection is one of the governor's most important informal powers. The speaker names all committees and their chairs. By tradition these selections are made in consultation with the governor. The governor also designates his choice for speaker pro tempore, who will normally serve as his House floor leader. By House and Senate rules, the speaker and pro tem positions are determined by roll-call votes.

In earlier months Folsom had astounded political observers by choosing J. Bruce Henderson as his president pro tem. Probably no political leader in the state was more intensely opposed to more parts of the Folsom program than Henderson.

J. Bruce Henderson's father, William, was an Ohioan who fought in the Union army during the Civil War. After the war he bought large tracts of plantation land in Wilcox County, became active in Reconstruction politics, and in 1874 was elected probate judge.[13] J. Bruce inherited the land and added to it; by the 1950s he owned more than eight thousand acres around Millers Ferry and Camden. (One farming expert who worked in Wilcox County in the 1950s placed the figure at seventeen thousand acres.) At its peak one hundred families worked on his property.[14]

Henderson's actions as a public figure were a passionate defense of his position as a major Black Belt planter, in some ways guileless and innocent, in others cynical. Of course an advocacy of one's interests is the essence of politics, but Henderson had a peculiar talent to transform in his mind a defense of his personal political and economic position into a crusade for good government.

Henderson defined "good government" largely as a situation in which no one drank and where blacks did not vote, worked hard for a subsistence wage, and knew their place. Albert Boutwell, a first-rank Birmingham Big Mule politician of the 1950s and early 1960s, described him as "devout and dedicated." Then Boutwell felt it necessary to add, "He was not a heartless man." As evidence, he cited Henderson's authorship and advocacy of a law designed to bring about systematic treatment of venereal disease, but Boutwell and everyone else on Goat Hill (the capitol) knew why Henderson had pushed that bill. Venereal disease was a major affliction among the people working on his plantation, cutting into the efficiency of his operations.[15] Two other problems slowed the pace of work—pellagra and liquor. His solution to the pellagra problem was (quoting a Wilcox County resident) "to build a fish pond for the niggers—they liked to fish." Apparently, whites also liked to fish because Henderson established a schedule regulating the pond's use by race. Henderson's solution to the liquor problem was prohibition—he was a strict teetotaler and one of the state's leading drys.

His way of elevating everything he did politically in pursuit of his own interests to the level of grand philosophy made him an irritating, if steadfast, ally; any deviation from a Henderson position earned the transgressor anguished, hand-wringing diatribes or letters, but one always knew where Henderson would stand on virtually any major issue, and one rarely had to worry about his changing a position by compromise.

He was a hard, grim, dignified man with a square face, rimless glasses, and slicked-down hair. He arose at three or four o'clock in the morning, and more than one Camden resident recalls receiving business calls from "Mr. Bruce" at those hours. No hint of humor appears in his voluminous correspondence.

Most people believed that Folsom's peculiar choice for president pro tem had been Joe Poole's condition for supporting Folsom in the runoff (Henderson had been Poole's campaign manager). In a letter to Henderson dated March 11, 1950, Poole claimed that Folsom had agreed to make Henderson his president pro tem in return for Poole's support in the runoff. Henderson, however, opposed Folsom in the runoff. Folsom denied that there had been such an agreement and added: "They [Poole and Boozer] didn't have any other place to go."[16] Folsom indicated that he appointed Henderson because he hoped to gain the cooperation of the conservative-dominated legislature. He saw it as a harmless gesture of friendliness, since he would not be obliged to keep the president pro tem as a permanent floor leader. That is how two of his closest aides, who were appalled by his choice, also remembered it.[17] Two highly experienced journalists who supported Poole cast further doubt on the theory that Folsom agreed to select Henderson in exchange for Poole's runoff support; they believe that Poole's assistance to Folsom arose from an agreement they had struck early in the campaign to each support the other if he made the runoff. Poole suggested the deal, never dreaming that he would lose the primary.[18] The journalists' version tends to support Folsom's account that he appointed Henderson as a gesture of goodwill toward conservatives.

Folsom's organizational blunders were not confined to the Senate. According to tradition, the speaker, although elected by the House, was appointed by the governor. He made two mistakes in his selection: indecision and the choice of an individual who did not support the governor's programs in the stolid manner expected of Alabama speakers. It was the norm for governors-nominate to announce their choices for speaker soon after the primary. Instead, Folsom withdrew from the political scene for a Florida vacation, where he became the joy of photographers, posing in wildly flowered shirts and shorts. One picture showed him in that garb standing next to a man wearing a dark suit, white shirt, and tie whose head barely reached Folsom's chest. The contrast in size and attire, plus Folsom's gangly, pale legs, was ludicrous, and many Alabamians were not amused.

Some suggest that Folsom went to Florida to rest from what was probably the most tiring campaign schedule undertaken in the state's history. In addition, Folsom's mother had died in the middle of the campaign, a grim fact that may only have fully registered after his victory. Also, Folsom was entangled in an affair that had produced a child, and he probably spent some of his time away from Alabama politics trying to control that potentially dangerous situation.[19] Finally, it did not occur to him that his choice for the speakership would be challenged because of the tradition that the governor's choice was automatically approved. His leaving Montgomery or the state at crucial decision-making junctures was a pattern that would recur many times during his years in office.

The 1946 gubernatorial election was not the first lost by the state's elite, and the Big Mules had always been able quietly to stifle an unfriendly governor's most objectionable policies in the legislature. The task had been deftly handled by skilled and experienced Black Belt legislators. Elites in other states were also well schooled in the techniques required to neutralize errant chief executives. In Louisiana the standard procedure was, in T. Harry Williams's words, to "absorb him and thus render him harmless. The first move . . . was to show him social attention, to demonstrate to him that, after all, gentlemen liked him and wanted to help him in the difficult job ahead."[20] But in the late months of 1946 it must have become evident to the Big Mule leaders that Folsom was different, that he could not be absorbed, and that it would be better to fight him openly. He was an alien presence which the elite wanted exorcised. His challenge to their power was real, and they would try to obliterate him. Control over the legislature was the key to achieving that goal.

The fight began with the selection of the House speaker. Before Folsom could name his choice, two conservatives, Chauncey Sparks's speaker Charles Normal and W. L. Martin, declared their candidacies. A freshman representative from Barbour County named George Wallace also let it be known that he was available for the speakership.

Another candidate, Bill Beck from DeKalb County in North Alabama, entered the race. Beck had not originally been a Folsom supporter. He apparently had favored Poole and had switched to Folsom when Poole had. Despite this questionable background he appeared far superior to the other two serious candidates, and the governor-elect threw all his influence behind Beck in what became a titanic battle as conservatives pushed for Normal and Martin. While the recorded vote (96–0) shows overwhelming support for

Beck, interviews indicate the real margin of victory to be only four votes. Folsom was forced to expend substantial resources at the beginning of his term to achieve Beck's election.[21]

So Folsom stumbled into his first legislative session having made an unfortunate choice for president pro tem and having had to fight in the House for what should have been his automatically. To make matters worse, Lieutenant Governor Clarence Inzer, the Senate's presiding officer, represented urban Boss interests. The law firm of which Inzer was an active member during his term as lieutenant governor represented on a regular basis Alabama Gas Company, Louisville and Nashville Railroad, Republic Steel Corporation, and many similar corporations.[22] With Inzer and Beck making the committee assignments, designating committee chairs, and wielding the gavels in their chambers and Henderson the governor's de facto Senate floor leader, the game was over before it began.

Despite the fact that Beck would appoint a large percentage of North Alabama legislators to committee chairs and vice chairs (see Table 1), weakening the Black Belt position, the Black Belt–Jefferson County delegations would control half the House votes. Unlike the other regional delegations, especially the northern representatives from Folsom's own region, the coali-

Table 1. House Chairs and Vice Chairs by Regional Base (Percentages)

	Black Belt	Jefferson County	Mobile County	North Alabama	Wiregrass	Other Counties
Chairs						
1947–50	18	9	0	36	18	18
1951–54	40	13	0	27	13	7
1955–58	27	13	7	40	7	7
1959–62	53	12	0	18	0	18
1963–66	37	16	5	37	0	5
1967–70[a]	32	16	11	21	5	16
1971–74	29	10	5	33	0	24
1975–79	29	14	10	29	5	15
Vice chairs						
1947–50	27	27	0	46	0	18
1951–54	27	27	7	33	0	7
1955–58	40	20	0	20	0	20
1959–62	41	12	0	24	0	24
1963–66	32	5	5	42	5	11
1967–70[a]	26	21	5	26	5	16
1971–74	24	14	19	19	5	19
1975–79	29	14	9	29	5	14

a. First session after reapportionment.

tion could and would maintain voting solidarity, leading to defeat of many gubernatorial proposals in the House even with Beck choosing to chair the Rules Committee.

Moreover, within three months of his election Beck would split from Folsom on his major program positions—representation, voting rights, and basic civil rights. Despite these disagreements, Beck, by our calculation, voted for Folsom's program 67 percent of the time in the first legislative session and 63 percent of the time in the second.

Interviews with legislators of that era, discussions with Folsom, and newspaper coverage from the period present a convincing picture of Beck opposing Folsom in exchange for Black Belt promises of support for his gubernatorial race in 1950. The legislators claim his relatively high support figures represent Beck's realization that the promised support would never be forthcoming and that personal self-interest dictated returning to the Folsom program, for North Alabama and Wiregrass support would be vital to a statewide election bid without Black Belt support.

The situation in the Senate was a disaster. Folsom totally misjudged his ability to work with Henderson and the strength of Henderson's convictions. As Table 2 indicates, Henderson stacked the committee chairs with Black Belt senators, but vice chairs were more "equitably" distributed. Admin-

Table 2. Senate Chairs and Vice Chairs by Regional Base (Percentages)

	Black Belt	Jefferson County	Mobile County	North Alabama	Wiregrass	Other Counties
Chairs						
1947–50	42	3	3	23	3	24
1951–54	47	3	3	23	7	16
1955–58	40	3	0	33	7	17
1959–62	35	3	3	28	10	27
1963–66	33	3	7	20	10	26
1967–70[a]	23	23	10	26	13	7
1971–74	20	15	15	25	5	20
1975–79	18	12	12	29	12	18
Vice chairs						
1947–50	33	3	0	37	3	23
1951–54	37	3	3	40	3	13
1955–58	30	3	3	20	7	37
1959–62	45	0	0	31	10	14
1963–66	40	0	0	43	7	10
1967–70[a]	26	19	7	26	3	20
1971–74	35	25	0	20	5	15
1975–79	12	35	6	24	6	18

a. First session after reapportionment.

istration bill after administration bill would die in committee, and one administration appointment after another would meet defeat. As in the House, Black Belters, directed by Henderson, led the attack. Our calculations of Henderson's support scores show him supporting the governor's programs 14 percent of the time in the first session and only 5 percent of the time in the second session.

The First Session

The tribulations Folsom would face for the next four years were vividly illustrated in his first major legislative test in the Senate. It concerned his appointments to Alabama Polytechnic Institute's (Auburn University) Board of Trustees. Auburn is the state's land grant university, and as such it houses the Agricultural Extension Service, which employs agents in each county, a network tied inextricably to the massive Alabama Farm Bureau Federation. This system encompassed huge wealth and power and still does today. The Farm Bureau Federation, the Extension Service, and Auburn were so intertwined that it was quite realistic to think of them as a single entity. County agents not only supplied a wide variety of technical and educational assistance, but also wielded considerable power to help or hurt individual farmers—for example, by determining how much cotton they could plant. Agents were not supposed to use their position for political ends, but they had in fact been combatants in many important state and local elections, legislative clashes, and state referenda for several decades.[23]

On February 15, 1947, the executive committee of the State Association of Soil Conservation District Supervisors charged in a meeting with Folsom that the Extension Service director was undermining the Soil Conservation Service program preparatory to a takeover attempt. Plans by the supervisors to introduce a resolution on the matter on the floor of the 1946 state Farm Bureau meeting had resulted in the threat that if they pursued it they would be accused of being Communists.[24]

On February 18 Folsom sent telegrams to all local superintendents of schools in which he requested their views "as to whether the Extension Service has provided effective and wholehearted cooperation in educational programs for rural people."[25] Over 60 percent of the superintendents answered his request, and by a margin of 2 to 1 they indicated that the Extension Service had not cooperated with them. The fact that their negative responses put them in some political jeopardy underscored the intensity of their feelings.[26]

The Auburn board consisted of ten members, with the governor as an ex-officio voting member. When Folsom took office, there were four vacancies on the board with a fifth soon to be open. He recognized the place held by the Auburn–Extension Service–Farm Bureau coalition in the state's power structure, and he openly expressed his desire to hobble it and bring better service to the small farmer. Majority control of the board offered him an excellent opportunity. His four appointees, announced early in February, were Gould Beech, Reuben Wright, who was Ward McFarland's senior law partner, Guy Lynn of Huntsville, and Dr. Joe Davis of Albertville. In another time with another governor the latter three would probably have been automatically accepted by the Senate, but these men were Folsom's nominees and Gould Beech, his speechwriter, who was still editor of the *Southern Farmer*, served interests contrary to those of the state's agriculture establishment. The *Southern Farmer* represented the tenant and so-called family farmers. Its publishers and Beech's friends, Marshall Field of Chicago and Aubrey Williams, a native Alabamian and former National Youth Administration head for Franklin Roosevelt, were widely perceived as radicals or worse. Williams had openly fought the Boswell Amendment both before and after its passage.

News of Beech's nomination broke on a Sunday morning, and Extension Service officials, Farm Bureau executives, and other agribusiness leaders rushed from church to emergency meetings, where they began planning how best to oppose Beech. It is easy to understand why they opposed him. Beech was friendly, thoughtful, quick-witted, and very articulate—far different from his taciturn and leaden opponents. Grover Hall, Jr., described his "earnest and reasoned solicitude for the underdog" and his deep concern for tenant farmers' "squalor and miseries." "When you have said something which rawhides his own viewpoint about human values," Hall wrote, "the large hazel eyes widen and whiten and he has the aspect of an eagle batting his eyes. His lips get thinner, his pronounced drawl speeds up to three-quarter time and you have a cataract of spirit, statistics and historical precedent to cope with."[27] Yet he was far from the Communist subversive portrayed by so many. He had served as a consultant on agricultural matters for the "Bourbon from Barbour," Governor Chauncey Sparks, and in 1946 he wrote speeches and platforms for thirty-six moderate to conservative office seekers. One evening six candidates for the legislature faced each other in a radio debate all armed with notes drafted by Beech. He was a populist, but he was also a pragmatist.

On February 21 Folsom delivered a cleverly worded but impolitic chastisement of the Extension Service and its supporters in an address before the Auburn student body. The speech was broadcast on radio statewide. It began innocently enough, but, after congratulating the Alabama citizenry on the quality of their land grant university, he said: "Recently I've been hearing a few complaints about more taxes. Every time I hear anybody hollering about taxes, I ask him how much money he made during the war. You might look around and see who's hollering in your community. . . . The average citizen isn't worrying about taxes. He's worrying about whether we in Alabama are going to build a first class state. He's thinking about roads and schools and colleges." Reviewing Auburn's various programs, he moved in for the kill.

> Auburn has got to be one institution. The college, the experiment station, and the extension service are part of one institution. Auburn has one president. One board of trustees. One job. It gets its money from one place. The people. . . . We want the extension service to have all the money and the county and home agents it takes to do a good job. . . . We want the extension service to serve everybody. That means all the people. . . .
> . . . The extension service has got to get out of politics, and stay out of politics. And I mean all kinds of politics. Local politics. State politics. National politics. My kind of politics. Your kind of politics. Government politics, and farm organization politics. The farmers in every Alabama county have got enough sense to run their own farm organization.[28]

According to newspaper accounts, the speech was enthusiastically received by an audience of six thousand students and faculty. It was followed by an Auburn board meeting at which Folsom's nominees, not yet approved by the Senate, sat as full voting members, a customary and proper procedure. The newly constituted board then unanimously adopted a statement highly critical of the Extension Service—a scaled-down version of Folsom's speech. This statement, together with the speech, intensified agricultural establishment opposition and broadened it to include all Folsom nominees and not just Beech.

On March 1 Folsom called a special legislative session to act on his Auburn nominees *and* to call a constitutional convention. He had been expected merely to call a session to unfreeze a budget surplus for distribution to the schools. He had, of course, advocated constitutional revision throughout his campaign, but his sudden call for a convention appeared impulsive. Meanwhile, as if to confirm Folsom's charges, Walter Randolph, president of the Alabama Farm Bureau Federation, filed suit in the Lee County Circuit Court to enjoin Beech, Wright, and Lynn from serving on the board prior to Senate approval.

The legislature met on March 3. In a very short address Folsom appealed to the lawmakers to "give the people a chance to decide on whether we need to rewrite our Constitution," and he underscored his support for his Auburn board nominees.[29] The atmosphere was tense, and it was clear that both his constitutional convention and his nominees were about to be savaged.

The campaign being organized against the governor disturbed many of the newspapers that just a few months earlier had opposed his election. A *Birmingham News* editorial asserted that "the Farm Bureau would like to make it appear that it is fighting to prevent radical elements from taking over farm organizations within the state. But that charge appears a little far-fetched, and it is given further denial by the unanimous lineup of the Auburn trustees in its accusations against the Extension Service."[30] A *Montgomery Advertiser* editorial stated: "Unfortunately for Auburn the major forces in this state which oppose Folsom's program have chosen that institution as a battleground. They are fighting a bitter delaying action to prevent the governor from taking the Extension Service out of politics. . . . Apparently they prefer to see the Extension Service continued as a political machine, doing its chores through the medium of a Farm Bureau which it dominates regardless of the wishes of the real dirt farmers of Alabama."[31]

The day after Folsom's speech Senate galleries were packed with Extension Service and Farm Bureau members creating an atmosphere that one Folsom leader described as like a "deep freeze."[32] The Senate, led by J. Bruce Henderson, confirmed two interim appointments made by Governor Sparks and withdrawn by Folsom (Earl McGowin and Birmingham business leader Frank Samford) by a vote of 24–6. The McGowin confirmation was meaningless because the term to which he had been nominated had expired, but it served to demonstrate the intensity of feeling against Folsom in the Senate. A petition quickly distributed and signed by fifteen hundred Auburn students strongly supporting Folsom's position was shown to the senators, but it had no impact.[33] At Beech's request Folsom withdrew his nomination and named in his place Senator V. S. Summerlin. The next day, with Extension Service and Farm Bureau members squeezed out by six hundred marching, placard-carrying pro-Folsom Auburn students, the governor withdrew the other two controversial nominations.[34] He then nominated Representative Roberts Brown of Lee County and Probate Judge W. L. Parish of Clanton, but the Senate abruptly adjourned sine die without informing the House or the governor, ending the shortest special session in the state's history. It was a humiliating defeat for Folsom. Trying to put the best face on things, he told reporters, "It's good for a fellow to get a spanking once in a while. It helps him keep his feet on the ground."[35] After the Auburn debacle Folsom was no longer a credible force in the legislature, if indeed he ever was.

Beech remained in Alabama for a time working with Folsom in several capacities, but, his reputation in tatters, he finally departed for Texas, where he would in later years become a successful real estate investor.

Having allowed his informally granted legislative authority to be taken from him, Folsom had to rely more and more heavily on patronage, state contract authority, and various slush funds to influence lawmakers. Later, because of a tightening of the merit system (civil service), tougher low-bid laws, and a new ethics law, a governor's command over patronage resources with which to reward friendly legislators was severely diminished. Folsom in his two terms and all governors through the 1960s possessed control over more resources than any before or since. For example, governors of that period could distribute roughly $20 million per year in road construction contracts almost anywhere in the state, and other state contracts for such items as automobiles and office equipment added millions of dollars to that figure.

It is virtually impossible for the observer outside of government systematically to track the use of all these resources, but detailed records were kept which accounted for the distribution of the largest and most important single category of patronage, road construction projects.[36] Many legislators and newspaper reporters interviewed for this book spontaneously cited road construction administration as one of the most important, if not the most important, areas of gubernatorial discretion and power in the legislature. Time and again, these sources outlined the same rationale of road construction allocation by the governor, and it did not matter which governor was being discussed. When asked by what criteria the governor distributed road construction projects among Alabama counties, a former highway director (a gubernatorial appointee) gave a typical response: "Highway construction is closely related to the governor's percent victory [in the Democratic Party primary] in a county. Legislative support is also important. Need comes in third."[37]

Descriptions of Alabama road construction that arose in interviews received convincing support from documents in governors' office files (Folsom, Patterson, the Wallaces, and Brewer) housed in the state archives. These documents fall into the following categories: letters from the governor to legislators thanking them for their support on particular bills and informing them that the construction of a specified stretch of road would be forthcoming; memoranda from the governor to the highway director instructing him to build roads for campaign supporters or friendly legislators; and letters from county officials reminding the governor or highway director of his political obligations and suggesting highway construction as a way to redeem himself.

Judging from a detailed examination of their files, the post–World War II governors spent more time on road construction decision making than they did on any other activity, with the possible exception of civil rights concerns. Interviews with Folsom, George Wallace, and Highway Department officials who served under them reinforced this observation. Wallace and Folsom exhibited an encyclopedic knowledge of road construction matters, including detailed information on the location and condition of the state's roads and whether they had built or improved them. Highway Department officials reported that Wallace often spent more than an hour at a time day after day with his highway directors, all this in addition to frequent telephone conversations and memoranda. No state chief executive would devote so much time to a subject that did not interest him.[38]

Once Folsom tried to punish a legislative delegation by stopping a project. He had consented to construct a bridge in Montgomery County, but it developed that the Montgomery lawmakers were opposing him on almost every important issue. He called Highway Director Ward McFarland and asked, "What's the status of that bridge?" McFarland replied, "We've got a contract on it." Folsom asked, "What would happen if we cancel the contract?" McFarland said, "We'd get sued." Folsom ordered, "I'll tell you what. Build the bridge without steel." McFarland was horrified. "We can't do that. It'd collapse," he said. Folsom considered that possibility for a moment and then responded, "Don't put in much."[39]

A 1948 legislative investigating committee also found evidence that road locations often had been based on considerations other than need. One part of their report read as follows: "There is an established custom in Alabama, over a long period of years, for highway contractors to make sizeable donations to political campaigns. One highway contractor testified that in the last ten years he had donated approximately $15,000 to political campaigns. Another contractor who had been in Alabama only a short time stated that he had found this to be an accepted custom in Alabama."[40] A 1964 U.S. Bureau of Public Roads investigation of the rewarding of consultant engineering contracts for road construction work in Alabama found a pattern similar to that discovered by the 1948 Alabama legislative committee.

Government jobs were also an important source of gubernatorial influence in the legislature. Upon winning the 1946 and 1954 primaries, Folsom was deluged with letters from lawyers, legislators, businessmen, and others claiming to have helped him in the primary and asking him to appoint them or others to positions ranging from cabinet spots to state liquor store jobs. Those close to Folsom, such as J. A. Carnley, S. Fleetwood Carnley, O. H. Finney, and Bill Drinkard, received similar messages.

Every opening in even the most obscure post created intense interest and activity among legislators. In reviewing the files, one is often struck by the contrast between the low-level positions being sought and the weighty influence brought to bear from the legislature and other sources. Openings for prison chaplains, alcoholic beverage license inspectors, and menial Highway Department jobs were all the subjects of high-level contention. State legislators, powerful judges, and important lawyers devoted so much energy to such routine matters because an influential's image was enhanced by his ability to obtain positions for loyal campaign workers or friends of friends. The ability to distribute jobs to the faithful allowed an individual to create his own small "machine."

Legislators could be influenced with a wide variety of rewards, as is suggested by a file entitled "A Guide to the Legislature" in the Folsom personal files in the state archives. A card in the front of this file reads:

> John Gaither, June, 1948—secured job in Revenue Department for son. November, 1947, secured Mercury
> Kendall, Bob—secured pipe to be used in his house. Shipped to City of Evergreen, June, 1948
> Perry, Crisp—June, 1948—secured second hand auto from Grimes Auto Company—complete set of hydrolic brakes
> Glover, Ben—countless number of times 1947, 1948, mainly rowboat and paddles
> Kimbrell, Fuller—1947—secured car
> Fite, Rankin—1947—secured car
> Barnett—1947—secured car
> Harvey, W.—secured car
> Hardwick, Guy—fishing tackle wholesale, May, 1948
> Lowe, Bob, October, 1947—hunting in Wyoming, Dixie in July, 1948
> Mize, Bennie—May, 1948, helped in settlement on case in Board of Adjustments also helped get payment from Highway Department after money was frozen
> Lowe—Boutwell—carried on trips with Building Commission.

The "secured car" notations do not mean that the state of Alabama bought automobiles for the individuals indicated. In the years immediately following World War II new cars were in short supply, and sometimes political pressure accelerated the purchase of one. The "Dixie" mentioned in connection with one legislator was a state-owned yacht which was in heavy demand for fishing expeditions and parties.

The cards in this file gave brief descriptions of the career and interests of legislators. The back of each card lists people appointed to executive branch and local government positions on the recommendations of particular legislators. The descriptions are too obvious and brief to be of much use, and the favors appear to have been done near the beginning of Folsom's term. The cards were not kept current because, once Folsom and his aides developed a feeling for the legislators, they did not need written records. During the first set of interviews for this book done in 1973, Folsom was asked to characterize each member of the legislature in both terms, and he was able to describe most of them in great detail. When his appraisals of whether legislators had supported or opposed his programs were compared to roll-call votes, he proved to be extremely accurate. Those few legislators he could not remember turned out to be moderates who supported some of his programs and opposed others.

All the methods discussed so far by which Folsom influenced legislators were more or less legal except for some relatively minor merit system and low-bid manipulations, and, according to countless interviews and news items, they were standard practice among all Alabama governors of the period. It is of course much more difficult to gauge the frequency with which illegal agreements were struck between Folsom and legislators, but it is clear from virtually all informed accounts that many lawmakers were not averse to selling their votes. In his descriptions of legislators Folsom frequently mentioned that particular ones could be bribed: "The trouble with ole'——," he once said of a well-known representative, "is that when you bought him he wouldn't stay bought. The next day he'd be back for more. I liked the kind of man that when you bought him he'd stay bought."[41]

The largest single source of cash for influencing legislators was probably money extorted from liquor companies who sold, or wanted to sell, their brands in state stores. Many such companies were willing to spend tens of thousands of dollars each year to maintain access to the state system. The intermediaries between government officials and the liquor companies were the so-called liquor agents. Given the sensitivity of these positions the appointments of all agents were subject to the governor's approval. A highly public example of a slight breakdown in this arrangement occurred in 1950 when the Seagram Company balked at firing its agent, who for reasons that were unclear suddenly became unacceptable to Folsom. Seagram products were instantly "de-listed" by the ABC Board and ABC Board Chairman William P. Screws made clear to the company what was required for their products to reappear on the state store shelves. Once the company agreed to hire Folsom's choice (James Key of the Strawberry Pickers), Seagram products were immediately relisted. When asked whether politics had been part of the arrangment, Screws replied, "Of course there are politics. All such appointments are political."[42]

A percentage of the money that flowed from many of the liquor companies through most liquor agents was stored in a safe in the office of one of Folsom's most trouble-prone aides. Estimates of the amounts contained in the safe varied from thirty thousand to eighty thousand dollars. One day a secretary made off with the money, and of course the theft could not be reported to the police, but the money was easily replaced.[43] Funds from the safe went to legislators in envelopes containing one hundred dollar bills. The envelopes ended up in the legislators' mail slots at the capitol, among other places. Two Folsom brothers and Ross Clark made many of these transactions.[44]

Besides their payments to executive slush funds, the liquor companies apparently spent money in great quantities to influence legislators directly. Legislators so inclined were provided with virtually limitless quantities of their favorite brands delivered to their hotel rooms when the legislature was in session. J. Bruce Henderson was once told by a Birmingham senator that if he would merely soften his opposition to the liquor interests, he would find cash showering down on him through the transom of his hotel room. Henderson was so disgusted by the pervasive presence of liquor dollars routed directly to legislators and indirectly via the governor's office that he once proposed that the ABC Board manufacture liquor itself and sell it at cost; he felt that the political impact of the liquor interests was worse than the appalling effects of alcohol on society.[45]

In his use of legal and illegal means to influence the legislature, Folsom was following a pattern set by other Alabama and southern governors. His administrations differed only in the relatively consistent use he made of these manipulative techniques for idealistic ends.

The ethical situation in which Folsom found himself was complex and subtle, although he had little difficulty resolving it. A chief executive trying to follow an ethical course of behavior in a corrupt political system that he is trying to improve has two choices. He can perform his functions according to the letter of the law and be ignored by the majority of lawmakers who are being influenced by forces representing the status quo, or he can use illegal tactics to bring about reforms to make the system less corrupt. In Folsom's time there was a third choice, which was to use legal rewards such as road construction contracts to bring about modest changes, but Folsom was not interested in modest change. A plaque in his office carried an inscription of the words of city planner Daniel Hudson Burnham: "Make no little plans; they have no magic to stir men's blood, and probably they will not be realized. Make big plans; aim high in hope and work, remembering that a noble, logical diagram once recorded will never die, but long after we are gone will be a living thing, asserting itself with ever-growing insistency."

By standards set forth in the Alabama Constitution and by the most relaxed democratic canons, the political system in Alabama in the 1940s and 1950s was corrupt at its core. The legislative apportionment established in the 1901 constitution favored Black Belt counties at the expense of northern, southern, and urban counties, and that was the conscious plan of the authors of that document. As the decades went by, the state rapidly became more urbanized, and the malapportionment increased accordingly. When Folsom became governor, there had been no reapportionment since 1901, even though the Alabama Constitution specifically called for reapportionment every decade.[46]

The 1940 census found the Alabama population to be 2,832,961. Dividing this figure by 35, the number of senators (and senatorial districts), gives 80,942, the number of citizens who should have been represented by one senator under a standard of one-person, one-vote. Table 3 shows how far from this standard the Alabama Senate had fallen. The pattern was clear. In the most extreme case, a District 16 Black Belt citizen's vote was twenty

Table 3. Malapportionment of the Alabama Senate, 1940

Senatorial district	Population	District Underrepresented or Overrepresented
District population less than 45 percent black (North)		
1	81,872	under
2	76,028	over
3	95,579	under
4	66,317	over
5	84,197	under
6	99,916	under
7	63,319	over
8	51,832	over
10	69,816	over
11	76,036	over
12	105,560	under
13 (Birmingham)	459,930	under
15	77,894	over
29	63,003	over
31	90,421	under
34	43,996	over
District population over 45 percent black		
9	67,662	over
14	54,992	over
16	22,661	over
18	46,765	over
19	64,019	over
20	35,736	over
22	26,279	over
24	32,722	over
26	47,464	over
27	72,230	over
28 (Montgomery)	114,420	under
30	55,245	over
32	44,718	over
35	67,577	over
District population less than 45 percent black (South)		
17	100,353	under
21	92,460	under
23	51,857	over
25	88,111	under
33 (Mobile)	141,974	under

Source: Hallie Farmer, *The Legislative Process in Alabama* (University: Bureau of Public Administration, 1949), p. 31.

times more influential than a District 13 Birmingham voter's. Moreover, because of discrimination against blacks, much smaller proportions of citizens voted in Black Belt counties; thus the Black Belt voter's vote was even more influential than these figures suggest.[47] House figures told a similar story. There were originally 106 representatives, which meant that a single member of the House would have represented 26,726 citizens on a basis of one-person, one-vote. Nineteen out of twenty-three Black Belt counties had House members representing fewer than this number—ten counties fewer than 14,000 citizens per representative.[48] As in the Senate, this malapportionment was even greater if only voters were taken into account.[49]

There was another effect of malapportionment in the Senate, widely remarked upon but more subtle than the gross effects shown above. In proportion to their numbers Black Belt counties had more single-county senatorial districts and far fewer three-county districts. North and South Alabama had all but one of the three-county districts. Counties sharing a senatorial district nearly always traded senators from term to term. For example, District 1, which included Lauderdale and Limestone counties in North Alabama, would alternate with a senator from Lauderdale one term, a senator from Limestone the next. Meanwhile, single-county districts tended to return the same people. The result was that inexperienced senators from multicounty districts tended to face veterans from single-county districts armed with a mastery of parliamentary procedure. Furthermore, Black Belt counties had more highly disciplined political infrastructures than most non–Black Belt counties and were thus more likely to return the same individual term after term.[50]

Occasionally, attempts had been made to fulfill the Alabama Constitution's requirement for reapportionment. Few such bills were ever voted out of committee for House or Senate floor consideration, however. A reapportionment bill did reach the House floor in 1939, but it was defeated 60–31. The defeat was administered by a coalition of Black Belt counties and overrepresented rural counties scattered throughout the state. Urban counties tended to support the bill.[51]

In 1947 and 1949 Folsom attempted to pass the so-called sixty-seven senator bill, which would have provided one senator for each county, bringing about partial reapportionment. The votes on that bill in both the House and Senate were quite different from those in 1939; representatives and senators from the Black Belt, Birmingham, and Mobile teamed up to oppose the other counties. For example, in a September 18, 1947, House vote 83 percent of the votes could have been predicted according to that pattern, far better than one could have done by assuming that county representatives would have voted simply according to whether they would have benefited mathematically from the change. Similarly, in an August 9, 1949, Senate vote on the same bill 85 percent of the votes could be explained by a Black Belt–Birmingham–Mobile Big Mule alliance. It is a measure of the stability of the Black Belt–Birmingham–Mobile Big Mule alliance that the urban members made only token efforts to reapportion. Furthermore, opposition by this alliance at the committee level kept bills calling for total reapportionment on a basis of one-person, one-vote from reaching the floor of either chamber in both Folsom terms. However, interviews suggest that sentiment in Mobile, Montgomery, and Birmingham in favor of reapportionment grew through the late 1950s and early 1960s.[52]

Combined with the material in chapter 3, these data on malapportionment support the conclusion that Folsom had entered a political system unconstitutionally skewed in favor of a wealthy minority, and a system in which large numbers of citizens were kept from voting by deceptive laws, terror, and fraud. Folsom's objectives were to bring about reapportionment and universal suffrage. He envisioned that this newly constituted political structure would then slowly eradicate discrimination. But he was trying to break into a closed system. He wanted to end malapportionment, voting discrimination, and similar evils, but those very problems of the system kept him from accomplishing those ends. Ultimately, federal court action was required.

The political system was corrupt, and Folsom's basic goal was to end that corruption. Thus there is some basis for arguing that his use of illegal rewards to influence the legislature was justified. But one factor was missing that might have made his use of those techniques justifiable: the possibility of success. Given the entrenched forces for the status quo, the extra margin provided by illegal rewards could have had little effect toward achieving the basic changes that he pursued. And any lesser goals, such as improved roads or better schools, did not justify his resort to illegal inducements.

The Regular Session

Folsom began the regular 1947 legislative session having been narrowly victorious in a speakership fight which he should have won without difficulty, having made a poor selection for his Senate pro tem, and having lost the Auburn board of trustees battle. His credibility as a power in the legislature could hardly have been lower, but he managed to diminish it even further by operating in the legislature on the basis of inaccurate information, at least in the early months. The first major conflicts in the regular session (technically, they occurred in a special session within the regular session) concerned sales tax changes and the allocation of surplus income tax funds that had built up during World War II. Folsom wanted to divide the surplus funds roughly in half between education and welfare, and he wanted to eliminate sales tax exemptions on tobacco, gasoline, liquor, and other items.[53] The quality of the information he was receiving on those matters is indicated by memoranda from his "executive investigator," W. LaRue Horn, who had determined that as of April 1 the governor's program had a good chance of passage. The legislature, however, voted to allocate all the money to teachers' salaries and none to welfare, by votes of 93-0 in the House and 34-1 in the Senate. The lone dissenter was J. Bruce Henderson, one of the state's largest landholders, who wanted the money used for property tax reduction.[54] Speaker Beck joined the majority in the House to defeat the governor's proposal.[55] Votes on the sales tax changes came later in the session in July. The sales tax bill was opposed by business concerns, such as the Gulf, Mobile and Ohio Railroad, Alabama Dry Dock and Shipping Company, International Paper Company, the Chamber of Commerce, and many more, all of which sent representatives who testified before the House Ways and Means Committee. But modified versions of the changes desired by the governor were approved.[56]

In addition to suffering from poor information, Folsom's attitude toward the legislature in his first term was typically that of an outsider-ideologue chief executive. He looked upon his election as a mandate—he was going to bring his platform to fruition against any opposition, and the legislature was "the opposition." He was heard to say, "If they [the legislature] don't give me what I want, I won't give them what they want."[57] According to one of his ablest cabinet members, Folsom in his first term did not realize that "the biggest prima donna in the whole world is a first term legislator,"[58] and well over half of the legislators were freshmen. Furthermore, many second- and third-term lawmakers were neither modest nor cooperative. Folsom approached newspapers the same way. He summarized his attitude toward the press with the remark, "I was elected and only two papers favored me. The power of the press—shit."[59]

Combined, Folsom's belief in his mandate and his insensitivity toward opponents' positions gave him a destructive "take-it-or-leave-it" attitude. The cabinet member quoted above observed that "if some representative would want to insert just a comma into a Folsom bill, the Governor would explode, 'Why that SOB is against my whole program.'" Then, his subsequent actions toward that legislator would generate vigorous antiadministration behavior. Folsom also broke important informal norms by failing to consult relevant lawmakers concerning executive appointments. Senators and representatives slighted in this way missed no opportunity to express their displeasure. Most observers agreed that even though the legislature was solidly against him, he could have developed far better working relationships than he did. He seemed to thrive on controversy. He did not seem happy unless he was standing in the midst of a colorful, loud, messy free-for-all.

Peculiarly, despite this behavior he enjoyed excellent personal relationships with most legislators and reporters, including many far removed from him on the ideological or interest-group spectrum. One such opponent recalled that "Folsom's door was wide open to every member of the legislature, in contrast to ———, for example, who was extremely difficult to see, who hated the legislature, and who was too busy chasing women to have much to do with the legislature."[60] Folsom loved to throw parties for everyone in and around government, and he enjoyed participating in legislative meetings, sometimes sitting by the speaker or the lieutenant governor as they presided, sometimes on the floor, moving about, just one of the boys. It is probably safe to say that no other Alabama governor has ever shot craps with legislators on Goat Hill.

A number of references to Folsom's drinking have cropped up in this narrative, beginning with his wine making as a young man, his drunken conference with Kenneth Griffith concerning his 1942 gubernatorial bid, his astounding drinking feat in Chauncey Sparks's headquarters the night of his 1942 defeat, and his reactions to the deaths, in quick succession, of his wife, brother, and mother. By 1947 alcohol had become a large part of his life. Opinions about his drinking in the first term vary over a relatively narrow range. Some describe it as barely affecting his performance, while others see it as interfering with his effectiveness occasionally. Albert Boutwell, who subscribed to the latter view, found that, because of Folsom's erratic behavior, his loyalists were sometimes reluctant to make commitments because they were not sure that he would live up to them. Nevertheless, Folsom's tactical sense could impress even Boutwell, who was a clever and tenacious politician. Folsom had nominated Boutwell's leading Jefferson County rival to a judgeship. Boutwell had tied up an administration-backed national guard appropriation bill in the Finance Committee, and Folsom wanted it badly. Folsom came to Boutwell and proposed that the judgeship be given to someone more acceptable in return for Boutwell's support of the appropriation. Boutwell agreed. He told this story as one professional politician admiring the handiwork of another, and the fact that they represented entirely different interests and were far apart ideologically made no difference.[61]

After the fiery first special session in January until at least the beginning of August there was surprisingly little proadministration versus antiadministration rhetoric used in the legislative halls. Folsom's key reform bills, such as poll tax elimination, were quietly stifled, and his appropriations bill zipped through with, if anything, less than the usual conflict and modest changes on the order of less than 5 percent. Even the Auburn board controversy came to a peaceful settlement of sorts. Joe Davis was finally confirmed in June by a vote of 34–0, but Representative Roberts Brown was rejected 18–15 with

Henderson leading the opposition, saying, in an ironic choice of words, that Brown was "prejudiced" against the Extension Service.[62] Virtually all the newspapers were highly critical of Brown's rejection, citing his standing in the legal profession, his good work in the House, and his war record.[63] Later Folsom renominated Brown, but his confirmation was lost in a logjam at the end of the session.[64]

The relative peace between the administration and the legislature continued through the end of summer as the income tax surplus allocation amendment went to the voters for approval. Folsom's only attempt to defeat the measure was a mildly worded radio address in August. His apparent inattentiveness is perhaps explained by the fact that immediately after the speech he rushed to California in a National Guard airplane, where he publicly courted California Governor Earl Warren's daughter Virginia, whom he had met at a National Governor's Conference. His trip had been preceded by lengthy daily long distance telephone conversations, but the romance quickly ended.[65]

At the end of August, following an intense campaign in support of the referendum by teachers groups, business organizations, and labor unions, the amendment passed by a 4–1 margin. Folsom responded graciously, referring to the result as "a great step forward for education in Alabama."[66]

After the summer lull, open hostilities between the governor and the legislature resumed during Senate consideration of one of his most important proposals, a $40 million road construction bond issue. It had moved through the House with ease during the summer, but the measure ran into stiff opposition in the Senate, where conservatives had a stronger voice. On September 4, Folsom delivered an impassioned plea on its behalf in a statewide radio address, and two days later he sent a blistering letter to the Chamber of Commerce resigning from it because it opposed the bond issue.[67] Those efforts only served to underscore his impotence in the upper house.

The opposition began openly to voice its opinion of the governor from the floors of the legislative chambers. For example, Representative Wallace Malone, a Houston County banker and a close friend and frequent correspondent of J. Bruce Henderson, charged that Folsom was "a monumental failure . . . not competent to administer the affairs of this state."[68] Representative J. W. Brassell, who was not an administration ally, cautioned against such extreme rhetoric: "If you continue this fight against him you will wind up by sending him to the U.S. Senate or maybe to the vice president's chair."[69] If awards were given for political prescience, Brassell would be a recipient. He was incorrect about the offices involved, but in that one sentence he summed up much of what was to occur in Alabama politics for the coming decade.

All of Folsom's major bills were defeated in the 1947 session. They included poll tax elimination, reapportionment of the legislature (which was only the modest "sixty-seven senator" proposal), a bill that would have removed all state government executive branch policymakers from the merit system and made them gubernatorial appointees—affecting upwards of two thousand positions—the $40 million highway bond issue, his Auburn board appointments, and a constitutional convention.[70]

Senator James B. Allen of Etowah County, like a shark smelling the blood of a wounded swimmer, introduced a constitutional amendment designed to permit the legislature to call itself into special session. Under existing provisions the legislature could convene itself only to institute impeachment proceedings against the governor; all other special sessions had to be initiated by the governor. Senator Allen's "self-starter" was approved in both chambers by overwhelming majorities.

At first glance, the self-starter appeared to be an innocuous change, but neither the conservatives nor Folsom regarded it as such. The governor viewed it as the most serious threat to his power in either term.[71] Conservatives were disturbed at the prospect of Folsom running the executive branch without legislative oversight for a year and a half (the legislature met biennially). He had already shown what he might do by supporting tax reassessments of large corporate properties, executed by his thorough and competent commissioner of revenue, Philip Hamm. (A more detailed account of this and other administrative actions is given in chapter 7.) Goodyear Tire and Rubber was one of the hardest hit. Lieutenant Governor Inzer, who had helped secure the passage of the self-starter amendment, acted as attorney for Goodyear in a hearing held by Commissioner Hamm, but his efforts were unsuccessful. The author of the amendment, Senator Allen, was a member of a law firm retained by Alabama Power Company, the Lousville and Nashville Railroad, Equitable Life Assurance Society, Indemnity Insurance Company, and other large property holders. Other legislators representing similar interests were afraid that Hamm's initial reassessments were just the beginning (an accurate judgment), and they wanted to be able to quickly reverse such outrages in the legislature.

The intensity of the attacks on Folsom increased. Grover Hall, Jr., in a civic club speech described Folsom as "washed up" and as a "monumental fraud."[72] Vicious lies about Folsom's sexual proclivities were circulated, aimed especially at the clergy. At the annual Alabama Farm Bureau convention, Representative Walter Givhan of Dallas County (Black Belt), and a Farm Bureau spokesman, blasted Folsom for vetoing a bill that would have permitted a quick restructuring of the state's election laws in the event of a Supreme Court decision against voting discrimination. He described Folsom's advisers and policies as "red" and a threat to "orderly government."[73] Givhan went on to spell out the nature of the plot being hatched by the governor, Aubrey Williams, and Gould Beech. They would bring about universal suffrage and with black backing they would try "to dominate us and they will, unless the farmers do their part." House Speaker Beck followed Givhan to the podium and, after endorsing Givhan's views, added that "the white people of Alabama must look to their interests. Governor Folsom has swung to Aubrey Williams and Gould Beech and that threatens white supremacy and orderly government in Alabama."[74] At no time in the state's recent history has a House speaker turned on the chief executive in this manner. Givhan's and Beck's rhetorical excesses were too much for Grover Hall, Jr., who, while agreeing that orderly government in Alabama was menaced by the Folsom administration, denied that the cause was radicalism. Instead, the problem was the "fabulous incompetency" and "pennyweight political opportunism" of the Folsom administration, a problem that would not be solved by Givhan's and Beck's "extravagant, fanciful utterances."[75]

The Self-Starter Campaign

The self-starter was, up to a point, a clever device proposed by one of the wiliest parliamentarians ever to sit in the Alabama legislature or, later, the U.S. Senate, but it contained a fatal weakness. Since it was a constitutional amendment, voter approval in a statewide referendum was required. Perhaps Allen and other supporters of the proposal felt that since Folsom had lost the income tax referendum so badly and had suffered so much negative publicity during the legislative session, the self-starter would be greeted with enthusiasm by the voters.

Folsom believed that the self-starter, if enacted, would destroy his ability to bring about meaningful reform in state government; he had to defeat it. And he was confident that the legislature's conservative majority had challenged him at his strongest game, a version of electoral campaigning. The suds bucket was taken off the shelf, the Strawberry Pickers were reconstituted, and Folsom bought a new suit and headed back to the stump. To his opponent's surprise, he not only addressed the self-starter issue but also transformed the campaign into a broadside counterattack on the Big Mules. He began his "report to the people" state tour in the Wiregrass, speaking in Luverne, Troy, and Elba. "Yes, I'm the man who wasn't supposed to be governor. The people are not supposed to have a governor because the governor is supposed to represent the special interests."[76]

Reviewing the Auburn board debacle, he said, "They began to yell impeachment then. [A few legislators and interest group leaders had mulled over the possibility and rejected it as impractical, but Folsom rarely lost an opportunity to exaggerate this.] They wanted to throw me out of your office—throw me out of the office to which you elected me. Just think of it. They wanted to throw me out because I wasn't supposed to be governor."

While acknowledging that he had made mistakes, especially in his choice of legislative leaders, he reserved most of the blame for the defeat of his programs for Alabama Power Company, the Tennessee Coal, Iron and Railroad Company, and "other big monopolies." He blamed the "special privilege" groups for defeating his road program and observed that they did it "just because they said it would give 'Big Jim' Folsom too many marbles." This was an entirely plausible explanation because he could have influenced a substantial number of legislative votes with $40 million. Almost as an afterthought he turned to the self-starter. "I called the legislature into session twice, and they blocked everything you wanted. If you want them to call themselves together to block your program that's all right with me."[77]

On the second day of the campaign he added "them lyin' dailies"—the "great daily newspapers"—to his long list of villains. "They've got a new song to sing, now. They're singing the song of the boys who are doing the squealing," referring to the Big Mules. "If I would dance to their tune, you'd see big fine editorials about what a great governor 'Big Jim' is. But I'm not dancin' to their tune—I'm dancin' to *your* tune."[78]

One of Folsom's peculiarities was an anglophobia, which surfaced briefly in 1946 and reached full flower during the self-starter campaign. Comparing his $40 million road bond issue to the popular and constructive Marshall Plan, he ranted, "If we can dump millions of dollars overseas, we can afford to spend a few million for our own needs. We loaned England $3 million and now they have started whining for some more."[79] By mid-November he had bridged from this theme to snide asides aimed at Senator John Sparkman and any congressmen who had supported the Marshall Plan. He expressed puzzlement over the "dumping of dollars" into England by the United States and added, "Maybe your congressman can explain it when he comes to you next spring seeking reelection—one of your senators, too, will be coming around for reelection."[80] Of all the countries receiving assistance from the United States, only England was regularly mentioned in his frequent attacks on foreign aid.

During the self-starter campaign, he resumed his habit of "resting" before a speech, lying flat on his back in a truck bed, on a sidewalk, on the rostrum, or on courthouse steps. He had apparently done this once when he was genuinely tired and suffering from stomach cramps and had been caught by an alert photographer, and from then on he continued the practice to "show the damned newspapers."[81] Newspaper photographs of him reclining in various unlikely locations scandalized the state and embarrassed his supporters. In Fayette one of his cabinet members, Fuller Kimbrell, who was familiar with this routine, slipped a chair under the governor before he could sink to the sidewalk. Kimbrell was not about to have his governor sleeping on the sidewalk in his home county.

Some weeks prior to the beginning of the self-starter campaign, Folsom had attended a celebration of "Air Day in Texas" as guest of honor. (He was a strong believer in the future of private aviation, foreseeing a time when single-engine aircraft would be almost as widely used as automobiles. Many of the great number of small airstrips in Alabama were constructed under his auspices.) In accepting Governor Buford Jester's invitation, Folsom telegraphed: "Tell Governor Jester that I want a date with the prettiest girl in Texas." Upon his arrival in the Lone Star State, he drunkenly tumbled out of his airplane into the arms of an Air Day official. He came late to the banquet that evening, "refused to take his place at the speakers' table," wolfed down a steak "from a table near the door," and ambled back to his room, where he passed out, making himself late for the judging of a beauty contest. Air Day officials were obliged to use a pass key to arouse him. At breakfast he ordered beer and proclaimed, "The only thing better than beer is whiskey." His escapades generated heated protests from clergymen throughout Alabama.[82]

With his jovial endorsement of beer and whiskey ricocheting around the state many assumed that his prespeech "rests" were caused more by alcohol than fatigue, and doubtless many were, but his desire to "show the damned newspapers" should not be forgotten. The consensus among people close to Folsom was that drinking only slightly impaired his performance during the rigorous self-starter campaign.

The self-starter campaign also featured a good deal of kissing. In 1946 he had done much kissing, and far more women than babies, but it was of greater interest to the press when he became governor, especially when the newspapers were engaged in trying to discredit him. He certainly provided them with enough ammunition. As he traveled the state, each newspaper would feature a "Kissin' Jim" story, often set aside from the self-starter campaign feature. There were two major themes: Folsom surprising a blushing maiden and matrons lying in ambush for the handsome governor. Often he lifted his targets by the shoulders and bussed them firmly on the lips.

Although they pretended to be horrified by his resting, drinking, and kissing, Folsom's opponents were delighted that he was behaving so self-destructively. They were convinced that voters in Bible Belt Alabama would finally turn against him, but they were mistaken; it would be fourteen years before he finally went too far. He was somehow above the sanctions that would have been imposed on a normal politician. People did not seem to mind, and indeed they expected him to operate according to a unique set of rules. One reporter described it as an innocence that he radiated. It might also be termed an other-worldliness. In fact, his other-worldliness made him attractive to voters in a way probably never seen in Alabama. People sensed that this giant, with all his clowning, had an almost mystical, as well as a humane, sense of where the state should be headed.

As the self-starter campaign moved along, Folsom broadened his attacks on opponents real and imagined. In Marion County he attacked Representative Smith Dyar, one of the few real populists in the legislature and a sincere administration supporter, because he had voted for a bill regulating the administration's profligate use of state-owned equipment. He also intensified his rhetoric. The Big Mules, now called "Got Rocks," were portrayed as swooping down on Goat Hill in their long, black limousines, dressed in fancy clothes, to keep the people's mailbox roads from being constructed. He described in vivid language how them "lyin' dailies," owned by the Got Rocks, howled in pain when Folsom went against them.[83]

Folsom, too, traveled in a limousine, and in a speech in Elba he characteristically turned that fact to his advantage. In the midst of a tirade against "the big rich boys who drive to town in the big limousines," Folsom stopped and glanced nervously at the long, black vehicle in which he traveled. "Of course, I have a big limousine myself, but it is *your* limousine, and I thank you for it," he said. Then as if some waggish gnome inside him was goading him along, he added, "I have a new Packard ordered, too, and I want you to see it because it belongs to you."[84]

Self-starter advocates responded ponderously and ineffectively to his campaign. Perhaps because they felt that Folsom was doing so badly, it was not until November 13 that they began to organize. Their attacks on Folsom featured phrases like "educational campaign," "home rule government," and "fundamental principle of democracy."[85] A week later they were still organizing and still talking to one another, doing little more than convincing the convinced.[86] In one of those organizing sessions Senator Allen expressed the belief that the state's newspapers, which had been suffering so under Folsom's attacks, would carry the day for the self-starter. J. Bruce Henderson agreed, suggesting that an educational conference for newspaper editors might facilitate the process. It was clear from comments of this sort that they still had not grasped the nature of their opposition or the changes that were occurring in the political process.

Folsom had long since written off the newspapers as a significant force in Alabama politics, although he cared somewhat more about their judgments then he admitted publicly. A large segment of his support came from people who paid little attention to the press, and even when his supporters were temporarily influenced by the newspapers, he was able effortlessly to short-circuit their stiff-backed editorial attacks with charm and country humor. "I don't care what you say about me, boys," he joked to reporters, "just spell the name right."

Folsom's activities represented opportunities for skilled reporters to exhibit their writing prowess. For example, during the self-starter campaign, Rex Thomas penned this vignette:

> I stood in a drugstore at Abbeville, Ala., waiting to get a long distance call through. Across the street on the courthouse steps, the "Strawberry Pickers" were beating out a bouncy version of "Keep Them Cold Icy Fingers Off a Me."
>
> "The Speech" ambled through the crowded Henry County courthouse yard, shaking hands with the grizzled, blue-shirted farmers who had come to hear him. They followed him as he strolled across the busy street and into the drugstore.
>
> The six-foot-eight-inch giant walked over to me, leaned his super-structure against my lean five-foot-seven chassis and boomed in a pleasant voice:
>
> "Boy, we got 'em three to one in this county."[87]

The self-starter advocates' organizational sessions did not help, and their radio broadcasts continued to sound more like doctoral dissertations than campaign speeches.[88] Meanwhile, in a typical Folsom radio address, he began by asking listeners to open their windows and yell to their neighbors that Big Jim was on the air. As he waited for their return and filled the airwaves with small talk, throughout the state windows would shoot up, and the news would fly from house to house together with invitations to those lacking radios to come and listen. (In the 1950s, when he turned to television, he would occasionally address the viewing public early Saturday morning during childrens' shows. He would open his speech by asking the children to wake up their parents and tell them that Big Jim wanted to talk to them.)

Folsom's ability to personalize his radio speeches was almost uncanny; it was nearly as though he were in the room with his listeners.

> Let's talk about what's going to happen on January 6. I know a lot of you mothers are listening in. You probably just finished the dishes. You won't have much time to rest because there's ironing to be done. And by that time you'll have to start cooking again. But this so-called self-starter amendment is important to you.
>
> Why did a little clique in the legislature plan this amendment? They figured they could do more damage if they could come to Montgomery any time they wanted to. . . .
>
> Here's what they said to the people of Alabama when they killed the road

program. They said to you, "Go ahead and wallow in the mud until Jim Folsom gets out of office." They don't care if the school bus gets bogged down. They don't care if you can't get to the church.[89]

Beck, Henderson, Boutwell, and Allen, who had surfaced as the leading proponents of the self-starter measure, realized by January that a more plain-spoken approach was needed, but by then it was too late.[90] In a January 4, 1948, editorial just before election day, Grover Hall, Jr., took such an approach as he presented the Big Mule position and urged the voters to ratify the self-starter amendment.

> Submission of the amendment expresses, almost unanimously, the revolt and revulsion of the legislature for the repugnant misuses of the governor's office.
>
> First shocked, then bewildered, then aroused by the spending and racketeering of the Folsom Administration, the legislature sought to remedy the chaos and quell its source. . . .
>
> The amendment would deprive the governor of not one single power. His powers would remain intact. It would simply give the legislature power to act decisively to protect your state government from the pig snout orgies and ravages of Folsom's unfit band. . . .
>
> Perhaps the strongest argument in favor of ratification is a negative one. That is to say, the effect of a Folsom victory upon Folsom.
>
> Ratification is an act of self defense.
>
> It is clear that Folsom would construe the amendment's rejection as a mandate to go on as he has. That means humbling the dignity of his office, loose spending of public money, loose and inept administration and possibly a new revenue session of the legislature.[91]

The self-starter was voted down by more than a 60–40 margin. Hall wrote, "A javelin was thrust at Folsom, he caught it in his paws and snapped it in two," and he ruefully mulled over the vagaries of politics. "Folsom and the legislature are opposites in all respects. But they were elected by the same people on the same ballot." He suggested that the key to the contradiction lay in Folsom's charismatic personality. "No other politician could fill the City Auditorium here as Folsom did Saturday night. He is the foremost box office attraction since Tom Heflin."[92] But, Hall reflected, Heflin ultimately defeated himself when he attempted to bolt the Democratic party. What comparable error would Folsom commit? What would bring Folsom down?

CHAPTER 6

Civil Rights and Remaining First-Term Legislation

I can't think of anything worse than slavery. That's the reason I was for one man one vote, the right of the black man to vote, and women on the jury.

James E. Folsom

Folsom's two gubernatorial terms coincided with two crucial periods in the nation's civil rights history. The Dixiecrat split occurred during his first administration. After a time of relative calm and public inactivity during the Gordon Persons administration, Folsom's second term marked the beginning of the southern reaction against *Brown* and related Supreme Court decisions. During both terms, in a sense still debated, Folsom worked for an expansion of civil rights for blacks, poor whites, and women.

There is widespread disagreement concerning the reasons behind his efforts on behalf of expanded civil liberties. Some found Folsom a populist or a liberal governor who believed in a pure democratic process with all adults voting on an equal basis, a man for whom all forms of discrimination by government were anathema.[1] Others suspected that Folsom was a sly segregationist, an image he projected in his 1962 gubernatorial campaign.[2] Still others characterized him as a moderate for his times.[3] And, finally, some portrayed him as a combination of opportunist and clown.[4]

Folsom's public statements and actions in both terms provide strong and fairly consistent support for the first view: Folsom's populist-liberal beliefs were untainted by racism and had as their central aspect a deep faith in equality. These beliefs, which can be traced to his childhood and adolescence, motivated his major efforts in government and politics. His populist-liberal outlook was reinforced by his CWA experiences and by his father-in-law J. A. Carnley who, in addition to being a Populist in the fiery tradition of William Jennings Bryan, was a racial moderate.[5]

Folsom's early election campaigns had no racial overtones, and race issues arose in 1946 only in the later stages of the runoff campaign as his desperate opponent struggled to reverse a faltering effort. Even before being sworn in, Folsom faced his first major civil rights test, the Boswell Amendment referendum. His opposition was not as vigorous as it might have been, but it was unambiguous, and he made his position clear during the gubernatorial primary campaign, not after.

Race and National Politics

The year 1948 brought a presidential election and a watershed in the nation's civil rights history. In January few people of any political persuasion believed that Harry Truman would survive the November election. Attitudes toward him in Alabama varied from suspicion and distrust among the Bosses to complete antagonism in Folsom's crowd. The Bosses disliked his economic liberalism and his orientation to northern cities, labor unions, and possibly minorities, although they were not sure concerning the last point. In October 1947 the President's Committee on Civil Rights had recommended a strong civil rights program, but Truman had not yet declared his intentions on the matter.

Folsom had made his position toward Truman clear during his first year in office when he went out of his way to welcome to Alabama the leader of the most left-leaning sections of the Democratic party, former vice president Henry Wallace.[6] Wallace criticized Truman's overly antagonistic approach toward the Soviet Union and his failure to bring about domestic reforms. When reporters inquired about his feelings toward Folsom, Wallace replied, "He's the only prominent Democratic Leader that's had nerve enough to introduce me during the last six months. So, of course, I'm for him."[7] Many of Folsom's speeches at this time were equally critical of Truman, and, like Wallace, whom he appeared to be mimicking to some degree, Folsom concentrated on foreign policy.

Introductions of Henry Wallace and occasional speeches, however, did not satisfy Folsom's desire to have his views known. After all, few people really cared what a young governor of a relatively small state had to say about the president. Another vehicle for the expression of his views suggested itself one night to a wildly drunken Folsom and one of his aides who was suffering from delusions brought on by the antihistamines he was taking for an allergic condition. Folsom would pursue the Democratic party nomination for president of the United States! He announced his plans to his cabinet early the next morning. At first, some of them thought that Folsom merely intended to become the state's "favorite son" candidate, a reasonable option open to any governor, but Folsom made it clear that he was pursuing the presidency in earnest. At times he said that he merely wanted to be a favorite son candidate, but the rest of his rhetoric belied that intention. His radio address announcing his candidacy was a classic populist foreign policy statement and a bitter attack on big business and the Truman presidency.

> Who's running our party in Washington? . . . The head of our party is a nice man. But he's not running our party anymore. And he's not running our country. He's let himself get hog-tied. He's got some men hanging around the White House who don't care anything about him, or the party, or the country. They're thinking about themselves and how they can make a million dollars off your sweat.
> But taking money out of the farmer's pocket isn't the worst of it. Look at the three departments that will lead us to war or peace. There's the Defense Department. It's headed by a Wall Street lawyer [James V. Forestall]. Then there's the State Department. It's headed by a professional soldier [George C. Marshall], a good man as long as he stuck to being a policeman for democracy. . . .
> Then there's the Commerce Department. It's supposed to build up our foreign and domestic commerce. It's headed by a monopolist [Averill Harriman]. . . .
> If I were President I'd use the old corn shuck mop on the monopolists, the Wall Street lawyers, and the State Department fancy pants. And I'd send the professional soldiers back to the department where they know their job. . . .
> Monopolists, brass hats, Wall Street lawyers, tea sippers. They're not real Democrats. . . . What have they got in common with the peace-loving, God-fearing people of the Cotton Belt? What do they know about the farmers in the wheat fields? . . .
> . . . Look at what they're doing in the name of democracy in Washington. They're running all over the world dumping billions on top of billions. They're trying to bribe foreign leaders to vote a certain way. They're carrying billions in bribes in one hand, and a sword of fear in the other.
> Now, if spending 20 or 30 billions more would help democracy in the world or bring peace, I'd be the first to say it was worth it. But you can't bribe and threaten the world into peace. Here's the proof. Look at the countries where our agents have been handing out bribes and guns. The kings and the dictators are getting stronger. But the Democrats are getting weaker. . . .
> Now, I mean what I say about the leader of our party being a nice man. . . .
> But the monopolists, the brass hats, the grain speculators and the Wall Street lawyers have got hold of him. They have decided to keep him. . . .
> The bunch that's captured our President are doing a lot of talking about stopping Communism. They're blood brothers of the Communists. They're power mad just like the Communists. These agents of Wall Street monopoly are just like the Communists in another way. They believe in rule of a few. They don't trust the common people.[8]

Most of Folsom's cabinet members and aides were uneasy about becoming associated with his presidential campaign, but they humored him, while winking at reporters behind his back. At first, reporters and editorial writers treated the story with surprising seriousness, although they were highly critical of his radio address. Of seven major southern newspapers cited in a *Montgomery Advertiser* editorial, only the *Richmond Times-Dispatch* took advantage of the story's potential for humor: accompanying a standard headline ("Folsom Seeks State Backing for Presidency") the paper ran a photograph of Folsom wearing a sarong.[9] Soon, however, many Alabama dailies were following the *Times-Dispatch*'s example, turning Folsom's most powerful weapon, humor, against him.

Meanwhile, the day before his announcement of his candidacy and his anti-Truman speech, the state Democratic executive committee hinted that an antisegregation plank in the national Democratic party platform might produce a bolt by southern delegations. The committee adopted a resolution instructing convention delegates to "resist with all their ability and power any and every attempt to insert in the [1948 platform] any proposal that would directly or indirectly favor or allow any Federal legislation which would abolish or tend to abolish racial segregation."[10] Mississippi Governor Fielding Wright had begun to advocate secession from the party if a civil rights plank became part of the platform.[11] Folsom ignored these ominous developments in his presidential announcement.

The meaning of his omission was not lost on segregationists. The Jefferson County Democratic Committee immediately adopted a resolution supporting Truman "in view of recent developments."[12] It added, however, the qualification that continued support for the president was contingent on the exclusion of a civil rights plank from the 1948 platform. Then in a burst of human fellowship the committee created a subcommittee to "combat racial and religious hatreds." On the same day Birmingham Police Commissioner Eugene (Bull) Connor announced his candidacy for delegate-at-large to the Democratic national convention (the slot that Folsom was pursuing) and called for President Truman's renomination, the preservation of southern traditions, and the extermination of Communists.[13]

In a speech two days later Folsom responded to the state party leaders' actions with clear opposition combined with indirection. He scored the executive committee for trying to "dictate to candidates what they ought to stand for" at the national convention, and he expressed his opposition to bolting the Democratic party.[14] Then he listed an eighteen-point platform which ignored the segregationists except for two points that, loosely construed, could have been interpreted as an endorsement of states' rights (for example, "I am for local responsibility in the government of all the people.").

On February 2, Truman recommended federal legislation banning lynching, protecting voting rights (including poll tax elimination), ending segregation in interstate transportation, and creating a fair employment practices commission and a joint congressional civil rights committee. Truman and the

Democratic party had been hurt by his unwillingness to support actively the creation of a fair employment practices commission two years earlier in the face of southern opposition. In retaliation, black leaders had supported Republicans in the 1946 elections, and the Democrats had lost control of Congress. Black leaders had forcefully taught Truman a lesson; he had to recognize their interests and those of white liberals in the party, such as Henry Wallace. Furthermore, Communist propaganda focusing on the mistreatment of blacks in the South was hurting the United States all over the world.

Most Alabama and other southern political leaders were enraged by the president's actions, but Folsom and Senator Lister Hill were silent.[15] A few days later the Southern Governors Conference was held in Florida. Folsom vigorously opposed talk of a bolt, but the other governors adopted a resolution that suggested that one could easily occur. The governors appointed a committee to meet with the Democratic national chairman. At that meeting they asked whether Truman's civil rights proposals could be withdrawn from Congress and whether convention rules could be modified in such a way as to favor minority (segregationist) interests. The answers were negative, and the meeting ended in failure for the segregationists.

The battle lines in Alabama were changing rapidly that February. During the latter stages of his self-starter campaign Folsom had been making increasingly cutting remarks about Senator Sparkman's support of foreign aid. Sparkman, a racial moderate, was up for reelection in 1948, and Folsom decided that Sparkman had to go. According to William Barnard, who cites Sparkman as his source, Gould Beech "had spoken with the Senator in February and had warned him that unless Sparkman changes his views on foreign policy, he would face opposition in the primary if Beech himself had to make the race."[16] According to the *Montgomery Advertiser,* Beech also contacted Lister Hill and "demanded with the transfixed serenity of an evangelical snake worshiper that Hill join the Folsom 'crusade.'" And Ross Clark, described by Grover Hall, Jr., as "that Folsom agent who wears suits the color of a black satchel," tried to convince former congressman Lafayette Patterson to run against Sparkman, but to no avail.[17] Reuben Newton of Jasper was apparently close to entering the race, but ultimately decided against it. Finally, Folsom settled on his revenue commissioner, Philip Hamm, an effective administrator but a poor election campaigner. This split among the state's handful of racial moderates delighted segregationists.

Two less visible contests were more important to civil libertarians and segregationists. One concerned delegate selection to the Democratic national convention and the other the choice of Democratic party nominees to the Electoral College. Both groups would be picked in a May primary.

Like the others, the next event of those confusing early months of 1948 had been percolating for quite some time, but it came from a totally different direction. In March a woman suing as Christine Putnam Folsom (known as Christine Johnston from an early marriage) asked the Cullman Circuit Court to issue a declaratory judgment establishing her as Folsom's common-law wife and her twenty-two-month-old son as his.[18] Folsom claimed that the suit was merely a ploy designed to discredit him politically, but that was a lie, as he readily admits today.[19] He was the father. Folsom had known Christine since late in 1944. He had appeared with her many times in public and had presented her to many people as his fiancée. But after her pregnancy he had allowed or had ordered his aides to buy her off against the advice of her attorney and author William Bradford Huie, who had encouraged her to file suit.[20]

Christine Johnston ultimately accepted a financial settlement. The money to pay her came from bribes to the ABC Board. A Birmingham businessman paid board members twenty-five thousand dollars for the privilege of participating in an arrangement in which wine was shipped into Alabama in tank cars and bottled there. The money was transferred to a Cullman businessman, who decided that there might be a way to extend the money. He paid Christine ten to fifteen thousand dollars, gave her a Buick bought at a discount, and pocketed the rest. Another Birmingham businessman who some months earlier had paid a similar sum for what he thought would be a monopoly on the tank car deal found that he had what amounted to an unwanted partner. He told the entire story to a *Birmingham News* reporter named Hugh Sparrow, who wrote it and submitted it to his editors. At the last minute the full story was squelched by the second man in the tank car arrangement, who appealed to the editors on some unknown personal basis. The paper ran the story, but in expurgated form.[21]

It was a massive scandal; papers throughout the nation made it front page news. While the sheer silliness of Folsom's presidential bid would have caused it to disintegrate on its own, the paternity suit accelerated the process.

Folsom, however, was unbowed. Nine days after the paternity suit first made front page news, the governor surfaced in Manhattan at the Barbizon School of Modeling. The students of that institution had voted him "The Nation's Number One Leap Year Bachelor." He was met on the street in front of the school by one hundred girls, whom he began kissing in rapid succession. A crowd estimated by reporters at twenty-five hundred quickly collected on the sidewalks and in the street.[22] Traffic backed up for blocks in both directions while police attempted to persuade the governor to move inside. In one photograph Folsom had grabbed a woman reporter by the shoulders and was sweeping her sideways in his direction—her notebook and pen appear to be floating in mid-air, and she has a look of surprise on her face that combines both horror and embarrassment. He went for a second reporter and moved toward a third, but she ducked away and he returned to the models.

A male reporter worked his way close to Folsom and shouted, "What do you think of the New York ladies?" "Best in the world," Folsom yelled back and then paused to kiss another. "Outside Alabama, that is." He bussed another. "They're the prettiest in the world—outside Alabama." Another. "The best I've ever seen—outside Alabama."[23]

Finally, he made his way inside the school, where he was met by two hundred more models, and he started over. After Folsom accepted a scroll commemorating his Number One Bachelor status, a motorcycle escort led him and a select bevy of the young women to a restaurant for lunch. "He looked down the long table at which some 25 models were seated and shouted: 'Give them all a drink on the taxpayers of Alabama.' He called to a waiter: 'Bring on the cornpone and black-eyed peas.' The waiter said he was sorry he couldn't oblige, and Folsom capitulated: 'Well, then, bring me some of that Yankee food.'"[24] Scheduled to visit the Empire State Building after lunch, he declined, saying that he was "tuckered out."

Asked years later why he had made the New York trip in a time when he was embroiled in a paternity suit and struggling to have his presidential bid taken seriously, Folsom replied, speaking with special clarity, "I wanted to go on the O-ffensive." Grover Hall, Jr., bemoaned his fate in having "a peglegged Achilles for an adversary." "What would be a scandal to politically exterminate a dozen Sparkses, Dixons, Hills and Sparkmans falls as a gentle rain upon Folsom's shoulders, coagulates and becomes adoration. . . . The psychologists can confine themselves to establishing what Folsom-in-general gratifies in you and you and you in this post-war, atomic era. Us, we're darkly preoccupied with the source of the knave's inexhaustible luck."[25]

Hall, the *Montgomery Advertiser*'s editor throughout much of Folsom's gubernatorial career, was a sharp observer and a superb reported whose fluid prose could inspire or anger his readers, but just as frequently could be breezy and funny. Occasionally, he failed—his humor, for example, sometimes degenerated into childish name-calling—but he was so clever he could even make a trick like name-calling work. He was as perceptive, stimulating, and skillful as his Pulitzer Prize–winning father, and, like his father, he was not a tool for Alabama's top leaders, but he lacked the good fortune to be given a target that was as easy to savage as the KKK. Grover, Jr., was damned to a time and place in which he found himself defending institutions, practices, and people repugnant to Americans who believed in democracy and human dignity.

As it turned out, Hall was right about the paternity suit: the scandal had little long-term effect on Folsom's career. Hall described Folsom's withdrawal from his presidential pursuit as having "occurred silently, like a snowflake falling in the river." Folsom had not "renounced his candidacy—he . . . let it expire in response to what might be described as a negative mandate." Hall again bemoaned his luck. Folsom had stumbled into an attack on Truman when the president was still popular in Alabama. "That Truman later emerged a Southern enemy and caused the rest of us to join Folsom in his hostility is just another example of the man's incessant luck," Hall wrote. Making matters worse, few voters remembered that Folsom's original attack on Truman had been mounted from the Henry Wallace left.[26]

In a peculiar way, by accelerating the destruction of his presidential aspirations and Hamm's senatorial race, the scandal had a salutary effect on the delegate selection campaigns of those promising loyalty to the national party. Folsom began to place less emphasis on Truman and more on a classic argument long used by southern liberals and populists opposed to racial discrimination. He asserted that the real issues were ones of economic well-being and social justice and the threat to those values by elite dominance of the state and nation, and that the Big Mules were using race to distract voters from those issues and to keep many citizens from voting at all. He continued his criticisms of foreign aid, especially aid to dictatorships, and he criticized Truman's civil rights program in the language of states' rights, saying that it would lead to increased federal power and could even mean that federal troops would someday invade Alabama, turning it into a police state.

While not entirely attractive to Sparkman and Hill, Folsom's modified approach was harmless to them. It permitted them to turn their attention away from Folsom and toward the common enemy. Lister Hill entered the convention delegate race and endorsed Truman, a move which required more than a little courage since it followed so closely on Truman's civil rights revelations.[27] In his view, the Democratic party had been good to the South during the Depression, whereas the Republicans would have been a disaster. Furthermore, the South could expect no better treatment from the Republicans because the GOP's civil rights programs were, if anything, worse than Truman's—it remained the party of Lincoln. A southern split from the Democrats would virtually guarantee Republican victory, given Truman's unpopularity nationwide.

Hill's argument was a solid, logical counterpoint to Folsom's high-flying, sweeping populist oratory. Three weeks after Hill filed for convention delegate, however, Sparkman called for Truman to refrain from seeking the nomination, pointing to Truman's supposed unelectability. Sparkman suggested that Dwight Eisenhower, who was being courted by both parties, would make an excellent choice for the Democrats. Soon after Sparkman's announcement, Hill withdrew his support from Truman and echoed the junior senator's call for the general's nomination. Their opposition to Truman was based mainly on his political weakness rather than on his civil rights program.[28]

On April 5, Gessner McCorvey called a meeting of the Democratic executive committee, which, under his leadership, voted to bolt the party should the convention adopt any part of Truman's civil rights program. It ordered all candidates for convention delegate and alternate to file a statement of their intentions concerning a potential bolt. The committee also endorsed the candidates for electors who had pledged not to vote for Truman.[29]

McCorvey was becoming an increasingly important segregationist leader. He had led the successful referendum campaign for the Boswell Amendment and was emerging as a major architect of what was to be the Dixiecrat bolt. He had been elected state party chairman in 1939 with Governor Dixon's support. Folsom could probably have eased him out early in 1947, but he declined to do so, even though he knew full well what interests McCorvey represented.[30] As Folsom explained later, the other candidates for the 1946 gubernatorial primary had all tried to be the first to file, and since they all came rushing forward in a jumble, they had to share the headlines. Folsom wanted to add mystery to his campaign, and he wanted the headlines all to himself, and so he delayed to the last minute. This also deluded his opponents and the press into thinking that his campaign was an ill-prepared afterthought. So that he could file at any time, he had the documents notarized several weeks in advance. When he filed with the secretary of state, however, she refused to accept the documents because they had been notarized several weeks earlier. Folsom knew she did not have a case, but he was badly frightened. After driving all night from Montgomery to Mobile, he met McCorvey at his office and asked the chairman what his status was. McCorvey inquired only if he had publicized his candidacy since obtaining the notarization. Folsom replied that he had not, and McCorvey informed him that he could have had the papers notarized last year and it would have made no difference. "The old man was so forthright on the thing," Folsom said later, "that I never forgot, so I didn't oppose him [for reelection]. Also, I was in the fight over the speakership which was much more important, and the Dixiecrat thing hadn't come up yet—McCorvey was just rabid on the Dixiecrat stuff."[31] Folsom's refusal to eliminate McCorvey was typical of his basically humane, decent approach to politics, which separated him from someone like Huey Long who would have replaced McCorvey without a twinge of conscience.

Many state politicians, especially moderates from North Alabama, were appalled by the actions of the state executive committee at its April meeting. Although much that followed went as expected, Chauncey Sparks surprised many when he declared his intention not to bolt. Sparks made clear his opposition to Truman's civil rights proposals and swore that he would do everything in his power to fight them, but he felt that a walkout would not be seemly.[32] Moderates were delighted that Sparks, with his impeccable conservative credentials, would join the loyalist cause. Attorney General Albert Carmichael also refused to bolt.

By the second week of April it seemed that lines had been drawn between loyalists and bolters (the term "Dixiecrat" had not yet appeared), but the divisions were not that simple. There were at least three groups: Folsom loyalists (populist-liberals), segregationist loyalists (such as Sparks), and bolters. Even these categories are too simple because many, if not most, of the "Folsom loyalists" were moderate, flexible segregationists. It must have been enormously confusing to the voters. A list published in the April 27 *Montgomery Advertiser* illustrates the problems. The list was divided between candidates endorsed and not endorsed by Folsom. The "Folsom endorsed" category included Attorney General Carmichael and State Senator A. L. Patterson, both of whom were running for convention delegate. Carmichael was a moderate and Patterson would soon leave Folsom for the Senate conservative bloc. On the other hand, the "not endorsed" group combined the likes of Chauncey Sparks and Lister Hill with Gessner McCorvey and Wilcox County's reactionary J. Miller Bonner.[33] Folsom's failure to endorse Hill probably had to do with his desire to dominate the liberal wing of the Alabama Democratic party.

Folsom's campaign for his slate of candidates barely creaked along. He traveled about with Philip Hamm, who was still going through the motions of running for the Senate, and State Senator Broughton Lamberth, who was a candidate for national committeeman. Folsom appeared tired and dejected, and his speeches lacked the verve that had energized his recently won self-starter campaign. After speaking, he would introduce Lamberth, who would merely acknowledge applause without even speaking for himself; then Folsom would introduce Hamm, who would bore the audience for a few minutes and end by apologetically and hesitantly distributing his publicity cards. It was a dismal performance all around except for the ever-professional Strawberry Pickers, who were on the state payroll at the time.

The results of the May primary and the June runoff split the convention delegates roughly in half between loyalists and bolters, but *all electors* were pledged to vote against anyone favoring civil rights reform. Folsom failed to win election as a delegate, but Hill won handily. Hamm and Lamberth were defeated, and congressional candidates oriented toward Folsom were defeated in every district. It is difficult to imagine that such a disaster could have been suffered by the man who had engineered the brilliant self-starter victory. The press and Folsom's political opponents interpreted this loss as proof that his career was at an end, which encouraged them to continue attacking his legislative programs with little thought that their actions might be used by him in 1954 reelection campaigning.

Some have wondered why Folsom, Hill, and Sparkman did not cooperate in open opposition to the bolters, but Folsom was not the type to cooperate with another Alabama politician who regarded himself as Folsom's equal or superior. In addition, Folsom saw himself as the leader of the opposition to the Big Mules; Hill and Sparkman were far too moderate for his taste. Nor should Folsom's attitude toward Sparkman's support of foreign aid be overlooked. Folsom felt strongly that Sparkman was wrong on that issue. By setting Hamm against Sparkman, Folsom indicated that he was trying to dominate both Alabama senators.

Given Folsom's attitudes toward them, Hill and Sparkman were not likely to have anything to do with him on an issue of any importance. Even if Folsom had not been trying to dominate them, they probably would have regarded him as an unreliable ally in a fight as dangerous as this one.

The day after his primary defeat Folsom surprised the state by marrying. He and Jamelle Moore quietly slipped out of Montgomery to a small private ceremony at the Rockford Baptist Church in Rockford, Alabama. Bill Lyerly was the only Folsom associate present. News of the wedding hit the front pages of the state's papers and for days stories about their honeymoon plans and interviews with the new First Lady shared front section coverage with the growing Dixiecrat movement.

While the marriage surprised the state and even most of Folsom's family, Rachael and Melissa had been told in advance. Only the exact date had been withheld from them. Jamelle had occasionally spent time with the girls since first meeting Folsom, and they had become fond of her. The girls' only concerns were whether they would still be allowed to fall asleep in Folsom's huge bed listening to him read stories and tell tales and whether Aunt Ruby and her daughter Cornelia would continue to be part of their home life.

The Democratic party convention in Philadelphia was far worse for the bolters than they had imagined it could be. After defeating southern platform amendments, the convention also rejected the administration-backed civil rights plank and voted 651½ to 582½ to accept an even stronger position, whereupon Convention Chairman Sam Rayburn, paying no attention to Bull Connor's furious efforts to be recognized ("Bull was hollering like the devil's own loudspeaker") gaveled a recess.[34]

The civil rights plank adopted by the convention committed the party to "continuing efforts to eradicate all racial, religious and economic discrimination." It asserted that "racial and religious minorities must have the right to live, the right to work, the right to vote, the full and equal protection of the laws."[35]

Immediately after these events Grover Hall, Jr., who was on the convention floor, wrote these anguished lines which summarized what would be a large part of the moderate southern view of the civil rights struggle for the next twenty years: "The South asked this Democratic convention for understanding and forbearance, and received a savage blow on its face in return. . . . It was not an act of any sinister leaders, any opportunistic big city sewer voices or New Deal pinks—it was the rank and file of delegates from all over the country. . . . It is clear that we of the South are alone, quite alone with our oppressive and gathering problem. . . . The attitude of this convention towards Alabama and the South this afternoon was cold, forbidding and contemptuous."[36]

When the convention reconvened and the roll call of the states for presidential nominations began, Handy Ellis announced that those pledged to leave if a civil rights plank were adopted were carrying out their promise; so half the Alabama delegation and a group from Mississippi departed. Remaining with the loyalists was George C. Wallace, who was there as an alternate for a bolter who was too ill to attend. The loyalists from Alabama and nearly all others from the Confederate states who stayed voted for Georgia's Senator Richard B. Russell; no one from Alabama voted for Truman.

On July 17 southern Democratic party dissidents held a convention in the Birmingham, Alabama, municipal auditorium. The Alabama delegation was rich in urban and Black Belt Bosses and their representatives. Frank Dixon was keynote speaker. Mississippi, South Carolina, and Louisiana sent similarly influential groups, but Virginia, Florida, Tennessee, Kentucky, Texas, North Carolina, and Arkansas had little official representation. Overall, few congressmen, senators, or governors were there. Arkansas Governor Ben Laney, an early dissident organizer, traveled to Birmingham, but refused to venture out of his hotel room, participating in the convention only by pouring cold water on the intoxicating spirit of rebellion with an announcement that southerners should not split from the Democratic party. Folsom performed his official duty by appearing briefly to extend an official welcome. He remained only long enough to read a pro forma attack on Truman which contained no words of support for the conventioneers themselves. They nominated South Carolina Governor Strom Thurmond and Mississippi Governor Fielding Wright for president and vice president, respectively.

To have any chance of success, Dixiecrats had to expand from their southern base, but their convention was a poor start. A *Montgomery Advertiser* editorial described it as "entirely negative." The "inflamed and uninspired leaders did little more than bellow and cry 'nigger.' "[37] Years later,

George Wallace, with his emphasis on states' rights and populist economic themes similar to those used by Folsom in 1946, would largely succeed where the Dixiecrats had failed.

The myths and images that the Alabama elite used to justify their hold on power and maintain the status quo—including Social Darwinian ideas of rule by the "best" and a natural, immutable hierarchy with blacks at the bottom and poor whites next—have already been discussed. In their dealings with the federal government, however, the leaders of the elite added another element: states' rights. This doctrine, as expressed by segregationists, held that the federal government was threatening to become a dictatorship, and one way to avoid that happening was to invest and maintain as much power in state governments as possible.

For most states' rights advocates the signs of uncontrolled growth of the federal behemoth lay all around: federal antilynching laws had brought the federal government into police activities guaranteed to the states by the Constitution; federal elimination of the poll tax would involve the national government in the administration of elections; and a variety of laws with origins in the New Deal had resulted in federal control of the economy. Whatever its merits as a theoretical idea, states' rights became a code phrase for southern politicians who wanted to avoid direct discussions of segregation, voting discrimination, discriminatory hiring practices, and so forth. Strom Thurmond, for example, one of this nation's most determined segregationists, declared that he was "not one whit interested in the question of White Supremacy," and that he would campaign exclusively on the issue of "sovereignty of the states as against Federal government interferences."[38]

Barnard emphasizes that Dixon, McCorvey, Henderson, and the like were not evil men, cynically manipulating public opinion for their own selfish ends but that they truly believed that their ideas represented a closely reasoned and highly principled philosophical defense of freedom. It should be added, however, that their high principles rarely, if ever, caused them to deviate from paths that served their personal economic interests and the political interests of the groups they represented, something which occurred frequently with Folsom. The elite myths and political-economic self-interest would go hand-in-hand until the mid-1950s, when the interests of urban and Black Belt Bosses diverged. Then inconsistencies between white supremacy and political-economic self-interest would be resolved in favor of the latter, and pragmatic leaders would arise to replace segregationist idealists as the dominant political spokesmen.

Now that Truman had committed himself to a relatively strong civil rights program, he cleverly froze Republicans into a corner, isolating them from black voters by calling Congress into special session before the election to consider civil rights bills. Southern congressmen and senators, including Lister Hill, succeeded in killing the bills. In the presidential campaign Truman blithely ignored the very real and solid Republican support of civil rights bills in both chambers and further ignored the fact that the senators most responsible for defeating the civil rights bills were from his own party. He hammered away at the "do-nothing" Eightieth Congress controlled by Republicans with devastatingly effective rhetoric.

While Lister Hill played the anti–civil rights role expected of him, he seemed to lack enthusiasm for the prosegregation fight. In a Labor Day speech he called upon the South to consider other rights along with states' rights. He emphasized the contributions the federal government had made to human welfare in Alabama: statutes outlawing child labor and sweat shops and guaranteeing unions the right to collective bargaining; provisions for a minimum wage and decent working hours; housing programs; the GI Bill of Rights; Social Security; and many more. He underlined repeatedly that these programs had not been created by advocating states' rights.[39]

As the November 1948 election approached Alabama citizens who wanted to cast their votes for Harry Truman faced a dilemma: no electors pledged to the president appeared on the Alabama ballot, since the Dixiecrats had won all eleven elector slots in the May primary. State Senator Joe Langan of Mobile, one of Folsom's few supporters in the 1947 legislative session, assembled a statewide rally of "loyal Democrats" in Montgomery in mid-August to develop a strategy to get a slate of electors pledged to Truman put on the November ballot.[40] More than two hundred persons were expected at the meeting, but only thirty to thirty-five attended, and most of those were labor leaders with whom Langan had close ties. At the meeting and in speeches around the state Langan spoke harshly of the Dixiecrats, comparing the Alabama voter's inability to vote for the candidate of his choice to the situation he might find in a Communist country.[41] Langan's group decided to seek a writ of mandamus forcing the Dixiecrat electors to vote for Truman. Folsom actually filed the suit in October before the Supreme Court, but the court refused to consider it.[42]

Even after the election, with Truman victorious, Folsom continued to fight. In early November he filed suit in district court to force Alabama's electors to vote for Truman, and he sent telegrams to the electors asking them to support Truman voluntarily.[43] Neither attempt worked. A few days later a number of North Alabama state legislators and private citizens filed two state court suits. Those efforts also failed. Stubbornly refusing to admit defeat, Folsom filed two more suits, one before the Alabama Supreme Court, the other before the Supreme Court, and again he lost.[44] His suits focused on two points. First, he stated that it was customary—almost common law—that party electors cast their ballots for the nominee of the national party winning in the state. Second, and more important, he pointed out that in 1945 the Alabama legislature had passed, and Governor Sparks had signed, a law requiring electors to vote in that manner.[45]

While some have charged that Folsom took these and similar actions because he hoped to build a strong constituency among black and poor white voters,[46] Folsom gave other reasons in a speech delivered on November 1. He began by observing that Alabama voters did not have the "privilege of voting for or against the nominee of the Democratic Party." This was a tragedy in his eyes because "the only real and honest progress the South has ever made has been under the leadership of the Democratic Party. It is the only party which has favored us according to the actual needs of our people, and not the whims of the more fortunate monied interests. It is the only party which has brought relief in welfare, health, rural electrification, highways, social security, and many other humanitarian measures."[47]

Up to this point Folsom sounded little different from Lister Hill, but Folsom quickly moved to a second theme which placed him in a different category. He charged that majority rule—democracy—was being denied the Alabama voters and that the persons responsible represented a cunning, selfish, and bigoted elite, which he likened to the worst dictatorships in history.

Without denying that Folsom may have been thinking about future elections as he fought the Dixiecrats (a very risky and doubtful proposition given that movement's enormous popularity), it must be said that one of Folsom's most basic beliefs was that it was his responsibility and his historical place to fight elite attempts to downgrade the quality of democracy. He considered himself a crusader in the battle for human rights.

Voting Rights

In January 1949 the United States district court in Mobile declared the Boswell Amendment unconstitutional, and conservatives feared that the Supreme Court would uphold that decision, as it ultimately did. The Boswell Amendment had required new voting applicants to "read and write, understand and explain any article of the Constitution of the United States." The court found that in practice only blacks were required to submit to questioning. Furthermore, the court argued that the phrase "understand and explain" was too vague to be applied and that no other parts of the amendment offered guidance as to its explanation. Finally, even if such guidance had existed, the registrars, being laymen, were not qualified to determine the validity of answers.[48]

Horace Wilkinson, a leading Dixiecrat, had expected such a decision. He had been working on another disfranchisement device which would have turned the Democratic party into a private organization unregulated by state law but open to anyone who believed in "states rights, white responsibility, and the right to reject a ballot."[49] Essentially, Wilkinson's plan would have required Democratic candidates to reject all ballots cast for them by voters who refused to swear their belief in states' rights and white responsibility. This would, in his view, have the effect of disfranchising Negroes, Republicans, Socialists, and Progressives.

This was too much even for McCorvey, who in a letter to Frank Dixon (with a copy to Wilkinson) expressed the feeling that "if something along this line could be done, it would be fine," but he was certain that the federal courts would quickly declare it unconstitutional. Then McCorvey presented his thoughts on what could be done following the Boswell decision: "I am just afraid we are going to have to . . . recognize that we will simply *have* to permit negroes to vote in our primaries under the set-up now existing. I think we have a splendid protection in the way of our poll tax, insofar as large numbers of these negroes are concerned. The negro race generally, is so thriftless and shiftless that the average negro is not going to pay $1.50 in February for the privilege of voting next November, and by retaining the all-important cumulative feature of our poll tax, it will only be a few years before these negroes are practically eliminated as voters, even though they register."[50]

McCorvey then recounted a chilling anecdote which revealed his feelings about civil rights better than any dozen public statements he could have made.

> Relative to the mentality of our colored friends, let me just give you a little incident that brought the matter home to me very clearly. We have an old cook, Eliza, who has been with my family and my wife's family for over forty years. . . . She is the type of old faithful family servant that we all love. However, some days ago, when I was discussing our troubles on this negro voting proposition, my wife remarked that she could talk to Eliza from now until Doomsday and that she could never convince Eliza that there would be any harm in her selling her vote for $10.00, if somebody wished to buy it. Emily says that old Eliza would feel that her vote belonged to her and that she would have just as much right to sell her vote as she would have to sell a puppy belonging to her, and that is the way, I am sure, the average negro, even most of the good negroes, would look at the proposition.[51]

The Supreme Court quickly upheld the district court ruling. Folsom told reporters that he was "cheered" by the decision. "I opposed the Boswell Amendment in the election and I think the Supreme Court decided right."[52]

McCorvey responded with a new constitutional amendment that based voter registration on character and citizenship. No person would be allowed to register unless voting registrars had determined that he or she possessed "good character" and understood and embraced the "duties and obligations of citizenship under our republican form of government."[53] McCorvey's new amendment came to be known as Boswell, Jr.

The 1949 Legislative Session

Folsom and the Dixiecrats expected that civil rights issues would be more heavily stressed in the 1949 legislative session than they had been in 1947, and that they would be deeply intertwined with more routine matters. In January 1949 Folsom began a series of conferences with legislators in an attempt to build a coalition favorable to his program, which remained essentially unchanged from 1947 except for a stronger emphasis on civil rights and reapportionment.

Folsom rounded out his coalition-building efforts by conferring with county and city officials on the subjects of roads and increased local autonomy. Most local officials were more concerned with these matters than with state-level power struggles. Local officials working in concert could, in one journalist's description, "all but crucify a legislator, politicalwise, businesswise, and otherwise."[54] Changes of any consequence in government structure or revenue systems at the local level required legislative approval and often state constitutional amendment. At that time half the amendments to the 1901 constitution concerned matters in a single county or city. Generally speaking, the legislature would approve any local government's request for change if that request were supported by a majority of the legislative delegation from that area, and the legislature would reject requests opposed by the local legislative delegation. This veto over local government changes represented power that legislators were loath to relinquish. Folsom favored home rule as a matter of principle, and he let local administrators know that he could be counted on to push it if the cities and counties supported his road bills.

He tightened his control over road construction projects by naming the veteran highway administrator Henry S. Long as right-of-way agent in the Highway Department.[55] Even with Long's appointment, though, by the end of 1949 Folsom was apparently not entirely satisfied with the degree of control he had been able to exercise over road construction locations. The main problem was that approximately one-third of the construction done in the first three years of his term represented commitments made during the Sparks administration. In addition, there were hints that Highway Department officials under merit system protection were not making the kinds of decisions that he wanted.[56] When stories surfaced to the effect that the governor was going to increase his control over road construction location and do a more effective job of rewarding friends and punishing enemies, O. H. Finney did not bother denying them.[57] Hugh Sparrow found one example of how he rewarded friends in the $125,000 Alexander City bypass that was constructed in 1948 on a right-of-way flanking land owned by a Folsom loyalist, Senator Broughton Lamberth. Alexander City residents called it the "Broughton Lamberth Highway." Later the state paved a section of road that cut through another piece of Lamberth property. In both cases the value of the senator's property was enhanced considerably.[58]

Folsom continued to use patronage rewards to cement his power. His strong supporter Representative George Wallace was named to the State Planning Board, replacing Representative Wallace Malone, a major antiadministration leader. His efforts in patronage distribution were not always successful, however. He unaccountably failed to appoint Senator A. L. Patterson's choice for Lee County probate judge, even though Patterson had been a fairly strong administration supporter. Embarrassed at his lack of standing with the governor, Patterson broke with him publicly.[59]

Prior to the 1949 legislative session Folsom spoke on the radio and stumped the state over a two-month period to gather public support for his programs. In his major address before the legislature he declared:

> This body should give its earnest consideration to improving present voting qualifications.... This study should not be approached with the idea of disfranchising any of our population. Restrictions imposed by prejudice and intolerance have been declared unconstitutional.... It is inherent in a democracy that a person who exercises the full rights of citizenship should be allowed to vote.... Our population is 60 percent white and 40 percent Negro. We are gradually affording the Negro opportunity to make substantial contributions for the benefit of the total population. We must strengthen the cornerstone of opportunity for them. We must remember—that which is built upon prejudice or ill will cannot survive in a democracy.[60]

Meanwhile, Dixiecrats were busy raising money and writing new legislation. They held a posh fund-raising banquet in Birmingham which John Temple Graves promoted in one of his columns. He wrote that "among the guests will be the ghosts of Woodrow Wilson, Theodore Roosevelt, Thomas Jefferson, and Andrew Jackson." Grover Hall, Jr., could not tolerate such fatuous imagery; he composed a satirical response which included a seating chart in which, among other outrages, he placed the KKK leader next to the spirit of Roosevelt, who had once made Booker T. Washington responsible for federal patronage in Alabama. He also wrote clever dialogue for banquet guests living and dead. The Dixiecrats ended Hall's imaginary banquet by staging a walkout on their wraithish guests.[61] Real, living Dixiecrats were not amused.

Folsom sensed that his quiet, behind-the-scenes efforts at coalition building were not enough to bring about the legislative successes he desired. Thus, toward the end of March he began a series of rallies that combined the best features of the self-starter campaign and President Harry Truman's fight against the "do-nothing" Eightieth Congress. By April Folsom's legislative opposition had revealed a shiny new look. A seventeen-member Senate group calling itself the "economy bloc" announced that it intended to disembowel Folsom's programs in the upcoming session.[62]

Folsom continued his radio addresses and personal appearances, sometimes accompanied by the Strawberry Pickers. The emergence of the economy bloc seemed to inspire him to refine his theme of elite domination of state government. In an April 3 radio address and his first message to the 1949 legislature on May 3, he presented two of his most penetrating critiques of the status quo, complete with a historical analysis tracing the drafting of the 1901 constitution by what he described as Wall Street–controlled carpetbaggers (a partly erroneous but powerful symbol) and the evil effects of legislative malapportionment and barriers against universal suffrage. The economy bloc became the "carpetbag bloc" and "special privilege slaveholder bloc" representing exclusively the interests of railroads, steel trusts, and oil companies.[63]

When the legislature opened, the governor proposed a set of bills that was audacious even for him. His budget was 45 percent greater than the one for the preceding biennium, and he asked for $61 million in new taxes, together with an $80 million road bond issue, plus poll tax elimination and other civil rights reforms. He later admitted in interviews that he had requested much more than he expected to receive, hoping that compromises would give him a significant portion of what he wanted.[64]

The Senate lost no time in attacking the governor. By a vote of 17–9 Senate rules were changed to route gubernatorial messages through the Rules Committee, a body dominated by conservatives, rather than directly onto the Senate floor. Such messages included appointments, executive amendments to bills, and vetoes. Accompanying the passage of this change was much talk of bottling up Folsom's appointments until the next governor took office two years later, and in fact the Rules Committee immediately began to bury all Folsom appointments.[65] Senator Guy Hardwick of Houston County, a moderate, predicted, as Representative Brassell had two years earlier, that continued rock-hard opposition to all of Folsom's programs and appointees would make a martyr out of him, guaranteeing his reelection in

1954.⁶⁶ A *Montgomery Advertiser* editorial endorsed Hardwick's warning, and another editorial a week later made the same point, observing that the paper, "for all its aggrievement over Primo C. Folsom, has always been careful to point out that some of his program embodies enduring aspirations of the people" and that conservative rigidity and failure to compromise would only work in Folsom's favor. "The people often embrace demagogues when the respectable leaders are first given the chance and fail to respond to their wants and needs."[67]

Ignoring such warnings, both the House and Senate immediately proceeded to dismantle Folsom's program.[68] Nearly all the votes were overwhelming—outcomes such as 68–32 in the House and 26–8 in the Senate were the norm.[69] That summer the Folsom supporters in the legislature introduced approximately fifty-six administration bills of varying importance. Nearly all of them were obliterated. The handful that passed were so severely amended that they barely resembled the originals. Furthermore, the Senate refused to confirm any of Folsom's nominees for boards and commissions except for one nominee to the Auburn University Board of Trustees.

The economy bloc was almost completely successful in maintaining the status quo. On the other hand, Folsom supporters stopped McCorvey's modified Boswell Amendment, passed a law requiring the unmasking of the KKK, and defeated most of the more than seventy bills introduced by the economy bloc.[70] One of those would have taken control of the prison system away from a gubernatorial appointee and turned it over to a board.[71] Seventeen others taken together would have required that no agency spend money not appropriated to it by the legislature (many agencies received funds directly through earmarked taxes, fees, and other so-called open-ended appropriations). Finally, legislative cuts in executive branch budget requests were relatively modest, averaging approximately 10 percent, and while the Senate refused to consider Folsom's board and commission nominees, state law permitted them to assume their offices until they were rejected by the Senate.[72]

As it had in the previous regular session, the legislature passed a bill requiring an anti-Communist loyalty oath for public employees. The lawmakers apparently believed that Communists were attempting to undermine Alabama state government in general and the schools in particular and that they would refrain from signing such an oath. Folsom vetoed it, as he had done in 1947. Similar bills had been enacted in Oregon, Massachusetts, New York, and eight other states, but none had been met by a veto. To Folsom the oath violated the First Amendment of the Constitution, a point lost on the legislators, who had been stampeded by the red scare that gripped public opinion at that time. With this unpopular action Folsom demonstrated once again that he cared more about protecting civil rights than he did about public opinion.

The leaders of the economy bloc came out of the 1949 session with severely tarnished reputations after they made a mistake that made them appear both greedy and inept. After a month of cutting Folsom's huge revenue and spending proposals, they introduced a bill in late June that provided for the construction of 99 bridges at a cost of roughly $15 million. Not surprisingly, nearly all economy bloc members supported it, for the bridges were in their districts. Later J. Bruce Henderson added 14 bridges, and a few days after that 22 more were added, which brought the number to approximately 135 (newspaper reporters lost count) at a total cost of some $20 million. Some bridges were added by proadministration legislators in an effort to make the bill look as ungainly as possible, and, doubtless, to obtain some bridges for their districts should the bill pass. It was killed, however, and the economy bloc's image of opposing Folsom purely on the grounds of fiscal conservatism was never the same.

The economy bloc's ability to kill Folsom's programs is easy to understand. It represented a firm majority in both chambers, and its numbers included presiding officers who could route the governor's bills to unfriendly committees for a quick burial or drop them onto the floor of the chamber to suffer public execution. It is somewhat more difficult to understand how Folsom's slender forces could destroy so many economy bloc measures. The answer is that the Alabama legislature probably provided greater opportunities for obstructionist tactics, including filibustering in both houses, than any legislative body in the nation. By simply insisting on the reading of the journal, minorities could eliminate five hours of each day, and there were countless other ways to filibuster.

Most of the administration's strength lay in the Senate, and four men in that body were responsible for the major damage to the economy bloc: Tom Blake (Calhoun), Rankin Fite (Marion), Broughton Lamberth (Tallapoosa), and Joe Langan (Mobile). Of these, Langan was widely regarded as extremely able, and Fite, whose career would stretch into the Wallace era, was in the process of developing into one of the most talented parliamentarians ever to appear in the legislature. In addition, Guy Hardwick, who would be lieutenant governor in Folsom's second term, emerged as a tough and articulate moderate.

Folsom ended the year 1949 with three of his most memorable speeches. The first was a rip-roaring, hell-raising attack on the opposition delivered before the National Convention of Young Democrats in Chattanooga.

> It is a long established fact that the Republican Party is a do-nothing party. . . .

> In the last few years we've seen arise here in the South an off-shoot of the Republican Party. They call themselves the Dixiecrats. . . .
> They are easy to identify, because birds of a feather always flock together. You've got the Dixiecrats, the KuKluxers, the race baiters, and some of the selfish interest groups of the big corporations. They're right in there rubbing elbows together, spreading their filth, their lies, their old and ancient hatreds. And what are they trying to do? They're trying to boil up hatred of the poor white people against the Negroes. They're trying to keep the poor white from progressing by keeping the Negro tied in shackles.[73]

The second speech preceded a regional cabinet meeting held in Birmingham; it was broadcast over a statewide radio hookup. He devoted half his time to civil rights matters, including the subject of blacks in the criminal justice system. Beginning with an observation that Henderson, McCorvey, and others of their persuasion were fond of citing, he mentioned that blacks, who constituted 35 percent of the population in Alabama, were responsible for 65 percent of the prison population. While Henderson and his friends took this as prima facie evidence of the inherent moral inferiority of blacks, Folsom suggested a different interpretation.

> Negroes, due to lack of economic opportunity, education, and life in general do not have the same chances as do the rest of our people. I do not believe . . . that they have been given a fair deal at the hand of justice and jury in this state. There are sections of Alabama where a Negro doesn't stand a Chinaman's chance of getting fair and impartial justice on an equal footing with white men.
> The fee system and the niggardly treatment of Negroes at the bar of justice, are tools which are used to keep the poor white and the Negro subservient and submissive. The method is as ancient as was used in the Middle Ages.[74]

Probably the best example of Folsom as a friend of minorities and the poor and opponent of the elite came in his Christmas radio message.

> Under the extensive freedom of a democratic country, there emerges a pattern of life which creates economic barriers among people. And as a democracy grows in years and expansiveness, there comes about a controlling minority group. That group controls because through advantages and opportunities it obtains great portions of wealth. Wealth means power, and power, influence. And so often that influence becomes an evil thing, in that it is used for a few, and not for the good of all. It is for that reason that we must have laws to establish control over power and authority, control over forces which are based on self-gain and exploitation. And it is necessary that we have laws to establish a measure of assistance and help for those who are not able to grub out a meager, respectable living. . . .
> Our Negroes who constitute 35 percent of our population in Alabama—are they getting 35 percent of the fair share of living? Are they getting adequate

medical care . . . ? Are they provided with sufficient professional training . . . ? Are the Negroes being given their share of democracy, the same opportunity of having a voice in the government under which they live?

As long as the Negroes are held down by deprivation and lack of opportunity, the other poor people will be held down alongside them.[75]

Despite his failures in 1949 and realizing the impossibility of achieving complete reapportionment, the governor pushed on in June 1950 to call a special session to amend the Alabama Constitution to obtain one senator for each county. He also called for placement of women on juries and vaguely expressed support for civil rights for blacks. The session lasted only four days, and the legislature voted down his proposals decisively. The *Montgomery Advertiser* credited Governor-elect Gordon Persons with organizing some of the opposition, but, regardless of Persons's intervention, there was no likelihood that Folsom's bills would have been passed.[76] Only days later, Folsom called the legislature back into session, this time to concentrate on reapportionment alone. Although this session lasted somewhat longer, the result was the same. By October he had called a total of five special sessions in that one year. All ended in failure.[77]

Folsom's efforts to expand civil rights were not confined to court suits and legislative activity. In 1949 his legal adviser warned Jefferson County voting registrars about discriminating against blacks. He noted that the rejection rate for blacks was forty-nine times higher than it was for whites and observed that he doubted that such a discrepancy was due to objective differences in qualifications. He also reminded the board members of the criminal and civil penalties that they could suffer if a successful legal suit were brought against them. Then the chairman of the Jefferson County board, a Folsom appointee, accused his two colleagues of purposely slowing the registration process in order to discourage black applicants. Following that, Folsom appointed an advisory committee to investigate such allegations. Soon blacks began to be registered in increasing numbers.[78]

Each Alabama county had a three-member board responsible for voting registration, with one member of each county board named by the governor. The other two were selected by the independently elected state auditor and commissioner of agriculture and industries. Folsom appointed some people who would register anyone of voting age, but in some counties the governor found it difficult to locate anyone willing to perform that way. The Jefferson County example indicates that at least one of his appointees followed his wishes, and interviews in Tuscaloosa suggest that he did well there also. Overall, however, he was not very successful.

In 1940 the percentage of adult blacks registered to vote in Alabama was less than 1 percent, as compared to a 5 percent average for the South. In 1947 Alabama had reached 1 percent and the average for the South had grown to 12 percent; by 1952, Alabama was at 5 percent and the South 20 percent; by 1956, Alabama 11 percent and the South 25 percent; and by 1958, Alabama 15 percent and the South 28 percent. Alabama's registration rate was somewhat lower than one would expect based on demographic factors alone.[79] About this period Folsom said: "My strategy was to get blacks registered in the white counties, and then the rest would take care of itself."[80]

Folsom feared that Alabama and the other southern states would find themselves in federal court for violating their citizens' civil rights. He viewed voting rights, reapportionment, and public education as the most likely targets of federal intervention. Because of these concerns and his personal beliefs, he sought to correct state deficiencies in these areas. For example, in 1950 Folsom and Attorney General Albert Carmichael, a Lister Hill ally, refused to join eleven southern states in filing friend of the court briefs in support of Texas in that state's efforts to uphold the principle of "separate but equal" education before the Supreme Court. Both men underwent severe criticism for this.[81]

One of Folsom's last acts in his first administration was the appointment of a woman, Annie Lola Price, to serve on the Alabama Court of Appeals. No woman had ever held such a position in Alabama, and at that time women still could not serve on juries. The governor's legislative allies had made anemic attempts to correct this situation, but they had made no concerted effort, nor had Folsom himself. In meetings with women's groups at that time he made no attempt to hide the fact that he was more concerned with achieving passage of his budget bills and other civil rights legislation.[82]

Folsom's first-term civil rights record was a distinguished one. At enormous risk to a political career which he prized highly, he opposed, with surprising success, Big Mule attempts, backed by an overwhelming white majority, to tighten their control over blacks. And with far less success but amazing audacity, he attempted in many ways large and small to extend the bounds of freedom for blacks, poor whites, and women. As we have seen, Folsom regarded his civil rights and "pocketbook" bills as elements in a total, coherent program for aiding the working and middle classes and, more important, giving them tools with which to help themselves.

CHAPTER 7

Folsom and Administrative Power: First Term

> Booze and poorly judged appointees blunted his idealism. He wasn't enough of an administrator to get it together.
>
> Congressman Carl Elliott

> We discussed everything I did. . . . And we discussed things in advance. He knew things I didn't know and gave me many ideas.
>
> Philip Hamm

Folsom's only administrative experience prior to becoming governor was as CWA director in Marshall County and as an insurance executive. All accounts indicate that he did well in both capacities. In those experiences he depended on his personality, style, and enthusiasm but not on administrative skill for success. In both settings he relied upon skilled and loyal staff people and colleagues to clean up after him and handle detail work as well as aid in decision making. Both experiences instilled in him a set of attitudes which left him ill-equipped to serve as chief executive of the state. He came to overestimate the value of intuitive judgment in policy formulation and decision making and to believe that the energy and verve that he brought to his early relatively small-scale administrative enterprises would permit him to control the executive branch. Furthermore, he developed a profound faith in the value of personal loyalty (and his ability to inspire it and detect its presence), which caused him to ignore incompetence and improper behavior. The weak or nonexistent policies, poor decisions, and general confusion that resulted from these attitudes damaged his credibility in the eyes of influentials and the public.

Experience may be the best teacher, but experience unguided by reflection—that is, experience that is merely repeated by rote in different circumstances—often produces mistakes. Folsom was unaware that he had been working in ideal circumstances in Marshall County. There he had been part of a newly formed agency in which regulations were fluid; he had had a competent, highly dedicated staff who believed in what he was attempting to do and who provided some structure to guide his undisciplined energy; and the area under his purview had been relatively small and self-contained and its problems relatively uniform.

From his insurance work, Folsom took to the governor's office the popular but discredited view that businessmen (especially small businessmen) bring to public life a special set of "businesslike" attitudes that produce a tight, efficient administration.[1] The fallacy of this belief is that there is very little relationship between the situations in which a small businessman functions and those a governor must face. A governor must deal with pressure from clever and energetic interest group representatives or the demands of temperamental legislators, powerful independently elected officials such as the lieutenant governor and attorney general, and career bureaucrats infinitely more knowledgeable about their areas of expertise than a governor can ever be. All these are new to a small businessman in his first elected position. Furthermore, devotion to the survival and growth of a struggling business allows little time for an entrepreneur to do the kind of thinking about politics and government that would help him in the governorship clearly to decide where he wanted to take the people of his state and how he might accomplish his objectives.

Folsom knew the directions in which he wanted Alabama to move, but, like most small businessmen turned public administrators, he had little sense of how difficult it would be to achieve his goals. Small businessmen in their first governmental experience tend to treat public office as if it were a simple matter of selecting the "right people" (usually people like themselves, without governmental experience), issuing orders to them, and then attacking select problems themselves while ignoring the expertise available among career professionals within the government. Often the result is failure. All this was certainly the case in Folsom's administration.

As governor, Folsom hired subordinates who were politically loyal (based on their efforts on his behalf in the campaign), with little or no concern for their ability or honesty. Having serene confidence in his personnel choices, he paid only casual and intermittent attention to what his appointees did thereafter. He freely delegated authority. Concerning himself mainly with issuing broad policy guidelines, he assumed that their implementation would be automatic, for his appointees were loyal to him, and the people of Alabama had given him a mandate for change. With some important exceptions, he was completely uninterested in day-to-day administration unless it had implications for influencing legislation or there were pleasingly complex political intrigues involved. On those occasions when administrative or operational details caught his eye, the results were often disastrous. For example, early in his first term he decided that the state was spending too much on motor oil. He ordered that "burnt" (used) oil be saved and reused, together with new filters. The damage that resulted from this practice is not known precisely, but it is believed to have been considerable.[2]

Most long-time observers of Alabama politics believe that Folsom's weakest quality as an administrator was his judgment in choosing subordinates. The best that one can say about his selections is that they were uneven. Many were honest, hardworking, and idealistic individuals, such as O. H. Finney, S. Fleetwood Carnley (Folsom's brother-in-law from his first marriage), Bill Lyerly, Philip Hamm, and Gould Beech, but by most objective accounts a majority in both terms were opportunists for whom government service represented little more than a chance to line their pockets or make business contacts. For example, one of Folsom's key appointees told a reporter that he "wasn't about to live on any $6,000 a year" that the state paid him—he regarded that as "cigarette money."[3] This attitude was common, and when persons with such a perspective were given authority, the results were predictable.

Folsom's administrative decisions were somewhat more complex because ideology intervened more often, but probably the greater part of his administrative decisions were made according to the same standard as his personnel choices, that is, he rewarded those who had helped with his election. Those who helped bake the pie helped eat it. One of his appointees stated: "Folsom's aides were amateurs. I told him that he needed people around him who knew administration and suggested Roscoe Martin [a leading public administration scholar] of the University of Alabama political science department. He said, 'Was he fer me?' I replied that I did not know how Martin had voted. Folsom shot back, 'I've found from long experience that if a man isn't loyal to ya the more he knows the worse off ya are.' The people he surrounded himself with were simply people who happened to pop their heads up at opportune moments. He depended on loyalty."[4] This individual went on to explain that a politician's ego is at stake in politics, and so he feels a need to surround himself with people who he believes are personally loyal. He might have added that Folsom relied blindly on loyalty: the earlier a person had supported him the more loyal the person was in Folsom's mind. Folsom never fully understood that early support might have been a calculated gamble—hard work on a campaign in exchange for the possibility of holding power and making money if Folsom won. For many the gamble paid off handsomely.

Folsom justified his Jacksonian spoils approach to staffing and administrative decision making with his oft-repeated dictum, "You can't take the politics out of politics," a verity masquerading as quip and tautology, but one which justified excesses that most citizens would find intolerable. The result of Folsom's spoils administration was a parade of scandals and waste unequaled in this century for its openness, if not magnitude. When asked how Folsom's terms rated in honesty, legislators, cabinet officials, reporters, and other informed political observers invariably responded that they were average. The only differences, they suggested, were that other governors maintained tighter control over their subordinates, who kept their actions more private and did not offer elaborate ideological justifications for what they did.

Personnel Choices

With notable exceptions, Folsom's personnel selections fulfilled every criticism ever made of the spoils system. An Alabama political scientist observed that one of the main features of Folsom's terms was "administrative confusion and an inability to get administrative talent. Nearly everyone with administrative talent had been opposed to Folsom except those who wanted to sell him asphalt. Folsom's associates were small town boys sharing only one characteristic—a love for strong drink."[5] They were also very young; estimates of the average age of his appointees vary between thirty-three and thirty-six. As a group they possessed a reputation for open dishonesty unequaled in recent times. One House member who was close to Folsom portrayed them as quite honest or uniformly crooked, depending on the standard applied. One major Folsom appointee, he said, was a paragon of integrity: "He took no more than he put into a campaign."[6] The representative then went on to specify this amount as the man's contributions to all campaigns, including the governor's. There was no hint of sarcasm in his voice; he regarded this administrator as a man of the highest integrity.

It is difficult to determine the exact importance to Folsom of the persons close to him, partly because they played radically different roles as office managers, speech writers, bag men, cabinet officers, and so forth, and partly (and more importantly) because his relationships with most of them changed constantly. The following were leading figures in his first term:

—W. H. (Bill) Drinkard, a Cullman mortician, part owner of a funeral home chain, and an insurance executive, was finance director, the single most important appointive administrative post in Alabama government. The finance director is roughly the equivalent of a secretary of the Treasury and director of the Office of Management and Budget combined. Drinkard also served in a number of other capacities in both terms, including member of the Pardon and Parole Board. He was one of Folsom's earliest Cullman supporters.

—Bill Lyerly, a young man fresh from military service, had no governmental experience, but became Folsom's chief of staff, which meant that he was an administrative aide with many of the responsibilities he had held during the campaign. He also held other positions in both terms, including highway patrol chief and executive secretary.

—O. H. Finney became Folsom's executive secretary, essentially the same position he held when Folsom worked in Marshall County.

—Philip J. Hamm, who had a degree in social sciences, had considerable low-level administrative experience in various educational institutions and the Tobacco Tax Division of the State Revenue Department. He became revenue commissioner, an extremely important position. Hamm was one of Folsom's oldest boyhood friends and had assisted in his earliest campaigns.

—Kenneth J. Griffith of Cullman was one of Folsom's earliest supporters and an extremely able attorney. He became Folsom's legal adviser, and he was later appointed Cullman County probate judge.

—Ward McFarland, a lawyer with a degree in business administration, became the state's highway director. He possessed few qualifications for the position, but he learned the full potential of the office more quickly than many would have liked. McFarland also served as docks director in the second term. He was one of the governor's earliest supporters, extending back to 1942.

—Bryce Davis of Cullman, yet another early supporter and a lumberman, became chairman of the Alcoholic Beverage Control Board.

—S. Fleetwood Carnley, Folsom's brother-in-law and an Elba attorney, became director of the State Department of Industrial Relations. He was named a circuit judge in 1950. Rather high-handedly, Folsom named him to both positions without consulting him, arguing that, had he asked Carnley before the fact, he would never have taken the positions.

—Frank Boswell, who at the age of forty-nine was one of the oldest members of the Folsom team, had long experience in prison administration and became director of the State Department of Corrections and Institutions.

—Gould Beech served as a speech writer and for a short time as a member of the ABC Board. His appointment to the Auburn University Board of Trustees was refused by the Senate, and he held that post only for about one month.

—Loula Dunn was the straight-spined, forceful, stern, and competent longtime head of the State Department of Public Welfare. She was the only holdover from the previous administration in an important appointive office. Folsom kept her partly because of her ability, partly because of the excellent legislative connections she had developed, and, many suspect, partly because he was as frightened of her as everyone else was.

—Herman Nelson, who was a career Highway Department employee, became assistant highway director in the first term and returned in the second as highway director.

—J. B. (Jake) Mitchell, who had been Cullman County sheriff for eight years, was named public safety director.

—Brooks Glass, a Gadsden insurance man, became director of the State Department of Commerce.

—R. R. Wade, president of the Alabama Federation of Labor, was named state labor director.

A goodly number of Folsom's appointments were logical: Wade, Boswell, Nelson, and others were fully, even impressively, qualified for the responsibilities they were given. And some, like Carnley, who seemed to lack sufficient experience for their positions grew quickly into their unfamiliar roles. But many lacked both experience and the ability to grow, and a considerable number who possessed adequate experience were bedeviled by drinking problems that at times exceeded even Folsom's.

In several instances Folsom's first choice for a position was excellent, but alcoholism interfered. For example, Ward McFarland was not the leading candidate for highway director. Folsom had been considering Herman Nelson, a widely respected road construction expert, but just as Folsom was about to appoint him, Nelson went on a three-day drunk and then soon after did it again. Folsom needed a reliable person in that sensitive post, and Nelson just would not do. He continued with the Highway Department as assistant highway director, though he periodically disappeared for binges. Realizing that he was destroying himself, Nelson went to Ward McFarland and said, "Life is just too gay for me in Montgomery. Could you return me to my old position [in a smaller town]?" McFarland agreed. Nelson was able to conquer his drinking problem in less hectic surroundings, and he returned in the second term to do an excellent job as highway director.[7]

Alcohol brought more than one man's public career to a grim and miserable end. Montgomery was a city of limitless temptation for the influential. Lobbyists were happy to provide whatever was wanted. Temptation (and this old-fashioned word is the correct one in this context), combined with the pressures of office, was more than some could tolerate. Often, upon being returned to the familiar environments of their homes in small towns, they recovered and took up productive careers usually in some private endeavor. One such individual, who took to washing down powerful pills with large quantities of bourbon, began carrying a gun, telling people in dark, conspiratorial tones that he would "get his enemies before they got him." He once appeared in his office promptly at 8:00 o'clock and, finding that no one else had arrived on time, began calling their homes, only to find that the time was 8:00 P.M. One day, which was to be his last in office, he was found atop the governor's desk wielding an American flag mounted on a staff tipped by a sharp brass point and screaming to all who came near, "You'll never take me alive!" He was gently overpowered by highway patrolmen. Folsom forced a liquor company to make him an agent at twenty-five thousand dollars per year, and he used the money to reestablish himself in private business.[8]

Folsom's family members, most of whom had helped in his campaigns, were not forgotten when appointments were made. By March 1947, in addition to Carnley, one brother, two brothers-in-law, a sister-in-law, a cousin, and a cousin's husband were all on the state payroll. Jamelle Moore, who would become his second wife, was given employment in the Highway Department, and later her father was also employed in several capacities.

Fred Folsom, another brother, served in various positions on and off official payrolls. He had worked in banking, the auto industry, and the seed loan program as a civil service employee. After his retirement he worked for his brother doing "confidential work," including handling cash (both incoming and outgoing), manning the governor's office whenever Folsom was absent, keeping track of legislative votes, and the like.[9] Many describe Fred Folsom as one of Big Jim's "satchel men." Ross Clark performed the same function. Both men were essential to Folsom, who had absolute faith in their loyalty and the advice they gave.

When Folsom took office, letters poured in from people wanting administrative jobs. One to O. H. Finney from an executive of the Slocomb National Bank dated January 6, 1947, indicated that the bank was anxious to see someone from its part of the state appointed to the Oil and Gas Board. In the last paragraph the writer declared, "May I say that the bank was the only bank in this section that was 100% for the governor."[10] Claims of this sort were carefully investigated by persons working under Folsom's direction. His campaign organization had been so disorganized that no formal list of supporters had been kept. Only those known directly by Folsom were immediately repaid for their work via his patronage powers.

Some who had helped in the campaign were uninterested in a government position, but they did want rewards of other kinds. Writing in the *Dothan Eagle* at the time of the 1946 inauguration, Nat Faulk described the case of a Charlie Creech who was pictured as being "close to the administration," but he was not interested in a job, he told Faulk. "He has a lending and insurance business in Andalusia and wants to stick with that," Faulk wrote. "He said, though, that so long as insurance is going to be written for the State along with bonds for employees, he won't turn down any business of that nature if offered to him."[11]

Apparently, altruists like Charlie Creech were in short supply. Since not enough appointive positions were available to reward the faithful, merit system employees were pushed out by threats, sudden transfers to other towns, and similar tactics. They could have obtained formal hearings and fought those tactics, but most decided they would lose and simply resigned.[12] When even this crass pressure did not open enough jobs, Senator David U. Patton, in July 1947, proposed a bill which would have removed as many as two thousand positions from the merit system.[13]

Folsom's personnel choices and the way he made them must be viewed in perspective. No other Alabama governor chose key people much differently. It is difficult to tell someone who has contributed thousands of dollars to a campaign or spent hundreds of exhausting hours working in it that he is "not qualified" for an administrative post. And there are few other ways available to reward campaign workers. Nor can we ignore Folsom's desire for loyalty. Unfortunately, all too often in sacrificing technical expertise for loyalty Folsom obtained neither.

Folsom's administrative style with its stress on politics in administration, his tendency to ignore administrative detail, and his spoils approach to staffing did not bode well for efficient and honest government. It is not possible to review all areas of government, but we can focus on areas of special concern to him, areas where we would expect to find close supervision and appointments based on ability and knowledge.

Alcoholic Beverage Control

The ABC Board was a three-person commission, appointed by the governor, responsible for overseeing the operation of state liquor stores and privately run bars and the sale of beer and wine by private concerns. The board had the authority to approve or block the sale of particular brands in the state. A single decision could mean tens of thousands of dollars in profits for a given company.

Mainly due to alcohol shortages caused by World War II, state store customers had a disgusting array of choices at the time Folsom took office. He took advantage of this situation very effectively during the 1946 election campaign. Asked during the runoff what he intended to do about the ABC Board, he replied ponderously and reflectively: "Whiskey was a problem in times of old, whiskey was a problem during Prohibition, whiskey was a problem during the war"—by this point reporters who were as yet unfamiliar with his speaking style were leaning forward expectantly—"and whiskey's going to be a problem tomorrow."[14] He was so right.

Folsom's first choice as chairman of the ABC Board was Bryce Davis.

Immediately after taking office Davis informed all distillers selling in Alabama that they would be expected to employ as their Alabama representatives only those people acceptable to the ABC Board (standard operating procedure in virtually all administrations before and after Folsom). A drastic shift in business toward companies employing Folsom loyalists was apparent three months after the inauguration. Many persons experienced sudden increases in business or became liquor company representatives for the first time in their lives, including a Cullman druggist (a close friend of Davis), Roy Drinkard (Bill Drinkard's brother), and George Martin (a former labor union organizer and administration supporter).[15] In the rush to cash in on lucrative contracts some Folsomites were stuck with obscure, slow-selling brands known only to winos or gourmets. That, however, did not keep the ABC Board from buying those products despite the fact that they could be sold only through price reductions resulting in considerable revenue loss.

In April 1947 the independently elected Public Service Commission, headed by Gordon Persons, who would follow Folsom as governor, began an investigation of ABC Board activities. It heard testimony from a Gadsden trucker named B. C. Holloway who had submitted the low bid for an ABC hauling contract and who was persuaded by Davis to withdraw the bid in return for a promise for a larger contract later. Holloway was then double-crossed and ended up with nothing. One implication of this testimony was that Davis knew who had submitted the low bid before the sealed bids were opened. The investigators asked how he had managed this. A secretary for the board testified that, upon receiving the sealed envelopes containing the bids, she had placed them in a locked cabinet. She and Melvin Dawkins, an ABC Board member, testified that when they formally opened the envelopes, they showed signs of having been tampered with.[16]

Stories about the hauling contract manipulations were broken primarily by the *Birmingham News* reporter Hugh Sparrow, a dogged, muckraking investigative reporter uniformly hated by those governors whose terms coincided with his long tenure with the *News*. Sparrow columns casting Folsom in a positive light were a rarity. Folsom later referred to him as "Ole' Hugh, the greatest press agent I ever had—I was in his columns all the time."[17]

Davis apparently overbought liquor by overwhelming margins. A cabinet member discovered this and informed Folsom, and Folsom quickly asked for Davis's resignation.[18] Folsom would later say that he was so impressed by the potential for dishonesty in ABC dealings that he decided to change board members every year. "In the second term I made the mistake of not changin' them enough," he added.[19]

Alcoholic beverage regulation involved more than brand selection. Two major issues of 1946 and 1947 concerned juke boxes and draft beer in bars, forbidden by ABC regulations and state law, respectively. The reasons for the ban on draft beer are a mystery, but the logic behind the juke box regulation was that music, especially bebop, combined with the mind-altering qualities of alcohol, could drive otherwise levelheaded, hardworking people to crazed antisocial behavior. Folsom campaigned on both issues in 1946. He ridiculed the prohibition of draft beer as stupid, and concerning juke boxes he said, "If the rich man can have music with his champagne in his country clubs, the poor man should have music with his beer."[20] In November 1946 he stated, "I'm just common folks. Common folks have just as much right to dance as rich folks." He then added a stirring tribute to the superior taste of keg beer.[21] The next day the Alabama Methodist Conference issued a statement in opposition to draft beer and juke boxes.[22]

The juke boxes were ultimately approved, but not before the sudden "resignations" of all three ABC Board members (Lamar Kelly, Melvin Dawkins, and J. P. Faulk) late in January 1948. They were quickly replaced by Lowell Gregory, Oliver Taylor, and Gould Beech. Beech resigned one month later due to personal reasons. He was replaced by ABC administrator Otis McRight, who had been hired in 1947 to replace the incumbent administrator Herman Whisenant, who had been fired. Taylor and Gregory were fired in October 1948, and the turnover rate continued high until well into 1949. By August 1949 Folsom had appointed his fourteenth ABC Board member. A number of these individuals resigned for personal reasons which had no relation to their performance on the board, and Folsom probably fired several others on mere suspicion. On the other hand, one of his ABC appointees wrote a letter to the liquor companies to the effect that they had to pay him an extra twenty-five cents per bottle for all liquor sold in the state. Folsom fired him.[23]

The ABC appointments and resignations slowed in the last year of his administration. When asked if his later appointees were honest men and efficient managers, Folsom responded that he doubted it, but that he had given up trying to find such people. He said that he believed that he had settled on individuals who may have done a "little dealing under the table," but nothing that landed them on the front pages. In talking about one ABC Board member Folsom commented, "He was about the best one, year in and year out, that we ever had. He always looked after my personal interests to see that my expenses were taken care of—when we had extracurricular expenses, you know. He saw to that."[24]

Purchases

Each year the State of Alabama bought tens of millions of dollars worth of automobiles, trucks, tires, typewriters, office equipment, and similar items. In September 1947 a small but typical scandal broke when Ralph Eagerton,

Big Jim with scrub brush during 1946 campaign speech. Two members of the Strawberry Pickers are sitting behind. (Alabama State Department of Archives and History.)

The Strawberry Pickers, circa 1946. (*Alabama Magazine.*)

Sam Englehardt, mid-1950s.
(*Alabama Magazine.*)

Albert Boutwell, mid-1950s.
(*Montgomery Advertiser.*)

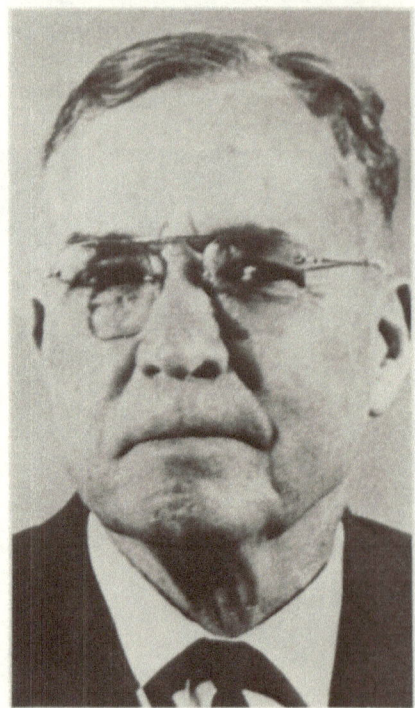

J. Bruce Henderson.
(*Montgomery Advertiser.*)

Big Jim and Jamelle Moore Folsom during first term. (Melissa Folsom Boyen.)

Governors' breakfast in New York City, December 3, 1949, the day after dinner given by the Democratic National Committee to launch 1950 Congressional campaigns. Folsom (seated center) with Governor G. Mennen Williams of Michigan (left) and William M. Boyle, Democratic National Chairman, being interviewed by reporters. (ACME photo, from collection of Melissa Folsom Boyen.)

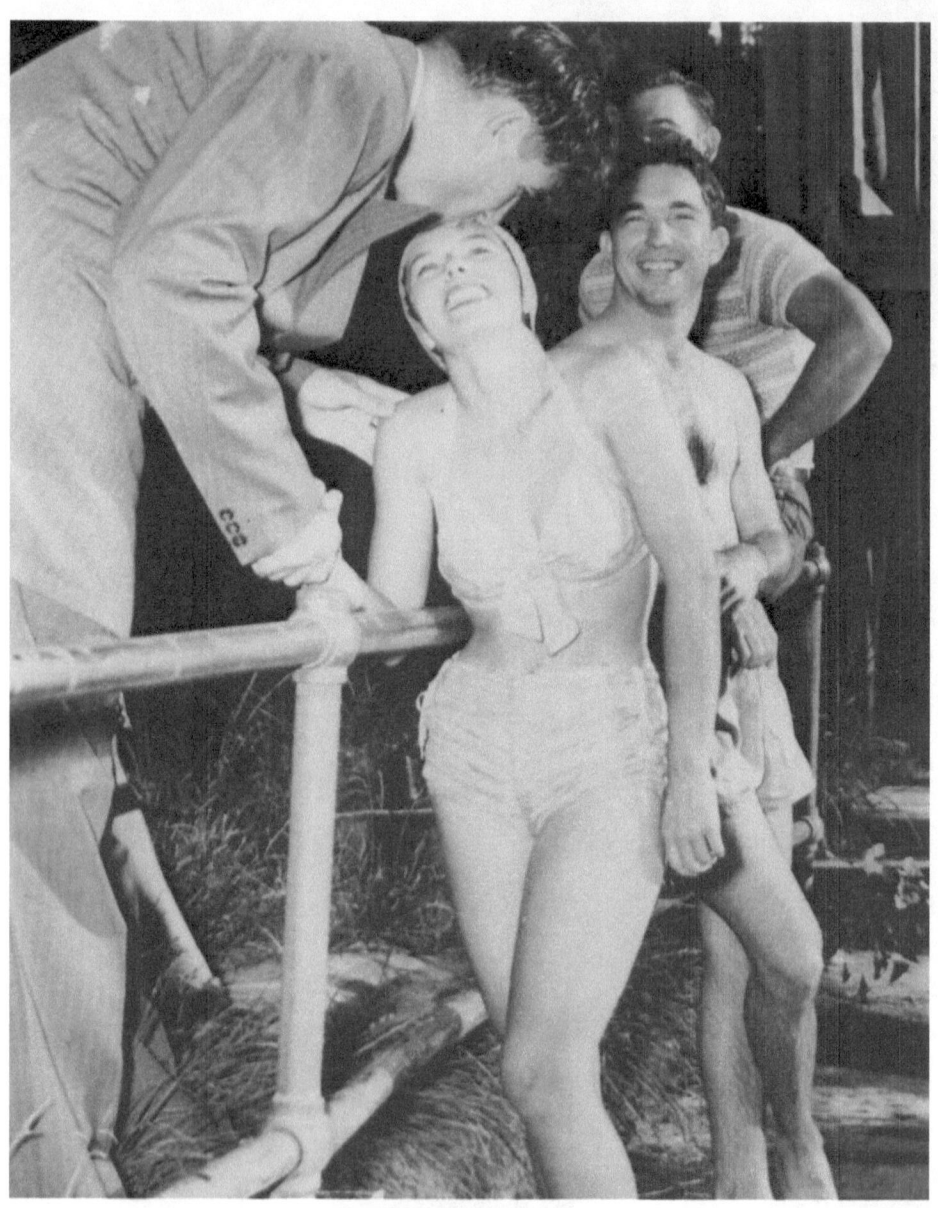

"Kissin' Jim," early in first term.
(Alabama State Department of Archives and History.)

Big Jim, taken just a few days before his defeat in the 1962 primary. (Photograph by Bob Kyle.)

Big Jim, 1974. (*Montgomery Advertiser.*)

"Walking Tall" poster photograph, 1974 campaign for governor. (*Montgomery Advertiser.*)

Big Jim and older Alabamian, first term. (Alabama State Department of Archives and History.)

The 1954 campaign. (Photograph by R. E. Hogan, Talladega, Alabama.)

1954 car caravan forming in Cullman. (Photograph by R. E. Hogan, Talladega, Alabama.)

Big Jim, 1954. (Photograph by R. E. Hogan, Talladega, Alabama.)

chief examiner of public accounts, challenged an arrangement in which Finance Director Bill Drinkard, acting as de facto state purchasing agent, awarded a contract for auto batteries to a Birmingham company. The contract price was $6.75 per unit, but a few days after it was awarded, Drinkard increased the price by $1 per unit. Drinkard justified the increase as a way to insure that the state had an adequate supply in the face of postwar shortages.[25] Chief Examiner Eagerton was not impressed with that explanation, and he forced a repeal of the extra dollar. Throughout most of 1947 Drinkard himself served as state purchasing agent, a practice which the attorney general ruled contrary to merit system regulations. When the attorney general ordered him to appoint a purchasing agent, Drinkard selected an individual who had scored sixth on a merit system examination, when by law he was supposed to pick from the top three.[26]

Eagerton and his office (and journalists) were barely able to keep up with Drinkard. *Alabama Journal* reporter Geoffery Birt found a string of irregularities in the purchases of state automobiles. In the first year of Folsom's term sixty-four cars valued at $62,162 were bought from the Hartselle Motor Company, owned by Drinkard's brother. Birt reported allegations that sometimes, after sealed bids were opened, a "misplaced" envelope would be found, and it always seemed to contain the low bid. Such revelations apparently did little more than remove the low-bid facade, for by March 1948 it became clear that the state's auto parts purchases were not even being let for bids. Drinkard defended this practice by arguing that all auto dealers charged identical catalog prices (which would not have been true of large state orders) and that it did not matter to taxpayers which businesses received government contracts.[27]

Drinkard's defense is reminiscent of that employed by George Washington Plunkitt, a turn-of-the-century Tammany Hall politician, who gave this definition of "honest graft":

> Everybody is talkin' these days about Tammany men growin' rich on graft, but nobody thinks of drawin' the distinction between honest graft and dishonest graft. . . . Yes, many of our men have grown rich in politics. I have myself. . . .
> Just let me explain by examples. My party's in power in the city, and it's goin' to undertake a lot of public improvements. Well, I'm tipped off, say, that they're going to lay out a new park at a certain place. . . .
> I go to the place and I buy up all the land I can in the neighborhood. Then the board of this or that makes its plan public, and there is a rush to get my land, which nobody cared particular for before.
> Ain't it perfectly honest to charge a good price and make a profit on my investment and foresight? Of course, it is. Well, that's honest graft.[28]

Plunkitt went on to argue that the taxpayer was not hurt by his actions because whoever owned the land would charge the highest possible price to the government. He did not mention that the land's previous owners were greatly harmed, nor did he indicate that when government officials were permitted to take advantage of their power in this manner, they might tend to make decisions for the sole purpose of creating opportunities of which they could take advantage.

In March 1948 Eagerton issued an audit which charged overpayments totaling $1,728.21 by the generous finance director. He had overpaid Goodyear Tire and Rubber Company for batteries and the Meyercord Company for tobacco and playing card tax stamps.[29] Irregularities were also found in Drinkard's dealings with companies selling roof coating and plastic cement and primer. The examiner discovered that specifications for bids often named the brand (even when that was not important for product performance), thus restricting the firms from which bids could be accepted. When this sort of manipulation failed and bids from the "wrong" dealers turned out to be low and for some reason envelopes containing low bids could not be "accidentally" discovered, Drinkard or purchasing agents working directly under him blithely rejected the bids, issued invitations for new ones, and accepted new bids that were usually higher than the originals. The examiner's report also criticized many other phases of the finance director's operations.

Folsom was only mildly bothered by reporters such as Birt and Sparrow who exposed such faults in his administration. He liked reporters in general, and because they lacked adequate time and resources, their stories were sometimes vague and easily refuted. Furthermore, few voters read long, technical stories, and he could brand their investigative work nothing more than vindictive attacks by them "lyin' dailies." When their stories became too vivid and well documented, Folsom would often fire an offending administrator and rehire him in a different capacity a few months later.

Eagerton, however, irritated him. Perhaps it was the examiner's greater resources, legal and analytical; once he caught an administrator in shady dealings, it became a serious matter with potential legal repercussions, including jail. Or perhaps it was Eagerton's alien dedication to administrative reform, which held that you could take the politics out of politics. One Sunday morning in the governor's office early in 1948, Folsom engaged Eagerton in a shouting match that became so heated that visitors could hear Folsom's voice far down the corridors of the old capitol building.[30] Out of spite, Folsom even tried to have Eagerton's brother drafted for military service.[31] When that failed, Folsom turned to a ruse that did him real credit as a political tactician, if not as an efficient administrator.

After seeing one of Eagerton's highly critical reports that focused on the Highway Department and a report issued by a Montgomery County grand jury based on Eagerton's work which was equally critical, Folsom appointed a five-man investigating committee which at first glance appeared to be an independent group.[32] Included were Speaker Beck, who by this time was being described by the *Montgomery Advertiser* as a "clamorous and vehement assailant of the Folsom administration"; Senator Guy Hardwick, who was not identified with either Folsom or the economy bloc; Ed Rodgers, of the Alabama Road Builders Association; Senator Robin Swift, another determined Folsom opponent; and Chris Sherlock, whom Folsom had outpolled in the 1942 gubernatorial election.[33] The group appeared to be heavily loaded against Folsom, but in its final report the investigating committee defended Highway Department actions and attacked the grand jury and Eagerton. The committee accused both of generating public "distrust in their government without just cause," and it also portrayed them as "rumor mongers" who were "making mountains out of mole hills."[34] The report was a whitewash, and the reason was clear. Three of the five members including Swift were former highway directors. While serving as Sparks's highway director, Swift had been roundly criticized by the *Birmingham News* for having the state construct a road near some of his coastal property. The Folsom administration was not building roads where Swift and the other committee members would have built them, but the criteria being used were no different than standards they had applied or supported in the past and hoped to again.

Despite Eagerton's findings and the press's revelations, administrative trickery and manipulations continued. The conservative legislature could easily have stopped those practices with a few clearly written statutes. For example, it could have enacted strict bid procedures and passed them over Folsom's inevitable veto, but it did not. The most likely reason it did not is that key legislators' districts were benefiting from the abuses or hoped to in the future.

The administrative scandals were so common that they almost became routine. Attempts were made to extend the liquor agent system to purchases of road construction machinery, paint, school textbooks, and many other items. Insurance policies covering such state properties as the Mobile Docks were also subject to manipulation, often involving Folsom family members, such as Cecil and Fred Folsom and Ross Clark.

As stated earlier, nearly all Alabama governors before and after Folsom hired line and staff personnel and awarded government contracts by standards little different from his. Interviewees experienced in the ways of Alabama politics found the honesty of Folsom's terms of office to be average. The Folsom administration, however, lacked the style to handle patronage politics gracefully. As one reporter observed, the Folsom administration "appeared worse than most because they were so clumsy. In the first year, pay-offs were made by check. There were photostatic copies of pay-off checks floating all over town. Folsom himself received little or no money or pay-offs or things of that sort because he never cared much about money. . . . Folsom's attitude about stealing was that he didn't want to know too much. Everyone else would know what was going on, but Folsom would stick his head in the sand."[35] When asked about bribe taking among state politicians in general, this reporter replied: "Most politicians—the majority of them anyway—are not dishonest—don't take pay-offs—mainly because they're respected businessmen who don't want to be caught."[36] He added that one's definition of dishonesty depends on one's view of politicians taking advantage of governmental positions to benefit their business interests. Such behavior was standard practice when Folsom held office.[37]

Folsom as an Administrator

For every statement that can be made about Folsom as an administrator a counterstatement can also be made, or at least many exceptions noted. Working with him was a different experience for every administrator, depending on, among other things, what areas of government were of interest to him. Highway construction was his first administrative concern, and he spent more time overseeing that area than any other. Most line officials in other departments found him to be in many ways an ideal chief executive; he would occasionally indicate the broad directions toward which he wanted them to move and then leave them alone for considerable stretches of time. But even in policy areas that he usually left to others, he would suddenly probe very deeply. Often the result was of the sort illustrated by the case of the "burnt" oil, but sometimes his impact was quite beneficial.

One of his better administrative interventions concerned a clinic in Birmingham that was partly state funded and operated by Dr. Thomas Spies. Spies's major concern was preventive medicine, and he emphasized nutrition (especially among poorer patients); this is common approach today, but was apparently quite unusual in the late 1940s. The doctor and his colleagues found themselves in conflict with the Jefferson County chapter of the American Medical Association, which was working against the clinic in the legislature. This opposition by the medical establishment attracted Folsom's attention partly because Spies seemed the underdog in the struggle. One day, Folsom walked into the clinic unannounced and began talking to patients in the waiting room. He also talked to Spies and Dr. Louis Friedman, who taught at the University of Alabama Medical School and worked part-time with Spies and later became one of Folsom's closest cronies. The governor was so impressed by what he heard that he sternly warned the medical establishment not to interfere with Spies. He also spoke to the presidents of the Alabama Power Company and several Birmingham banks who in turn extended their mantle of protection over the clinic.[38]

Folsom was also interested in improved welfare administration, and, according to one official, he had a positive impact there as well: "Prior to Folsom there were no objective welfare qualifications—everything hinged on who you knew politically. Folsom encouraged the establishment of objective criteria."[39] This emphasis on efficient administration was at odds with his standard political approach, but apparently he felt that certain critical tasks, such as aiding the poor and elderly, required a measure of objectivity. Even here, however, he was not consistent. While encouraging the systemization of welfare, he also permitted O. H. Finney to write a constant stream of memoranda to Loula Dunn asking for special consideration for particular individuals.

For line officials whose work areas especially interested him and for many staff aides, he could be an exasperating superior. One of them said, "Folsom was wearing on people—he didn't mean to be inconsiderate, but he could be irritating."[40] Folsom could indeed be wearing. One aspect of this quality was his incredible energy; he was almost impossible to keep up with. A great many stories about him begin, "The phone rang at 3:30 A.M., and it was *him*."

Folsom's energy level was phenomenal. People who worked closely with him became burnt out, and after a year or two they tried to insulate themselves from him, some by physical separation, others by drinking. One of his cabinet members separated himself from the governor so completely that a highway patrolman was dispatched to locate him. Folsom's telephone calls were not being returned (his secretary claimed that he was "out of the office"), and so the patrolman climbed on a ledge and walked along the outside of the building to peer into his office, where he was working busily at his desk. He was fired soon thereafter.

Folsom's lack of consideration was well documented. Once a group of legislators and administrators accompanied Folsom in a state plane to a meeting at Fort Benning, Georgia. On their way back, they were surprised to discover that the plane was landing in Mobile. Folsom had been drinking, and on an impulse he had instructed the pilot to land there. He had called ahead to have one of the state yachts readied, and he dragged everyone out to the ship, not even allowing the men time to call their wives. They sailed around in the Gulf for three days, drinking heavily and washing their underwear in a sink. This was but one of the many ways that he demonstrated who was in charge.[41]

His capriciousness and immaturity, often amplified by heavy drinking, grated on his aides. Sometimes he could be funny, but on other occasions he embarrassed those around him. He plowed through life unaffected by others' judgments of his behavior unless family members were present. The public kissing continued until his marriage in 1948, and it became like an old joke repeated too often. It also began to backfire. Once a blind girl visited his office, and when he attempted to kiss her, her seeing-eye dog leaped to her defense, scaring the governor away. "Miss Auburn" for 1947 refused to allow the governor to kiss her before a crowd of six thousand. She turned him away twice, the second time after his speech when she retreated from him across the stage. According to newspaper accounts, "Chagrin was written all over his face as he stood with hands on hips and watched her walk away." Later, it took her male escort to prevent Folsom from trying again.[42]

Still, Folsom's eccentricities could be quite winning. A short time after his nomination in 1946 he and a group of Alabamians went to a Veterans of Foreign Wars convention in San Francisco, a city he knew well from his merchant marine days. Folsom and a few Alabamians began walking, and he led the uneasy group into a dilapidated part of town in which saloons frequented by sailors were concentrated. They entered a frightening looking dive, and Folsom immediately sat down at a table with a gang of sailors and began exchanging seafaring stories with them. The talking went on for hours as the number of seamen around him grew larger. Neither he nor any member of the Alabama group told the sailors who Folsom was. It never occurred to Folsom to take advantage of his newly won position to impress strangers. The Alabamians walked back to their hotel with new respect for their governor.[43]

Soon after his inauguration, Folsom, Bill Lyerly, and others traveled to Washington, D.C., to confer with the president. Lyerly was extremely proud of the fact that he had served in the Ninth Infantry Division in World War II and had seen a great deal of action. Folsom and President Truman were in the Oval Office with Lyerly waiting outside. Then Truman invited Lyerly inside. As they shook hands, the president asked Lyerly if he had served in the war, and Lyerly proudly told him that he had indeed and that he had served in the Ninth. Truman asked, "Did you see any combat?" Lyerly was horrified that the president would not have known that his beloved Ninth was in the thick of battle, and he began to stammer and stutter, at which point Folsom and Truman started laughing. Folsom had arranged the joke with Truman in advance, knowing the effect it would have on his aide. On another occasion in Washington Folsom arranged to have Lyerly serve as General Omar Bradley's personal assistant for an evening. It was a great honor for Lyerly. During the evening Bradley asked, "Where did you serve, soldier?" Lyerly responded, "In the Ninth Infantry Division, sir." Bradley asked, "Did you see any combat?" Big Jim had struck again.[44]

It is ironic that an idealogue like Folsom should have surrounded himself with individuals who were out to profit from the public trust. He could not understand people in public life whose sole ambition was to enrich themselves. It was proper for them to take enough to make ends meet, but he was sincere in his disgust with people whose attention in public office was focused exclusively on making money. To him public service represented an opportunity to make important changes. At one point he became especially frustrated with one of his cabinet members' excessive financial manipulations, and he turned to Lyerly and asked plaintively, "Bill, explain to me about ____." He really understood, but he just found it hard to believe. In this particular case he was willing to accept a trade-off between the individual's enormous ability and his exorbitant opportunism. But it is more difficult to understand why he hired so many "despoilers, knaves, and mediocrities" (Grover Hall, Jr.'s description of Folsomites), and why he allowed them to remain. One such person, described by a former cabinet member as a "reprobate" and a "wheeler-dealer," held at least eight different positions in the first term and by all accounts failed at every one by virtually any standard of honesty and efficiency. While shifting him from one to another of his eight jobs, Folsom commented that this individual "would steal a nickel off a dead man's eyes and then kick him in the ass because it wasn't a quarter."[45] In his second administration Folsom placed him in one of the most responsible positions in the government.

Grover Hall, Jr., once described Folsom as chastely dishonest, and there is a sharp gleam of truth in the phrase. While it does not excuse his dishonesty, Folsom used patronage and ill-gotten funds to influence legislators to vote for a constitutional convention, reapportionment, elimination of the poll tax, and other praiseworthy legislation. He used additional resources at his disposal to benefit cronies and relatives and to support his love of good living. His lapses in this latter category were unsystematic and casual. They were childlike in the sense that a six-year-old empties a cookie jar knowing that the shortage will be discovered sooner or later, and when the inevitable happens, he blames it on the cat. The only difference is that Folsom rarely tried to deny anything.

The legislature appropriated enormous funds for Folsom's personal use through the temporary clerk hire fund, the mansion fund, and the contingent fund. According to state law, the contingent fund was for "repair and upkeep of the governor's mansion and the operation thereof, as well as expenditures for public or official entertainment incident to his office and for such transportation as may be necessary for the governor's use."[46] The law also required a strict accounting of all money spent. Items from a 1950 audit of the contingent fund convey a sense of how he managed those resources.

—In March 1949 Folsom and sixteen others stayed at the Statler Hotel in Washington, D.C., and ran up an $802.26 bill. Few of the sixteen were there in an official capacity and, according to the audit, three were New York models.

—The sum of $4,700 was withdrawn from the contingent fund for "incidental entertainment at the mansion." No documentation and no other justification was provided.

—There were "numerous instances of travel" where no effort was made to itemize expenses or even provide a justification for the purpose of the travel.

—Folsom and Governor Sparks were charged with using the contingent fund to pay for such personal expenses as laundry and groceries in direct violation of the law.

—Unspecified silver items were bought as gifts.[47]

Folsom was also infamous for his mansion fund expenses, but there is less justification for criticism on this score. A comparison of Chauncey Sparks's and Folsom's expenses during twelve-month periods from 1945 to 1946 and 1947 to 1948 shows expenditures totaling $10,068 and $14,758, respectively. Given the high inflation rate of that period and wartime austerity, these figures are not far apart. Both seem rather high, but they include expenses for receptions and other public functions held in the mansion.[48]

Much of Folsom's ethical misconduct was on the order of traffic ticket fixing, and in fact he attempted this very offense at least once. One of his friends had been convicted of drunk driving and with the conviction went an automatic six-month suspension of his license. He appealed to Folsom for the return of his license, and Folsom ordered Lyerly to do it. Lyerly refused, citing the law. Folsom replied, menacingly, "Bill, there's a law that you forgot about. It's the law that I'm the governor and I can fire you whenever I want. Do you know about that law, Bill?" Lyerly replied, "Yeah, I know about the law. I'll give him his license." Still, Lyerly used every delaying tactic at his disposal. Finally, after six months the man's license was reissued. Lyerly returned to Folsom and said, "Governor, you know that guy that lost his license? Well, it's been taken care of."

In addition to being highly energetic, eccentric, a poor judge of people, a sometimes connoisseur of political intrigue, and erratically honest, Folsom was chronically suspicious, listening to and occasionally acting on gossip of the most dubious accuracy, but he was also unbelievably naive and optimistic about the people who surrounded him. He was capable of keeping them on, especially those who had supported him from the earliest days, through one scandal after another.

Notable Exceptions

When they were appointed, Philip Hamm and S. Fleetwood Carnley appeared in training and experience to be almost completely inadequate to their assignments, but they quickly developed into two of Folsom's best administrators by even the most rigorous standards of honesty, efficiency, and creativity.

Hamm had had only modest administrative experience in various educational programs, and he had worked as a minor functionary in the State Revenue Department, which he headed in 1947. This was no background for the chief of the state's central tax collection agency, a position which required as much technical expertise as any in government. Hamm, though, was willing to learn, and, backed by a first-rate staff, he became a creative administrator. His position as an outsider gave him the perspective from which he could view old problems in ways that would be difficult for more experienced people submerged in old modes of thinking. Hamm plunged into his new responsibilities by organizing a series of "seminars" in which his able merit system staff subjected him to a cram course in public finance.[49]

Hamm was one of the few administrators with whom Folsom worked closely. "We discussed everything I did," Hamm said. "Like when I sent crews to Washington to photostat income tax records. I told him all about that. And we discussed things in advance. He knew things I didn't know and gave me many ideas [such as] naming things to look out for. In fact, I think he suggested sending those boys to Washington."[50]

Soon after assuming office, Hamm modified procedures for collecting sales taxes. The usual procedure was for state revenue examiners to collect tax payments from store owners immediately after performing their audit. Hamm changed it so that the revenue examiners merely performed audits and reported the results to the central office in Montgomery, which then sent statements to merchants. The new arrangement permitted the addition of internal checking procedures that were not possible under the previous system. In addition, Hamm felt that the old system smacked too much of the king's tax collector dunning hapless yeomen.[51]

In September 1947 Hamm launched a campaign to collect delinquent state income tax payments beginning with the 1945 returns. This campaign generated an additional $1 million in revenue from 1945 returns alone.[52]

His biggest concern was property tax reform. It happened that the legislature's Interim Committee on Revenue published its report "The Alabama Revenue System" the very month Hamm took office. Among other faults in the state's revenue system, the committee found "extreme inequalities of many types in the assessment of properties of different kinds and values, and among different areas."[53] The committee, which was dominated by businessmen-legislators, also found that small property owners were much harder hit than larger ones. In addition, the committee criticized the revenue system as a whole for its regressivity.

Given the conservative nature of the legislature, it is surprising that the report was ever issued. Perhaps its authors did not believe that Hamm would take it literally. His first step was the reassessment of corporate property values. The Southern Railway Company, the first to undergo reassessment, saw its assessment increase from $18.25 million to $25 million; assessments of Goodrich Tire and Rubber in Tuscaloosa increased by 200 percent and Goodyear Tire and Rubber in Gadsden by 66.7 percent.[54] The lieutenant governor and several attorney-legislators represented a number of corporate property owners in their appeals to Hamm, but there is no indication that they produced a single change. Simultaneously, Hamm moved in another direction against inaccurate assessments by applying a previously unused section of the State Tax Code which empowered him to reject local nominees to a county board of tax equalization.[55]

The state's largest property owners were horrified at these developments. In October 1947 Hamm was the topic of a discussion at a luncheon meeting of Associated Industries of Alabama, probably the state's most prestigious business group. The meeting delegated Barrett Shelton, publisher of the *Decatur Daily*, to investigate the revenue commissioner. He reported his findings in a letter to Frank Dixon in which he described Hamm as "fairly smart but extremely radical." Hamm's dislike of fraternities in his student days at the University of Alabama was also a black mark against him in Shelton's letter. He was summed up as "a small bore school-teacher politician with an innate suspicion and hatred of those who have acquired success." Shelton closed the letter by bemoaning the reassessments to which several Decatur businesses had been subjected.[56]

In interviews Hamm remembered his reassessment battles clearly: "There was a fellow in Tuscaloosa named Foots Clements. He had a housing project that was assessed at $20,000 and I didn't raise it much—just up to $300,000 [Hamm smiled], and he came into my office raising hell and tellin' me that he was goin' to take it to court. And I told him, 'You borrowed $750,000 to build that son of a bitch. Last year your total rent was $105,000. Now you don't want the public in Tuscaloosa to know all that. You are either cheaten' one way or another. You're not goin' to take anything to court.' "[57]

It was no accident that a member of one of the law firms representing property tax complainants, State Senator James Allen, was the author of the self-starter. As Folsom beat back that attack, Hamm doggedly continued his reassessments while carefully keeping his own operations starkly immaculate. He applied merit system rules instead of trying to bypass them and consistently achieved a clean bill of health from the examiners of public accounts.[58] Large landowners continued to complain, but it was clear that for a long time they had been underassessed compared to small property holders and therefore had no basis for legal appeals. Hamm's handiwork was rigorous and fair. The landowners had no more chance against him than Folsom had against Ralph Eagerton, for Hamm was no radical, Shelton's analysis of him notwithstanding. The largest property owners, though, continued to flail away at him in the press, if not in court. For example, the *Montgomery Advertiser*, representing their interests, launched this tirade: "The scandalous Slappity-Hap, with the look of a cretinous panda in his eyes, and his revenue commissioner, Phil Hamm, with the look of a frightened panda in his eyes, are on the make again with their slicker strategems."[59] The *Advertiser* then portrayed industrialists as threatening to leave Alabama, refusing to build additions to plants already in Alabama, or refusing to enter the state in the first place. As it turned out, however, businesses continued to expand and move into Alabama; even after Hamm's reassessments, property taxes were far lower in Alabama than they were in the Northeast and Midwest.

Like Hamm, S. Fleetwood Carnley, director of Industrial Relations, had little in his background that prepared him for his governmental responsibilities. As director, Carnley had responsibility for workmen's compensation, the state employment service, coal mine inspections, and the administration of protective labor laws.

When Carnley came into office, the employment service was returning to state control after the war years. He found that the compensation and employment sections had functioned independently for years, often with little communication between them. He was responsible, largely through his open, caring style, for the reintegration and smooth operation of both sections and the reassertion of state control. His duties frequently took him to Washington in search of operating funds, and he proved successful in those endeavors. He also developed systems for locating employment for returning veterans and graduating college students. His job placement centers helped combat a "brain drain" that plagued Alabama at that time. And he brought about fairer and more efficient workmen's compensation administration.[60]

Carnley had a wide range of legislative as well as administrative goals. He was especially interested in extending unemployment compensation laws to include benefits for sick or disabled workers, reinstituting regularly scheduled coal mine inspections, tightening coal mine inspection requirements, and passing and enforcing rigorous child labor laws. He succeeded in passing approximately a dozen bills at a time when most Folsom administration legislation was being voted down by overwhelming majorities. A large part of his effectiveness probably lay in his earnest, guileless approach. Legislators dealing with him could be certain that bills he drafted had no hooks or tricks.

The Pardon and Parole Scandal

Ideals were much less important to Folsom the chief executive than they were to Folsom the chief legislator. When he paid attention to them, as he did in dealing with welfare, public finance, and industrial health and safety reforms, his performance as an administrator tended to improve. When his administrative efforts were unguided by ideology, the worst elements of patronage politics reigned supreme. This is not to suggest that an ideologue is automatically a competent administrator, but it does indicate that having some notion of what one wants to accomplish helps and, failing such direction, administrative processes drift. The classical ideal of efficient administration, that is, the businessman-politician's call for businesslike management, is a hollow standard if only because the measurement of efficiency and even its definition in government is usually difficult, if not impossible. What made Hamm and Carnley so effective was not that they elicited more work per hour out of their staffs but that they had clear ideas of what the programs under their purview should look like measured by rather simple, commonplace standards which, it happened, were consistent with Folsom's brand of populist-liberalism. In addition, both Hamm and Carnley were highly motivated individuals who required little guidance or supervision, although apparently Hamm worked more closely with Folsom because of the governor's interest in taxation. And neither was hobbled by hidden agendas for self-enrichment.

The efforts of Folsom and his administrators in the fields of liquor control, financial management, and state purchases were fraught with problems, but Folsom's worst performance as chief executive was not in any of these areas. That place is reserved for the decision making on pardons and paroles that occurred in the last year of his first term. His abysmal performance there is especially tragic since there was so much room for improvement in this and related elements of the criminal justice system, and Folsom's deeply held beliefs provided at least rough guidelines by which the improvements could have been accomplished.

The granting of pardons and paroles had for decades been a particular area of dishonesty in Alabama state government: pardons and paroles were often bought with bribes of cash, property, and sexual favors. According to a *Montgomery Advertiser* editorial, paroles were widely "used by governors to buy and pay for the votes of lawyer-legislators."[61] One reporter told of a prominent North Alabama lawyer during the second Bibb Graves administration who was typical of many wealthy dealers in pardons and paroles. "He had many farms given to him when, say, some farmer's kid would cut someone up and they'd throw him in jail—the farmer would give him a farm and he'd give the kid a pardon or parole."[62] In Folsom's first term, however, the system reached extremes of venality and irresponsibility that were unequaled in the state's history.

Pardons and paroles were granted by a three-person commission called the Pardon and Parole Board. Its structure was similar to the ABC Board in that its three members were appointed by the governor to serve staggered terms. Part of Governor Frank Dixon's sweeping state government reorganization in 1939, it had been created to remove this critical part of the criminal justice system from politics, that is, from control by the governor.[63]

Trouble began on October 1, 1949, with the appointment of Bill Drinkard, fresh from his work as finance director, to the Pardon and Parole Board. His vote combined with that of Glen D. Vinson (appointed by Folsom in 1948) constituted a majority. As required by law, board members had from the beginning in 1939 developed rules and procedures to guide decision making. On November 18, 1949, on a motion by Vinson and over the dissent of the third member, Howell Turner, the board abolished all rules and regulations. Drinkard and Vinson then began to grant pardons and paroles, in the words of a report issued by a special pardon and parole legislative investigating committee, "without reference to the merits of the individual cases considered."[64]

Basing its report on the sworn testimony of four hundred witnesses, the investigating committee concluded that "hardened criminals with long records of conviction, escape and delinquency, were released upon society, without any evidence of a desire or intent on their part to reform. . . . Criminals convicted of heinous crimes were released after only a few days' imprisonment. Prisoners were released without pre-parole investigation. . . . Parole was often followed quickly by full pardon without reason or justification."[65] Many of the individuals freed were unstable and violence prone. Folsom chose to portray these findings as part of a smear, a "gigantic conspiracy" designed to hurt his chances for reelection in 1954, but they were based on solid evidence.[66]

Under Drinkard and Vinson there was a sudden and massive increase in the number of pardons and paroles granted. During the four years from October 1, 1945, through September 30, 1949, there were an average of 136 temporary paroles, 383 permanent paroles, and 84 pardons granted each year. From October 1, 1949, through September 30, 1950, there were 470 temporary paroles (a 246 percent increase over the average of the previous four years), 928 permanent paroles (142 percent increase over the average of the previous four years), and 112 pardons (33 percent increase over the average of the previous four years). In the three-and-one-half-month period October 1, 1950, through January 15, 1951, the pace accelerated at an even faster rate.

During some especially busy periods of the Drinkard-Vinson reign, the

Pardon and Parole offices were sometimes (to quote Geoffrey Birt) "as busy as Macy's on Christmas Eve."[67] According to the investigating committee, "the hall corridors and grounds around the Pardon and Parole Building became so packed with pardon and parole seekers that the board's operations deteriorated into uncontrollable confusion." The mobs of pardon and parole seekers and their attorneys and families "could not all get in the Building and spilled over to the outside."[68] State government workers who normally parked in the vicinity feared for their persons and automobiles, and so they prudently parked blocks from their regular spots and walked circuitous routes well around the area.

Sometimes Drinkard and Vinson granted pardons because in their judgment a prisoner's record was so awful as to suggest that he could not succeed as a parolee! In Drinkard's words, "I feel if a man can't make parole, he ought to have a pardon."[69] Drinkard explained this apparent irony with impeccable logic: If a prisoner was so crime prone that he would quickly commit parole violations and be returned to jail, there was little reason to grant him parole.

In the 1951 legislative investigation, witness after witness testified that pardons and paroles were being sold for as little as a few hundred dollars for relatively minor offenses or thousands for more serious crimes.[70] Release could be purchased very cheaply. For example, one man was pardoned after serving fewer than seven months of a twenty-five-year sentence for killing his brother-in-law. It cost twenty-two hundred dollars for his release from prison and another one thousand dollars for the restoration of his citizenship rights, or a total of $133 per year for the remaining twenty-four years of his sentence.[71] The highest price for a parole documented by the legislative investigating committee was six thousand dollars.[72] Birt's "Macy's" simile was apt, but he should have added that it was the bargain basement.

Political access was also a route to pardons and paroles, sometimes working by itself, sometimes in conjunction with bribery. Cabinet members, local political leaders, campaign managers, and legislators were implicated by name. There was, for example, the case of a Pike County man who was convicted of receiving stolen property and sentenced to four years imprisonment. He wrote a letter to Folsom on October 22, 1949, outlining his situation: "I have only fifteen (15) days . . . to get my business rounded up and be ready to go to Draper [Prison]. This fifteen days will be up on the first day of November." He asked that he be pardoned before having to enter prison. His justification was not that he was innocent or that there had been extenuating circumstances connected to his offense, but rather that "I worked all through your first campaign (one before run-off) for you. I had from one to three sound outfits on road at all times. I paid out of my own pocket for all of this except gasoline and oil."[73] He was paroled on November 18, 1949, and pardoned on May 18, 1950.[74]

Title 42, Section 1, Code of 1940 required Pardon and Parole Board members to "devote their full time to their official duties." When Folsom gave the position to Drinkard, he told him that it was a soft job that would require no more than one day per week, which was close to the amount of time he in fact spent on the job. Much of his schedule was apparently taken up hunting and fishing. Vinson testified that "it was hardly possible to sit down in the Drinkard office without sitting on a fish hook or a shotgun."[75] The legislative committee found that Drinkard had "studied few of the cases and was familiar with few of the files."[76] Vinson was much more attentive to his responsibilities, but his job performance was hampered by heavy drinking.

The whole point behind the creation of the Pardon and Parole Board in 1939 was to remove it from the governor's direct influence. The investigating committee, however, concluded that Folsom's impact was considerable, and Drinkard and Vinson, while denying Folsom's influence on specific decisions, blamed the policy of mass prisoner releases on the governor.[77] Vinson testified that he had followed Folsom's instructions to release convicts who lacked sufficient funds to hire counsel.

On his last day in office Folsom accepted Vinson's and Drinkard's resignations and publicly reprimanded them for having released too many prisoners, but soon thereafter he was quoted as saying that the one black mark against him was that there were more prisoners behind bars when he left office than when he first became governor. He added, "I publicly stated that day I went into office that one-half the prisoners were political prisoners."[78] He made the same remark later in interviews. He believed that the criminal justice system was so biased against the poor (especially blacks) that he would have been justified in releasing even more prisoners than he did. Indeed, when he spoke of these events, he hardly mentioned Drinkard and Vinson—as if the Pardon and Parole Board had not even existed. He accepted full responsibility for the releases, and he still saw himself as releasing "political prisoners." In a 1973 interview he said, "My only mistake was I didn't free all the prisoners."[79] One Folsom administration member who took no part in pardon and parole activities said, "Jim always had the philosophy that the court system had put them in because they lacked a proper defense. He always said that there were no lawyers in the penitentiary."[80] Folsom also advocated enrolling released convicts in the National Guard, a proposal which prompted the *Alabama Journal* to recommend psychiatric treatment for him.[81]

The legislature's investigating committee clearly revealed the nature of pardon and parole decision making in the Folsom administration. Indeed, the committee's report, as first written, was a bit too clear for the legislature. Part of the report had named a number of legislators who had received fees ranging from fifty dollars to one thousand dollars (ten to twenty cases each) in pardon or parole cases. They were attorneys, and those fees were well within the norm for legal work of that sort. In fact, if anything, they were rather low. But the legislature wanted this section eliminated and voted to cut it from the report. In so doing, it debased the authority of the entire report and made the named legislators appear guilty of abusing their positions of public trust. Grover Hall, Jr., wrote, "If it thought so little of this offending paragraph, the inference is left that the remainder of the report is less than authoritative."[82] Even before Hall could get his words into print, Folsom had used their action as a vehicle for charging that the report was politically motivated.

Law enforcement authorities heard the testimony and read the legislative report, but, considering the dozens of individuals who were part of one of the largest political scandals in the state's history, amazingly little was done. A Montgomery County grand jury indicted only Representative J. Emmett Wood, Roy Drinkard, Thomas Vinson, and Frank Boswell, charging them with perjury before the legislative investigating committee. In all four cases either the defendants were found innocent or charges were dropped. Representative Wood won a mistrial chiefly on the basis of a defense against perjury charges to the effect that he was bordering on delirium tremens at the time of his testimony and really didn't know what he was saying.[83] It appears that many influentials, pro- and anti-Folsom, were uninterested in pursuing a just conclusion. By mid-1952 the entire matter had just disappeared from view.

From the beginning Drinkard made no secret of his intention to use his position as finance director for personal gain, even going so far as to inform reporters of this fact. Folsom's objections to Drinkard's open dishonesty and greed led to loud, angry arguments. In one of them Drinkard was heard to scream, "You big son of a bitch, you send me back to Cullman and I'll take you with me."[84] But, damaging evidence that Drinkard may have held notwithstanding, the characteristic that most protected him was that he had provided Folsom with some of his strongest early election campaign support. Bill Drinkard and his family contributed considerable amounts of cash and time when the few people who even knew of Folsom's ambitions were mainly ridiculing or ignoring him. Folsom found him a sincere and hardworking aide who occasionally went a little astray.

Blindness to the faults of early supporters is a classic weakness of even the most cold-blooded politicians. Still, this explanation is not entirely satisfactory; it places too much burden on this one factor. Folsom was not completely ignorant of events in his administration, especially when they appeared daily on the front pages of newspapers.

Considering the statements of those interviewed for this study, it is unlikely that Folsom profited financially from this mass release of more than two thousand prisoners. The specific cases of his direct involvement in decision making on pardons and paroles documented by the legislative investigating committee described Folsom as intervening on behalf of individuals who contributed time or money to his 1946 campaign. The October 22, 1949, letter to Folsom cited above stressed the writer's strong support for Folsom before the 1946 primary. In the only other case of Folsom's involvement documented in detail by the committee, the governor told Broughton Lamberth to stop participating in pardon and parole matters and specifically to stop demanding fees for assisting pardon and parole seekers. Beyond that, we have Vinson's testimony, interview subjects' recollections, and Folsom's own assertions that he allowed the process to continue primarily out of grossly misguided populist zeal.

The pardon and parole scandal had, in important ways, much the same tone as Folsom's calling and recalling special legislative sessions for a constitutional convention and his thrashing at the bloodied and then moldering corpse of the Dixiecrat movement. He had a way of becoming fixed on an idea, almost hypnotized by it, and when this happened, he was at his most self-destructive. Had Folsom been merely dishonest, he would not have allowed hundreds of heinous criminals to be released prematurely, attracting headlines day after day for almost the entire last year of his administration. His quick dismissals of ABC Board members only suspected of misdeeds, and especially his prompt firing of Bryce Davis, another early North Alabama supporter, for relatively small misdeeds reinforce this argument. Despite his Jacksonian-spoils justification for what his aides did ("With everything equal I want a friend to have it") and despite his oft-repeated disdain for what newspapers printed, Folsom objected to excessive greed, especially when reporters were attracted. His sensitivity to having his administration portrayed on the front pages as a den of thieves varied dramatically from time to time, but he reacted to such publicity often enough to fire dozens of people in both terms.

Folsom's ideological reasons for allowing the prisoner releases provide an additional reason for his failure to fire Drinkard, to wit, Drinkard was doing what Folsom wanted him to do both as finance director and as a Pardon and Parole Board member. Folsom wanted to reward his friends, and he also required fairly large amounts of cash with which to bribe legislators and buy off Christine Johnston. The problem in both cases was that Drinkard bungled administratively. His contract awards were tainted, and his release of prisoners could not have attracted a more negative press and public reaction. This still does not explain why Folsom did not fire him for incompetence, but there appears to be no case in either term when he dismissed anyone purely for that reason.

Finally, Folsom believed that politics permeated the entire administrative process. He had little hope that objectivity could obtain in any governmental situation. To a considerable degree, he saw Drinkard practicing the same kind of politically motivated decision making that his predecessors had, and this was largely an accurate perception. He viewed newspaper criticism as similarly motivated.

Folsom objected so strenuously to the criminal justice system as it operated against the poor that one must wonder why he did not try to reform it instead of using temporary "solutions" such as releasing prisoners prematurely. This is particularly puzzling given his tendency to think in terms of fundamental systemic changes aimed at basic societal problems. This was the whole point to his advocacy of a constitutional convention, reapportionment, elimination of the poll tax, and similar measures. At the beginning of his second term he championed the creation of a comprehensive public defender system, but he could have done so much sooner. He did attempt some criminal justice reforms in his first term. For example, he helped to bring about the eradication of the corrupt fee system by which local law enforcement officials were paid on what was essentially a piecework basis, which meant that they had an incentive to arrest as many people as possible. But he clearly could have done much more, especially as he was familiar with the field of law enforcement by virtue of his family's work in that area and his first father-in-law's background as a lawyer, judge, and trusted political adviser.

Public administration as it existed as a professional field in the 1940s and many administrative reforms in the first four decades of this century, such as civil service, operated under the assumption that politics and administration were separate functions, with politics being the formulation of basic policy (usually by the legislature) and administration the execution of that policy (usually by the executive). The objective of public administration under this assumption was to execute basic policy in an efficient, nonpolitical manner. A theory propounded on the planet Mars could hardly have been more alien to Folsom's modus operandi and that of most other Alabama governors. In his view, a winner should govern, and in so doing he should reward those who helped him gain power. Folsom's Jacksonian-spoils explanations for his actions were not lame post hoc justifications for mistakes. After all, he acknowledged making very few mistakes.

In addition to his beliefs about the virtues of the spoils system, his administrative style was a mixture of his lack of self-discipline, invalid lessons learned from early administrative successes, belief in the small businessman as government official, an intense need for the personal loyalty of subordinates, an inability objectively to evaluate the performance of subordinates (especially those he believed to be loyal), and traditional Alabama politics as practiced by most governors before and since Folsom. Basic policy directions were guided, rather consistently, by his populist-liberal viewpoints when he cared about a particular policy area enough to bring them to bear.

CHAPTER 8

Electoral Politics and Civil Rights, 1950–1954

> Mama used to tell me, "when boys throw mud on you, don't rub it because it just smears it. Let it dry, and it will fall off."
>
> James E. Folsom

The 1950 Democratic party primary centered more on the aftermath of the Dixiecrat movement than it did on the contest for the governor's chair. Since the Alabama governor could not succeed himself, the governorship and control of the legislature and state Democratic executive committee were at stake. Because they had so successfully taken advantage of their commanding position on the executive committee in 1948, the states' righters concentrated their energies on maintaining control of that body.[1] Surprisingly, they found themselves in a weak position.

Several factors worked against these former Dixiecrats. First, public opinion had soured toward them. By denying voters the right to choose between Truman and other candidates, they had gone too far, as they had also done in crushing Folsom's legislative programs. Second, the congressional district system of electing executive committee members gave loyalists an advantage. Widely known states' rights leaders resided almost entirely in the Black Belt, Birmingham, and Mobile. States' rights candidates elsewhere were unknown to the electorate and were competing with widely recognized and popular loyalists. Even in Birmingham and Mobile loyalists were able to field very attractive candidates. Third, Hill and Sparkman joined together with Folsom, Congressmen Albert Rains, Carl Elliott, Bob Jones, Edward deGraffenreid, and George Grant in opposition to the Dixiecrats.[2]

In a 1950 speech that could have been written by Folsom two years earlier, Hill charged that the Dixiecrats were agents of the Republican party whose mission was to break up southern Democratic parties from within so that the GOP could take over the presidency and Congress and thereby repeal social and economic gains made during the New Deal.[3] Fittingly, *Talladega Daily* editor Tom Abernathy, the leader of the 1950 states' rights campaign, would work for Eisenhower in 1952 and run for governor as a Republican in 1954. This came after a 1950 statement that "I, for one, seek no allegiance with the Republican Party, which brought the shame and degradation of the first Reconstruction upon Alabama."[4]

Dixiecrats also faced formidable opposition in the gubernatorial race. One candidate, Philip Hamm, was of course a Folsomite, but he was not seen as a contender. The two men who seemed to have a strong chance, Gordon Persons and Chauncey Sparks, were loyalists and segregationists. Persons's opening campaign speech stressed his solid opposition to Truman but his loyalty to the national Democratic party and his belief that segregation laws were in no need of change.[5] The best-known Dixiecrat candidates were Henderson and Bull Connor. Their basic approach to the campaign was exemplified by Henderson's declaration that the structure of Alabama government was threatened by "the fire of socialism, communism, or Trumanism, unless we extinguish the torch that is poised to set the blaze." Henderson charitably identified Folsom (who was only running via his surrogate Hamm) as a Trumanist. He named no socialists or Communists.[6]

A split between states' rights segregationists and loyalist segregationists developed, with the differences appearing to be primarily stylistic. R. F. Hudson, the urbane publisher of the *Montgomery Advertiser* and *Alabama Journal,* wrote to Henderson informing him that his newspapers would endorse Sparks despite Hudson's personal agreement with the Henderson platform.[7] Tensions also developed between Henderson and one of his closest allies, Joe Poole. Ill feelings had first arisen after Poole's 1946 defeat (Henderson had been his campaign manager), but their differences grew into an outright split during the 1950 primary campaign. Henderson's refusal to moderate his self-destructive emphasis on prohibition despite Poole's efforts to convince him otherwise, irritated Poole and other potential supporters. Poole feared that Henderson's sole objective in seeking the governorship was to push a prohibition referendum through the legislature. Poole informed Henderson that his fanatical rigidity was isolating him from business, farm, and even temperance groups who were in no mood to back a loser.[8] As Henderson read Poole's last written attempt (a five-page single-spaced letter) to convince him to moderate his views on the hopeless prohibition question, he scribbled marginal notes, the last one of which began: "I have no alternative but to follow my own convictions in all moral matters."[9]

This letter also pointed to a weakness of the gubernatorial campaigns of Big Mule Black Belt candidates that surfaced in every campaign thereafter—severe underfunding. In it Poole described in detail how his 1946 gubernatorial campaign treasury had run short, and he accused Henderson of not supplying his share of needed funds.[10] Poole then informed Henderson that he was making a "first installment" contribution to Henderson's 1950 gubernatorial campaign of a paltry one hundred dollars and that he planned to make later expenditures that would amount to no more than two thousand dollars.

Loyalists won over half the seventy-two executive committee places in the first primary without a runoff. Three weeks later, they won six more seats, increasing their majority to nearly 60 percent. In the governor's race, to everyone's surprise, Hamm made it into the runoff with the front-runner, Gordon Persons, but Persons had far outdistanced him, and Hamm declined to contest the runoff. Lister Hill, in a little-noticed campaign, was running for renomination to the Senate against a states' rights candidate named Lawrence McNeil of Birmingham. Hill swamped his opponent.

As Folsom prepared to leave office, he issued a "four year report to the people" in which he outlined his vision of his administration and the future:

> There has been four years of progress in some fields but very little progress in others.
> There has not been much progress in the fundamental liberties.
> It is not really important that several thousand miles of roads have been built for the people during the past four years, and it is not of great significance that teachers' salaries have been almost doubled nor that the reforestation program has been greatly advanced. What really concerns the safeguarding and promoting of democracy for our people, is whether or not every man so entitled is given the right to vote.
> We ha' e to face up to the fact that 35 percent of our people are Negroes. We cannot stick our heads into the sand and let the world march by without direction, without planning. . . . Many of them who are qualified to the letter of the law have been maliciously kept from exercising the right to vote. That is not democracy in any man's language.[11]

The Persons Administration and Civil Rights

Many voted for Persons because he promised tranquility and honest, efficient administration of executive functions. Folsom had tired voters just as he had exhausted people who worked close to him. Persons's administrative style, it turned out, was virtually identical to Folsom's in its use of patronage politics, except for pardons and paroles, but he certainly provided tranquility. He enjoyed extremely friendly relations with the legislature largely because he attempted little that was not favored by safe majorities. Only in the area of civil rights was the Persons administration remarkable.

In his gubernatorial campaign Persons had advocated poll tax elimination and legislative reapportionment. His initial proposal to kill the poll tax was defeated, but his compromise measure limiting the cumulative feature (upon which Gessner McCorvey placed so much faith for effective disfranchisement) to two years was approved by the legislature and ratified by the voters. He also sponsored a sixty-seven senator reapportionment plan which was pushed vigorously in the Senate by Wilcox County's J. Miller Bonner, who had preceded Henderson into the Senate and replaced him when Henderson ran for governor. Like Henderson, he feared Folsom's return, and the reapportionment bill, an awkward concoction likely to be rejected by the voters, was designed to rob Folsom of one of his prime issues. Bonner also proposed enactment of a bill which would have made it unlawful for an office seeker to violate a campaign pledge. "If Big Jim couldn't lie he couldn't run," Bonner charged. To which Folsom responded, "He's a fine, distinguished old gentleman. When I get to be 73 years old I'll be belly aching about the good work the younger generation is doing myself."[12] The hapless Bonner had no reply. The legislature passed the reapportionment bill, but Bonner's campaign honesty plan made the lawmakers nervous as they contemplated some of their own campaign pledges, and it sank quickly from view. Persons expended little effort on behalf of the sixty-seven senator plan (a constitutional amendment), and it was defeated by the voters.

The governor and his legislative leaders also resurrected an updated version of McCorvey's Voter's Qualification Amendment, known as Boswell, Jr. This was roughly the same legislation that Folsom's supporters had killed in 1949. Reapportionment and Boswell, Jr., were connected. Some Birmingham legislators were dissatisfied with the malapportionment that was part of their alliance with the Black Belt. They insisted that some sort of reapportionment was their price for support of the Voter Qualification Amendment.[13] It would appear that they were outfoxed by Bonner, since reapportionment was killed by the voters and Boswell, Jr., was passed.

Persons signed a version of another bill violating civil liberties that Folsom had stopped in his first term. This one required Communists to register and prohibited them from holding either elective or appointive public offices.[14] Other bills with a similar orientation fared less well during the Persons administration.

Sam Engelhardt, the senator from Macon County and brother-in-law of Wilcox County's Senator Bonner, submitted a bill which would have carved his county into two parts, black and white. He also offered a bill which would have transformed public schools into private ones; failing that, he suggested the possibility of eliminating the public schools and replacing them with a statewide television network.[15] Macon County had one of the highest percentages of blacks of any county in the state, and it was the home of

Tuskegee Institute and a veterans hospital, both of which employed large numbers of well-educated blacks. Engelhardt, who owned sixty-five hundred acres of rich farmland (worked by some seventy-five tenant families) and various business concerns, was one of the county's wealthiest citizens. He was convinced that drastic measures were required to defend his holdings against the rising tide of black aspirations and power. Engelhardt, a square-jawed, gruff but friendly, blunt-talking individual, openly stated that his entire reason for being in politics was to keep Macon County from being governed by blacks who, he believed, would quickly strip him of his property through tax reassessments and similar devices. In the early 1950s Engelhardt became the Black Belt's major spokesman and tactician, leaving the doctrinaire and wordy J. Bruce Henderson increasingly isolated.

Just as Engelhardt was gradually replacing Henderson as the major spokesman for Black Belt segregationists, Jefferson County Senator Albert Boutwell, a leading anti-Folsom legislator and one of the economy bloc's founding fathers, was supplanting Frank Dixon as the major spokesman for the urban-based segregationists. Like Engelhardt, Boutwell saw the problem less in the steamy ideological mode of Dixon and Henderson and more as a professional politician trying to respond to the interests of his constituency.

Boutwell was short and of average weight, and he often smoked cigars, which did not fit the peculiarly delicate quality of his face. An excellent parliamentarian who was voted hardest-working legislator of 1949, he was always an efficient Birmingham Boss tool. Boutwell represented Birmingham corporate interests as a lawyer and as a senator, a common combination of roles in those days. A Burkian conservative, Boutwell placed special emphasis on the need for maintaining order in any political community. He believed that dangerous instability lurked always close to the surface, and he feared rapid change. These beliefs meshed well with his sponsors' economic interests, especially those sponsors concerned with maintaining segregation. Yet as the years went by he began to feel that segregation would not last long and that there might even be something ethically wrong about it. Boutwell, a self-made man in the best sense of that term, also cared about the many factory workers and poor in his district. He possessed a moral sensibility of which his segregationist allies were only dimly aware. Those who sensed it interpreted it as weakness.[16]

A critical difference between Jefferson County and Black Belt Big Mules was that the former had much less to lose with the fall of segregation. Black Belt planters correctly felt that their entire fortunes—indeed, their identities—were being threatened. From this point alone it was predictable that Jefferson County Bosses would be more likely to compromise on segregation than their Black Belt counterparts. The difference could be easily detected in Boutwell's determined but nevertheless distant support of segregation in the 1950s versus Engelhardt's impassioned, angry, do-or-die approach. In interviews Boutwell traced the Birmingham–Black Belt alliance to the great numbers of Birmingham residents who, like Boutwell himself, had been born in the Black Belt. Even though Birmingham was industrial (in Boutwell's words, "Jefferson County *was* big business—U.S. Steel"), its cultural ties to the Black Belt were not quickly broken. The increasing divergence between them arose partly because over the years Birmingham residents moved toward the requirements and needs of an urban industrial existence and away from the rural Black Belt culture. In addition, the lower percentage of blacks living in Jefferson County compared to the Black Belt meant, in Boutwell's words, "that something could be done without dominance by the blacks."[17]

In 1953 the legislature created the Alabama Interim Legislative Committee on Segregation in the Public Schools in anticipation of adverse Supreme Court decisions. The committee was chaired by Boutwell, who was just beginning to question the rationality and morality of the South's stand on segregation. Just as the committee was completing its work, the court delivered its decision on *Brown,* and the committee, unsurprised, included it in a report issued in October 1954. The document was written in a cool, distant, analytical tone, consistent with Boutwell's legalistic-technical approach to most problems; it was far removed from the race baiting of which at least one of the committee's members was capable.

The fundamental assumption underlying this report, and one accepted by a great number of Alabama whites, was that "there is in Alabama a basic sympathy and understanding between the races which is genuine and sincere. There is no dormant hostility between them."[18] The report argued that coerced integration would upset that pacific situation and produce a shocking level of destruction throughout society. Blacks would suffer most. Parents of black children sent to integrated schools would be fired, their leases would be terminated, and the least stable of both races would react violently.[19] Psychological damage to black children living through such turmoil would be incalculably large. In this connection, the report paused to deny the Supreme Court's finding that segregated schools damaged black children psychologically and socially.

The report held out the hope of compromise: integrated schools could be created in addition to all-black and all-white schools. Parents of either race would be free to send their children to either a segregated school of their own race or to a special integrated school. This system was labeled "freedom of choice"—a usage which should not be confused with later applications of that term—and it became one of Boutwell's major legislative pursuits when Folsom became governor a second time.

The report did not endorse such extreme measures as abolition or abandonment of the public school system. Its basic strategic proposals were, first, to give the legislature flexibility by eliminating state constitutional controls on educational funding and procedures and, second, to give school officials protection from lawsuits by making them judicial officers and furnishing them with the attorney general's legal protection.[20] The report stressed that neither proposal required fundamental constitutional changes. The most important constitutional change recommended was the elimination of the prohibition against integrated schools, while making clear that no one would be forced to attend integrated schools or operate integrated schools. Changes would also be made to insure that the legislature would be able to fund private education.

Investigations

In Alabama it is not unusual for a newly inaugurated governor to "discover" in the first two or three months of his term that under the previous administration the use of state automobiles was abused, contracts were awarded without proper low-bid procedures being followed, incompetents were hired for important state jobs, and the former governor's family grew rich off the state treasury. These "discoveries" are announced to the press in tones of sanctimonious horror, and they are accompanied by forced resignations of whatever rascals remain left over from the previous administration. These events are quickly followed by the appointments of statesmen loyal to the new governor. Suddenly the incumbent loses interest in revealing the previous administration's misdeeds, lest it remind the press and public of current practices.

The Folsom administration's disorderly and shabby approach to governance and personal enrichment was bound to attract more than the usual casually executed, public relations oriented inquiries. The year 1951 started with just such an investigation, but this time the Internal Revenue Service joined in the probe. Despite extensive efforts, the results of the Persons's administration investigation were quite ordinary, and the legislature's special pardon and parole committee's actions were never responded to by the state or county criminal justice systems. The IRS conducted grueling audits of the entire Folsom family and many high-ranking administrators only to find a few relatively minor infractions.

The average politician would have been thankful that so little resulted from these entirely legitimate investigations, but Folsom responded as if Persons, the legislature, and the IRS were nailing him to a cross. He was to use this as part of his defense after his arrest by the state highway patrol on a drunk-driving charge. Patrolmen spotted his car weaving back and forth on

Highway 31 north of Birmingham. As he was being arrested, Folsom declared, "You'll have to shoot me to take me to jail," but he went quietly. He was booked in the Jefferson County jail, held for one hour, and then, with photographers recording the event, released under a three-hundred-dollar bond. He was acquitted in court, after producing more than a dozen witnesses who testified that they had seen him shortly after his arrest and that he had not appeared drunk to them.[21] From the time of his arrest Folsom portrayed this relatively simple event as a Big Mule attempt to ruin his reputation. He claimed that after this incident and especially during campaigns he sometimes had to have friends fly him between Cullman and Central Alabama locations to avoid the police traps set up for his car in and around Birmingham.

The year 1952 was a time of speculation about Folsom's political future. Editorial writers and politicians were beginning to rethink their conclusion that Folsom's political career was finished, but there was still virtually universal agreement that if he ran in 1954, he would land in Buck's Pocket, a part of Alabama and a state of mind well known to him. Buck's Pocket, a beautiful gorge near Guntersville in North Alabama, is considered a haven for defeated political candidates. A newspaper article describing the scenic wonders of the place stimulated a telephone call from Folsom to Grover Hall, Jr., which Hall featured in a classic piece entitled "No. 9 'Long Distance from Alex City'":

> Folsom—Hi there.
> Ed.—Hi.
> Folsom—I want to set you straight on what that fella . . . wrote . . . this morning on Buck's Pocket. Take it down and give it to the AP.
> Ed.—Go ahead.
> Folsom—I take exception to what he said about Buck's Pocket being a real place. I've been there plenty of time on my own accord. That's pure geography. But the voters sent me there lots of times. And that's pure North Alabama mythology. That fella is trying to get literal.
> Ed.—Okay.
> Folsom—Have you written my 9th political funeral yet?
> As a matter of fact, that labor of love had not been performed. We make haste to repair the deficiency:
> James Elisha Folsom, who, like Napoleon, escaped a place named Elba to assume high office, will in all probability never be Governor of Alabama again.[22]

The 1954 Campaign

For Folsom the 1954 campaign began the day he left office in 1951. He and Jamelle returned to Cullman, and there he turned again to the insurance business, supervising twenty-one district agents and occasionally selling policies.[23] Jamelle Folsom's major concern was the raising of what would be a large family. Rachael and Melissa had been joined by a brother, James Elisha, Jr. (Little Jim), in May 1949. A year later Andrew Jackson (Jack) was born and then one year later Jamelle Alabama (Bama), to be followed in 1954 by Thelma Ebelene (Scrappy). Joshua Melvin (Josh) would be born in 1956, Eulala Cornelia (Lala) in 1959, and finally Melody Dunnavant Folsom in 1970.

Throughout the 1951–54 period, the Folsoms attended every political meeting, civic club function, and social event they could, traveling throughout the state in preparation for the next campaign.[24] Virtually the only time Folsom spent with his children was during church and regular Sunday afternoon trips and while doing household chores such as yard work with Rachael and Melissa.

Once the formal campaign began, the Folsoms continued to work together. Jamelle made all the stops, appeared with Folsom on every platform, sang with the Strawberry Pickers (her rendition of "You Are My Sunshine" is still well remembered), and distributed literature to the crowds after her husband's speeches. Their marriage and her presence in the campaign quieted the type of negative personal publicity that had plagued the 1946 campaign.

In 1954 Folsom faced what appeared to be a tough group of opponents: J. Bruce Henderson, James Faulkner, James B. Allen, Elbert Boozer, Henry Sweet, Winston Gullatte, and C. C. (Jack) Owen. But none of them was able to develop momentum. Boozer was becoming a perennial candidate best known for committing colossal oratorical gaffes. Four years earlier he had unaccountably told an Auburn audience that he knew they were proud of the fact that the University of Alabama, Auburn University's arch rival, had beaten Auburn during the previous season's football game—an especially strange remark considering that Auburn had won that contest. In 1954 he advocated a change in the state pardon and parole law which would have made difficult the sort of wholesale release of hardened criminals which Folsom had permitted in his first term. Unfortunately for Boozer, his proposal had been made law three years before.[25] While Boozer at least had the virtue of providing suspense for his audience, Henderson merely bored his with such statements as "All we need to do is to spend the state's present income wisely and put first things first."[26] Jimmy Faulkner, a Bay Minette publisher, ran a twenty-four-hour talkathon which galvanized listeners into contributing $2,567.50 to his Decency Fund. James Allen, a leading Folsom opponent in the state Senate (and later United States senator) ran a similarly lackluster campaign despite his endorsement by a majority of major newspapers.

Only Henry Sweet, who had served as Folsom's director of state docks until he was unceremoniously fired, managed to stir even mild interest with his charge that Folsom had as governor accepted more than $50,000 in kickbacks from insurance companies in return for state contracts. As evidence Sweet displayed copies of bank deposit slips and personal checks belonging to Folsom, but he never securely connected those documents to bribery. He tried to use Folsom's public image as a poor country boy to suggest that the large sums at Folsom's disposal could only have been obtained by illegal means, neglecting Folsom's many years as part owner of an insurance company. Sweet also charged that Folsom's brother-in-law Ross Clark, another owner of the insurance company, who was then under indictment for federal income tax evasion, was involved in the scheme. After tantalizing the press for more than three weeks with illegally obtained photostats of various documents, many of which were printed in newspapers, he produced an affidavit signed by F. O. Pierce, former state representative from Barbour County, who swore that he had paid Ross Clark $12,000 of the $15,000 in commissions he had allegedly received from the state. If Pierce had indeed paid that amount, he was guilty of overpaying as well as bribery; state officials who were buyable could be bought for far less than 80 percent of the take. Sweet also exhibited copies of Folsom's state income tax forms which reported incomes far lower than had been shown by the deposit slips.[27] None of Sweet's charges was ever substantiated by state or federal law enforcement officials including the federal Internal Revenue Service, which audited Folsom several times (resulting in a $330 refund).[28]

Sweet was seeking revenge, and not without justification. While serving as state docks director in Folsom's first term, he was in Savannah, Georgia, attending a meeting of people connected with ports. Folsom tried to reach him by telephone without success. Folsom was running a fever of 102, and he was becoming increasingly irritated. He had Bill Lyerly call and ask the desk clerk to page Sweet. Sweet did not respond. Lyerly then asked the clerk if he could see Sweet in the crowd, and, unluckily for Sweet, the clerk spotted his name tag. Then, on Folsom's instructions, Lyerly told the clerk to inform Sweet that he was no longer docks director. The deed was done, and soon the clerk returned and cheerfully told Lyerly, "He's coming to the phone now."

Folsom responded to Sweet's detailed but ineffectively presented case with remarks still repeated in Alabama political circles: "I wouldn't let none of them fellows down in Montgomery get rich. If anybody was gonna get rich, it was gonna be ol' Big Jim. I plead guilty to stealing. That crowd I got it from, you had to steal it to get it."[29] He would bellow, "Shore I stole. I stole to build hospitals. I stole to build schools. I stole to build roads." Pointing dramatically at members of the audience, he would add, "I stole for you—and you—and you."[30] One of his campaign aides viewed Folsom as having "a genius way of handling attacks. He would say, 'Well, my opponent didn't really mean that. He's just runnin' to get ready to run. He's got to have somethin' to say. . . . ' He would treat attacks with gentle toleration and disdain—treat his opponents as children run amok. He'd say, 'Brother, if you believe everything they write in them lyin' newspapers, you are confused.' "[31]

When opponents charged that he had used the office of governor for political advantage, his response was to appoint a committee "to see if you can take the politics out of politics."[32] The committee consisted of three men who understood better than most what the role of politics in politics or in the governor's office was—his regional campaign managers Fuller Kimbrell, George Wallace, and Charles Pinkston.[33]

In one of his best speeches Folsom combined evasive answers to critics, high drama, humor, and poetry.

> My enemies have made it cloud up a lot of times on me, and on my program, but they haven't made it rain. Right after I got home from Montgomery after four years I was notified that they were going to investigate me, and the suds-bucket fund from the 1946 campaign. They looked and they looked, and they asked questions and they checked my bank account. I guess it was overdrawn; it usually is!
>
> Anyway, after three years of investigating with a cost of at least a hundred thousand dollars they gave me a clean bill. But they had tried, mind you—they had tried to find something wrong. But they couldn't do it.
>
> And then they put me in that "Big Birmingham Jail" and kept me for a whole hour. I sure enough thought it was going to rain, 'cause, boys, it was shore mighty cloudy. But again they had tried to make it rain, and had made it mighty cloudy, but it didn't rain.
>
> My opposition not only persecuted me and my family, but they persecuted the boys who worked for me and helped me put over your program. They persecuted them for their faith, just like in the olden times in Europe when a man was persecuted and imprisoned for his beliefs and for his faith. And they carried them off before the king's judge, and they tried them without a jury, and away from home—before the king's men they tried them. It was just like the poet Byron wrote:
>
>> There are seven pillars of Gothic mold,
>> in Chillon's dungeons deep and old,
>> And in each pillar there is a ring,
>> And in each ring there is a chain,
>> That iron is a cankering thing,
>> For in these limbs its teeth remain,
>> With marks that will not wear away. . . .
>
> And they left marks upon the boys who helped me, and who tried to help you—marks that will not wear away. They tried them, again and again, but what did they find? Nothing! Why did they find nothing? Because there was nothing for

them to find. But they tried them just the same—tried them to prove to you that there was something, when all the time they knew there was nothing.

And folks, during this campaign it has been cloudy several times. My enemies have tried to make it look like rain, but the clouds they have made are nothing to compare with that big black cloud that is going to rise up out of the south about the fifteenth of April. There's going to be thunder and lightning and that cloud is going to roll just like it's bound to rain, but folks it ain't going to rain.

Now, that reminds me of the time when I was a boy and had rather catfish instead of plow—but about the only time I got to go catfishing was when it was too wet to plow. One day I was plowing along, and out of the south a little thunderhead got mixed up with another thunderhead, and they turned awful black, and there was a loud thunder and I just knew it was going to rain—yes, sir, I could already feel the catfish a-biting my hook, so I stopped my mule and started taking out to go to the house.

From across the field I saw my pa coming in a trot—he was waving his hand. And he was shouting something, but I couldn't hear him. Then about that time a little breeze come up out of the west, and that big bad cloud began to break up and that breeze brought the worst message any young catfisher ever heard—for by that time my pa was in hearing distance—and I can still hear him say, "Jim, Oh, Jim, hitch up that mule, boy—it ain't going to rain."

So, on election day, folks, I want some plowing done. I want some votes plowed into those polls—I want some Jim Folsom votes plowed in on election day—'cause, folks, it ain't going to rain![34]

The major impression that one comes away with in reading this speech is its sheer beauty. Folsom's use of the rain simile is extraordinarily powerful even though it is completely illogical. He weaves it in and out of the colorful narrative, ending with a homey anecdote with which every hardworking person can identify. Throughout, rain is a negative thing brought against the forces of good ("the boys who helped me, and who tried to help you") by the forces of darkness, but suddenly at the end, rain is something to be hoped for by a young boy who more than anything wants to escape hot, arduous labor to go fishing. But he finessed the problem and transformed plowing into voting in the minds of his listeners, who by this point were so overwhelmed by Folsom's incredible theatrics and rhetoric that logic had been shortcircuited. Effective political symbols need not be logical.

This speech was not only illogical but also factually incorrect on several points. The investigations had nothing to do with an overdrawn bank account, but, with a dextrous turn of phrase, he transformed serious charges into a joke. Several of his associates had been found guilty of income tax evasion and other charges, although most of them were minor. There was, in fact, plenty for the investigators to find, but again, when powerful symbols are being used by a master showman, matters of fact are of little importance.

The 1954 Folsom campaign was a moderated, better-organized version of his 1946 effort. His platform was very similar to the one he had used eight years before, and all his tricks and artifices remained, honed fine.

Comparing the 1946 and 1954 campaigns, reporter Rex Thomas described the latter as "a more mature, more serious performance. 'Kissin' Jim has almost become 'Preachin' Jim.'"[35] This was not to say that Folsom's campaigning had become entirely becalmed. His use of humor was still amazingly brash if not always original. He carried a book containing "country" jokes. As the campaign rolled along he began to feel that this source was running dry, a judgment which he shared one day with a reporter who was riding with him to a rally. The reporter said that he had a story Folsom might enjoy but he doubted that he would be able to use it publicly. It concerned a man who frequently returned home late at night drunk. His wife would fuss at him every time he did, but this only made things worse. The more she fussed, the more he drank. She was almost ready to admit defeat until her mother advised her to reverse her tactics and be completely pleasant to her carousing husband. That night as he was about to enter the house, staggering and singing, his wife leaned out the window and said, "Come on in, sweetie." He looked up at her with bloodshot eyes and said, "I might as well. I'll catch hell anyway when I get home." The reporter was shocked to find that Folsom used the story in his speech.

On another occasion—opinions differ on whether it was in 1948 or 1954—Folsom used this incredible piece: "Folks, you know my enemies been fishin' for Big Jim for a long time, and they've used all kinda bait. Awhile ago, a friend told me, said, 'Big Jim, they gonna hook you this time, they fixin' to get an attractive blonde, and they gonna dress her up fine and put perfume on her, and they gonna throw her out and troll her past you.' Now, folks, you know what I told my friend? I said, if that was the way my enemies aimed to catch me, if that was the bait they were gonna use, they were gonna catch Big Jim every time!"[36]

How could he say such things without alienating voters? As an experienced newspaper reporter explained it, "He could get away with what other politicians, even today, wouldn't touch with a ten foot pole. That was because he had a kind of big teddy bear image—in a peculiar way, a kind of sense of innocence. Everyone knew that he drank, but even the strict 'drys,' felt that somehow because it was him it was different. It didn't have the sinful air that it would with the ordinary politician."[37]

Rex Thomas noted that the 1946 and 1954 campaigns had different audiences. The 1946 audiences had consisted almost entirely of working-class people wearing bib overalls and heavy shoes, while the 1954 crowds were much closer to being a cross-section of society, including considerable numbers who arrived in "sleek new, big cars" wearing "tailored suits and French cuffs."[38] Many interviewees believed that Folsom interpreted his increased popularity with monied elements as their conversion to populism, a belief which, though mistaken, contributed to his increased flexibility and greater effectiveness in his second term. Others suggest that he saw their support for what it was—getting on the bandwagon with a sure winner—and that the flexibility that he demonstrated in his second term was simply due to his greater experience and maturity. The broader support behind Folsom in 1954 was reflected in the campaign's central slogan: "Y'all Come."

While Folsom welcomed support from all segments of society, he did not forget where his greatest strength lay. He feared being too closely identified with those interests he had spent his career opposing. One way he distanced himself from them was by avoiding them at rallies. When he finished speaking, he would dive into the crowd, moving quickly past obviously well-heeled people, seeking out the poorest-looking individuals, with whom he would shake hands and talk.[39]

Folsom expressed himself in even simpler, plainer terms in 1954 than he had in 1946. For example, a constitutional convention to bring about reapportionment became a "fair vote" convention—"so you folks can have your fair share of votes in the legislature."[40] His emphasis on highways remained, but, again, he presented it more skillfully. He told a variation on an old political story to illustrate the importance of road building.

> One day a traveling salesman picked up a farmer and they were riding along on this nice blacktop road out here between Sumiton and Empire. The salesman started talking to the farmer, but the farmer didn't say anything; he just held his mouth tight and listened and nodded his head. The salesman talked about coal, crops, and the weather; he even talked about the atom bomb, but the farmer didn't say a word, just nodded his head. Then, out there at old man Sam Barnett's house, where the blacktop ends, the road got powerful rough, and bumpy, and dusty—you've all been over that road and know what I mean. Now when that traveling salesman hit that unpaved road, he said, "Right back there is where Jim Folsom went out of office." The farmer hadn't said anything, but he started rolling his window down, then he reached up in his mouth and pulled out a powerful big chew of tobacco, then spit hard, and said, "Yes, and brother, by grabbs, right back there is where Jim Folsom is going back into office."[41]

Folsom would tell his audiences, "In 1946 I told you that I was going to pave Highway ____ and Route ____ [fitting the roads to his locale], and now I'm back and they're paved. Isn't that right brother?" Someone would invariably nod. "Listen at him nod his head," Folsom would say, delighting the crowd.[42]

On education he said: "Folks, on education. Shore I'm for education. I've got six chillun and the good Lord willin' I'm gonna have six more. Shore I'm for education."[43]

He continued his use of visual aids, begun with the suds bucket and mop eight years before. He never equaled the bucket and mop, but many remember his effective use of two galvanized pipes, one ¼ inch in diameter, the other 2½ inches. The small one represented patronage received by North Alabama in the previous administration, the larger one flatland (Black Belt) patronage.

Buster Hogan of Talladega, a Folsom campaigner and former *Birmingham News* photographer, was using visual aids of his own. He obtained a huge dilapidated 35mm movie camera of the sort used to film commercial motion pictures. The camera was inoperative except that it was capable of emitting realistic whirring sounds. Attached to the camera was a microphone (also a dummy) and a power cable leading to a 1936 Dodge station wagon which contained the camera's "power source," a broken-down Maytag washer which, when activated, produced loud motor noises. A professional sign painter decorated this equipment with a "national Movietone News" logo complete with gold leaf. "Photographers" then used this convincing looking and realistic sounding equipment to provide campaign news "coverage." The sole function of this charade was to legitimize the campaign and attract crowds of real reporters. Periodically, the logos were changed to represent "Pathe News," "Twentieth Century–Fox," and, in a burst of inspiration, British and French national television. The "British" camera operator was an Alabamian who spoke Greek but supposedly no English. To talk to him reporters and bystanders had to work through Hogan, who "translated," making his broken Spanish sound as much like Greek as he could. Apparently, no one thought to ask how a non-English-speaking Greek could be working for British television in the United States. More logically, a French-speaking Alabamian became the French television cameraman. Only Hogan and his "technicians" were aware of this amiable little fraud. Even Folsom, pleased that his campaign was receiving such widespread publicity, was unaware that not an inch of film was being shot.[44]

Bill Drinkard is credited with perfecting what was probably the most dramatic device of the campaign, the automobile caravan. The campaign formally opened with the Folsom family leaving their Cullman home by car and picking up, car by car (together with trucks and tractors), a parade of supporters that finally extended more than twenty miles. Each vehicle was decked out with banners, flags, and signs. Similar caravans would carry Folsom into the state's larger cities throughout the campaign.

Perhaps the major difference between the two campaigns was that Folsom's still loose-knit organization worked not only for his election but for the election of a slate of pro-Folsom legislative candidates. Probably no other gubernatorial candidate in the state's history—certainly no anti-establishment candidate—has attempted to do this on his own. The one-party, multifactional nature of Alabama's political system makes it difficult for a gubernatorial candidate to accomplish much beyond winning his own election. Few have the extra resources to go beyond that because they are obliged to devote so much attention to building and maintaining their own organization.[45]

It would be easy to exaggerate the cohesiveness with which Folsom ran his 1954 slate campaign. While on one hand he declared that "Jim Folsom is running for every office from constable on up," he also stated that he was "not trying to tell the people who to elect. . . . There is no Folsom slate."[46] His reluctance to admit the existence of a slate was partly due to his track record on endorsing candidates for public office; he had endorsed candidates in every statewide election since 1946, and nearly every one had lost. He operated more quietly behind the scenes in 1954. In some cases, office seekers attached themselves to him in their campaigns, often to their advantage, without receiving his formal endorsement. Alabama voters seemed to shy away from the idea that he was organizing a machine, and so his nonslate was probably the most effective way for him to proceed.

Few admitted to having voted for Jim Folsom in 1954—it seemed somehow a slightly disreputable thing to do—but he won without a runoff, taking 51.4 percent of the vote, a remarkable victory considering the importance of localism and the fact that he faced so many worthy opponents, scattered so widely through the Mobile area, the Black Belt, the southeast, and the northeast. Simultaneously, the voters selected majorities in both chambers that could be counted on to support his ambitious programs or at least counted on not to automatically oppose them as had been the case in the first term.

His response to his victory carried a peculiarly sarcastic tone: "It looks like they've conceded. Even the newspapers. That's nice of 'em."[47]

CHAPTER 9

Second-Term Legislative Relations and Civil Rights

Nothing just happens. Everything is arranged.
James E. Folsom

A week after Folsom's 1954 Democratic primary victory, the Supreme Court delivered its decision in *Brown v. Board of Education*. Folsom realized immediately that his hopes for reapportionment and a constitutional convention were finished; he knew that his legislative "majority" would dissolve over racial quarrels. "[The decision] created a hell of an uproar, and I knew that one-man-one-vote reapportionment was dead. . . . So I began working for something that was practical that I could get to such as Tombigbee, interstate, inland docks, deep water docks, mailbox roads."[1]

Late in 1954, at a Florida conference, southern state governors issued a defiant resolution protesting school integration and what they saw as the Supreme Court's efforts to remove control of the schools from the states. Governor-elect Folsom refused to sign the document.[2] A month earlier in an interview held in Mississippi he had observed that one of his prime objectives in dealing with the school integration controversy would be to "build some decent schools for Negroes, to get them out of the outhouses and barns."[3]

Folsom's 1955 inaugural was as colorful as the one in 1947 had been. His inaugural address was devoted almost entirely to civil rights: "I am here with one chief mission. To see that you the people may have and hold your freedom."[4] In addition to his familiar calls for a constitutional convention, an end to the poll tax, and so forth, he advocated creation of a comprehensive public defender program.

While the inaugural celebrations and speeches appeared to be a rerun of 1947, Folsom's legislative opponents were facing a new man as far as parliamentary technique was concerned. The governor-elect met with legislators in Cullman and Elba well before the new year began. Then, with great care and skill, he selected his legislative leaders, House committee chairmen, and House committee members. His choice for House speaker, Rankin Fite, had proven himself a loyal and extraordinarily able legislative strategist in the Senate during Folsom's first term. Fite ran unopposed and upon election immediately named himself chairman of the powerful House Rules Committee. As his House floor leader Folsom selected the quick-witted, hardworking Etowah County (Gadsden) representative George Hawkins. (Today Hawkins has a picture of Abraham Lincoln hanging above his desk in his law office, not a common sight in a state which proclaims itself the "Heart of Dixie.") In the Senate his president pro tem, elected unanimously, was the big, blustery, hard-drinking Broughton Lamberth. Lamberth was the least sophisticated of the three. Ideologically, Hawkins and Fite could be described as moderate populist-liberals. This and their North Alabama origins oriented them rather closely to Folsom's programs. Lamberth was not ideologically inclined, but he was personally loyal to Folsom. The two were cronies, fond of driving through Montgomery streets, careening along at dangerous speeds with Lamberth at the wheel and Folsom reclining next to him, his bare feet stuck out of the window. Folsom was also blessed with the election of Guy Hardwick as lieutenant governor. Hardwick demonstrated his positive attitude toward Folsom by appointing Lamberth as chairman of the Senate Finance Committee and vice chairman of the Senate Rules Committee.

As Tables 1 and 2 indicate (see chapter 5), Black Belters and their Jefferson County allies still held a large share of committee chairs and vice chairs. The pro-Folsom leadership, however, placed the key committees in the hands of Folsom supporters and also strengthened the position of North Alabamians. Fite, Hawkins, and Lamberth were basically supportive of Folsom's programs in their own votes. This support, which in the first session was at or above the 90 percent level for all three legislators, diminished to approximately 60 percent for Fite and 40 percent for Hawkins and Lamberth after Supreme Court decisions made desegregation the major issue in Alabama politics. Like many legislators, they would distance themselves from Folsom on racial and civil liberties issues and stay with him on bread-and-butter issues.

Pocketbook Legislation

Folsom's first serious legislative test came in the special session that he called for the last week of January to pass his three-part road program. House Bills 1 and 2 would have increased the gasoline and diesel taxes two cents, and House Bill 3 would have created an immensely powerful Alabama highway corporation with the authority to borrow unlimited amounts of money and to pledge future revenue for repayment of the bonds. The highway corporation would consist of the governor's executive secretary, the state highway director, and the state finance director, all three of whom were gubernatorial appointees. A toll road bill sponsored by two Folsomites was introduced in the Senate. Although Folsom had not included toll roads in his program, he did not object to them. Taken together, the bills would have provided an estimated $100 million in road construction during Folsom's second term.

The bills shot through the House Ways and Means Committee with only one dissenting vote, and when they were brought to the floor on February 1, they were cosponsored by forty-six legislators, only eight short of a majority. The first vote came on an amendment to the gasoline tax which cut the tax increase from two cents to one cent. The administration could muster only three additional votes and watched the amendment pass 54–49. Quickly, Joe Dawkins, a Folsomite legislator since the days of the first term, received permission from the speaker to change his vote from aye to nay; anyone voting against a bill could move for its reconsideration, and by changing his vote Dawkins was able to do just that. Immediately after Dawkins's motion was accepted, George Hawkins moved to adjourn. Administration forces were stunned at the tax reduction, but they immediately set about changing the results. Folsom, together with lobbyists representing financial institutions, bonding concerns, road machinery companies, and road construction contractors, worked on crucial representatives. Within the week all three bills had been passed.

The passage of these bills in the House was a textbook example of how it should be done and illustrates one of Folsom's favorite sayings: "Nothing just happens. Everything is arranged."[5] It actually began with Folsom's success in supporting legislative candidates friendly to his programs in the 1954 Democratic party primary. In the effort to pass the bills themselves he employed a combination of rewards and carefully formulated threats. Telegrams were sent to county officials suggesting that unless county legislators supported Folsom's road programs, new roads might not be constructed in their counties for the next four years. Simultaneously, to dramatize the point, road maintenance activities suddenly stopped in those counties. Some votes were bought with cash. One Folsom aide reported: "Every legislator in the governor's office wanted something in the form of graft." He quoted them, burlesquing their panicky voices in a squeaking falsetto: " 'I've got to have some money. I've got to have some money. It costs so much to stay down here.' And it did."[6]

Folsom also softened opposition to the highway corporation bill by gracefully consenting to three amendments—the addition of two independently elected officials (the attorney general and state treasurer) to the corporation leadership, a limit of $100 million on the amount of tax anticipation bonds that could be issued, and the addition of competitive bid provisions on the bonds.[7]

Winning over the Senate was a different matter. There Folsom did not enjoy the advantage of a presiding officer with a fast gavel or a floor leader as able as George Hawkins, or as large a majority as he had in the House. To make matters worse, the "antis," as they came to be called—the reincarnation of the economy bloc—were led by several extraordinarily able individuals, most notably Albert Boutwell.

After four years as an economy bloc leader in Folsom's first term and four more as Gordon Persons's floor leader, Boutwell stood—with eight years of legislative experience, a deep love of complicated political strategems and tactics for their own sake, and the resources of Birmingham's Bosses—as a formidable anti leader. Boutwell and the other major anti, Sam Engelhardt, made an effective combination. Boutwell was quiet and introspective, a man for whom political trickery was an art form. Engelhardt was louder and more open and a better public speaker. Different as the two men were personally, and different as their political interests would come to be in later years, their objectives were very similar in the middle 1950s. Engelhardt and his Black Belt colleagues and Boutwell's wealthy urban backers wanted to maintain a subdued black work force and low taxes. The only politically significant difference was that Engelhardt was more concerned with disfranchisement and segregation, since Macon County was 80 percent black.[8]

Because of Folsom's weaker strategic situation in the Senate, his programs did not fare as well there as they had in the House. Indeed, things went rather badly, and the situation was not improved by Folsom's stupid threat against Engelhardt after Engelhardt had caused a three-day delay in consideration of the road bills. Expressed in Engelhardt's words but not denied by Folsom, the threat was: "If you don't go along with my highway program, I'm going to get a new board of registrars in Macon County and register every damn nigger in the county."[9] There is disagreement among interview subjects and newspaper accounts as to whether Folsom delivered the message personally and meant it seriously, but there is no question that Folsom said it and that the message was understood by Engelhardt as being of serious intent.

Engelhardt kept Folsom's words to himself for two weeks until the bills were to be brought before the senate Finance and Taxation Committee. His explanation for the delay in making them public was that he was "waiting for Folsom to take it back." "But he hasn't done so," Engelhardt lamented primly, "and I feel the good people of Alabama, both white and colored, should see the tactics being used by the governor."[10]

Committee negotiations were intense. Dramatizing his lack of able supporters in the Senate, Folsom relied not on a senator but his finance director, Fuller Kimbrell, to represent his interests there. At issue were the nature of the bonds, whether revenue anticipated (which Folsom wanted) or general obligation (which the antis wanted); the size of the bond issue; and the amount of the gasoline tax increase. The revenue anticipated bonds did not require a public referendum, while the general obligation bonds did, and the revenue anticipated bonds carried higher interest rates. The Senate finally decided to offer $40 million worth of general obligation bonds and increase the gasoline and diesel fuel tax one cent. There would be exemptions for farmers using diesel fuel and a promise exacted from Folsom not to retaliate against counties represented by antis.[11]

At first, Folsom seemed to accept the Senate compromise gracefully. He told one adviser that he probably could have held out for more, but he decided to compromise and so "leave no sore toes."[12] A few days later his mood turned sour. At a joint House-Senate meeting which legislators thought was called as a celebration of the bills' passage, Folsom suddenly lashed out at the antis, selecting, for reasons that were not clear, Wilcox County Senator Roland Cooper (who had replaced J. Miller Bonner) for particular abuse, referring to him as a "round rock," meaning reactionary, countrified, and slick.[13]

Despite this outburst, Folsom is widely viewed as being far more effective in his dealings with the legislature in his second term than the first. "He was more pliable in the second," said a former legislator who served in both terms.[14] "Folsom got along with everyone—even his enemies," recalled another.[15] Still another said, "He was popular with the legislators. They would be in a hotel room. There would be a knock at the door. Folsom. 'Give me a drink of whiskey, boys. What y'all talkin' about?'"[16] He was on surprisingly cordial terms with legislators with whom he seemed to be in continuous bitter public conflict. He would come to their homes on convivial visits, threatening delicate antique chairs with his immense weight and chasing heavy slugs of bourbon with water drawn directly from a kitchen sink, mouth to the tap. And he was generous in allowing them to use state aircraft and other equipment and programs under his control. Boutwell agreed with these descriptions. "Everybody loved old Jim. Folsom could get along with anybody."[17] Speaker Fite remembered, "Folsom did not suggest legislative strategies, but he would listen to you. Those of us on the floor would absorb as much as possible and bring it to him. In the second administration he was much better informed."[18] One of Folsom's aides suggested that his increased effectiveness was partly due to the fact that legislators had become accustomed to Folsom's eccentricities.

Folsom's enhanced legislative abilities and improved relations with lawmakers reflected a recognition that people could be against his programs without being against him personally, and not an improved understanding of the legislative process itself. One of his floor leaders said, "Folsom had a comprehensive knowledge of politics, but he never seemed to grasp or want to grasp legislative procedures."[19] A key senator reinforced this image: "He had no conception of constitutional requirements. He spent most of his time philosophizing and trying to organize public opinion pressure. . . . [He was more interested in] going on the road than in doing the hard work necessary to accomplish something concrete."[20]

On March 1, 1955, Ross Clark, Folsom's brother-in-law and close adviser, placed a .22 caliber pistol to his forehead and killed himself. Clark had been a cofounder of the insurance company of which Folsom was part owner and for which he worked as North Alabama representative. The two had been very close for twenty years. A jovial individual, he had shown no obvious suicidal tendencies. Apparently, he was despondent over being found guilty (he pled nolo contendere) two months earlier of evading $6,711 in federal income taxes for the years 1947–49 and 1951. He was required to pay that amount plus a $2,500 fine. Folsom's brothers Fred and Cecil also pled nolo contendere to the same charges involving lesser sums. Folsom believed that Clark was hounded to death by the Internal Revenue Service.[21] Folsom took Clark's death as he had his wife's, brother's, and mother's—badly. According to a close Folsom aide, Clark was a "father image to Jim." He continued, "He was a man that Jim went to especially early in his career. He was an ultimate source of advice. Folsom talked to him like a father. [Clark] wasn't a deep thinker, but he had great political sensitivity."[22] His close friends believed that to some degree Folsom blamed himself for getting Clark in over his head. His drinking, which had already reached titanic proportions, got worse.

Later in March Folsom called a special session of the legislature to consider old-age pension reform. It promised to be a confusing session. Conservatives and many members of the administration wanted educational matters to be considered first. Conservatives sought enactment of additional segregation laws in the wake of Supreme Court decisions, while many Folsomites were worried about school financing.[23] Folsom was more concerned about pensions because, among other reasons, he believed that education forces were sufficiently well organized to take care of themselves, a lesson he had learned in the 1947 fight over the distribution of the budget surplus. He also respected State Superintendent of Education Austin Meadows as a skillful advocate of educational interests. So, while he favored higher pay for teachers and increased funding for construction programs, in public statements he was quite vague about how these goals would be achieved beyond proposing a bond issue of unspecified amount.[24] He told legislators that once he had enacted his three "musts" (road programs, expanded old-age pensions, and legislative reapportionment), he would cease involvement in legislative matters and "step aside."[25]

The governor also wanted to deal with pension matters first because he knew that a combination of educational funding needs and segregation issues could produce endless parliamentary confusion that would strangle everything else. He did not want the state's elderly to lose out in such a melee, especially since they were suffering particularly severe pension shortages due to flaws in Social Security regulations, tight appropriations, and the Persons administration's Relatives Responsibility Act. That statute made elderly pensioners ineligible for support if their immediate family could supply assistance.[26] Folsom had two major objectives: to repeal the Relatives Responsibility Act and to increase pensions. The latter goal required sin and luxury tax increases, a graduated tax on insurance premiums (with state-based companies given a tax break), and a corporate franchise tax increase. Business groups such as the Alabama Chamber of Commerce, Alabama Power, Mobile ship-building concerns, Alabama Farm Bureau Federation, Associated Industries of Alabama, coal-mining companies, pulpwood and paper companies, and insurance companies worked vigorously to defeat the bills.[27]

The first concrete anti move came in the House with the attempted passage of a resolution that would have kept the bills out of the administration-dominated Ways and Means Committee, but it failed.[28] There was also action in the upper house, where Folsom testified before the Senate Finance Committee, which met in his office. The governor spoke as an expert witness, that is, as an insurance agent. He characterized insurance company threats to leave the state if the insurance premium tax passed as a bluff. Even if some of the larger companies packed up their actuarial tables and pulled out, there was little reason to worry, Folsom argued, because it would leave the field open for smaller Alabama concerns. He need hardly have added that one such business was his own. "I feel mighty sorry for those poor, helpless 14 billion dollar insurance companies. [They] have a first mortgage on the world," he sneered.[29]

By the end of March the House had approved virtually all of the Folsom tax proposals, and a few days later the Senate Finance Committee voted out large portions of the package except the corporate franchise tax, which was indefinitely postponed. The insurance premium tax was cut, and the liquor tax was increased over what the governor wanted. If it had been his first term, Folsom might have regarded this as a triumph—indeed, that is how it was treated by the press in 1955—but his standards were higher now. The next day he attacked the "fistful of senators from a fistful of counties" who were attempting to bottle up the corporate franchise tax bill and who had blocked progress in the legislature "down through the generations." These "despots would sentence 50,000 aged to rag picking and the other half to the garbage can. What for? To glorify themselves before the paragons of privilege, hoping to be petted on the head like a waggy tail dog."[30]

Folsom followed his tirade with a resolution introduced by Senator Garet Van Antwerp III to stack the Finance and Taxation Committee with enough additional members to take control. This proposal was greeted by a thirteen-hour filibuster on April 6 and ten more hours the next day. Folsom responded with a televised appeal to the electorate on public television urging them to pressure their senators to break the filibuster.[31]

Meanwhile, Broughton Lamberth suggested that if conservatives would allow the franchise tax to be voted on in the Senate, the administration would drop the Finance and Taxation Committee stacking plan. They agreed to it, and the Senate approved nearly all of Folsom's old-age package with only modest amendments. Folsom and his legislative leaders had performed brilliantly.

Only a few days after completion of this special session, Folsom called another for a constitutional convention and legislative reapportionment, but conservatives were successful in delaying action on both.[32]

Soon after this abortive special session Folsom became entangled in labor issues. He had pledged during the campaign to repeal the state's right-to-work law, but he was not eager to begin. There was powerful opposition to repeal in the legislature, and, worse yet, many of his legislative supporters and legislative aides were unfriendly to organized labor. Those opponents included Rankin Fite, who was almost rabid on the subject, Senator Harlan Allen of Cullman, who owned a lumber mill which he did not want to see unionized, Broughton Lamberth, O. H. Finney, and Folsom's legal adviser, Murray Battles. Other Folsomites, including Senators Escar Roberts and E. W. Skidmore and Representatives Joe Dawkins, A. K. Callahan, and Ryan deGraffenreid, strongly favored repeal.

As the House began consideration of the right-to-work repeal in May, several major labor disputes broke out at Southern Bell Telephone, the Louisville and Nashville Railroad Company, and a host of textile mills. Issues concerned health and welfare benefits, wages, and union recognition. Violence exploded on all sides. Workers cut telephone wires, burned railroad equipment, and bombed some buildings. In turn, union organizers were confronted by armed thugs in Huntsville, Cullman, and Sylacauga.[33]

Folsom came down on the side of the unions. In Bessemer, when the telephone company asked the Jefferson County police commissioner to escort strike breakers into their facilities past a phalanx of picketers, the commissioner refused. When other Jefferson County officials appealed to Folsom to use the National Guard, he also refused and used the situation as a vehicle to blame the violence on the state's right-to-work laws. He also announced that he intended to seek legislation that would permit state government to take control of the telephone company, resolve the strike, and operate the company in the public interest.[34]

Folsom then introduced another right-to-work repeal bill, but it was buried in the House in a series of delays and stalls led by Speaker Fite and supported by many Folsomites. Folsom was finally forced to abandon the bill "for the sake of harmony."[35] Union supporters Callahan and deGraffenreid responded by introducing an innocuous looking bill pertaining to the relationship between "masters and servants," which the Speaker carelessly referred to the Judiciary Committee. The bill would have partially repealed right to work, a feature accidentally revealed at the end of the committee hearing.[36] The speaker then quickly killed the bill.

Meanwhile, conservatives went on the offensive, introducing a flood of antiunion bills, including Roland Cooper's anti-NAACP bill, which required that group and others organized like it to pay special fees that would have hampered organizational efforts. The bill almost slipped past union supporters (they did not call Cooper the Wily Fox from Wilcox for nothing) until they discovered it would apply to unions as well as civil rights groups. They were able to exempt unions, but they had no objection to hindering the NAACP.[37] An important part of union leaders' strategy in those days centered on a labor-black coalition, but that plan foundered on intensified racial strife.

Civil Rights and Schools

In May the Supreme Court handed down the second *Brown* decision, which called for a case-by-case treatment of school desegregation cases. Alabama segregation leaders were pleasantly surprised by the decision. The *Montgomery Advertiser,* in concert with most other southern newspapers, saw the coming of "generations of litigation," which, though awkward and expensive, was viewed as better than forced school integration.[38] Several vague points in the decision, such as the court's failure to set deadlines, were also seen as working in favor of the segregationists.

Nevertheless, the second *Brown* decision called for integration sooner or later, and Folsom quickly lost control of the Senate and soon thereafter the House as legislators rushed to submit bills that would prove their undying opposition to the Supreme Court action. At the end of June the Senate shouted adoption of a resolution urging Congress to reveal "what part, if any, the Communist Party had in writing the U.S. Supreme Court school decisions." This resolution was the product of a compromise. The original had called for the impeachment of the justices and the election of their successors. Its sponsor, Senator Albert Davis, compared the justices to the rulers of Nazi Germany and the Soviet Union.[39]

The ever-imaginative Sam Engelhardt had a more serious intent when he submitted his School Placement Bill. The basic idea for the bill was offered by a Tuscaloosa high school student when he participated in the American Legion's Youth Legislature.[40] Engelhardt and a group of conservative lawyers turned it into a sophisticated attempt to circumvent Supreme Court decisions. The bill purported to enhance school administrative efficiency by providing a system in which students would be assigned to schools on the basis of school faculty and facilities; the students' abilities, psychological stability, home life, and morals; the social environment; and other factors. The system set up an entire administrative framework for accomplishing the testing and other decision procedures specified in the bill.

Folsom disliked the bill, but he was obliged to move carefully. He and School Superintendent Austin Meadows were sponsoring a $150 million school bond issue and a sales tax increase earmarked for education, and segregationists were holding both bills hostage against passage of sound school segregation measures such as Engelhardt's. News of Engelhardt's proposals had been circulating as early as March. Throughout the months of bargaining, Folsom had responded as diplomatically as he was able. He publicly observed that those "guided by blind prejudice and bigotry" always made more noise than fair-minded people and that he did not find anything "seriously wrong" with the Engelhardt bill.[41]

Of all the issues that arose in 1955 the most complex was educational funding. If funding had been the only problem, it would have been difficult enough, but tax reform and racial issues were also part of it. The schools were in poor shape. Pay levels were close to the worst in the nation, and much improvement was needed in textbook distribution and school lunches. Property taxes, the classic school funding source, were underutilized in Alabama compared to other states.

Since the beginning of his first administration, Folsom had been trying to rationalize the property tax system. It was one of his few interests in administrative reform, and he viewed the school funding situation as a perfect vehicle for improvements in property tax administration. Property tax assessments were erratically executed, and tax breaks for businesses made the system even more inequitable. Tax specialists believed that bringing all property owners to the same level and tightening assessments would net the state tens of millions of dollars. In June administration leaders introduced a bill to that effect. Black Belt plantation owners and Birmingham industrialists were outraged. Senator Van Antwerp and Meadows did not help their cause when they asserted that the higher taxes could be used to improve black schools, which would permit the state to argue in court that schools were indeed separate *and* equal. A Black Belt senator replied, "We don't *want* the black bastards to learn to read and write."[42] Thus property tax reform was terminated.

Folsom then turned to direct administrative reform combined with political pressure on assessors. He tried to establish training programs to make assessments more reliable and accurate, but lack of training was not the problem. Tighter assessments would hurt the elected assessors' political positions back home. Folsom also said that he would end those reform attempts that would cut into fees that assessors received under the current system if they would cooperate to improve assessment equity and accuracy. Even this more realistic approach failed.

The Van Antwerp–Meadows argument that separate and truly equal schools would short-circuit Supreme Court decisions did not fool segregationists. The Supreme Court had said in *Brown* that, among other destructive features of segregation, the experience of being discriminated against was itself damaging, regardless of the quality of the school that one was forced to attend; thus "separate but equal" or even "separate but superior" was no longer legally valid. Segregationists (and Van Antwerp and Meadows) were aware of this, and they continued to delay passage of the funding bills.

Meanwhile, Folsom and Meadows were having trouble agreeing on the next step. Meadows wanted a 1 percent sales tax increase, elimination of sales tax exemptions, and, since the state income tax was a major source of school funding, an end to the deduction of federal income tax payments in the calculation of the Alabama tax together with the introduction of income tax withholding. Folsom agreed about ending sales tax exemptions and federal income tax deductions, but he opposed Meadows's other proposals. Education-oriented legislators introduced Meadows's program. Many of the existing sales tax exemptions benefited agriculture and industry, and legislators representing those interests opposed any changes. They did not simply use standard negative tactics such as the filibuster; they also fired back a barrage of tax proposals to complicate the situation. Legislators, Meadows, and Folsom bargained and bickered through July with no result. Then Representative Joe Goodwyn proposed the so-called Goodwyn Plan, a progressive corporate and individual income tax which contained something for everyone: since most of it would be paid by individuals, corporations could live with it; since it contained a graduated scale, liberals found it acceptable;

since it did not hit agricultural and industrial operations, as elimination of sales tax exemptions would have done, those interests could tolerate it; and since it would provide considerable revenue, education groups were delighted.

Meadows launched a massive lobbying effort, and under his direction five thousand teachers invaded Goat Hill. Under their dour gaze the House and Senate quickly passed slightly different versions of the bill. Following House-Senate conference action, the Senate conservatives who still opposed increased taxes of any sort pounced on the bill, further altering its composition. The House accepted their changes. They created an absurdity that would be rejected by the voters in the referendum that was required. Banks and insurance companies were exempted from the tax, and the legislature was given the power to define and redefine personal income subject to the tax. Meadows and the legislators working with him (many of whom were Folsomites) knew that they had been duped, but they had little choice but to support the mongrelized Goodwyn Plan.

The referendum campaign went badly. Folsom, for whom education was an important but not the highest priority, worked little for it, and, indeed, when Meadows predicted that its defeat would cause schools to close, Folsom publicly disagreed, saying that he could keep them open. What was worse, segregationists argued that racial unrest made it unwise to provide further funding for schools that might have to be eliminated if integration became a reality and that too much was being spent on black schools that were run by a governor who did not believe in segregation.[43] The Goodwyn Plan was voted down by an overwhelming margin, as were nineteen other constitutional amendments; only the one amendment that Folsom opposed passed.

A month later Folsom called a special legislative session for January 1956 to consider school funding and the authorization of a constitutional convention. When the session began, school officials warned that without additional funds the schools would be closed in March. Neither Folsom nor the legislators were moved by these dire predictions, and Folsom denied their validity as he called for a study of school financing by a twelve-person committee of experts, a proposal which was rejected by the House. The behavior of the governor and the legislators suggests that they had passed the Goodwyn bill simply to satisfy pressure from school groups, while knowing that the voters would kill it.

Meanwhile, in the summer of 1955, as the legislature had effectively stalled the funding bills, support for the Engelhardt School Placement Bill had grown—and had in fact become an avalanche. Returning to an old theme and trying to avoid an argument over race, Folsom labeled the bill a piece of class discrimination. "I wouldn't want to sign a bill that would let rich folks send their kids all to one school and the poor folks to another school."[44] But while believing in the basic truth that segregation was more a class issue than a racial one, he seemed to sense that he should say more. "I just never did get all excited about our colored brothers. We have had them here for 300 years and we will have them for another 300 years. I have found them to be good citizens and if they had been making a living for me like they have for the Black Belt, I'd be proud of them instead of kicking them and cursing them all the time."[45]

The placement bill, which slipped effortlessly through the Senate, ran into trouble in the House. The speaker demonstrated that he could play the hostage game as effectively as any by referring the Senate bill to the Committee on Elections, chaired by Folsomite James Branyan of Fayette. Simultaneously, he refused to allow debate on the House version of the placement bill. An attempt to force floor debate failed because it did not attain the necessary four-fifths, but the vote showed that Folsom's support was eroding among the representatives from outside North Alabama. Joe Dawkins, who led the administration's fight, justified the vote to block Engelhardt's bill by citing the Senate's blockage of administration bills not on direct opposition to segregation.[46] Finally, an agreement was reached that freed both placement bills, and the House quickly passed its version of the bill by 97–3. The Senate, concerned about NAACP legal probes in Macon County, quickly passed the House version by an overwhelming majority.[47] Folsom did not veto it, but he refused to sign it; a veto would have been easily overridden. With few exceptions, this was to be his pattern throughout the second administration. Segregation bills passed by a slender margin or containing some other weakness were vetoed. Others were pocket vetoed. The rest became law without his signature.

Immediately after his defeat on the School Placement Bill Folsom again sought approval for his beloved constitutional convention, and again his proposal was unceremoniously crushed by the legislature.[48] He was defeated yet another time when his veto of a bill which imposed heavy license fees for NAACP memberships in Wilcox County was overridden; however, Folsom's supporters had blocked the original bill, which had statewide application. His bill to permit women to serve on juries was killed in the Senate after having passed the House.[49] Likewise, his poll tax elimination bill was defeated, and his public defender program never left committee.

There were a few oases in this dreary landscape. Three minutes before the end of the session the governor pocket vetoed Engelhardt's bill allowing the Macon and Wilcox County boards of education to fire any teacher who advocated or belonged to an organization that favored integration.[50] More significantly, Folsom's legislative leaders managed temporarily to stop Boutwell's "freedom of choice" plan, which had germinated in the senator's interim school segregation committee. This bill was designed to replace Engelhardt's School Placement Act should it fall under federal court attack. Boutwell's measure contained a double trigger. The first, the tripartite school system of white schools, black schools, and integrated schools, as outlined in the committee's report, would be activated in the event that the School Placement Act were struck down, and the second would consist of nothing less than the eradication of the public school system if the tripartite school system were in turn struck down. The second trigger would be sprung partly by excising all references to "segregation" and "public" schools from the constitution.[51] In effect, the legislature would have created a system for public funding of "private" schools.

Boutwell's radical plan was not as popular as Engelhardt's placement bill. Many felt that the Supreme Court would slap it aside effortlessly. Most school officials, including some in the Black Belt, opposed it because their jobs might be lost under the totally unknown new system. And some segregationists were unhappy with the integrated third school, fearing that such an institution would ultimately serve as a model for the entire system. The latter were assured informally that no integrated third schools were really contemplated.[52] Nevertheless, conservative doubts, combined with Folsomite delaying tactics, stalled Boutwell's efforts to secure his bill's passage.

Other Legislation

Folsom's legislative objectives in 1955 were extraordinarily ambitious. He tried to broaden representation on the State Board of Health, which was monopolized by physicians; make disbarment decisions appealable to the courts (they began and ended with the Bar Association); create a public defender system (opposed by lawyers who made fees from taking indigents' cases); destroy the local (county) option to be wet or dry; change the court to which Public Service Commission decisions were appealed from Walter B. Jones's First Circuit Court (consistently proutility) to Rowan Bone's Court of Appeals; allow women to serve on juries; abolish the poll tax; give eighteen-year-olds the vote; and relax barriers against black voting. The governor was defeated in these and many similar measures, but he occasionally won. His appropriations bills, which featured generous increases for health and welfare programs, were passed. The Industrial Development Commission, which he advocated and which was one of the few of his programs enthusiastically endorsed by business, whizzed through. And his legislative leaders succeeded in repealing a Persons administration statute that had taken control of the state docks from the governor.

Folsom's attempts to limit the authority of physicians and attorneys in areas that they believed to be their private preserves but which had important implications for the public were nothing new. For example, in his first term Folsom discussed with a representative the appointment of a particular dentist to the State Medical Board. The legislator objected that the man in question was not a member of the Dental Society, to which Folsom replied, "That's exactly the kind of man we want."[53]

His objections to doctors' monopolizing public policy on health paled beside his endless struggles against the legal profession. He was most concerned with attorneys who served in the legislature while continuing their practices. In his view, this was more than a serious conflict of interest with lawyer-legislators voting on behalf of clients instead of constituents. To him it represented a violation of the principle of separation of powers because lawyers, as officers of the court and as legislators, were serving in two branches of government simultaneously. "There are three branches of government just like a three-legged stool I used to carry around."[54]

The range and detail of his interests in the 1955 session were matched by the care he took in lobbying legislators. His skilled leaders facilitated his efforts, but, despite his heavy drinking, he gave close personal attention to legislative matters through much of the session. One highly experienced merit system employee recalled that "some committee chairmen became so dependent on the governor that they wouldn't even call a meeting unless they first checked with him."[55]

While Folsom's command of legislative affairs in 1955 impressed even hardened foes, his comprehension of public policy was sometimes amazingly naive. Once Jake Jordon, the chief budget officer in the Department of Finance, was awakened at five in the morning with a call from the governor's mansion. "Get over here, Mr. Budget Officer," Folsom commanded. Jordon found Folsom clad only in long underwear, already drunk. The only other person there was Pitt Tyson Manor, a political manipulator skilled in ingratiating himself with influentials in the state and federal government. Folsom told Jordon, "The education problem—I've got it licked. I know how we can deal with it." Jordon then dutifully and reluctantly asked what the solution might be. Folsom replied, "We are going to double the tax on coal and iron ore, and that will take care of it." Jordon, whose knowledge of the state's tax system was legendary, calculated that Folsom's plan would net an additional six hundred thousand dollars per year, a fraction of the millions of dollars needed to upgrade the educational system. After having informed Folsom of this fact, he asked where the governor had gotten the idea. Folsom replied, "Oh, Pitt Manor told me." As they left the mansion together, Jordon asked Manor why he had so badly misled the governor, to which Manor replied, "Oh, he was bugging me about the education thing, and I just told him the first thing that came to my mind." Such was the quality of advice Folsom often took.

Civil Rights

The year 1955 was a time of intense organizational action by blacks who were searching for politically realistic tactics with which to fight for their rights. The group in Montgomery was probably as active as any in the nation. Alabama State University, nearby Tuskegee Institute, unions, businesses, and churches had attracted leaders of impressive talent and political sensitivity. In surveying areas where a battle might be waged, they decided to avoid education because they did not want to disrupt important court cases and because they feared that the legislature would close down the public school system. A protest against employment discrimination in downtown stores was another possibility, but it was decided that too many blacks were vulnerable to economic counterattack. They finally settled on the Montgomery bus system. It was ideal because approximately 70 percent of its twenty-five thousand patrons were black, and so the system depended on them to a degree that few other businesses did. The buses were segregated. When both races rode on the same bus, blacks had to sit in the back, whites in front. If all seats were filled and a white got on, blacks in the row closest to the front had to relinquish their seats if other seats in the black section were available. This was one of segregation's most galling manifestations, and it was often made worse by the all-white bus drivers (another issue), who by law possessed the authority of city police officers and who sometimes abused their power, humiliating their helpless black passengers.

Foremost among the Montgomery-area black leaders was the brilliant political strategist E. D. Nixon, the tall, handsome president of the union of sleeping car porters, NAACP executive, and head of the Montgomery Democratic Progressive Association. Nixon was portrayed by the *Montgomery Advertiser,* harking back to its postbellum style, as the local "NAACP Mau Mau chief." For some time Nixon had been casting about for a suitable vehicle for a protest. Three cases involving bus-related arrests had caught his attention, but he found that the subjects lacked the fortitude or the pristine personal background necessary to withstand the harassment and publicity that would be sure to follow an organized protest.[56] On December 1, 1955, Mrs. Rosa Parks refused an order by a driver to relinquish her seat to whites who had just boarded. After she had been bailed out and was being driven home by Nixon and liberal white political leader and attorney Clifford Durr, Nixon explained what he had in mind for her and she agreed to cooperate with him.[57] The next day Nixon began organizing a boycott of the bus system. Other black leaders sprang into action, printing and distributing leaflets and organizing alternative transportation for boycotters. Martin Luther King, Jr., who had arrived in Montgomery only a year before, did not participate at first, but he joined soon thereafter.[58]

The boycott was a stunning success, with approximately 90 percent of the normal black passengers refusing to ride. Instead, they walked, rode taxi cabs pressed into service by boycott leaders, hitchhiked, or convinced white employers to give them transportation. Virtually the only blacks to ride city buses were the elderly. In a series of organizational sessions the decision was made to continue the boycott; a name, the Montgomery Improvement Association (MIA), was selected for the boycott organization; a more efficient transportation system for former bus riders was developed; money raising was started; and a rally was organized. The rally, which attracted well over four thousand people, frightened many whites with its size, intensity of emotion, and tight organization.[59] The main speaker at this rally was Martin Luther King, Jr., in his public debut as the MIA leader.

Rally speakers outlined the MIA's demands: first, a new seating system that would not require blacks to vacate seats for whites; second, some guarantee of courteous treatment by drivers; and, third, hiring of blacks as drivers. The demands were, by today's standards, unbelievably moderate. They were well within the legal and social framework of segregation except, perhaps, in the fact that blacks were making demands at all.[60]

As so many segregationists after them would do, members of the City of Montgomery Commission (the equivalent of city councilmen) unwittingly cooperated with black leaders by providing reporters with a series of spectacles that reinforced some of the worst stereotypes of southern life. The city's first mistake was to use an obscure labor union control statute to indict King and other boycott leaders. The press gave this event wide coverage, and contributions to the financially pressed MIA poured in.

Negotiations between MIA leaders, city officials, and bus company executives began on December 8, and neither side budged. Talks continued through January with no progress.[61] Late that month the Montgomery Commission ordered city police to harass their opponents by arresting "hitchhikers" and "loiterers," that is, blacks waiting for MIA transportation, and enforcing even minor traffic violations by MIA drivers. Threats were voiced that white employers would begin firing employees participating in the boycott.[62] The police harassment began immediately. King was caught driving 35 miles per hour in a 25 zone; he was arrested, fingerprinted, and released on bond. However, the MIA was able to pay the fines for King and other drivers, and the arrests produced nationwide publicity for the boycott.

Folsom's role in the boycott is subject to some debate. According to Barnard, the governor "encouraged . . . Martin Luther King to broaden his demands of the bus boycott."[63] Folsom later denied this. His version of events was that he merely provided strategic advice to King based on his reading of a study of Mahatma Gandhi. "Whatever you do, if you haven't read that book, you go read it. Whatever you do, don't fight back. They'll put you in jail or whatever, but don't you fight back." Gould Beech had given Folsom a book about Gandhi (probably Jawaharlal Nehru's *Nehru on Gandhi*) some years earlier. Of course, by 1956 King had already studied Gandhi's passive-resistance tactics.[64] Folsom stated categorically that he did not encourage King to broaden his demands, because he was afraid that things were already moving too rapidly.[65] In addition to "advising" King, Folsom talked to city officials by telephone, trying to convince them to compromise, but it did no good.

The boycott brought a visit from New York Congressman Adam Clayton Powell, and his impending arrival at the Montgomery airport drew KKK protesters. Folsom's driver, Winston Craig, informed the governor of this situation, and Folsom ordered Craig to short-circuit potential violence by meeting Powell in the governor's best limousine. Folsom shrugged off warnings that he would be damaged politically by this act, and he compounded it by entertaining Powell in the governor's mansion.[66] They talked for half an hour over drinks, and as the controversial black leader prepared to leave, he asked Folsom, "How far can I go in talking about this?" Folsom responded, "As far as you want." Powell then announced to the press, "I just had a drink with the Governor. I doubt if I could have done that with the governor of my own state."[67] Over the years this apparently simple event took on enormous symbolic importance and was credited with contributing heavily to Folsom's defeat in his bid for a third term in 1962.[68]

Folsom's meeting with Powell is believed by some to have caused a breach between the governor and George Wallace.[69] This version of events is incorrect. As far as Folsom was concerned, the break began far earlier than that and far earlier than even Wallace suspected. It began in 1947, when Wallace voted for the self-starter. Even though Wallace supported most other Folsom administration programs, Folsom never again regarded Wallace as anything but an opportunist whom he could sometimes use. He took advantage of Wallace's growing popularity and impressive public-speaking and speech-writing abilities in the 1954 campaign, and of course Wallace benefited from the exposure that speaking on Folsom's behalf provided him. After the 1954 victory Folsom ignored Wallace when he asked for several little things—not for himself but for his brothers. Wallace could not understand why he was being snubbed when he was entitled to far more patronage than he was requesting. Neither he nor anyone else was told the reason.[70]

Despite his slipping popularity and the hardening of public attitudes toward political reform reinforced by *Brown* and racial turmoil, Folsom's call for a January 1956 special session emphasized the need to initiate a constitutional convention primarily for the purpose of reapportionment (this was the same session that considered education funding). None of Folsom's legislative leaders believed that a constitutional convention had the slightest chance of being approved, and Representatives George Hawkins and Joe Dawkins said as much on a television interview at the beginning of the session. During hearings on the measure before the House Rules Committee, Speaker Fite, who was also chairman of the committee, went home.

Folsom was beginning to resemble a boxer in one of the last rounds, worn and almost beaten but swinging back blindly, his gloves whistling through the air, hitting home only when his opponent becomes incautious. Hugh Sparrow suggested that Folsom wanted the session to end a failure so that he could use the defeat of his programs as an issue in a 1962 reelection campaign.[71] Identical speculation had occurred throughout Folsom's first term. Although some of this was little more than propaganda, there was probably some truth to it. Nevertheless, much of it reflected a common misunderstanding of the powerful ideological motivations that drove Folsom.

The day after Sparrow's column appeared, Folsom renewed the seemingly hopeless reapportionment fight. He issued a statement accusing the legislature of having "failed to keep its oath for half a century" in not bringing about reapportionment every ten years.[72] The day after that statement, over Albert Boutwell's opposition, the Senate Rules Committee passed the administration's constitutional convention bill. The bill was defeated on the Senate floor by 18–15, a loss, but a surprisingly strong proadministration vote given the times. It had taken the Black Belt–Birmingham coalition more than two weeks to defeat the constitutional convention this time; Folsom was still swinging and still dangerous even when his legislative leaders had lost their enthusiasm.

During the session the legislature passed a new batch of segregation bills. It was as if it could defeat the federal government by sheer volume of legislation. Included in this collection was the so-called nullification resolution, declaring the Supreme Court rulings "null, void, and of no effect" in Alabama. During a press conference Folsom observed that "all this clap-trap about the resolution is just like a hound dog baying at the moon and claiming its got the moon treed." He described it as "hogwash . . . a two-bit resolution."[73] Then he added, with elephantine coyness, that he would applaud it if it were passed by a constitutional convention. Noting the irony of a Folsom constitutional convention session ending by "nullifying" Supreme Court constitutional decisions, the *Advertiser* cracked: "Well might Folsom have said as Andrew Jackson said to his artillery in the Battle of New Orleans, 'Elevate them sights a little lower boys.'"[74]

But Folsom had not given up on reapportionment even if he had temporarily surrendered on the calling of a constitutional convention. On February 3, after much complex maneuvering, the House passed the Senate version of a reapportionment constitutional amendment by a vote of 74–23. It was a monstrosity that, among other things, would have drastically increased the size of the legislature so that physical additions to the old capitol building would have been necessary.[75] The bill was passed by a Black Belt–administration coalition. This was a way for the Black Belters to claim that they had complied with the constitution's requirement to reapportion. It was less clear what Folsom gained, but he was delighted with the result. "I'm mighty happy," he told reporters. "I've been working for this so long that now that it's passed I feel like I'm ready to retire. I'm gonna take one long vacation for about two weeks and then I'm going to take the stump for this bill. If it hadn't been for reapportionment, I never would have run for governor. And if it hadn't been for this issue, I'd never have been elected."[76] The voters defeated the proposal in November.

While all this was happening, racial tensions worsened. In January 1956 violence hit in Montgomery with the bombing of the homes of King and Nixon. Luckily, no one was seriously injured, but all of King's considerable oratorical skills were required to forestall violent retaliation.[77]

On February 1, Fred Gray, a black lawyer, recognizing that the Parks case would require many months or even years to wend its way from state to federal courts, fired another salvo with a new case (*Browder* v. *Gray*) concerning discrimination on Montgomery buses designed to go directly into the federal courts. The Montgomery city fathers retaliated by obtaining a grand jury indictment against Gray for "unlawful appearance as an attorney," a charge which could have ended in Gray's disbarment. This charge arose because one of the women in the suit had dropped out, telling reporters that she had been tricked into participating. This was why E. D. Nixon had been so careful in his selection of Rosa Parks as the pivot for the boycott. The indictment was quickly declared invalid for technical reasons.

Later in February, using a 1921 antiboycott law, a Montgomery County grand jury indicted eighty-nine bus boycott participants, all of whom were arrested and released on three hundred dollars bond each. Sometime later King realized that they should have gone to jail rather than pay the bond, an act that would have dramatized the situation considerably. Nevertheless, the mass arrests brought the best national news coverage to that point, yet more contributions, and the assistance of the national NAACP organization and the American Civil Liberties Union.

Meanwhile, Pollie Ann Myers of Birmingham and Autherine Lucy of Black Belt Marengo County had become engaged in legal actions concerning the University of Alabama. A committee of Birmingham blacks had been searching for black students to attempt enrollment at the university. Promised financial support from the committee, the two women sought graduate school admission, and they were accepted, but when university administrators discovered that the prospective students were black, they reversed themselves.[78] Myers and Lucy filed suit, and hearings began in June 1955. Judge Hobart Grooms ruled in their behalf, and the university appealed, but in October 1955 it lost again. The women attempted to register for the winter term. Myers was refused on vague charges concerning her "conduct and marital status." Lucy persisted through registration, only to be informed that she would be denied a dormitory room and the right to eat in the cafeteria, but she was nevertheless permitted to enroll for graduate study.

The university began to rumble like a volcano about to erupt. Crosses were burned, and motels and hotels began to fill with out-of-town and out-of-state visitors. Folsom selected this crucial time to take a fishing trip to Florida, confident that the state highway patrol could deal with any trouble that might develop. The historian Thomas Gilliam speculates that his escape was due to intense pressure being brought to bear by segregationists, especially after the Adam Clayton Powell incident, and, in fact, beginning around January 1956 he had begun to backpedal on racial issues. He was quoted as saying that he did not intend to "force black children to go to school with white children or vice versa," a sarcastic reversal on normal segregationist sentiments.[79] About the fishing trip he later said: "I thought nothing of it. I made the mistake of not calling out the troops or the military police at least. It wasn't a matter of fear—I just wanted them to get the racism off their chest."[80]

On Friday, Saturday, and Sunday nights just before classes began white demonstrators numbering approximately one thousand snaked around the campus and into town chanting "Keep 'Bama white" and "Hey, hey, ho, ho, Autherine gotta go," throwing rocks and firecrackers, battering automobiles driven by blacks, and harassing President Oliver Carmichael at his home.[81] Monday began the first full week of classes. It was a frightening, violent day for which university officials, city police, and the state highway patrol were almost completely unprepared despite the three nights of violence. Mobs at times numbering two thousand people, many unconnected with the university and encouraged by KKK and White Citizens' Council members, succeeded in driving Lucy from the campus.

Folsom later offered a variety of excuses for his inaction that weekend—inaction which he would come to regard as the most serious mistake of his career. Many wondered why, upon hearing news of the first or second or third riot, he had not broken short his trip and returned. The most likely answer, if this trip followed the pattern of so many others in this time of his life, is that he was so drunk that he was not capable of comprehending news even if it were conveyed to him accurately. One of his close assistants said, "Jim got drunk and went off to Florida." The same person claimed that during this period Folsom was consuming well over a fifth of bourbon per day.

J. Bruce Henderson was delighted with the students' actions. In a February 9, 1956, letter to Gessner McCorvey (who served on the University of Alabama board) he wrote: "There is something magnificent about the reactions and actions of youth. They may be wrong in 'form' and in the 'method' of protest but their actions are usually based on a fundamental and true concept of justice."[82]

The university board surveyed the situation and decided that Lucy had to be temporarily suspended for her safety and that of other students and faculty. Both houses of the legislature unanimously endorsed the suspension, and nearly every major newspaper except the *Tuscaloosa News* did so as well.

The Autherine Lucy case slowly came to a halt. In a press conference and later in a lawsuit her lawyers charged that the university board and administration had in effect encouraged the demonstrations so that they could justify Lucy's suspension. This was the mistake the hostile board had been waiting for. After brief courtroom sparring between Lucy's and the university's attorneys, the board, with board president Hill Ferguson abstaining and Folsom and Austin Meadows absent, expelled her, citing her "false, defamatory, impertinent, and scandalous" charges as the reason.[83] Legal action followed, but the board's decision held, and blacks were not permitted to enter the university until they filed past Governor George C. Wallace seven years later.

Historians agree that the Lucy affair strengthened the segregationist cause in Alabama and throughout the South.[84] One Alabama journalist who supports this view noted that "drinking, among other things, led to a great neglect of government [by Folsom]. His greatest failure was at the University of Alabama. If he had been there and told the KKK that if they appeared he would split their heads and had the National Guard there, the history of the state and indeed the history of the entire South might have been different. The University of Alabama thing was the second or the first big confrontation—Little Rock is the other. But Folsom allowed the mob to win."[85]

The Segregationist Forces

Objectively, things seemed to be going extremely well for segregationists. But beneath the surface, tensions among them were growing. Two days before J. Bruce Henderson wrote his euphoric February 9 letter to Mc-

Corvey he sent the following message to his friend Wallace Malone: "There are five corporations in Alabama that are so big and control so many of the raw materials and so much of the big banking and big credit in Alabama that they can absolutely and completely control the political policies of about 90% of the really big corporations in Alabama. For business reasons these five corporations have become the creatures of Lister Hill, the New Deal and Labor Racketeers. They have certainly prospered by the surrender."[86]

The lines of stress between Black Belt and urban Bosses (and even within Black Belt ranks) were becoming more severe with each passing month. In 1956, after a period of recession, Alabama's industrial production and manufacturing capacity were increasing rapidly, and business leaders wanted those developments to continue. Much future expansion depended on policy decisions to be made in Washington, D.C., and business decisions to be made all over the world. Racial discord, with its implications for labor problems, made the state look bad. Businessmen were also concerned with offshore oil, federal labor laws, federally supported nuclear power development and highway construction, farm housing programs, and many other similar matters. According to Gilliam, men like Henderson "could not comprehend how sensitive businessmen were to the public image of the South. A business and capital exodus that had been running from North to South might well be reversed if racial tensions increased or if violence flared. There were growing suspicions that the race crisis had already affected business."[87]

Yet another important development in this middle 1955-early 1956 period was the growth of a new set of organizations called the White Citizens' Councils. They began in Indianola, Mississippi, with a July 1954 meeting of one hundred planters, doctors, bankers, storekeepers, and the like, who were disturbed over the *Brown* decision. An organization of die-hard racists who were by and large uncomfortable with the violence and craziness associated with the Klan, the councils wanted respectability, although some members were not above encouraging violent behavior in others as they did in Tuscaloosa. In the first few months after the meeting in Indianola growth was slow, but by October the first council outside Mississippi was formed in Selma, Alabama.[88] Council growth accelerated in 1955 as new chapters sprang up all over the South. In Alabama membership figures were estimated at between twelve thousand and sixty thousand. Sam Engelhardt was selected to head the state council. Although they foreswore violence, the councils represented a serious threat to blacks. The Selma organization quickly set about screening blacks, searching for indications that they favored integration, and those who did were subjected to harsh economic sanctions—jobs were lost, credit was dried up, and renters were ejected. These tactics were soon employed by other councils throughout the state.

A councils rally was held in Montgomery in February 1956 during the bus boycott and just after the Autherine Lucy riots. At the rally, attended by many of the South's most prominent leaders, someone yelled repeatedly, "Where's Jim?" Jim wanted no part of it. He was in Birmingham attending a mental health conference.[89] The next day, when reporters asked Folsom if he approved of the councils, he replied, "I'm for white councils and black councils and red councils and yellow councils and brown councils, if there are any." And he added, "Nothing built on hate can exist for any length of time in a Christian democracy. I hope there's none of the councils who have based their beliefs on hate."[90]

Through March and April, while Folsom never approached being drawn into the segregationist frenzy swirling about the state, it was difficult to track his exact position. One reason was that he was engaged in a Democratic party primary campaign in which delegates to the national convention would be selected. One of his opponents was Representative Charles McKay, author of the nullification resolution. Folsom wanted to win the primary, which meant that he had to curb his civil libertarian tendencies, but he also had to say something negative about his opponent's handiwork. He hated the nullification resolution anyway, and so he relied on what for him was becoming a standby on matters concerning segregation, sarcasm. "A lot of people have been howling and raising sand about the situation and wanting to disobey the Supreme Court, so I figured they would be all for a [constitutional] convention. In such a convention they can even secede from the union, they can authorize me to call out the National Guard to go against the Federal troops. . . . They could authorize me to take over Maxwell [U.S. Air Force] Field, and I hope it could be done without firing a shot. You know, in the Civil War we took over an armory without firing a shot." Then he became more serious. "I got the hell beat out of me in 1948 in my race for delegate because I wouldn't holler 'nigger, nigger, nigger.' Put that in quotes boys, because I always refer to them as Negroes."[91] Folsom would later say that he was using the segregation issue to obtain a constitutional convention, while his opponents were using it to scare poor whites.

Sometimes on the stump his sarcasm would become mild equivocation, as it did when he maintained that since up to that point the State of Alabama had not been made party to a school integration suit (although the University of Alabama had), all the attention given to segregation in the legislature was a waste of time and effort. "Why had Alabama not been the target for such suits?" he asked his audiences. Because he had kept in close touch with the Negro leaders who had caused so much trouble elsewhere, he would answer, thus providing an indirect justification for the Adam Clayton Powell incident. Sometimes he addressed the Powell matter directly. His explanation hinged on two points: first, that he was trying to convince Powell to use his influence to see that no integration lawsuits were filed in Alabama; and, second, that Powell was Winston Craig's guest, not his.[92]

In the same speeches he often launched into slashing attacks on the White Citizens' Council, referring to it as that "nigger-hollering organization" and tying it to the Dixiecrats: "It's the same issues, the same faces, and they are singing the same song as they did in 1948 when they denied you the right to vote for the president of the United States. And anybody who would deny you that right will advocate mob rule and do anything else under the sun. The funny part about it is that most of these fellows doing all the hollering live with the Negroes, work with the Negroes and get their living made by the Negroes. . . . And most of them inherited those big plantations where they used to have slaves, and a lot of them wish they had slaves on them now."[93] But then one week after this speech Folsom said in response to questions from the Citizens' Councils: "I was and am for segregation."[94] In the middle of April he signed his first two segregation bills, one a mild version of Boutwell's freedom of choice plan which omitted the feature that would have eliminated the public school system, the other a bill to insure segregation of public parks.[95]

Despite his gestures in favor of segregation, Folsom and virtually every member of his slate were defeated.[96] It was "the most perfect race" he ever ran, Folsom declared a few days later. "I asked nobody to vote for me and nobody nearly 'bout did."[97] He wired a wry proposal to a fellow loser: "If anyone rumors we stole it, let's deny it to the bitter end."

Turmoil in the Councils

Sam Engelhardt constantly stressed that council actions were always legal and peaceful, and he was genuinely concerned about violent elements within the movement, even though the suffering he and his organization inflicted via economic pressure on individuals who were simply exercising freedom of speech was massive. Furthermore, by their extreme statements he and other respected community leaders seemed to encourage unstable individuals who were incapable of appreciating where a racist diatribe ended and a call to arms began. The councils fell more and more under the influence of vicious, anti-Semitic, anti-Catholic bigots who frightened Engelhardt and other establishment figures. A taste of what was to come occurred in April 1956 when six men attacked black musician Nat King Cole as he performed before a segregated audience in Birmingham. Luckily, they were removed before they could do him permanent injury. The incident received nationwide attention, and Engelhardt denounced the attack.[98] All the state's major newspapers joined Engelhardt's denunciation and bemoaned the fact that some of the councils were becoming little different from KKK klaverns.[99]

The relationship between the extremist and "moderate" wings of the councils remained more or less stable until President Eisenhower sent federal troops to enforce court-ordered school desegregation at Central High School in Little Rock, Arkansas, in September 1957. The South was more deeply shocked by this event than any other in the entire civil rights period. Klan violence exploded throughout the region. There were bombings, beatings, vandalism, kidnappings, castrations, and murder—much of it random with victims chosen merely because they were black. Alabama's political leadership became genuinely alarmed, and many, like Engelhardt, eased out of the councils. They wanted the violence and ugliness to stop. It encouraged federal civil rights suits and direct federal action, and it discouraged new businesses from locating in the state.

A Problem in the Folsom Camp

Folsomites were also having difficulties, but of another kind entirely—Folsom had become a full-fledged alcoholic. He often started drinking as soon as he arose and was deeply intoxicated by eight o'clock in the morning. He would continue drinking constantly through the rest of the day as long as he was conscious. On some occasions he and cronies, many of whom encouraged his drinking because it made him less alert and easier to hoodwink, would spend two or three days in a deserted cabin drinking constantly. These affairs were usually billed as fishing or hunting trips. He ate so little during these binges (although at this point it was difficult to distinguish between routine drinking and a binge) that a physician would administer vitamin injections. In the first two years of his second term he was able to moderate his drinking somewhat during legislative sessions. A Jefferson County House member said: "Folsom was at the Capitol working actively, often in the legislative chambers themselves on nearly every legislative day. . . . In the last two years of his second administration [Ralph] Hammond tended to run administrative affairs, but Folsom was active in the legislature even then. He was a very effective 'legislator.'"[100]

A distinction between the two halves of his second term is commonly made. Nearly everyone agrees that alcohol virtually paralyzed him in the second half. One of his House leaders, probably George Hawkins, is quoted as saying, "You'd have to catch him before breakfast if you wanted to talk to him about anything. . . . Many's the time I've driven like hell toward the mansion with the light just gettin' gray, tryin' to beat the dawn there, know-in' that the lighter it got the further away Big Jim was driftin'—because if you didn't get to the mansion before the sun did, he was gone."[101] Once Folsom was planning to call a special session, and he asked the League of Municipalities and other groups with which he was on good terms to prepare legislation they wanted passed. Then he "drifted away," forgot to call the session, and lost interest; it never was called.

Nevertheless, some legislators saw little of the governor's drinking even well into the second term. "I seldom saw him drunk in the legislature," said one North Alabama House member, who added that Folsom had a great memory for names, evidence that he could effectively manage an aspect of politics that even the most sober politicians find difficult.[102] Another North Alabama senator recalled, "Folsom did very little drinking in legislative sessions—I only saw him really drunk once when he fired ____. He drank mainly at night. I could go in to see him any time I wanted to."[103]

The Folsom children did not see him drunk during this time. They saw only social drinking at functions in the mansion. Their father kept the long but regular hours of a typical executive, seeing his family for short periods each day but keeping abreast of their activities. During this period he was often up well before dawn driving to Lowndes County, where he would fish for a short time and then return to the mansion for breakfast.

Some later suggested that as civil rights pressures increased and he recognized that his dreams of accomplishing major reforms were crushed with the backlash, Folsom turned to alcohol for escape. Others believed that Ross Clark's suicide caused the great increase in his drinking during his second term. An aide reported that after Clark's suicide "Folsom was never the same man. He was hardly ever in the office."[104] Soon after Clark's death Folsom informed O. H. Finney that he was going to call a special session on reapportionment and that he wanted Finney to set up appointments with legislators, one every fifteen minutes. The first, Woodrow Albee, arrived promptly at 8:00 A.M., but Folsom was not there. The second, third, and fourth legislators arrived, but Folsom had still not made it to the office. Fred Folsom called Winston Craig and was told that the governor had just left in an airplane for some unknown destination.[105]

Folsom's abuse of state airplanes earned him frequent media censure, although, legally, Alabama governors and their families did have use of those planes. Trips to football games throughout the South were common, as were such jaunts as shopping trips to Dallas department stores. Folsom's misuse of state aircraft was even worse than suggested by newspaper accounts. Airplanes, like alcohol, were a means of escape, and he often combined the two. Legislators dreaded invitations to fly with him because they never knew where they would end up or how long the trip would take. One state senator who was in Washington, D.C., with Folsom had to use all his considerable powers of persuasion to avoid being taken on a side trip to Argentina as he and the governor flew back to Montgomery. Legislators learned to evade flying invitations, but Folsom countered those tactics by making sure that the invitations were received. Legislators would return home in the evening to find highway patrolmen waiting in their front yards informing them that the governor wanted them at the mansion at dawn or before dawn the next day. They were sometimes told to prepare for a trip, sometimes not.

Folsom's National Guard pilots suffered even more than the legislators. He was infamous among the crews for his changes of destination in mid-flight. Once, on his way to California, he decided that Alaska would be more interesting. After several hours of flight in that direction and considerable drinking, he suddenly changed the destination to Mexico. At this point the crew revolted and headed back to Montgomery, which did not really matter because he was too drunk by then to know where he was or in what direction he was headed.

Folsom seemed always to be escaping—no one is sure from what. In the mid-1960s, when his career was a shattered ruin, he would literally drag one of his teenage sons from bed at two or three o'clock in the morning and announce that the two of them were leaving for Florida immediately. Folsom would sprawl across the back seat with a bottle, and his son, barely old enough to drive, would head southward in the dark. Folsom would periodically pass out, awaken an hour later, shout for his son to drive faster, drink more, pass out, awaken again, mumble garbled directions, and so they would make their way.

In Folsom's first term Fuller Kimbrell and a House member went to Folsom to lobby for a road, and after they had finished and Folsom was walking them to the door he declared, "Senator, they're tellin' another lie on me." Kimbrell, who could not imagine anything much worse than the lies and some of the truth that had already been told, responded, "Lord have mercy, Governor, what are they tellin' now?" Folsom drew himself up and said, "They tellin' I stopped drinkin'."[106] In the first term this was still funny. By the second, it was only funny from a distance.

Civil Rights in the Second Regular Legislative Session

Still sending wayward punches whistling through the air, Folsom opened the second regular session of his second term in May 1957 by calling for an end to the poll tax, creation of a constitutional convention, and the rest, but his address to the legislature at its opening was almost apologetic in tone. "I sincerely hope that you will come forth with a reapportionment bill that will give all the people a fair share of the vote in the Legislature of this state. . . . I think the time has come when women should be given the privilege and right to serve on juries." His comments on social welfare had the same wan, limp quality. "I would like to ask your serious consideration of a plan to provide some kind of medical care for indigent patients."[107] And more news stories suggested that he was frequently late for scheduled meetings, an indication that he was rapidly sinking into a near perpetual alcoholic stupor.

Segregationists seemed to be in a stupor of another kind as they blindly introduced still more bills in bewildering variety. There were so many that midway through the session a fourteen-member "super–segregation committee" chaired by Albert Boutwell and composed of members from both legislative chambers was formed to screen out the more peculiar items. Still, a torrent of bills issued forth from the super-committee, many of which became law. Folsom managed to pocket veto a handful of these bills at the end of the session, including one that would have required males to obtain permission from females before sitting beside them on a public conveyance, another to permit voting registrars to destroy records, and yet another to prohibit those blacks living in Tuskegee from forming a city of their own. In killing these and other bills Folsom said plaintively, "I have tried to softpedal racial legislation throughout my administration. All I want is for everyone to get along together without trouble."[108] Why did he behave this way? the *Montgomery Advertiser* asked. "It was," the editor wrote, "a remarkable thing for a politician to do, particularly against the flare of the army's operation in Little Rock. . . . [Folsom] is crude and abandoned in such matters as buying the pension vote, but he has never been a demagogue on the racial issue. Throughout both his administrations there is a conspicuous pattern of sympathy for the colored man's aspirations and a willingness to defy dominant public sentiment to uphold his viewpoint."[109]

One of the many bills that became law in 1957 was a piece of Engelhardt's Macon County "local legislation." Macon County blacks were registering to vote in increasing numbers, and it was becoming more and more difficult to stop them, especially since Engelhardt's council leadership encouraged the Justice Department to focus its attention on the affairs of the county. Engelhardt was feeling increasingly threatened. To keep blacks from taking control of the Tuskegee city government, he introduced what must surely be one of the weirdest gerrymanders ever conceived. He redefined the city boundaries to exclude blacks from voting. Somewhat like the original gerrymander in the early 1800s, Engelhardt's new Tuskegee was dragon shaped and had twenty-eight sides.[110] One Tuskegee white described it by observing that Engelhardt had "slipped up a couple of places and left about 15 or 20 Negro families inside the city limits. I guess he wanted to be fair about it."

Many Macon County whites, especially Tuskegee merchants, opposed the move for fear of retaliation, but officeholders and planters tended to favor it, reasoning that desperate times called for desperate measures.

Alabama blacks had just suffered a grievous setback in the cunningly wrought legal thrust by Attorney General John Patterson that had ended with the NAACP being banned from operating in the state (for eight years, as it turned out); so they proceeded carefully in the Tuskegee fight, launching a two-pronged counterattack. They took Engelhardt's plan to federal court and ultimately won the case. For more immediate effect and to attract news media attention they started a boycott against Tuskegee white merchants which ultimately forced more than two dozen of them out of business.[111]

Fearing that his redistricting bill would be struck down by the courts, the resourceful Engelhardt attempted to abolish Macon County by having it absorbed into adjoining counties, thus diluting Macon County black strength. However, his bill to that effect had to be approved by the adjoining counties, and none of them wanted any part of Macon County.[112] Folsom's opinion of this bill surprised no one. "If we are going to have something like that, then I think the other 13 counties should have the same opportunity, and we can do that by having a constitutional convention."[113]

As segregation bills of every shape and form flew in all directions through the legislative halls, North Alabama Senator Smith Dyar wrote a simple resolution condemning racial violence. His fellow senators were dumbfounded, and the bill disappeared in the Rules Committee, never to be seen again.

Other Legislation

As the 1957 legislative session began, observers saw education funding as the issue most likely to spark controversy and discord.[114] Austin Meadows was requesting large new increases which could not be met without tax increases, but Folsom, trying to implant in people's minds an image of fiscal conservatism for the 1962 election, declared himself opposed to any tax increases.

Probably the legislation that generated the strongest passion among Folsomites was Senator Joe Calvin's bill that would have required competitive bids on all state purchases and contracts exceeding five hundred dollars. The bill would have sharply reduced the governor's flexibility in awarding patronage. The first half of the session revolved around this issue. Administration forces used two time-honored devices to defeat it: misdirection and the filibuster. The misdirection was Folsom's widely publicized "plan" to sign an executive order requiring essentially what the Calvin bill contained, but lacking the full force of law. Then Representative Emmett Oden, an administration stalwart, offered his own mainly cosmetic bid bill; to his surprise, supporters of competitive bidding endorsed his bill, and he was forced to oppose his own legislation.[115]

Simultaneously, filibusters in both chambers entangled everything from almost the first day of the session to the last. The occurrences in the Senate on June 18 were typical. Seven administration senators (Broughton Lamberth, Richmond Flowers, Harlan Allen, Neil Metcalf, E. L. Roberts, Garet Van Antwerp, and M. H. Moses) were merrily tying the Senate into knots by speaking in two-hour shifts. On this occasion the orations concerned a motion from the Senate Rules Committee, which had reported out a special order calendar that had two reapportionment bills at the top. Competitive bid supporters had offered an amendment which replaced the first reapportionment bill with their bid bill. The Folsomites had retaliated with their talkathon. The next day a compromise was reached which "set aside" the bid bill and the two reapportionment bills until the twenty-second legislative day. The postponement served the interests of both administration leaders and opponents, the former because it delayed the bid bill and the latter because it delayed the reapportionment bills. Administration leaders got the best of the bargain because the reapportionment bills had no chance of passing, but antis could at least claim to their constituents that they had stopped the reapportionment bills. Placing the bid bill so far back in the schedule put it in jeopardy of being lost in the inevitable end-of-season log jam, and it also made it vulnerable to a pocket veto.[116] After a short recess and work on routine legislation, the House passed a compromise state purchasing bill 96–4. Some of the bill's features were the product of negotiations that occurred on the House floor in which Folsom took a part, moving among several clusters of representatives. He was very effective in securing the flexibility in the bill that he wanted while giving antiadministration forces enough to satisfy them.[117] In the first week of August the same bill achieved Senate approval. So ended the first half of the second regular legislative session.

The second half, like the first, had a timeless quality to it. Four bills were especially important: a $20 million highway construction bond issue; a corporate income tax increase to be earmarked for education; and two standard appropriations bills, one for education and the other for the remainder of state government. The latter two bills were by far the most important and were not subject to controversy, but they were caught up in the struggles over the others. Early in August the House by an overwhelming majority passed the corporate income tax increase, which disallowed federal income taxes as a deduction in calculating corporate state income taxes and produced an additional $7.5 million.[118] The governor had not opposed the income tax bill. The $20 million highway bond issue was a higher priority for him.

Folsom's Senate leaders maneuvered the highway bond issue onto the Senate special order calendar ahead of the corporate tax bill in hopes of passing the highway bill and exhibited no concern for the education bill's fate.[119] The major advocate of the corporate tax increase in the Senate was E. W. Skidmore of Tuscaloosa, who warned that he would block consideration of the appropriations bills until the Senate voted on his bill. Other senators were just as determined to stop the corporate tax bill. Corporate tax and road bond issue advocates would not permit the appropriations bills to reach a vote because once these essential bills passed, the legislature would adjourn immediately.[120] Somehow a prison reform measure and a bill creating inland docks managed to thread their way through this labyrinth and become law. The latter, one of Folsom's major pocketbook programs, had been bitterly fought by railroad interests, who stood to lose from the increased competition provided by expanded access to inland areas by ships and barges.

Skidmore followed through on his warning by holding off consideration of the appropriations bills and the highway bond issue as the session wound down toward adjournment; he demanded full readings of the appropriations bills, and he offered numerous amendments.[121] Another group headed by Senator Vaughan Hill Robison of Montgomery threatened to filibuster the bond issue in the same way, and still others who were opposed to the corporate tax bill threatened to filibuster it. Ultimately, Skidmore was stopped by two clotures in one day, and the appropriations bills were passed. The road bond issue and the corporate income tax increase both died.[122]

The second term had a schizophrenic quality. Folsom and the legislature fought bitterly over civil rights matters, and their confrontations were amplified and reinforced by frequent occurrences of race-related violence. But on pocketbook matters his relations with the legislature were fairly cordial.[123] A former governor remarked:

> Folsom had good relationships with most of the Jefferson County industrial leaders in his second term. He was very successful in his second term. He was not a vindictive person. He set a tone that was very pleasant. There was more real debate and less drawing lines and adamant, unyielding positions. He was not a grudge bearer. He succeeded in getting his road program, a broad old-age program, and the Industrial Development Board through. His main problem was a lack of stick-to-itiveness. He would announce some great-sounding program and two weeks later he and everyone else had forgotten it.
>
> His legislative leaders in his second term supported his programs very effec-

tively, especially Joe Dawkins in the Senate. He was very effective and very able. On financial matters he knew more than executive branch administrators. Most of his other Senate leaders were not leader types. In the House Fite supported Folsom's programs insofar as they did not conflict with his interests. . . . Folsom would simply turn his legislative program over to them and they protected it.[124]

The most prominent feature of Folsom's second-term legislative activities was his stand against segregation, which began in his first term and in many ways was strengthened in the second. He backpedaled occasionally, but, overall, everyone knew where he stood. Many black leaders wanted him to go further on their behalf, but a more common view was that provided by a major civil rights leader who remembered that when Folsom was governor, "it was a time when it was almost criminal to lean at all toward the blacks. In his blunt way, he came out for the blacks in many instances. . . . Folsom would come to my office many instances to talk to me about problems of state. . . . We'd talk about those damned rednecks . . . going to help them in spite of themselves. None of the liberal politicians—none of them—have done all they could. I sympathized with him under the circumstances under which he operated."[125]

Moderate to liberal whites assessed Folsom positively. One said, "Folsom wanted everyone to vote."[126] A North Alabama journalist said: "Segregation never made much of an impression on Folsom. He had the vision to see that the course of progress for Alabama, the U.S., and the world lay in harmony for the races. He recognized [before most whites] that the negro had been mistreated—not given opportunity to advance. . . . Folsom actually believed that all men are created equal."[127]

Segregationists of all stripes also had no doubts about Folsom. Sam Engelhardt and Albert Boutwell were certain that Folsom had sided almost entirely with the civil rights movement. And letters to Folsom on this subject were highly critical of his civil libertarian approach by a margin of forty or fifty to one. This count does not include the numerous death threats from segregationists that were forwarded to police.

Not everyone shared this view of Folsom. Some scholars, Alabama politicians, and reporters saw him primarily as an opportunist or eccentric, and both elements were part of his makeup. The most notable examples of opportunism occurred when he was trying to win the 1956 delegate selection and, as we shall see later, in the 1962 gubernatorial primary. But even in those cases he did not stoop to the race baiting favored by most of his opponents. Those who viewed Folsom as primarily an opportunist also pointed out that his advocacy of reapportionment was something that could be expected of any North Alabama governor who wanted to increase the power of his constituency and that most of his key programs that led to an expansion of the electorate would bring in new voters who would be loyal to him for the remainder of his career. Both arguments have an element of truth in them, for power was important to Folsom. But his actions as governor were hardly consistent with the hypothesis that power was his only motivation. A power-motivated person would not have pursued for so long the series of lawsuits against the Dixiecrat electors. He had to be aware that his four legal actions, in addition to the two filed by others, made him look foolish and probably lost him as much support as they gained for him. Many of Folsom's actions favoring blacks irritated large numbers of whites of all classes. Furthermore, Folsom did not expect the civil rights movement to succeed as rapidly as it did, which is to say that he did not expect to see significant numbers of blacks voting during his political career.

A rational North Alabama governor intent on nothing but maximizing his power would have pushed reapportionment, elimination of the poll tax, a constitutional convention, and the rest, but he would have avoided what the *Montgomery Advertiser* called his "candid and staunch solicitude for the colored man and his aspirations," and he would not have pursued any of those goals to the point where he would have come to look like a habitual loser unable to deal effectively with a legislature.[128]

Nor can his behavior be dismissed as simply eccentric. He did many things that can be accounted for only by reference to his eccentricity or to alcoholism, but his official actions as governor and even most of his campaign rhetoric were anything but eccentric; rather, they were consistent and coherent. And they related perfectly to his ideological beliefs and his upbringing in Coffee County.

Folsom's view of politics is that it is a struggle between rich and poor, with democracy and free speech the only weapons available to the poor short of armed revolution. His understanding of the civil rights movement was simply that blacks and poor whites are people, and in a democracy all people must have the right to vote, the right to a good education, the right to live where they want. Anything short of those freedoms permits the wealthy elite to rule absolutely. One of his many versions of this idea was to call his opponents "the slaveholders of Alabama—that's my opposition—the slaveholders is the big property owners, of course—those that had the Negroes in slavery by not allowing them to vote and the poor white in slavery by not allowing him to vote on account of the poll tax." He also believed that the "segregated school system was the key to slavery—the key to the poor man being shackled. That was the purpose of segregation—to keep the black man and the poor white man as second class citizens."[129] His attitude toward women's rights was part of this overall view. The key to his positive attitude toward the Equal Rights Amendment was that women are people and in a democracy all people must have equal rights.

Folsom insists that he was always opposed to segregation but that his overall strategic approach was to move slowly to avoid a "white backlash." Discussing the segregation resolutions passed by the legislature in his second term, he said defiantly, "Hell, we said, 'Let's let 'em all put one in and let them come through and then throw them in the wastebasket. Now those that got down in the pocket veto period, I threw all them in the wastebasket. . . . We'd filibuster until we had a stack that high [gesturing vaguely indicating a pile three or four feet high]. You ought to see those damned things."[130]

Folsom's attitudes toward civil rights and his related behavior were consistent with his community and family background, and they were deeply held. Although his public statements about segregation were rarely straightforward, he made clear his opposition to the status quo. He sought to free the political system to permit blacks and poor whites to exercise their full political rights so that they then might attempt to change things to their liking.

CHAPTER 10

Folsom and Administrative Power: Second Term

> There's been a lot written about what a highway program I put on, and I knew somethin' about road building and I had an opportunity to do it. But the thing I *initiated* was the inland docks—inland transportation and the Tennessee-Tombigbee.
>
> James E. Folsom

Folsom's first-term failure to produce reforms with the massive administrative power available to the governor was repeated, with minor variations, in the second term. Administratively, the second term did not reach the bilious depths or the rare idealistic peaks of the first, mainly because Folsom's personnel choices were older and more experienced than the group he had brought together eight years before. Many first-term Folsomites returned. Some of them were honest, others dishonest in varying degrees; some were competent, even brilliant, others completely inept; a few were idealistic, but most were utterly self-serving. Bill Drinkard returned, this time as conservation director, as did Bill Lyerly as director of the Department of Public Safety, Herman Nelson as highway director, Fuller Kimbrell (a senator in the first term) and then W. LaRue Horn as finance director, O. H. Finney as executive secretary, and Ward McFarland as state docks director. Other appointees included Pleas Looney, a skating rink operator and office manager of Folsom's Montgomery reelection headquarters, as Commerce Department director; Eugene Wells, a long-time union leader, as director of the Department of Industrial Relations; Murray Battles, a Cullman attorney, as the governor's legal adviser; Knox McRae, a North Alabama supporter, who held a number of positions including state docks director; and Harrell Hammonds, probate judge of Lowndes County, as ABC Board chairman.

Ralph Hammond, an author and first-term director of publicity and information, started the second term as press secretary. Hammond was a University of Alabama student in 1946 when he attended a Folsom rally and was so impressed that he helped to organize a Folsom-for-governor student group. In the second term he quickly emerged as Folsom's leading personal aide. Estimates of his importance vary considerably, but at the least, he was Folsom's prime speech writer, and in the last two years he became, by default, de facto governor at least as far as relatively small matters were concerned. He also controlled access to the governor over long periods of time.

It was a fairly standard collection of businessman-politicians and career public servants bright enough or lucky enough to have picked a winner before he looked like one. They were essentially indistinguishable from cabinet members and aides of the governors who preceded and followed Folsom.

Concerning staffing below the policy level, Folsom retained his dislike of the merit system. A few merit system employees were pressured to leave, but they resisted more effectively than others like them had in the first term, and Folsom quickly dropped efforts to remove them.[1] Memoranda suggest, however, that the Folsom administration never stopped trying to evade merit testing to hire unqualified but politically loyal personnel and place them under merit tenure protection. State employees not protected by the merit system, even ones who were difficult to replace because of their technical skills, were quickly fired.[2] They were often replaced with persons seemingly devoid of any marketable skills.

Folsom also continued to view state purchases as part of the spoils of victory. The Highway Department continued to buy disproportionate numbers of equipment and materials from Folsom family members, executive branch officials, and administration supporters at inflated prices without bids.[3] For example, Glenco Paving Company, formed soon after Folsom's reelection by an old Folsom friend, Rex Edwards, sold "plant mix" (a stone aggregate) to the state. In its first year of operation, the company sold eighty thousand tons, and as of July 1956 it was moving the material at the rate of five thousand tons a week. Glencoe gave Cecil Folsom a fifty-cent-a-ton "commission" on sales. Later estimates put Cecil's commission at seventy-five cents a ton. Bob Folsom created a corporation, Southern Supply and Contracting Company, which also specialized in doing business with the state, selling concrete and metal pipe, paint, steel forms, and so forth.[4] Other key administration members formed dealerships to sell automobiles, earth-moving equipment, gravel, asphalt, and nearly every other item and service that the state purchased. When bids were conducted, bidders were often told what figures they should submit. If sealed bids were submitted and there were doubts about what they contained, they were often opened and changed.[5] A study by the examiners of public accounts comparing the prices paid for standard products by the State of Alabama to prices paid by other states with competitive bid laws demonstrated that Alabama prices ran 20 to 30 percent higher.[6] With annual purchases of materials and equipment totaling approximately $15 million per year, these differences amounted to three to four million dollars wasted each year. Deposits of state funds were placed in particular banks as a matter of patronage.[7] Private roads were paved at state expense.[8] And liquor companies continued to pay kickbacks, sometimes as high as one hundred thousand dollars per year, for the privilege of selling their products in the state stores.

Patronage politics connected the executive branch and the legislature with complex and intimate ties even during the time of most intense conflict over civil rights. According to a North Alabama senator who voted with the administration on most matters, patronage politics was "75 percent of legislation."[9] By that he meant that 75 percent of the bills in the legislature revolved around not the merit a piece of legislation might have for the public but rather which legislators and executive branch officials would personally benefit from resulting contracts. The senator went on to say that, regardless of ownership, companies could scarcely hope to land a state contract without sweetening the deal with a bribe in some form. Such arrangements could be as crass as cash bribes equal to a percentage of the contract amount or as subtle as extra business given to a law firm or an advertising agency.

As though history were being written by a poet, it was left to Bill Drinkard to play the central role in the second term's major scandal. In August 1955 the governor announced that, due to a lack of maintenance, a number of state parks had been allowed to fall into such a deteriorated condition that several of them should be closed.[10] This statement prepared the way for timber-cutting operations in some parks by private contractors; the sale of the timber was to generate funds for park rehabilitation. Later in the month, contracts were let, without bids, to administration favorites Representative Bryce Davis, S. E. Belcher, and James M. Pinkerton, who were to cut timber at Little Mountain, Oak Mountain, and Bladon Springs parks, respectively.

Newspaper coverage of these transactions apparently alerted Tennessee Valley Authority (TVA) officials to the fact that land for Little Mountain Park in Guntersville had been deeded by TVA to the state exclusively for park purposes. Officials of the agency informed Drinkard that they wanted environmentally correct standards written into Davis's contract. When Drinkard rejected this call, the Guntersville Junior Chamber of Commerce took up the cause. In October it formally requested that Folsom stop the operation. Visits to Little Mountain by chamber members, the press, a state Senate investigating committee, and independent experts revealed that, instead of selective cutting of trees of one foot or more in diameter as specified in

Davis's contract, some areas had been denuded while others that needed thinning had been left untouched.[11] The executive secretary of the National Parks Association, Fred Packard, testified at a Senate hearing that he had "never seen a logging operation on dedicated land as destructive as the one" at Little Mountain. Operations at Oak Mountain Park also showed signs of administrative and operational irresponsibility. Beyond this, Drinkard employed a Folsom brother, a brother-in-law, and his second father-in-law in plush jobs managing lakes in public parks. This time when he was attacked by the press, Drinkard did not attempt to defend his actions with specious talk of honest graft. He simply denied that any favoritism was involved. Most of Drinkard's actions were taken with Folsom's full knowledge and support.[12]

As finance director, Fuller Kimbrell was the most important person with regard to patronage, aside from Folsom himself. He was sometimes referred to as the "assistant governor" in the first two years of the second term. One administration executive explained: "With no bid law the finance director was the Man. He had total control over spending and impoundment. . . . He took care of legislative appointments, contracts, etc. A man [legislator] wants to be a hero back home. Folsom didn't come to the office all that much."[13]

Representative George Hawkins, Folsom's House floor leader, who was planning a 1958 gubernatorial race of his own and was trying to cut a niche for himself, introduced a low-bid bill that Folsom and Kimbrell opposed. Kimbrell responded with a bill that contained two barbs. The first would have exempted any purchase over five hundred dollars deemed proper by a "purchasing committee." This committee would consist of the finance director, the highway director, state comptroller, and one representative each of the state's counties and cities to be appointed by the governor. Only the state comptroller was not a gubernatorial appointee. The counties and cities were represented because of Kimbrell's second barb, which would have applied the new law to county and city governments as well as the state. The primary idea behind Kimbrell's bill was to kill Hawkins's proposal, but Kimbrell would have been quite happy to see his version pass. It would have expanded his power enormously. Infuriated by Kimbrell's proposal, Hawkins accused him of seeking "life or death" control over all government purchases in the state, which would make the finance director "more powerful than the governor himself."[14]

Kimbrell's bill was very unpopular among county and city officials, and it was quickly buried, but it helped to entangle Hawkins's bill in complex legislative procedures. Then using "promises of roads, bridges, lakes, and proper appointments to the proper people," the governor induced a large body of Black Belt representatives to join most Folsomites in killing the Hawkins proposal. The Black Belters spoke convincingly about the need for low-bid requirements, but they too were more interested in patronage.[15]

Folsom became infamous for his lack of follow-through on administrative matters. On one occasion he summoned many of the state's top industrialists and budget specialist Jake Jordon to a meeting in Mobile. It was scheduled for one o'clock, and everyone, happy that Folsom had scheduled a meeting at a reasonable hour, arrived punctually. Everyone arrived, that is, except the governor. An hour and a half later, Folsom breezed in and, without apologizing for his lateness, began engaging members of the group in small talk about their wives and children and the weather. When he had completed his greeting, he said, "Let's get down to business." Then he paused, stared blankly around the room and said, "Aw, fuck it! I'm gonna play golf, so you tell Jake what you want and he'll get it for you." Then he left the room. Jordon turned to the group and asked, "Well, gentlemen, what do you want?" One of them replied, "We don't want anything. He called us up here."[16]

One of the reasons Folsom made such a poor executive was his view that administration was secondary to legislative concerns. This was exemplified when a North Alabama Folsomite senator found that a state official working in Marshall County was dishonest and asked O. H. Finney to have him replaced. Finney did so immediately with the senator's suggested substitute. But the official had support in the Montgomery delegation, and when it objected, Folsom fired the substitute and reappointed the original official. Soon thereafter the antis in the legislature proposed a low-bid law that Folsom opposed. The North Alabama senator promised to vote against the bill, but he began to waiver as a matter of conscience, and when he thought about the Marshall County affair, he began to lean strongly against Folsom. He communicated his intention to vote for the bill to Finney, and he was quickly invited to the governor's office. When he arrived, the office was full of people. The senator recalled, "He [Folsom] put his arm around me and patted me on the shoulder. I really felt it. 'You're going to stay with me on this low-bid vote aren't you?' Folsom said. The room fell silent. 'Ain't you got some roads up there you need built?' Folsom asked. He got on the phone and talked to Herman Nelson, 'Herman, ___ has some roads he needs built. Herman, you get to them!' That was the main thing I wanted—roads."[17] Folsom got the vote.

A card file maintained by Ralph Hammond contains many examples of similar transactions. Liquor contracts were given to some legislators, state buildings were constructed on land owned by others, and still others were permitted to sell goods to the state.[18]

Administrative power was also used to further Folsom's objectives in state Democratic party politics. J. Bruce Henderson kept records of as many of these transactions as he could detect. According to his notes, party influentials were given "a 4 lane Highway Brewton to Atmore"; promised a "Big Road Program in Marengo"; "offered a large State Deposit"; and given a "retainer fee of $5,000 for a [blurred] a total of $20,000." Another entry noted that "a county engineer was offered a job as division engineer provided he could get a new member of the State Democratic Executive Committee in his county to [blurred]."[19]

Folsom continued to influence regulatory bodies, such as the State License and Contracting Board (responsible for passing on the qualifications of contractors to bid for state contracts), the reconstituted Pardon and Parole Board, and the ABC Board. Memoranda from Folsom and O. H. Finney "requesting" favorable decisions on behalf of contractors friendly to the administration moved in a continuous stream to the contracting board.[20] The Pardon and Parole Board was pressured to reinstate Ward McFarland's civil and political rights, which he had lost upon his conviction for federal income tax fraud.[21] With regard to the ABC Board, Folsom personally supervised the use of money from liquor companies. The actual cash transfers were usually performed by his trustworthy and reliable brother Fred.[22]

The handling of resources under his immediate control was a bit more chaotic in the second term than in the first. The governor had three funds under his direct control, and the legislature placed few limits on their use. In 1956 the mansion fund was $60,000, the governor's emergency fund $100,000, and the departmental emergency fund $150,000 per year.[23] His mansion expenses averaged in excess of $9,500 per month. In contrast, Gordon Persons had spent an average of $1,587 per month. Without any written justification Folsom transferred sums ranging from $1,000 to $17,000 from the governor's emergency fund to the mansion fund.[24] He listed more than $30,000 for himself and Mrs. Folsom under the general category "expenses." No further explanations were provided.[25] Approximately $4,000 was withdrawn under the sole justification "expenditures for mansion services" and recorded as given to Senator Broughton Lamberth. Actions of this sort naturally attracted Ralph Eagerton's attention. In the course of the examiner's investigation, the mansion fund warrants disappeared from the comptroller's files, but Eagerton possessed duplicates, and so his investigation was not hampered.

Folsom so abused his use of National Guard aircraft that it stimulated an investigation by the air force. Folsom's response was to order every Alabama Air National Guard "jet, every C-47, and everything that can roll on wheels, much less fly, to fly to Jacksonville" for a "special weather mission" that would also include a "runway landing inspection" and runway "takeoff inspection later in the afternoon."[26] These activities were to take place the day of the Gator Bowl game.

As in the first term, there is no evidence that Folsom personally profited from the graft, "honest" or otherwise, that he surrounded himself with and participated in. The person who recorded his campaign contributions, considerable in the 1954 election, in which he ran as the favorite, said, "Jim could have been a millionaire from those donations. [But] Jim came out as a pauper."[27] A very conservative Jefferson County legislator believed that "Folsom never stole a cent for himself. . . . A man who is governor has to be in there by virtue of politics and planning. He becomes obligated, and the letting of contracts and appointments naturally don't go to enemies. The governor surrounds himself with men and you say, 'What does he want with that damned thief for?' Politics attracts that element. Folsom got himself surrounded by crooks."[28] In interview after interview both Folsom friend and foe reiterated this theme. Furthermore, Folsom continued under the close scrutiny of the Internal Revenue Service, and he had no significant problems with that agency's investigations.

Folsom continued to be an extraordinarily difficult person to work for. Reliability and promptness were never his prime qualities as an executive, but in the last two years of the second term his behavior became so erratic that people around him were surprised whenever he discharged his administrative responsibilities in a rational manner. Finney and Hammond spent considerable time writing apologies to VIPs who were refused appointments with the governor. One of the governor's staff recalled: "He was unpredictable when drinking. Things would get crucial, and he would go off on a binge. People were afraid to make decisions without him. People would come from Washington with appointments, and he would be gone. There was always turbulence."[29]

Folsom became progressively more abusive to those around him. In addition to the late-night telephone calls, sudden cross-country airplane trips, conferences for which he would arrive hours late, if at all, and similar insulting behavior, he would interrupt aides in mid-sentence with an angry "Ah, shut up!" On one occasion, when a man had taken the liberty of sitting on the arm of a chair occupied by Folsom's wife, the governor hit him with a chair. But almost no one resigned, even though actions of this sort aroused frenzied anger in them. A few of his close aides simply gritted their teeth and stayed with him out of a sense of duty. Others used the same tactics that had been applied in the first term to handle Folsom's high energy level, that is, they kept their distance or they drank. Still others remained close and withstood his abuse, but used his weaknesses to manipulate him. One friend believed that "Folsom was isolated by people who saw to it that he always had enough to drink. They ingratiated themselves with him and took a lot of crap in the process. They had no character."[30] According to a leading Alabama political reporter, "Folsom drank heavily in both administrations. He was often a victim of his 'friends.' You've got to be well fortified in your personal habits in politics. His friends tried and often succeeded in getting him drunk because they couldn't handle him sober."[31]

Folsom's public highjinks continued unabated. He attended a meeting of the Southern Governors' Conference near an East Coast navy installation, and the navy ferried the governors by helicopter out to an aircraft carrier, where they planned to demonstrate how jet fighters took off and landed from the ships. Everyone was there except Folsom, who arrived late, stumbled down the helicopter steps, staggered across the deck waving his big gray hat at the seamen, greeted an admiral with a jarring thump on the back and a hearty "Hi 'ya, boy!" and sat down amidst the other governors and a number of high-ranking naval officers. The demonstration began, but to everyone's horror the first jet catapulted off the carrier, splashed down into the water, and exploded. As the group stared at the pillar of smoke rising above the ship, Folsom slapped the man next to him on the knee and bellowed, "By God, if that ain't a show, I'll kiss your ass."[32]

At a dinner at the governor's mansion for state judges, including members of the Alabama Supreme Court, Folsom drank so much he passed out, sprawled flat on the floor. He had to be carried out bodily.[33] He attended a number of University of Alabama Board of Trustees meetings drunk.[34] For a Governor's Day celebration at the University of Alabama he flew the short distance to Tuscaloosa, and by the time he arrived he was unconscious.[35] Folsom was supposed to lead a Mardi Gras parade in Mobile. On the way he and his party stopped at several roadside bars. They never made it to the parade. He did the same thing on his way from Montgomery to an Auburn football game, stopping at literally every bar on the road. One Sunday in 1957 a group of Cullman citizens was scheduled to meet with him to ask for the construction of a road. They gathered in the local school at four o'clock. Folsom arrived on time, but after being assisted onto the stage, he stared blankly at the audience and slumped to the floor. His aides dragged him away.[36]

As his drinking intensified, he came to refer to liquor as "one of the necessities of life." Later it became simply "one of the necessities." One day he called a crony on the telephone and asked, "Do you have any of the necessities there at your house? I want to come over." His friend replied, "I only have four drinks." Folsom said, "That's not enough. Let me check and see what I've got. You just hold the phone." So his friend sat and held. The minutes ticked by and he was still holding when suddenly in walked Folsom carrying his bottle. He had completely forgotten the telephone.[37]

No one could predict where his attention would turn next or what subject would grip his imagination. Neil Metcalf, a strong Folsom supporter in the legislature, was a candidate for the national presidency of the Young Democrats. The election was to be held at the group's convention in Oklahoma City. Folsom decided that Metcalf, a leading candidate, should win, and he had nearly every Alabama legislator and state official of any consequence flown in to stack the vote.

At the convention Folsom was courted by New York Governor Averell Harriman, who was seeking the Democratic presidential nomination. They met in Folsom's hotel room with Folsom in his undershirt. Marshall Frady described the scene: "After a short exchange of pleasantries, it suddenly occurred to Folsom that Harriman was cultivating him. With his huge arm wrapped around Harriman's dapper shoulders, Folsom advised him, with a benign little tilt of his head, 'Now don't piss on ole' Jim's leg. You can't piss on ole' Jim's leg.' "[38] The full saying, which Folsom had apparently not bothered to complete, runs, "Don't piss on my leg and tell me its raining."

Soon after his arrival in Oklahoma City Folsom decided that Metcalf's cause would be aided by a party atmosphere. He tried to locate large quantities of liquor, but Oklahoma was a dry state, and he was unable to find a sufficient supply. He then ordered a National Guard C-47 to be loaded with forty cases of Jack Daniels and flown to the convention. A truck was rented to haul it from the plane to the hotel, but because of the state's strict prohibition enforcement no local driver would undertake the job; so, one of Folsom's aides did it. Not all the whiskey reached the hotel, however, as Folsom's temporary truck driver sold some of it in a back alley to fellow conventioneers at twenty dollars a bottle. Nevertheless, enough of it arrived at Folsom's suite to generate a riotous party that attracted enormous crowds.

Folsom also pursued his cause on television, where he appeared with Alabama Congressman Carl Elliott, Senator John Sparkman, Estes Kefauver, Michigan Governor G. Mennen Williams, and a state legislator named Pete Matthews. Folsom ambled onto the studio set with a large jelly glass of bourbon in his hand. When the program started and the camera focused on him, he decided that the glass might be misinterpreted (that is, seen for what it was), and so he explained in some detail that it contained not whiskey but "good ole Oklahoma branch water."[39] He punctuated his explanation with hearty thumps on Pete Matthews's back. As Folsom rambled on to other topics, Congressman Elliott, a man of liberal temperament but conservative personal tastes, eased downward in his chair to below camera range and crawled away on his hands and knees.

Deciding that reinforcements were needed for the Metcalf campaign, Folsom had Alabama college students quickly recruited and flown to the convention. But all of these determined efforts failed, and Metcalf lost. Folsom, in a dark mood, stormed away from the convention in his National Guard plane and left the students stranded in Oklahoma. Aides rescued them later.[40] Folsom blamed Metcalf's loss on a George Wallace television interview which included a vicious anti–civil rights diatribe. Folsom felt that Wallace's words so irritated northern Young Democrats that they voted against the Alabamian.

On a number of occasions Folsom, together with various members of his administration, legislators, businessmen, and journalists, flew to New York for meetings with industrialists and bankers to convince them to locate plants in Alabama or to sell bonds. In the second term these wild affairs featured nonstop drinking, weird all-night bus and subway rides, and confrontations with New York restaurateurs, one of whom, wielding a meat cleaver, chased an Alabama politico out of his establishment.[41] But even under these circumstances Folsom sometimes retained a measure of control. On one such trip the small number of Alabamians in his retinue who were there with serious intent wanted Folsom to attend a luncheon. Folsom responded, "Boys, if you want me to go, I'll go if you think I should in my condition. If you don't think I should, I won't."[42]

Even in this period of rampaging alcoholism, Folsom could be charming. A state senator's wife visited Montgomery and voiced a desire to meet the governor. A phone call brought an invitation from Finney. When the woman appeared in Folsom's office, he boomed, "Who in the hell is this? Where do you get so many pretty girls?" The senator recalled, "She was tickled. He was able to get close to people. She would vote for him from then on. And he could remember more names."[43]

Folsom never dropped the habit of reading history which he started as a youth. He demonstrated his knowledge when the French government donated to the American Legion a train car that had been used to transport troops in World War I. At the ceremony Folsom was scheduled to receive the French consul who was to present the car. Ralph Hammond and Bill Lyerly had each assumed that the other was having the governor's speech written, and they failed to discover this until Folsom was on his way down the capitol steps to the podium and he asked Lyerly, "Where's my speech?" Minutes later, Folsom launched into an address which included an outline of French-American relations beginning with the American Revolution. He included a detailed description of Lafayette's visit to Montgomery in 1826. One person who heard the speech recalled, "He ad-libbed a beautiful speech. He brought ole Lafayette from the Exchange Hotel right up to the capitol steps."[44] At the time only Folsom, Lyerly, and Hammond knew that the entire talk was extemporaneous.

Inland Waterways

Folsom counts his part in facilitating construction of the Tennessee-Tombigbee Waterway and in originating Alabama's inland docks systems as two of his best pocketbook programs. Both occurred in his second term.

Interest in construction of a canal between the Tennessee and Tombigbee Rivers extends back to the 1700s. The Congress first evidenced serious concern in 1874 when it ordered the army corps of engineers to perform an analysis of its potential. That study and three others that followed through 1932 concluded that the canal was not economically feasible. Then a 1938 corps review found the project to be justifiable, as did an updated version completed in 1945. Congressional authorization followed in 1946. The canal's estimated cost at that time was $120 million, and its benefit-cost ratio was 1.05. In other words, for every $1 spent (operating as well as capital costs) $1.05 in benefits would be generated. As a business investment the only thing keeping the waterway from being a losing proposition was little more than a nickel for every dollar spent. The $1 for costs would come from general revenues drawn from throughout the nation, while the $1.05 in benefits would be concentrated in Alabama, Mississippi, and adjoining states.

The waterway entailed "improving 170 miles of existing river channel, constructing 45 miles of canal, building five dams and ten locks, and excavating 112 million cubic yards of dirt and rock."[45] The benefit margin was especially thin when account is taken of the habitual practice of the corps of engineers to underestimate costs, overestimate benefits, and use discount (interest) rates in its calculations that were far lower than those businesses used in analyzing capital investments. The corps also followed another of its standard patterns by ignoring environmental damage that would require later expenditures to repair.[46] Even though the waterway was authorized in 1946, no funds were provided because the members of the House Appropriations Committee were uneasy about the small benefit-cost ratio. Later the Korean War delayed funding.

Folsom's director of the Alabama State Planning and Industrial Development Board was General Lewis Pick, former chief of the army corps of engineers. Early in 1956, with Folsom's full support and encouragement, he began lobbying influentials in Mississippi and Alabama on behalf of the waterway. As a result, later that year Alabama and Mississippi congressmen succeeded in convincing the corps to undertake yet another restudy. Completed in 1962, the study reported a benefit-cost ratio of 1.08, still very close to the break-even point. General Pick died soon after the restudy was initiated, but Folsom continued to push for the waterway. Early in 1957 he and Governor J. P. Coleman of Mississippi decided to institute a compact that would establish the Tennessee-Tombigbee Waterway Authority, which would, the two governors promised, undertake the project if the federal government failed to release funds for it.[47] Soon thereafter the Alabama and Mississippi legislatures approved the compact and appropriated a total of $180,000 for operating funds. After yet another analysis—this one producing a 1.24 benefit-cost ratio—and more delays, appropriations were finally voted by the Congress in 1971 and construction began the next year.

In 1978 internal corps of engineers documents released under the Freedom of Information Act revealed that the corps had been considerably less than objective in its many evalutions of the waterway. Benefit figures were calculated using barge traffic estimates based on a channel width of 300 feet, 130 feet wider than what Congress had authorized. Furthermore, in analyses performed in the period 1967–75 benefit calculations were based on a waterway length of twice the actual length of the project.[48] Cost estimates were similarly distorted.

The Tennessee-Tombigbee Waterway was the sort of project that people have in mind when they use the term "pork barrel." It was not worth its enormous cost, and it will benefit a small number of businesses and trade unions enormously. But Folsom, although his role was substantial, should not take all the blame for pushing it, because he was joined by virtually every other public official in Alabama and Mississippi (and later Tennessee, Georgia, and Florida) with a voice in the matter, and, judging solely by economic criteria, the Tennessee-Tombigbee Waterway will probably be beneficial to those states (although some environmentalists dispute this). Taken together they will be paying only about 10 percent of the costs, with the other forty-five states covering the rest, and they will reap most of the benefits. From such a perspective Folsom can take pride in the early part that he played in the waterway's development.

Folsom began thinking about a waterway compact in the 1930s.

> We have more potentially navigable rivers than any state. That came [to mind] when I was workin' WPA in Guntersville. They had a rally in Guntersville to try to build a canal in from Birmingham to Guntersville. The Chamber of Commerce got up some money and they hired a promoter to come and push the idea, and he stayed there until he spent all the money and they talked it up pretty good, but nothing ever came of it.
>
> Course, I'd been to sea and I knew the importance of canals—I'd been over to the Tennessee River and watched them lock boats through there. And it was just so important economically.[49]

Another reason Folsom liked the Tennessee-Tombigbee Waterway idea was that it promised to provide competition to that classic populist enemy the railroads, and indeed the railroad companies were in the forefront of opposition to the project.[50]

The inland docks are just what the term suggests—docks that are not on the Gulf Coast. The docks completed or begun during Folsom's second term are located in Decatur, Florence, and Huntsville on the Tennessee River, in Cordova on the Warrior-Tombigbee River, and in Columbia on the Chattahoochee River. It is unclear when the inland docks idea first appeared, but the first concrete planning was done by the Folsom administration, and the first specific proposals were shepherded through the legislature by Folsomites.

Folsom's enthusiasm for inland docks also derived from his experiences in Guntersville. Opposition came mainly from the railroads, but other business groups were very positively inclined toward the proposal. The legislature approved $3 million in general obligation bonds and a constitutional amendment permitting the state to embark on the novel program. The amendment was approved by the voters in December 1957.

The docks are not very large. The one in Decatur consists of two 231-by-50-foot docks, an 18,000-square-foot warehouse, an office, garage, and spur tracks to a major trunk line, together with access roads. Over the years it has become overgrown with weeds and has fallen into disuse. A local reporter explained that the docks were not important in and of themselves but because their construction was critical in forcing the railroads to build tracks (for fear of potential competition from barges) into the area, which in turn attracted the huge manufacturing plants now in Decatur. Folsom concurred: "The secret of the docks is to make the railroads equalize the freight rates. And that brought in the industry. . . . You get river rates. In other words, if you've got docks there are barge facilities, then the railroads, if they don't meet the rates of the barge lines, they've got to come down to those rates. And that makes Decatur."[51]

Folsom probably would have embarked on the inland docks program regardless of technical considerations since it so neatly included his ideological predilections in a package attractive to a large majority of business groups and labor unions, but it developed that the docks would be a sound investment. Analyses performed by independent consulting engineers showed that, while the docks (details vary from site to site) would barely break even considered as a business investment (construction and operating costs versus fees paid by shippers), they were still worth constructing because they would generate transportation cost savings and increases in real estate values near the docks, and they would attract new industry in the surrounding area.[52] Taking all benefits and costs into account, the benefit-cost ratios for the inland docks considered by the study were close to 2.0, thus justifying Folsom's enthusiasm.

With few exceptions, Folsom's attempts at major reforms during his second term failed. This happened not so much because of his personal eccentricities—the reason usually cited by interview subjects—but because the changes he desired were opposed by a large majority of the state's influentials. The Tennessee-Tombigbee and inland docks programs demonstrated what he could accomplish by remaining within the boundaries established by the state's elite. In these cases and others that concerned industrial development, success was achieved simply by showing business groups how state action would help them and for how little cost. Once that was accomplished, legislative and voter approval came easily.

This is not meant to understate his creativity and that of his closest aides who assisted in these programs. His advocacy of the Tennessee-Tombigbee compact was an imaginative stroke which dramatized a faltering program and probably accelerated its congressional approval, and from the state's point of view, if not the nation's, it will probably be beneficial. Proposals for individual inland docks projects had, by Folsom's account, been percolating around the state for several decades, but it remained for him to draw them together into a coherent, comprehensive set of proposals. Construction of the docks occurred soon after their approval.[53]

It is often said that much of the reckless behavior that occurred in Folsom's terms was due to his being fooled by unethical subordinates. Some former Folsomites became fiercely angry when describing such instances of dishonesty. There is no doubt that this occurred, but the point is misleading and usually overstated. It seems to lift responsibility from Folsom's shoulders for such events as the pardon and parole scandal and the purchasing irregularities that continued through both terms. At a minimum, he selected those responsible for those acts, and in general he was well informed of their activities. In explaining the frequent ABC Board turnovers in his first term, he complained that he had had difficulty locating honest people, but he also made it clear that he did not want honest people. He wanted people who would siphon funds from liquor companies to his bagmen without taking inordinate amounts for themselves. It is easy to believe that he had difficulty finding such individuals.

Folsom's subordinates fooled him less often than many believe. In virtually every case of questionable practices described above, administrators were either following Folsom's direct orders or were abiding by his Jacksonian-spoils policies. His awareness of his subordinates' activities was also demonstrated by his frequent firing of policy-level officials. But his attitude toward their activities was reflected in their frequent reappointment to other offices or in their being rewarded in other ways.

CHAPTER 11

The 1962 Election and Its Aftermath

> I never use any minority group . . . as a political football. It just isn't right, and I'm not going to do it. . . .
> I stand today, as I have always stood in the past, for complete segregation of the races in schools.
>
> James E. Folsom

The 1958 Democratic party gubernatorial primary had a large field of candidates, but George Wallace, John Patterson, and Jimmy Faulkner quickly moved to center stage. Faulkner's campaign made him sound too much like Folsom, who had become unpopular, and he was also burdened with the support of many prominent Folsomites, including Knox McRae, Bill Drinkard, Pitt Tyson Manor, and O. H. Finney. Even though Wallace had split with Folsom, he too suffered from his earlier close association with the governor and the support of many Folsom aides including W. LaRue Horn, Frank Boswell, E. C. ("Bud") Boswell, and Charles Pinkston.[1] Wallace ran a high-toned segregationist, industrial development, moderate populist campaign which centered on his pledge that "segregation shall be preserved with dignity and respect."[2]

Wallace had left the legislature to become a circuit judge in the Barbour County area and, to the degree that he could in that office, had attempted to maintain statewide visibility by engaging in the defense of segregation. But there was little that he could do. He did manage to wrangle invitations to testify against civil rights bills in Congress and issue an order against the removal of segregation signs from railroad stations, and, after federal officials had begun investigating grand jury selection procedures in Cobb County, Georgia, he promised "to invoke the full power and authority I possess and shall issue an order from the arrest of every member of the FBI or other federal police" who might attempt the same thing in Barbour County.[3]

Attorney General John Patterson had kept his distance from Folsom, and his record of anti–civil rights work was impressive. While legislators passed childish bills that were quickly struck down by the courts and Wallace engaged in posturing, Patterson won cases. Also, the tragic incident that had propelled Patterson into public life four years before was still fresh in the minds of many voters. His father, Albert Patterson, had been assassinated by minions of Phenix City, Alabama, gangsters less than a month after he had won the Democratic party nomination for attorney general in 1954. He had campaigned against the gambling, drug trafficking, and prostitution that were rampant in Phenix City. Quickly, the Democratic party executive committee had appointed John to take his father's place as the party's nominee for attorney general.

In 1958 voters were still responding to the elder Patterson's murder and the investigation that followed. Receiving Ku Klux Klan support, which to some degree he solicited, Patterson ran a hard-line segregationist campaign.[4] Wallace denounced the Klan and was endorsed by Jewish and black civil rights groups. He made it into the runoff, but Patterson defeated him with 55 percent of the vote. A short time after his loss, Wallace declared bitterly, "John Patterson out-niggered me, and, boys, I'm not going to be out-niggered again."

Just a few weeks before Wallace's term as circuit judge expired, agents of the federal Civil Rights Commission asked to see voting records in Wallace's district. Recognizing the political potential of this event, he took control of the records and announced, "If any agent of the Civil Rights Commission comes down here to get them, they will be locked up."[5] The agents responded with a federal court subpoena, but Wallace, amid loud publicity, still refused to surrender the records. Meanwhile, knowing that a contempt of court citation would soon follow, Wallace quietly transferred the records to grand juries in Barbour and Bullock counties and then called Civil Rights Commission agents and told them that the records would be available from the grand juries the next day. Despite this last-minute attempt at behind-the-scenes accommodation, Justice Department lawyers appearing before United States District Court Judge Frank M. Johnson, Jr., asked that Wallace be cited for contempt. Wallace, pushing for even more publicity, tried to plead guilty, but Johnson refused to cooperate. Johnson acquitted Wallace and explained the entire episode in his decision. Far from being a "fighting little judge," defying the court and the Civil Rights Commission, he said, Wallace had "through devious methods, assisted said [Commission] agents in obtaining the records."[6]

The Patterson Years

Folsom spent the time following his second term much as he had his previous four-year respite, managing his insurance affairs and various small properties and traveling around the state maintaining his visibility. However, he spent even less time at home during this period than he had before. He would arise before the rest of his family, and by the time they were up, he would be gone. While his drinking at home had increased, his children do not remember the wild excesses that persons outside the family do. He was still able to moderate his drinking when he was around his wife and children. His drinking at home tended to be of a social nature with the many political friends who visited constantly or quiet drinking alone. Often as he drank, he brooded over the people he had lost. For example, one of his children remembered coming upon him drinking on the front porch of the family cabin in Guntersville and quietly crying to himself. Something had started him thinking about the death of his first wife, and he sat there playing her favorite song, "Danny Boy," over and over.

He was not close to his family during this period. Although he encouraged his children to be active in any sports that interested them, such as tennis, he did not participate with them in those activities even though he was fully able. He and Jamelle often played tennis on the court he had built next to the house. He adopted a peculiarly passive role in dealing with his children. For example, he took no apparent interest in the quality of their schoolwork, telling them that average grades were good enough, and he did not attend Melissa's high school graduation, although Jamelle did. At the same time, he did watch over his family, even though he seemed distant. When they broke rules, such as driving a car without a license, he was usually aware of the incidents but let them know it only weeks or months later. He rarely punished them, for the simple expression of his disappointment was usually enough to keep them from repeating the offense. The children had always been made to understand that, as the governor's children, they were subject to especially strict rules of public decorum even when he was out of office. While a concern for manners seems out of character for someone capable of sleeping on a sidewalk during an election campaign, in some circumstances Folsom did care. And he imposed these standards on himself as well as his children.

There were exceptions to his pattern of passivity toward his family. For example, he refused to let Melissa attend the University of Alabama. His friend Dr. Louis Friedman made all the arrangements for her enrollment at the University of Arkansas, and he and Friedman drove a protesting Melissa there. Folsom would not explain why he did not want her at Alabama, but she later learned that her sister Rachael and cousin Cornelia had been blackballed when they had attempted to join a sorority and had experienced other slights because of the civil rights disturbances and Folsom's attitudes. Eventually Melissa left Arkansas and enrolled at the University of Alabama.

In 1961 Folsom was gearing up for a reelection campaign, but his aides were worried lest a racial explosion hurt his chances. Freedom riders, civil rights activists attempting to break interstate bus and bus terminal segregation, brought just such an explosion. In May freedom riders were attacked and beaten near Anniston and in Birmingham. Governor Patterson prefaced a press conference on the subject by observing that "Alabama isn't the Congo." Commenting on the beatings, the governor, a lawyer, a former attorney general, and the son of a man murdered in the streets, said: "When you go somewhere seeking trouble you usually find it. I lay full blame on the agitators who come in here for the express purpose of stirring up just such a thing. We can't act as nursemaids to agitators. They'll stay at home when they learn nobody is there to protect them. The state of Alabama can't guarantee safety of fools, and that's what they are."[7] Patterson evaded efforts by newsmen to get him to condemn the attacks. The strongest statement he would make was, "I don't condone that." As the reporters persisted, Patterson asked angrily, "Are you people in sympathy with the agitators?"[8] Governor Patterson had thus come close to placing the state seal of approval on thuggery.[9]

In late May a mob numbering some one hundred attacked freedom riders and bystanders in the Montgomery bus terminal. White men, women, and teenagers wielded baseball bats and bottles and threw bricks. In the course of the melee three men beat a twenty-one-year-old ministerial student senseless and then held him upright while a woman kicked him in the groin and beat him about the face and head until she became exhausted. Dropping him to the ground, they stomped and kicked him and then picked him up and threw him headfirst over a railing to the concrete several feet below. Only one police officer made an attempt to stop this and many similar beatings.[10] The federal government responded by sending four hundred marshals into Alabama.

Governor Patterson objected to the presence of the federal marshals, maintaining that they were unnecessary since state and local police were enforcing the law quite adequately.[11] The following day, however, a white mob attacked the Negro First Baptist Church, and there were numerous shootings into black homes and acts of vandalism by whites against black-owned property.[12] This was too much even for Patterson, who immediately declared martial law while also continuing to denounce the presence of federal marshals. "We consider you interlopers here," he said to the marshals, "and we feel that your presence here will only serve to agitate and provoke the racial situation." He accused a Justice Department official of encouraging the freedom riders and told him that he believed that they were Communist inspired.[13]

Folsom could have simply remained silent or he could have criticized both the governor for his tacit encouragement of violence and his failure to maintain order and the federal government for encouraging freedom riders, an approach taken by many newspapers in their editorials. He did neither. Instead, he telephoned the hated Attorney General Robert Kennedy and endorsed the marshals' presence. It was an amazing act of bravado. The next day he reversed himself, saying that since law and order had been established the marshals could leave, but reporter Bob Ingram wrote that the phone call to Kennedy would be remembered longer and would do Folsom great harm in 1962.[14]

It is ironic that Folsom, who in the past had used the classic populist theme of fear of outsiders so successfully, welcomed the federal marshal invaders, if only for a day, and that Patterson, who had supported John F. Kennedy's nomination for president, would attach himself so firmly to this theme. It is also ironic that George Wallace, the complete political pragmatist, should emerge as personifying the image of the southern civil rights opponent, for even as governor, Wallace's anti–civil rights acts would remain largely symbolic. Wallace capitalized on the forces set in motion and intensified by leaders like John Patterson.

The 1962 Election

A year before the 1962 gubernatorial campaign began, reporter Ingram discerned a note of uneasiness in the Folsom camp that had not been present in 1954.[15] Folsom's aides were worried about his drinking and about how his opponents would use the continuing racial upheavals. As it turned out, their concerns were well founded on both counts.

In addition to Folsom, the 1962 race included several strong candidates, such as George Wallace, Tuscaloosa Senator Ryan deGraffenreid (a widely admired moderate), Attorney General MacDonald Gallion, and Albert Boutwell. J. Bruce Henderson and Bull Connor were also running.

Race was the pivotal issue of the campaign. Folsom's statements on civil rights were the most moderate of all the candidates, but he was retreating from positions he had taken in earlier years. A draft of his opening speech, which he used throughout the campaign, reflected the changes.

> It is an historical fact that the only way to maintain segregation is to keep it out of court. I have successfully pursued this course in the past and I will do so in the future. . . .
>
> There are certain basic liberties that we need to be concerned with in Alabama today. For instance, the liberties of women are restricted. And old Big Jim is the last man in Alabama who would want to restrict the privileges of women. Today in Alabama they don't have the liberty . . . to serve on juries. For years I have advocated extending this liberty to women. . . .

I never use any minority group—women or otherwise—as a political football. It just isn't right, and I'm not going to now. Our white people and our colored people have lived together in harmony ever since we became a state. It has only been in recent years, when outside, as well as inside, rabble-rousers have created discord. . . . My policy has always been to settle these matters of discord before they get into the courts. Therefore, my record of preserving segregation has been the best of any Governor. . . .

I stand today, as I have always stood in the past, for complete segregation of the races in schools. . . .

. . . My own uncles from Alabama marched off, to the tune of "Dixie," to give their lives during the Civil War. . . . Three of them were killed. One of my Grandpas opposed the war and one favored it. That division remained in our family for many years. . . .

At the end of the Civil War, Abraham Lincoln, in world opinion the world's greatest American, stood before the assembled thousands in front of the White House. Here is what he said, "let us heal our wounds, let us receive the South back into the nation without vindictiveness. Please play 'Dixie.'"

The American Civil War is ended, long live America.

Alabama is the space State of the nation. Let us join the space age. Let us join together again in Alabama. I say to you forward march to victory. Please play "Dixie."[16]

When he first gave this speech, Folsom ad-libbed the following: "These freedom riders; I'd a put them in jail like they did in Mississippi. I would have put them sorry white folks in a cell with the blackest Negroes in Atmore Prison. I think those Negroes would have beaten them up. They don't like them either." He went on to say that when he was governor, there were no segregation cases in the courts, which of course was not true. "Old Big Jim can keep segregation," he concluded.[17]

Throughout the campaign Folsom continued to blame Patterson's mishandling of the freedom riders for increasing federal pressure on Alabama to end discrimination. His newspaper advertisements carried the same message. One read: "Folsom says: 'There will be no integration of public schools.' Folsom says: 'There will be no mixing of white and Negro children in our schools during the next 4 years while I am your governor.'"[18] Still, he felt the need to soften statements of this sort. "No man in his right mind can stand up here and say there will never be any integration," he maintained during a campaign speech. Then recognizing that he may have gone too far, he added that Alabama would be the last state in the union to yield. Whenever he mentioned race during the campaign, his comments shifted back and forth in this fashion. After promising to jail freedom riders, he would advise his audiences to follow Abraham Lincoln's prescription: "'Let's heal up our wounds and join the nation together. The Civil War is over.' Now, they shoot a man around the world in three hours, and they build those shooters in

Huntsville. Let's move ahead without hate or prejudice into the space age." Then he would say, "Segregation will be no problem. All the Negroes want is equal facilities."[19]

Senator deGraffenreid chose to obfuscate the race issue. The approach he took in a March 3 speech in Tuscaloosa was typical. "In the field of segregation, we have got to take the offensive. The only way we'll ever be able to preserve our customs and traditions is to go on the offensive and sell Alabama to the rest of the nation. We have got to have a man with the courage and determination to handle these problems, and you're looking at one right now."[20] In sixty-three words he had said nothing, which was precisely what he wanted to say.

Of the three leading candidates only Wallace, remembering his loss to Patterson, was clear about his intentions. He informed audiences that as governor he would not obey "any order of any Federal court that orders integration of any school."[21]

Folsom used the same campaign techniques that had served him so well in the past, and they generated some enthusiasm (as they did for Wallace, who borrowed liberally from Folsom for his campaign tactics), but they were not the novelty they had been and they were being presented to people for whom a Folsom rally was no longer a major source of entertainment. Television had become commonplace, and roads had improved (thanks in part to Folsom's policies) to the point that even persons living in remote rural areas could reach a nearby town for a movie, shopping, or church. Nevertheless, he plugged along, and audiences enjoyed seeing the old master at work even though his routines were becoming a bit threadbare. "The folks down yonder in Montgomery have been taking too much gravy out of the ham," he would say, "and I want to put it back into schools, roads, and hospitals where it belongs. You put in the ham, I'll do the grinding, and give the gravy to you." Then the "ham sack" was distributed while the Meat Grinders, under Roland Johnson's experienced direction, entertained.

Some fresh lines delighted his audiences. He admitted to having been closely associated with "wine, women, and song to which I plead guilty." At fifty-three, though, he said it had changed to "Metrecal, one gal, and sing along with Big Jim." He compared married life with Jamelle to a poker game: "I called her hand and she raised me eight of the best looking younguns you ever saw."[22] He also spoke seriously about such matters as increased industrial and agricultural development, reminding voters that he was responsible for bringing about the first practical steps toward construction of the Tennessee-Tombigbee Waterway, construction of the inland docks, creation of the Industrial Development Board, and a vast expansion of technical-vocational schools. But voters seemed more interested in hearing Wallace pledge to "stand in the door" of any school threatened with integration. Consequently, as the campaign moved along, Folsom devoted more of his time to defending his record by emphasizing his success in keeping civil rights issues out of the courts and promising that he would continue along similar lines in the future. He refused to indulge in race baiting, despite moves in that direction by Wallace. DeGraffenreid was also forced to devote longer sections of his speeches to segregation, but he continued to talk in vague terms. Like Folsom, he ran as honorable a campaign as a practical politician could under the circumstances.[23]

If Folsom's campaign techniques had changed little, his 1962 campaign was drastically different in tone. His innocence and radicalism were gone, replaced by middle-of-the-road opportunism, hardness, and slickness. Before the campaign he even emphasized that he would not run against the Bosses. "I want them all for me—the big mules, little mules, white mules, and black mules."[24] His 1962 fund-raising techniques also indicated that he had changed. Contributors were encouraged to join the $50-a-month club, the $100-a-month club, and so forth. When asked about this change, he responded, "I don't know anything about that. Shucks, we aren't taking anything less than $1,000."[25] The slickness evidenced in his speeches and interviews was not reflected in the operation of the campaign itself. Some supporters around the state were so disturbed at mistakes being made by the central office in Cullman that they suspected that campaign organizers were dangerously overconfident or, worse, that someone was sabotaging the effort.

Wallace combined his hard-hitting segregationist approach with a dual attack on Folsom's liberal approach to race and his alcoholism by reminding voters that Folsom had brought Adam Clayton Powell into the governor's mansion through the front door and had enjoyed drinks with him. Wallace vowed that no drinks would be served in the governor's mansion while he was in office. The *Montgomery Advertiser* reinforced Wallace's attack and endorsed him, arguing that if Folsom were elected, he would register all blacks to vote and, having achieved that, would abandon his office to armies of greedy aides who would loot the state as they had done in his second term while "he put in many full days at Hot Springs, Ark., taking the waters and perhaps doing other things of doubtful value to the state."[26] Other newspapers were more direct on the alcohol problem. A thoughtful *Andalusia Star-News* editorial entitled "Big Jim and Booze" speculated as to "whether booze had pinned the political giant's shoulders to the mat" and concluded that, while he was not an alcoholic, he was still experiencing "liquor troubles" that could destroy him.[27] In fact, Folsom was an alcoholic, but, as usual when there was something especially important to be done, he had sharply curtailed his liquor consumption prior to the campaign, and he had gotten himself into at least adequate physical condition with long, fast walks.

On the other hand, many people reported that he drank a great deal during the campaign. Several described incidents in which he was too drunk to climb onto the back of a pickup truck or to walk a straight line on a sidewalk.

As election day neared, most political observers were predicting that Folsom and Wallace would find themselves in a runoff, and that would likely have happened had it not been for Folsom's disastrous appearance on a statewide television broadcast the night before the election. The broadcast, consisting of a film, was supposed to have originated from Birmingham, but a strike prevented that, and so it was shifted to Montgomery. That afternoon, because he did not expect to appear on the broadcast except for a brief moment with his family, Folsom felt free to drink on his way to Montgomery. He was, by his own account, in "bad shape" upon his arrival in Montgomery; he took a nap lasting at least an hour and then had dinner, at which he drank moderately or not at all. His daughter Melissa spoke to him before the broadcast, and he was quite coherent. She said, "I didn't notice anything. I am convinced that he was OK before the TV appearance."

Just before the broadcast it was discovered that the film was not in the studio, and so Folsom decided to go on live with his family and ad-lib. A physician gave Folsom a vitamin shot, as he had many times in the past. Some who were there felt that Folsom was at that point not in good enough condition to attempt a broadcast, and they tried to dissuade him from going on. Others encouraged him. When he went on the air, he appeared to some to be drunk, but to others he seemed drugged. When he tried to introduce his children, he seemed to forget their names, running through several of their names as he tried to introduce each child. "Now, which one are you?" he asked one. As he gave up on introducing the children, a technician quickly put a film on—which appeared upside down. Jim, Jr., and Melissa, who were on camera with him, did not sense at the time how bad the scene looked to television viewers. They were aware only that it was somewhat awkward. His difficulty with his children's names was not noteworthy for them because he often absentmindedly ran through the entire list before getting to the name of the child to whom he was speaking. Melissa spoke to her father again after the broadcast, and he appeared to be completely in command of his faculties, asking her if she had arranged for a ride back to Tuscaloosa and engaging in general small talk.

Since this incident cost Folsom the election, it is natural that the events of that day would be exhaustively analyzed. The first question was, What happened to the film which was to be shown? It is likely that no one remembered to transfer it from Birmingham to Montgomery; there was speculation, however, that someone in the Folsom camp working for an opponent intentionally lost it.

The larger question concerned the cause of Folsom's behavior on camera.

Some thought that he had not recovered from his afternoon bout with the bottle, and a few even charged that traitors within the campaign had encouraged his afternoon drinking, as they had throughout the campaign. (According to this theory, these traitors were the same ones responsible for losing the film.) Others, though, thought he went on the air in that condition out of sheer stubbornness.

Another theory focused on the injection that he received. Some believed that the physician intended for the injection to backfire. They viewed him as a Rasputin-like figure fully capable of selling Folsom out. This explanation is improbable. The doctor was one of Folsom's largest financial contributors, and he was one of the few real populists attached to Folsom in the latter years of his career; he had a strong personal stake in Folsom. Nevertheless, the injection could have backfired accidentally.

A third theory about his condition was that he was drugged. Persons who were close to him that day and Folsom himself agreed that he was drunk that evening but not *that* drunk, and many hardheaded politicians and reporters who knew Folsom well thought he looked drugged, not drunk. Some believed that the drug was in the injection, but for the reasons given above this seems unlikely. It could have been administered in a glass of water or liquor or in his dinner. Supporters of the drugging theory pointed to what they viewed as an organized rumor campaign aimed at Folsom's drinking, claiming that the rumors surfaced in full force just before election day and drew a large audience to the broadcast to check on Folsom's condition. His children's memories of his condition before, during, and after the broadcast seem to discount the drugging theory. Still, someone might have administered a mild drug capable of rendering him confused but not incoherent.

A fourth theory is that a hematoma (a kind of bruise) in his brain, together with drinking and the fatigue that would naturally follow an arduous campaign, caused the behavior. On August 9, 1964, this hematoma would cause violent grand mal seizures and would require neurosurgery for its removal. Folsom would later decide that the hematoma, perhaps aggravated by an illicitly administered drug, had made him behave as he did. Folsom's physician, John T. Morris, declared: "It is my opinion that this brain lesion was the cause of Mr. Folsom's behavior on the night preceding the election of 1962. Jacksonian seizures, notoriously, come late following cerebral damage and/or scar tissue formation."[28] We may never know for certain where the truth lies.

Folsom missed the runoff by fewer than two thousand votes, an incredible feat considering what had occurred the night before. The count was very close and in doubt for many hours. While the count was continuing, a man representing someone very close to Folsom, but not Folsom himself, appeared in the office of State Democratic Party Chairman Sam Engelhardt, who was responsible for overseeing the count. Sensing that something peculiar was afoot, Engelhardt switched on a small tape recorder hidden in his brief case and quietly moved it toward the man, who offered virtually a blank check if Engelhardt would see to it that Folsom made it into the runoff. The chairman refused. When the man had left, he eagerly played the tape, but because the man had spoken in such soft tones, there was nothing to hear.[29]

As the count wore on and it became apparent that Folsom would lose, two of his closest aides, one of whom had supported him from an early point in his career, walked into Folsom's house in Cullman and announced, "Well, it's all over." They did not seem a bit upset.

Later that night, Folsom came down the steps from his bedroom. He was crying. He went outside, tore the campaign stickers from his car, and drove away. He was not seen again for two weeks.

After 1962

The next decade was a rough one for Folsom and his family. To his children he was a different person. He was usually absent, but even at home he drank constantly and in enormous quantities. He was very difficult to communicate with, and he angered easily. He underwent brain surgery after the difficult-to-locate hematoma was finally found, and then partly as a result of more drinking suffered another grand mal seizure in 1966. At that time his physician prescribed anticonvulsive drugs and urged him to stop drinking; aside from one episode of backsliding, he did so. Folsom recalled that the doctor told him to "quit drinking or die," and after the seizures he had little difficulty making the choice. Later in 1966 he suffered an automobile accident that left him with three bone fractures, but he recovered quickly from those injuries. In 1971 he underwent heart surgery for the implanting of an artificial valve.

During this period he engaged in a series of large-scale business ventures. He was extremely successful in common stock trading, but he became involved in two disastrous enterprises in the early and middle 1960s that, together with the sale of real estate at ridiculously low prices plus medical expenses, left him nearly penniless. The last major business in which he became involved was a locknut factory, which he purchased at a cost of one hundred thousand dollars. He quickly ran it into the ground with erratic pricing and other irrational policies that irritated customers. He seemed to throw money away.

Even as his health deteriorated and his wealth disappeared, he moved closer to his sons Jim and Jack. When they turned fifteen, they became eligible for their learner's permits. Each remembered being literally dragged out of bed in the predawn hours to take their father across the state to visit friends, to travel to their Gulf Shores cabin or, when they were staying at Gulf Shores, to run to the Florida border for liquor purchases. During these sometimes long trips, their father, for the first time in their lives, would talk to them about politics, past campaigns, and history. This was the way he had gotten close to his father, traveling with him at the age of four and five as his father made his tax collection rounds, and this was the way Uncle John had passed on the family history and his political ideals. The same pattern occurred with his third-youngest child, Lala. Each came to view Folsom as a dedicated populist with a deep respect for Alabama's yeoman farmers and workers and to understand the intensity of his beliefs and adopt many of his views as their own. As Folsom himself had, they absorbed those attitudes and beliefs through stories and tales of the past.

In the late 1960s the children began to see the effects of their father's business losses in their own lives. College became possible only if they worked their way through. Money for new clothes, home repairs, even food was often difficult to come by. The Alabama Constitution forbade the payment of a pension to a former governor, a problem that would be remedied by the legislature only in the late 1970s when it passed a statute allowing former governors to be named special consultants to the governor and to receive a state salary for their assistance. For more than a decade, then, Folsom had no pension on which to rely. Most of the old political friends were not around to help, the medical bills mounted, and there was still a house full of children, including Melody, born in 1970.

During the 1960s Folsom ran for various offices almost as a reflex action. He always hated to see an election go by that he was not contesting, for an election represented another opportunity to agitate for liberty and to damn the Big Mules and the lawyers. In 1974 he again ran for governor against George Wallace and a North Alabama state legislator named Gene McLain. He had few illusions about his chances of defeating Wallace, who was as popular then as he was any time in his career, but he sometimes fantasized about making it into the runoff against his old adversary and then beating him in an old-time political toe-to-toe. His real intent in running, though, was not to defeat Wallace but rather to limit his victory margin to make him look weak in Alabama and thus diminish his national strength. Part of his motivation was ideological, and another part was revenge for his 1962 defeat. That defeat seemed to prey on his mind more than he liked to admit. In an Associated Press interview he made no secret of his dislike for Wallace's place in Alabama history. He labeled Wallace "the god of the Dixiecrats and segregationists"[30] and privately referred to him as that "slaveholding son-of-a-bitch."

His was a low-budget campaign. Someone had printed cards for him. He had selected as his slogan "Walking Tall," after the popular motion picture of the same title. The front of the little pasteboard, about the size of a playing card, showed Folsom striding confidently toward the camera, and the back listed his campaign pledges: "(1) A convention for changed constitution. 'Not a smoke-filled room amendment'; (2) Equal rights amendment (ladies rights); (3) Abolish sales tax on all food; (4) Free hospital for all. Cradle to grave; (5) A law license and a legislative seat is a conflict of interest; (6) Blacktop every mailbox road in Alabama; (7) Running on the record."

Friends took turns driving him on one-week trips around the state, concentrating on North Alabama. The schedule was not an easy one. One April tour had him in Arab, Guntersville, Bridgeport, Stevenson, Flat Rock, and Valley Head on Monday; Fort Payne, Rainsville, Section, Dutton, Pisgah, Hennager, Sylvania, Fyffe, Chigger Hill, Geraldine, and Crossville on Tuesday; Boaz, Albertville, Oneonta, Blountsville, Summitt, Morgan City, and Hartselle on Wednesday; and so forth. The program was even fuller than this list suggests because he liked to stop at crossroads if he saw that he was ahead of schedule, and sometimes even when he was behind. At sixty-six years of age, he kept up this pace week after week, exhausting one traveling companion after another.

He did most of the driving himself so that he could be seen emerging from the car as the driver, thus demonstrating that, despite his many health problems, he was still vigorous and sober. His driving further tired his companions. He had always treated all mechanical devices as if they were products of alien black magic. To make a phonograph or radio work he would stab and twist aimlessly at the controls, all the while grumbling to himself until something happened (often the demise of the mechanism under attack). He drove much the same way, except that lives were at stake. At a stop sign he slowed down in the middle of the intersection and looked vaguely about, somewhat irritated that the sign had interrupted his train of conversation. He stopped at red lights regularly; once he had stopped and returned to his conversation (actually a monologue), however, the green was often not sufficient to bring his foot off the brake, nor were angry honks from behind. The turn signal indicator was a toy to be flipped back and forth at random. Certain he was immune to arrest, he sped down narrow two-lane roads at 75 to 80 miles per hour. "They won't make the same mistake they made back there in Birmingham," he said as he careened down a backcountry road. "They don't want to make a martyr the way they did before." Making fatigue even worse for his friends was the fact that he arose a little before dawn and kept moving until sundown. His companions, most of whom were younger and in far better health, were completely worn out by the end of a week of this, while he would be eager for another five days with a fresh recruit.

When he hit a town, he parked somewhere on the main street—no one would put a parking ticket on Big Jim's car—and worked one side of the street, while his companion took the other.

"How Y'all?"

"Who's your daddy?"

"What's your name?"

"Let's move the governor's chair back up to North Alabama! We want our share of the gravy."

"It's right there on the card. Free hospital care from cradle to grave. I built 'em in my first two terms as governor and now I'm goin' to free 'em."

"I don't want the salary, I just wants the expense account!"

When people first saw him, they would look away, but then they would realize who he was and would turn back and stare in awe.

Driving past the Bon-Ton barber shop in one town, Folsom remarked that he had given the barber a job when he was CWA administrator. "I had 2,600 working. That was too many. They liked to fire me for that. . . . When I was working for CWA I graveled these roads, and when I was governor I blacktopped them, and then four laned them."

In another town an old supporter and first-term ABC Board appointee, now seventy-six years of age, said, "People come in here and I say, 'Who you gonna vote for for governor?' And they say, 'I don't know. I don't know. But I sure ain't gonna vote for that Wallace. No sir, I ain't gonna vote for that Wallace.'" Folsom sat on the corner of a gray metal desk, swinging one leg and grinning. "That's what they sayin' eh?" "Yup. They're sayin', 'I don't know who I'm gonna vote for, but it ain't gonna be that Wallace.'" After conversations like this, Folsom would, for a few minutes, believe that he had a chance.

He stopped at a country store and gas station at a Tennessee Valley crossroads. A "Walking Tall" card was taped to the upper right corner of a Marlboro poster. The storekeeper was a handsome gray-haired former sheriff. An elderly man with thick glasses wearing dark blue striped trousers and a dark maroon narrow-lapeled coat and a man in his late thirties wearing tan work pants, heavy boots, and a thick cotton plaid shirt were sitting in the store.

The old man greeted Folsom, "the best governor this state's ever seen." Folsom interjected, "Well, I've built more roads around here than anyone. Bibb Graves started it and I almost finished it except for that bridge over yonder that Brewer started and George stopped. He's still tryin' to explain that bridge. Since Wallace has been in office, Montgomery has four lanes all around, and Dothan, and all over the Black Belt, but nothin' up here except what I built. We need another man from North Alabama." The younger man chimed in, "Yeah, that Wallace is nothin' but a little dictator." The others nodded in solemn agreement.

Folsom joined a group of men on the porch whittling and chewing tobacco. His baggy, wrinkled, stained, mended suit and heavy walking shoes fit the surroundings perfectly. Folsom distributed his cards, and the men read them slowly. One said, "These all look good, Jim, except for number four" ("Free hospital for all—cradle to grave"). They told him that he was "the best governor we've ever had." Folsom responded modestly, "I'm the only one from North Alabama since 1910."

Near Decatur he stopped at the spacious home of a long-time ally who, it developed, was a determined segregationist. "You maintained segregation better than any other governor," he said, admiringly. "You kept Autherine Lucy out of the University. All Wallace did was stand in the doorway while the niggers walked past him. You were effective. You got her expelled." Folsom replied, "I had nothing to do with her expulsion." "Sure, Jim," the man said, with an air of worldly sophistication. "No," Folsom said again, "I had nothing to do with it." "Sure, Jim, sure," the man repeated gently. Folsom insisted a third time, pronouncing each word slowly and distinctly, "I abstained on that vote. I had nothing to do with her being expelled." As Folsom was leaving, the man pulled a sheaf of bills from his pocket, peeled off three or four hundred dollars, and pressed them into Folsom's hand. "This is for your traveling expenses," he said. The man had greatly benefited from Folsom administration patronage, and he could not bring himself to believe that Folsom had opposed segregation in any way.

Later in the car Folsom angrily discussed black groups endorsing either Wallace or McLain with none of them supporting him. He was beginning to tell people, "We'll let George take half the blacks, that fella from Huntsville the other half, and I'll take the white majority. . . . George has been giving me hell all the time for the black vote and now he has it. I ought to give those black bastards hell all over the state, but that wouldn't be right would it?" Publicly he never went further than a few sarcastic remarks about the ingratitude of black leaders.

In Arab he was distressed to learn that some old cronies had died. "That's the trouble with campaigning at my age—all the old crowd's done died off, and I'm runnin' a young man's platform," he said, shaking his head sadly. "That's the sad part about goin' around."

He won about 5 percent of the vote in 1974.

After 1974 Folsom suffered a series of strokes which blinded him, a bout of bronchopneumonia combined with heart failure, and other medical problems. Through all these dangerous, frightening, and often painful episodes his morale remained extraordinarily high. During his recovery from heart surgery, he roamed the hospital visiting other patients and keeping their spirits up.[31] According to his physician his approach to his illnesses was "'onward and upward. Let's get the job done, whatever it is.' He has shown a remarkable tolerance and affection for people and disregard for the pain that he . . . has experienced. . . . He has not complained of his blindness. He is totally liberated from alcoholism. He has no stigmata of alcoholism."[32] In interviews Folsom never mentioned his blindness except indirectly in relation to such things as his inability to read, which was a major source of recreation for him prior to his strokes. His only other references to his physical condition concerned his need to take his "blood thinner" medication regularly.

His political philosophy remained unchanged, and politics continued to be of central importance in his life. His political activity, however, was largely limited to two areas. The first was his continuing concern over lawyers actively practicing law while serving in the legislature. Even though new ethics laws reduced the number of lawyer-legislators by requiring total disclosure of their firms' clients, Folsom continued to raise the separation of powers issue by instituting federal court suits and filing for governor in 1978 and 1982 as a way to garner publicity for his cause. He also questioned the propriety of public educators serving in the legislature while still part of the executive branch.

His second area of political activity was campaigning for Jim, Jr. (a member of the Alabama Public Service Commission and almost elected to the U.S. Senate), and Jack (who ran unsuccessfully for the office of commissioner of agriculture and industries) by visiting old friends and calling his old political contacts. During Little Jim's Senate race in 1980 a small motorcade and a series of speaking engagements through North Alabama were arranged for Folsom, and many of the older voters who had elected him to office came out to see their Big Jim and promise their vote to his son. Jamelle has campaigned actively on her own, making numerous trips to county courthouses and to people's homes for political teas. And the other children have been involved in the campaigns. Another generation of Folsoms has moved into the political arena.

CHAPTER 12

Folsom's Impact and the Web of Power

> Most of the world's decision makers, however powerful they may appear in journalistic accounts, must cope with the effects of decisions already made by events, circumstances, and other persons and hence . . . must act within narrow bounds.
>
> James MacGregor Burns

When running for office, most politicians take the position that their selection over their opponent will make a difference. They may argue that they will be more honest, caring and hardworking. Frequently, they promise that their new programs will solve such problems as the rising crime rate, that they will cut taxes or improve schools. Often they simply argue that it is time for a change and that they represent that change. Gubernatorial candidates are as likely as any to make such claims.

After an individual has been in office for a while, the public may perceive that changes are occurring. Crime rates may diminish, taxes may take a smaller bite out of pay checks, and educational test scores may rise. Those who voted for the officeholder may conclude that the changes they like are the result of his or her actions. Those who opposed the incumbent might credit other factors, such as the national economy, luck, or interest group pressure.

Some studies suggest that policymaking processes and decisions can often be explained in considerable detail with little reference to the individuals involved.[1] Even governors seem to have little personal impact on public policy.[2] A governor's freedom of action is limited by the social, economic, and technological forces that dominate his state and by public opinion.[3] Also, most state chief executives share the perspectives and interests of officials and interest group leaders with whom they must work. In such cases the impact of a governor is impossible to measure. Not all governors can be characterized this way, however. Through outstanding leadership and by virtue of being outside dominant interest group patterns, some are able to transcend the limits that constrain most governors. Many Alabamians believe that James E. Folsom had a large personal impact (for good or ill) on the direction of Alabama public policy; this chapter investigates that belief.

For any political figure to make an impact, he or she must in some sense have a perspective different from that of other government officials and major interest group leaders and the general public.[4] Folsom was drastically at odds with most other state policymakers and interest group leaders, and in the field of civil rights he was also completely out of step with the opinions of most voters. With few exceptions, other Alabama governors have mirrored prevailing attitudes on all important matters. They have had no interest in challenging the status quo except perhaps in one or two specialized areas. This gubernatorial conformity is not surprising since nearly all Alabama chief executives held one or more state offices before becoming governor. They were political insiders and wanted to remain so.

To make an impact, a politician must be more than just different. He must also be an effective leader. Folsom's record is erratic in this regard. His leadership was sometimes grossly inept, but he was effective often enough to justify the common belief that his eight years in office made Alabama a different place than it would have been had Handy Ellis or one of his 1954 opponents won and that it would have been a better place as far as civil rights was concerned had he been elected in 1962.

At least one additional factor must be present before a governor can have an impact; he should begin with some sort of substantial power base. The Alabama governorship itself is a mountain of power both legislatively and administratively. The powers are formally and informally granted and until recently included a substantial patronage base.

In Big Jim Folsom the State of Alabama had a governor who wanted to make drastic changes and whose goals were quite different from those of most other political leaders. At times he was capable of effective leadership, and he possessed sufficient formal power to have at least a chance of winning fights in the legislature and making administrative changes in the executive branch.

Of course, it is impossible to determine with certainty Folsom's impact on the state. No one can be sure what would have occurred had he not been governor. Nevertheless, with a few assumptions and a careful examination of his objectives and achievements, it is possible to arrive at conclusions which are reasonable, if not certain.

It is commonly assumed that because an event occurs during a chief executive's term of office he or she is the cause. In Alabama, for example, the increases in highway construction during Folsom's administrations are usually viewed as being the direct result of his efforts. But those increases may have been nothing more than the entire political system's response to the state's increasing urbanization and wealth and an expanded federal commitment to road construction, a set of conditions common to all other states at that time. Therefore Folsom's impact cannot be evaluated in absolute terms.

Folsom's impact will be judged from two perspectives. First, his performance will be compared to that of the governors who preceded and followed him. The concern here is whether the state and its people moved toward the objectives he established during his terms in office and, if they did, whether the changes were due to his actions or to processes set in motion before he took office. If his performance fit a preexisting pattern, his impact can be judged as minimal. Second, the performance of Alabama under his leadership will be compared to the nation as a whole. Since the entire southern region has generally fallen behind the rest of the nation in most areas of economic, social, and political development, Alabama's record will also be compared to that of the South.[5]

It is assumed that if Alabama merely kept pace with national and southern figures or fell behind, Folsom had no impact. Folsom may have had an impact only if in a given year in which he held office (and one year thereafter) Alabama improved its standing in comparison with national and southern averages. Since it is possible for a relative increase in Alabama's standing to have coincided with a Folsom term only accidentally (due to routine interest group interaction, decreased federal efforts, and so forth), each case in which he appears to have made an impact will be reviewed.

Reapportionment

Legislative reapportionment through a constitutional convention was the centerpiece of Folsom's attack on the Alabama power elite. If the federal courts had not intervened to force reapportionment in the 1960s, it still would probably have occurred because of strains that were developing in the Boss alliance due to the rapid growth of such industrial centers as Birmingham, Mobile, Gadsden, and Huntsville and the gradual shift of the population base to Jefferson County and North Alabama. In any event, Folsom's many attempts to bring about reapportionment and a constitutional convention failed.

Civil Rights

The poll tax and discriminatory voter registration were the chief means by which blacks and poor whites were kept from voting. They were Folsom's major targets in the area of civil rights. His first-term efforts to eliminate or

Table 4. Adult Blacks Registered to Vote,
Alabama versus the South (Percentages)

	1940	1947	1952	1956	1958
South	5.0	12	20	25	28
Alabama	<.5	1	5	11	15
Approximate difference	5.0	11	15	14	13

Source: Donald R. Matthews and James W. Prothro, *Negroes and the New Southern Politics* (New York: Harcourt, Brace and World, 1966), p. 148. Matthews and Prothro define the South as Mississippi, Alabama, South Carolina, Louisiana, Georgia, Arkansas, Florida, Virginia, Texas, North Carolina, and Tennessee.

reduce the poll tax failed. However, a drastic reduction in the poll tax occurred in 1953 during Governor Persons's administration, and it might be possible to attribute some credit for this development to Folsom's earlier efforts, but such a conclusion can only be very tentative.[6]

Table 4 shows that, comparing Alabama's performance to the southern average, Folsom's efforts to lessen voting discrimination were not very successful. There is no question that in some counties he appointed or influenced the appointment of officials who registered blacks in considerable numbers, but at the same time he completely avoided taking action in the Black Belt. By so doing, he wrote off large numbers of blacks. It is difficult to believe that his leading gubernatorial opponents would have accomplished even as much as he did, but by the strict standards being applied here, it cannot be concluded that Folsom had any impact in this area.

Folsom also wanted to end segregation in a gradual manner, but there was very little moderation in any form of segregation during either of his terms. Indeed, one could argue that through no fault of his own segregation was more pronounced in 1959 at the end of his gubernatorial career.

Folsom regarded his efforts on behalf of reapportionment and civil rights as more important than all his other accomplishments combined. He argued that his "agitating for liberty" helped to create a climate that prepared the way for later progress. There is no way to disprove his contention, but there is little direct objective evidence to support it. Later in this chapter Folsom's impact will be viewed through the perceptions of his political friends and foes.

Road Construction

Folsom is more closely identified with road construction than he is with any other policy area except reapportionment and civil rights. Many Alabamians believe that road building was his greatest contribution to the state. In 1946 when he took office, huge numbers of people were connected to neighbors, towns, doctors, and markets only by bumpy, often dusty dirt roads that were sometimes made impassable by heavy rains. Even many paved roads were narrow, crude, and dangerous. Folsom promised to build and repair those roads and make the people of the outlying regions an integral part of the state by giving them access to economic and political power centers. To do this he advocated drastic increases in appropriations for all types of road construction, with special emphasis on rural mailbox roads. He also introduced legislation to increase the governor's authority over the Highway Department and to increase the revenue base for construction.

The data for the period just after World War II show a nationwide pattern of spending increases for road and bridge building and maintenance. Alabama and the South followed this pattern. (See Figure 4.)

Figures on spending for construction alone (not shown in Figure 4) point to 1947 as a year when Alabama narrowed the gap between it and the South and nation. Careful examination of Alabama events, however, shows that the 1947 increases were due to increasing gasoline tax revenues from increased postwar driving, not Folsom's administrative action. And the 1942–46 construction figures were very low due to the war itself. Folsom introduced legislation to increase the revenue base for construction greatly, but his proposals were first gutted by Senate committee action and then killed on the Senate floor.

Figure 4 shows the difference between the total per capita spending on roads (construction and maintenance dollars) in Alabama and that in the nation and the South. One line represents the spending difference between Alabama and the South; the other line, the difference between Alabama and the nation. A data point located at zero would indicate no spending level differences between Alabama and the nation or the South. A negative number means Alabama is spending less per capita on roads than the nation or the South; a positive number would indicate greater per capita spending in Alabama. A drop in either trend line means Alabama is falling behind the nation or the South in its spending rate, while a rise indicates an upward movement in spending. Notice that throughout the 1940s and 1950s Alabama's rate of highway spending stayed behind national and southern rates.

Despite Folsom's reputation, Figure 4 suggests that it would be difficult to argue that his terms of office changed the course of state spending. During his first term, per capita spending remained virtually constant in Alabama, while it continued to grow in the South and the nation. In 1946 and 1947 the per capita gap between Alabama and the nation was approximately $1.00. By the time he left office four years later, the gap was eight times that amount. There was also a large increase in the gap between Alabama and

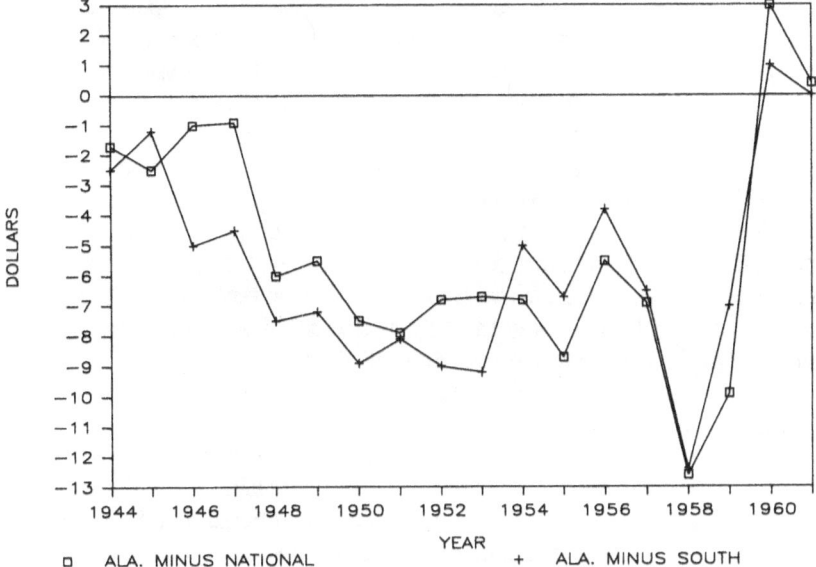

Figure 4. State Highway Funds per Capita

the South. Growth in all categories of highway spending occurred in his second term, but Alabama did not keep pace with national or southern spending patterns. Nevertheless, two years of his second term brought Alabama at least temporarily closer to the national and southern figures.[7]

From 1955 to 1956 the per capita gap in total spending between Alabama and the nation narrowed sharply. These changes occurred even though both the national and southern figures were rapidly increasing. Folsom's 1955 road-building proposals stunned even those accustomed to his grandiose visions. His program was scaled down in the House and again in the Senate, but he finally won a $50 million bond issue and a one-cent-per-gallon gasoline tax increase. Folsom was obliged to push hard for even the scaled-down version of his program, using routine log-rolling tactics with some legislators, bribing others, and threatening still others.

Folsom cannot be given all the credit for the 1955–56 increases. Federal matching funds served as a powerful inducement for all states. However, the 1955–56 increase was a large one, and it was at least partially due to Folsom's 1954 election of friendly legislators, his selection of competent legislative leaders, and a hard-fought battle. At a minimum, it is possible to conclude that he was responsible for a short-term acceleration of road construction.

In the period 1959–60, during John Patterson's term, Alabama actually moved ahead of both national and southern per capita spending levels. One reason for the move was that both national and southern spending had leveled off, but a second reason was Governor Patterson's successful advocacy of a $60 million bond issue. The financial backing for this issue was Folsom's one-cent-per-gallon tax increase.[8] Thus, Patterson must share credit for this additional spurt in construction and maintenance with Folsom.

Folsom's reputation as a road builder is especially strong in North Alabama, a region which before his election had been starved for good roads by a long series of Black Belt and South Alabama governors. Making matters worse, construction costs in the hilly, rocky north were often two or three times what they were in the remainder of the state.

The conventional political wisdom in the state concerning road construction is that the governor rewards counties that supported him in the Democratic party primary. North Alabama was largely responsible for voting Folsom into office, and conversations with politicians, journalists, and citizens throughout the state indicated a widespread belief that North Alabama was amply rewarded for its support. A county-by-county comparison of voting patterns for Folsom in the primaries and road construction completed in each county shows that those counties that had supported him in the primary did benefit substantially from increases in road construction.[9] These increases were more pronounced in his second term than his first, fitting the pattern of his program successes in the legislature. But counties that had not supported his election also benefited from increased construction, since the funding base had greatly increased. In North Alabama and the rural areas of the state, the change from the past was so dramatic that the perceptions of Folsom's impact have been magnified. Nonetheless the distribution of road-building activities was different under Folsom.

Public Assistance

Folsom's major concern in this area was for increases in payments to those over sixty-five years of age. Ever since his congressional campaigns, he had consistently supported such increases and in office he pushed for whatever increases he thought politically realistic. His basic objective was dignity for the aged. He also favored increases in other categories of assistance, such as unemployment compensation and payments to those injured in job-related accidents or incapacitated by job-related ailments, such as black lung and brown lung. In general, he supported larger payments under existing programs and increased funding of the state's share of federal programs, rather than initiate new programs.

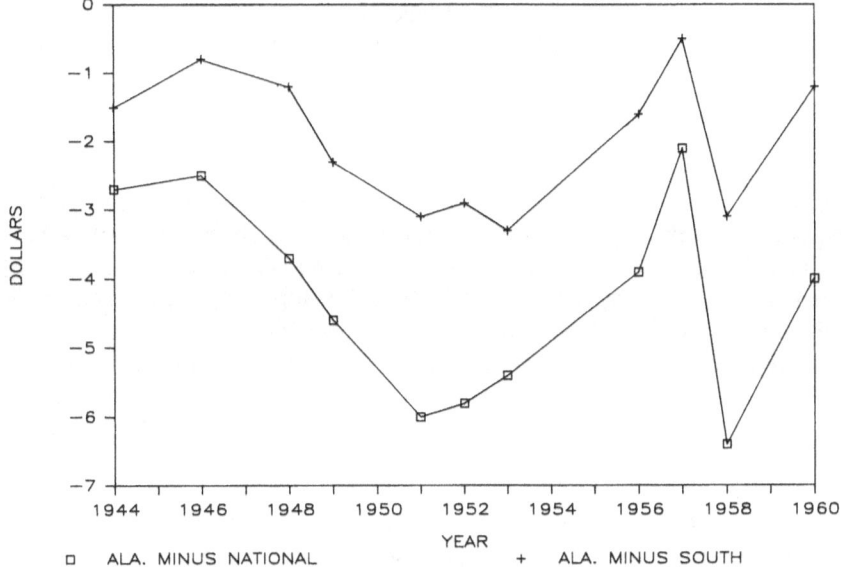

Figure 5. Public Assistance per Capita

Figure 5 plots Alabama per capita spending for public assistance compared to national and southern per capita levels. Public assistance spending increased over the years, but Alabama fell progressively behind the national and southern levels. Immediately after World War II and during Folsom's first term, Alabama's per capita rate lost ground. Alabama began to close the gap during the Persons administration, and the gap continued to narrow during the early years of Folsom's second term, only to widen again in the latter part of his term. The gap began to narrow again during the Patterson years.

It is clear that the figures did not move in the direction Folsom desired in his first term. One reason for this was that the legislature directed monies Folsom had intended for the aged to education. Under Persons, public assistance expenditures increased more slowly than they had under Folsom, but because national per capita spending leveled off, the gap between Alabama and the other states narrowed. This set of forces continued into Folsom's second term. Folsom's appropriations requests were much higher than Persons's, and he expended considerable effort toward winning these funds and tax increases to pay for them, but the legislature drastically reduced his appropriations requests and defeated most of his tax proposals.

Folsom was equally unsuccessful in both terms, and it seems safe to conclude that he had little direct impact on total welfare spending.

Industrial Development

Folsom advocated industrial development and industrial growth and actively pursued them throughout his second term. He is widely credited with accelerating the startup of the Tennessee-Tombigbee construction and creating the inland docks system and the Industrial Development Board. With all his criticism of the Big Mules, including the Birmingham industrial interests, industrial leaders indicate that he was a positive force on industrial development and never hurt their growth. He especially favored development of Alabama industry as a way to lessen out-of-state influences on Alabama's economy and saw the development of the waterway system and the inland docks as part of that process.

It is difficult to compare his industrial development programs with similar programs carried out in other southern states. It is also easy to imagine that most of Folsom's major opponents for governor, especially those tied to the Birmingham and Mobile Bosses, would have pursued industrial development as effectively as he did; however, his imaginative and energetic advocacy of the Tennessee-Tombigbee interstate compact and the inland docks construction would probably not have been equaled by others. The fact that the canal was not a viable project is not relevant to an evaluation of Folsom's personal impact. Therefore, he can be credited with making at least a marginal and possibly a substantial difference in this field.

Education

Except for general references to increasing the length of the school year, providing free textbooks, and establishing vocational schools, Folsom's major objective in education was to make more funds available to educational administrators so that they might improve facilities and instruction as they saw fit. A vocational training bill passed the legislature with his support, but the major effort on its behalf came from George Wallace. In higher education, Folsom's goal of breaking the Farm Bureau–Extension Service tie at Auburn failed.

An examination of all available data on education funding shows that in all categories of spending Alabama expenditures rose steadily after World War II. At the elementary and secondary school levels, two sets of data, per pupil expenditure and average salaries, typify this change (see Figures 6 and

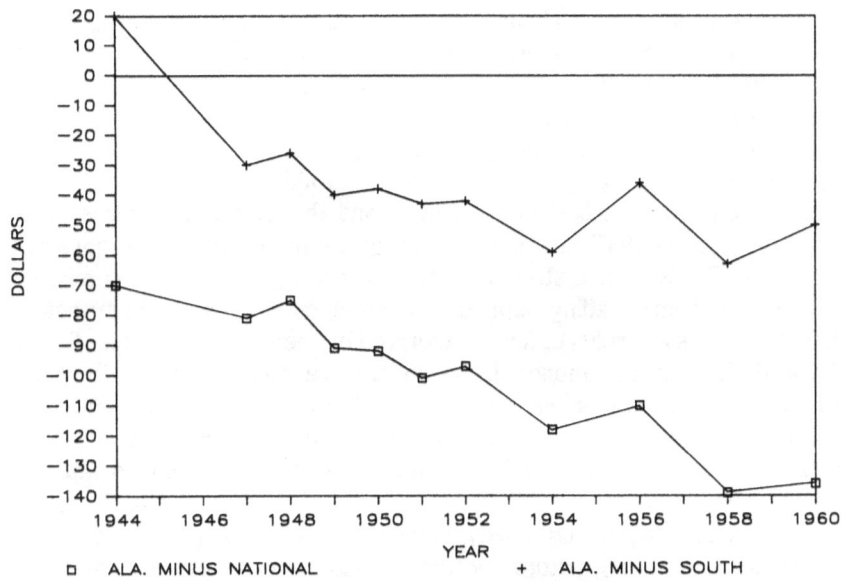

Figure 6. School Expenses per Pupil

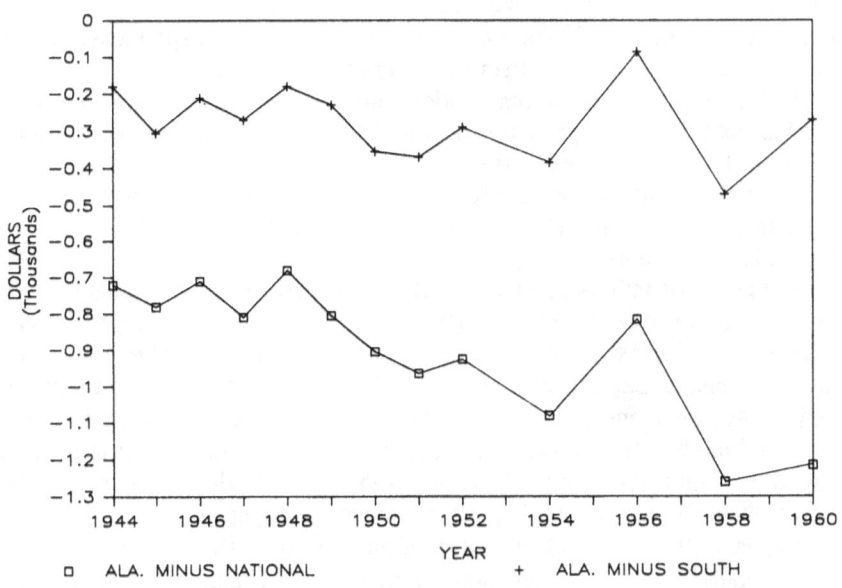

Figure 7. Teacher Salaries

7). The gap between Alabama and the South and the nation in per pupil expenditures narrowed between 1947 and 1948, 1950 and 1952, 1954 and 1956, and 1958 and 1960. The overall trend, however, was that of decline in comparison to the nation and near constancy with the South.

Salaries for school personnel was the biggest category in the expenditure figures. In this category only 1947–48 and 1955–56 saw any appreciable narrowing of the gap between the state and the nation. The surge in pay brought about in 1947 cannot be attributed to the newly elected governor, however. The evidence strongly suggests that it would have occurred had either of Folsom's leading opponents been elected. When Folsom took office, there was a surplus of funds generated by the state income tax. Folsom favored dividing the money between welfare and education. Teachers' groups and overwhelming majorities of both houses of the legislature wanted all the money to go into education. In this instance Folsom worked against educational interests, but even then he was advocating an improved position for education.

There was relatively little disagreement between Folsom, educational interests, and most legislators concerning regular appropriations for education. Teacher salary figures showed that Alabama had slipped far behind the nation and most of the South, and even the most dollar conscious conservatives realized that salaries had to be improved.[10] Journalists writing at that time and Folsom himself observed that legislators were responding more to educational interest groups than they were to the governor.

During the Persons administration, not only did educational interest groups continue their pressure on the legislature but Governor Persons supported a 1 percent sales tax increase for education. This brought Alabama closer to national and southern averages between 1951 and 1952, but the gap widened again between 1952 and 1954 even though the state continued to increase its funding.

As a result of actions taken in the 1955 legislative session, Alabama drew very close to the southern average for salaries and drastically cut the gap between itself and the national average. The gap in per pupil expenditures also decreased. Legislative reapportionment, an expanded road program, and old-age pensions were seen by Folsom as more important than education, and in 1955 he behaved accordingly, providing little more than verbal support for education. Indeed, he opposed a critical sales tax increase that was pushed through the legislature by education supporters.

It appears that Folsom had no impact on education. Dr. Austin Meadows, state superintendant of education for many years, including both Folsom terms, disagreed with this assessment. He argued that Folsom succeeded in raising the average citizen's expectations concerning what could be accomplished in the school system.[11] Perhaps he is correct. It could be that in opposing the sales tax increase for education in 1955 Folsom was opposing forces that he himself had set in motion in earlier years. But the evidence of Folsom's actions in both terms suggests that, although he favored increased appropriations for education, he had several other higher priorities.

The Overall Impact

Public policy in Alabama would probably have been little different had James Folsom never been elected governor. In his first term he sorely lacked administrative experience, and he faced a malapportioned legislature dominated by seasoned Black Belt and Birmingham legislators who had no trouble destroying his programs. A chief executive can accomplish little unless he succeeds in building the support of interest groups and legislators around each major part of his program. In the legislature each issue attracts a somewhat different set of supporters and opponents together with a bloc of indifferents who can be pulled in either direction by suitable rewards. In his first term neither Folsom nor his aides had the slightest idea how to use the resources of the governor's office to build such support. He had done a brilliant job of building voter support for himself in the 1946 primaries, but he seemed to believe that his task ended there and that from then on he had only to announce his goals and the legislature would swiftly enact them into law. He soon discovered otherwise. His chief response to legislative opposition in his first term was to appeal to the people over the heads of the lawmakers. These appeals succeeded only in antagonizing the legislature.

In the 1954 primary Folsom found a partial solution to his problems. He and his organization successfully campaigned for a legislative slate. He then took another big step toward legislative success with the selection of capable House and Senate leaders. He had also learned how to use state contracts and other resources to influence the legislators.

Even with such sound preparation, though, his second term was little more successful than the first. Several factors account for this. One was the intensity of his populist beliefs. His self-destructive opposition to the Dixiecrat movement demonstrated his standard approach to ideological opponents—he fought them openly, treated them with sneering disdain, and continued the fight long after it was over whether he or they had lost the battle. This approach was particularly evident in his fights for reapportionment and a constitutional convention. In his second term these goals were more important to him than anything else, with the possible exception of his own political survival. The *Brown* decision stimulated a ferocious public response which destroyed any chance he might have had to bring about his reforms.

He understood this at the time, but he continued pushing, throwing huge quantities of political capital into the hopeless fight—political capital that could have been used to make improvements in welfare, education, and other areas in which he had a sincere but less intense interest. Because of *Brown* the payoffs legislators demanded in return for their support for constitutional convention and reapportionment bills were probably much larger than they would otherwise have been, but he refused to give up—he was "agitating for liberty." In addition he became so distressed by the certain demise of his civil rights programs that he lost interest in other matters. He wanted nothing less than to be the leader of a revolution. When he could not have this, he sulked and drank and ignored other important matters.

Folsom did not see the status quo as a comfortable, satisfactory arrangement. He was outraged by a system that gave a white Black Belt citizen several times the voting power of his North Alabama or Wiregrass counterpart, that kept honest citizens from voting and attending decent schools, and that did not provide paved roads for great numbers of people. He wanted large-scale change in many areas of government. To accomplish this herculean task he needed to win the Democratic primary; organize a machine that would bring about the election of a sympathetic legislature; select efficient legislative leaders; provide continuous and consistent personal leadership; and differentiate between reachable and unreachable goals in order to avoid wasting his limited political capital. All of these together were necessary conditions for success.

The Changing Web of Power

The general idea that governmental decision makers respond to changing conditions around them suggests that the values, policies, and perhaps the membership of a state's elite must respond as well. The Alabama elite, which we have been calling the Bosses, ruled using two major techniques. First, in the late 1800s through 1901 they built a system that confined overt decision making to routine matters. Decisions directly affecting their major interests, especially basic political rules, were largely frozen and excluded from debate until the late 1940s. Second, since elections represented a threat to Boss domination of state government, the Bosses contributed large sums to the campaigns of candidates who would represent their interests, and they provided further support to winners by supplying their personal enterprises, especially law firms, their business. Once in office, Boss-supported legislators, lieutenant governors, and governors enacted statutes restricting voting rights and ignored the constitutional requirement of reapportionment.

At the time Folsom began his fateful 1946 campaign, the Bosses had for decades been limiting the scope of decision making in state government to routine housekeeping or pocketbook matters, such as budgets and road construction. Basic questions such as voting rights, desegregation, and reapportionment had been stifled. Folsom insisted on raising these long-suppressed issues in his campaign.

The Bosses lost the 1946 gubernatorial election, the 1948 self-starter, and the 1954 gubernatorial election partly because they had grown rigid and unimaginative and partly because Folsom was using strategies against them that they did not understand. Folsom introduced campaign techniques that permitted talented individuals to compete against better-funded establishment candidates with something approaching an even chance. Later, escalating campaign costs, due largely to television, would require that a winning candidate gain the support of interests able to contribute large sums or that he or she possess great wealth. In a sense, this would reverse the trend established by Folsom. It would become virtually impossible for a candidate to win with the kind of person-to-person shoestring campaign with which Folsom won in 1946. When Alabama's primary date was moved to September nonmonied candidates would have an even worse time because high summer temperatures make the kind of carnivallike outdoor rallies that Folsom used so successfully an uncomfortable ordeal.

Yet increased campaign costs by no means guarantee that any single monied interest can always win gubernatorial or senatorial elections. For evidence of this, one need only examine James E. Folsom, Jr.'s upset victory over incumbent Senator Donald Stewart in the 1980 Democratic party primary and runoff. Little Jim, thirty-one years of age with only two years in elective office (Public Service Commission), starting late, and with a war chest approximately one-tenth of Stewart's, was able to win nomination. Building on his father's name, his own positive image on the PSC, and person-to-person appeals, he used a few beautifully produced short television spots to sell himself. Stewart, who had only held the office for two years, having filled part of the late Senator James Allen's term, spent a fortune on ineffectively produced television commercials. Folsom was narrowly defeated in the general election by the Republican candidate, war hero Admiral Jeremiah Denton, who outspent him by a ratio of approximately five to one.

With its rapid urbanization, industrialization, and population growth, Alabama is a far more complex and pluralistic place than it was in the 1940s and 1950s. This should mean that there are sufficient sources of funding available from relatively diverse groups to permit at least two candidates for a given statewide office to run substantial campaigns with good chances for success.

In Governor Folsom's day, the Bosses were effective in stopping his initiatives in the legislature. In his first term their methods ranged from cruel slander to subtle parliamentary maneuvers. In 1955, having won an overwhelming victory in 1954, he was in an ideal position to defeat his opponents, but turmoil engendered by the civil rights movement neutralized much of his power. Although most of his reforms were defeated, Boss interests cooperated with the governor on the pocketbook and industrial development programs often cited as some of his greatest successes.

Elite legislators in 1946 held to a clearly articulated and at least superficially consistent body of beliefs which served to justify the status quo and their position as the chosen ones at the top. Elite myths emphasized the virtues of a hierarchical society with the best evidence of one's merit being one's position on the pyramid. These notions continued to be articulated and acted on well into the 1950s, but never again by government officials with the clarity and precision that could be found in the words of Frank Dixon, J. Bruce Henderson, and Gessner McCorvey. Dixon, the Birmingham industrialists' primary public spokesman, was replaced by the far less articulate but more flexible Albert Boutwell. Henderson, the most prominent Black Belt representative, was displaced by Sam Engelhardt, who was just as rigid as Henderson but capable of far more imaginative tactical moves. Like Boutwell, Engelhardt was uninterested in the ideological formulations that seemed so important to his predecessor. Governor Patterson, whose position in the Boss hierarchy was less clear but who represented establishment interests with regard to civil rights opposition, also lacked interest in ideological thought. George Wallace, with his populist-underdog approach to politics, was unsympathetic to the blue blood elitism of Dixon, Henderson, and McCorvey, and he chose to approach his battles from the position of a gallus-snapping demagogue, a fighter for the benighted poor whites, and defender of the state against the damnable incursions of the federal government.

In the 1950s urban elites became increasingly uncomfortable with the myths to which they and their predecessors had adhered since before the turn of the century, and they and some Black Belt groups found these values increasingly harmful to their business and political dealings outside the South. Reformulations of the declining values were being taken over by an increasingly marginal collection of biologists who "proved" the inferiority of blacks and the natural virtues of segregation, journalists who "discovered" and "documented" intimate links between Moscow and the NAACP, and lawyers who, by ignoring seventy-five years of federal court decisions and by rewriting American history, were able to invent hitherto undiscovered state powers. Government officials in Alabama often took such information and ideas and incorporated them into their public statements, but even at the height of racial turmoil, there was a dispirited, empty quality to their pronouncements even though they were superficially blustery and vigorous. They concentrated their attention on legalistic tactical points relating to interposition, the rights of demonstrators, and states' rights. The core of Engelhardt's thinking was that he wanted to keep what was his. Boutwell was an able lawyer who concentrated on fighting a holding action. Patterson was a first-rate legal tactician who simultaneously provided sub rosa, perhaps unconscious encouragement to mobs. Wallace happily wrung every possible political advantage from every twist and turn of events.

The architects of massive resistance against the civil rights movement in Alabama were philosophically and morally bankrupt, especially when compared (as they were in the nation as a whole) to civil rights advocates whose ideology embodied such mainstream American ideals as individual dignity, freedom of speech, and equal opportunity. Had the civil rights movement not been aided by the federal government, these differences in the quality of clashing ideals would not have mattered. Alabama and the rest of the South would probably still be segregated today. But it was precisely the increasing divergence between the elite-segregationist myths and mainstream American myths and the effective dramatization of these differences by civil rights leaders that attracted federal support.

The rapid changes in elite ideological tone from the 1940s to the 1960s were accompanied by demographic movements in the same direction. Through the period 1940–60 twelve Black Belt counties suffered precipitous population losses relative to the industrial counties. Only Montgomery County (the state capital), Russell County (part of the U.S. Army's Fort Benning complex), Macon County (veterans hospital), and Lee County (Auburn University and small industry) enjoyed significant growth. Furthermore, the kinds of voters attracted to these counties were not oriented toward Black Belt interests. Average Black Belt population declines except for these four counties were 12.4 percent in the period 1940–50 and 10.0 percent during 1950–60. During the same two time periods the largest five industrial counties had average growth rates of 29.1 percent and 21.5 percent. Per capita income growth increased in Black Belt and industrial counties by approximately the same percentage during 1950–60, but per capita income in the industrial counties rose from a much higher base. Thus in numbers of people and wealth the industrial counties were outdistancing the Black Belt counties. Furthermore, black population percentages, already relatively low in the industrial counties, diminished 4.9 percent during 1940–50 and 8.3 percent during 1950–60. This change helped to reduce racial pressures in the industrial counties.

The changing tone of the elite also correlated with changes in the backgrounds of those representing Boss interests in state government. Occasionally, someone as wealthy as Henderson would serve in office, but these were generally Black Belters. Few government officials representing urban elites were extremely wealthy in their own right. Boutwell, a self-made man, was typical. Comfortably well off financially, he did not command anything near the personal wealth or direct control over corporate wealth that the people he represented did. Boutwell and most other urban elite-oriented officials were from middle-class and upper-class families. These families encouraged their sons to attend college or work in the family business. In addition those families already politically active encouraged their sons to become involved in government. The involvement of their families in politics gave them an enormous advantage in successfully entering government. Individuals with working-class origins were relatively unusual in these ranks.

The complexities of corporate decision making make it difficult to discover elite origins. Nevertheless, a large percentage of corporate elite members probably had origins little different from those who came to represent them in government. This was partly because the large corporations in the state when Folsom was governor were relatively new and were administered according to rules that stressed accomplishment, competition, and merit promotion. As a result, these corporate elites and subelites functioned in a relatively open setting. The fluidity of their membership assisted the development of a strategic and tactical intelligence that made this group more adaptable to changing social and economic conditions than the Black Belt elite. Rigidity spells an elite's doom; flexibility promises survival.

Elites change—old elites shrink and new ones emerge as a result of social and economic change. Some groups in a society are associated with the emerging order, others with the social and economic system that is in decline. Elite groups in Alabama have risen and fallen with such changes. It is not much of an exaggeration to assert that when coal, limestone, and iron were discovered in Jefferson County, the Black Belt elite, which was then in the process of taking over state government, was doomed. The only thing that is surprising is how long Black Belt politicians were able to hang on to their power. They succeeded by structuring constitutional forces in such a way that political change had to be accomplished with their cooperation or through outside (federal) action.

At the point of Folsom's 1946 election the Boss alliance was functioning much as it had since 1901. Even though the alliance crushed Folsom's key programs with brutal ease, a significant change was occurring in Boss operations which presaged important structural movement in the future. That change was the 1948 withdrawal of support for the Democratic party by a large contingent of Bosses. Cotton Tom Heflin had been expelled from the political system for a similar act only twenty years before. Bosses supported the Dixiecrat party out of a growing dissatisfaction with the liberal national

Democratic Party. Dissatisfaction with the Democratic party was also based on federal court rulings that nearly rendered political parties useless in keeping blacks and poor whites from voting. Thus one of the party's control functions was gone.

The Black Belt elite also suffered from a decreasing ability to field and support attractive gubernatorial candidates. Chauncey Sparks was the last winner from the traditional Black Belt forces, and he was only victorious because of Bibb Graves's death. Joe Poole was an inept candidate; Gordon Persons supported the Black Belt in most of its objectives, but he seemed more closely allied with urban interests; Patterson supported Black Belt anti–civil rights interests, but he was far too liberal for them otherwise; and George Wallace, though from a Black Belt county, was highly suspect because of his close past association with Folsom and his own brand of populism. The Black Belt elite not only lacked attractive gubernatorial candidates loyal to them but also seemed unwilling or unable to provide them with the levels of financial support comparable to those that urban-oriented candidates were receiving. Making matters worse, they took to bickering among themselves, partly due to personal animosities but more importantly because some Black Belt economic interests were stretching far beyond the state's borders. Finally, in the 1950s everyone could see that the Black Belt elite was on the verge of losing control of its own counties as black voter registration steadily edged forward. And in the background was the near certainty that the federal government would eventually enter the arena to bring about completely unrestricted black registration.

This is not to suggest that no Black Belt interests are represented in establishment circles today. Despite a shift toward urban political power, the Black Belt still generates enormous wealth, and Black Belt interests are surely represented in the highest decision-making levels in the state, if not to the degree that they were in past years. Nevertheless, as we have suggested, increased population levels, urbanization, industrialization, education, and the like, have combined with black enfranchisement to increase group diversity, and this new diversity can now be accurately reflected in a properly apportioned legislature.

Legacies

It is difficult to sum up James E. Folsom's life and career. Simple, sweeping generalizations cannot capture any facet of such a complex, contradictory individual functioning, as he did, in an extraordinarily hostile environment. Almost nothing of importance can be said about him that does not need a qualifier.

Not surprisingly, the dominant patterns in Folsom's adult behavior—his addiction to politics as a way of life, his deep commitment to a populist-liberal ideology, his sense of humor, his eccentricity, and his alcoholism—can be traced, with little resort to exotic psychological theorizing, to his early years.

He was heavily dependent on others throughout his life despite the image he projected (containing a large element of truth) of being a lone warrior fighting under the people's banner, often without their appreciation or understanding. Even in the midst of his knight errantry, however, Folsom found himself in or created environments in which others felt compelled to be present to meet his basic needs. He acted as if his needs and satisfactions should rightly take precedence over the needs of others and that family and friends would naturally want to supply such aid. More often than not, his demands were fulfilled.

He loved to impress and dominate everyone around him. In a group, one way or another, he had to be the center of attention. In part, his size contributed to his ability to carry this off; it was impossible to ignore the existence of this huge figure with a booming voice. But more than mere physical presence was at work. He skillfully used his size and voice to control.

Prior to his blindness, he never just entered a room, he exploded into it. He would move through the doorway with a curious impatience, sweep his eyes about the room, raise his hand to all (as if assuming all were there awaiting his arrival), and send general greetings to everyone. "Deal!" he would bellow upon entering a truck stop or restaurant, as surprised customers looked up from their dinners. Like many tall men, he used touch and nonverbal cues to establish control. He might hang his arm heavily around the shoulder of the man next to him, firmly take the lower arm of one listening to him, draw it toward him, and maintain the grip throughout the conversation or monologue, kiss willing or unwilling women, or simply remain standing while others sat.

Still, he knew when not to go too far. In some settings he could be quite subdued. In annual meetings of a state honorary association attended by most former governors and many of the state's leading industrialists, jurists, newspaper publishers, and the like, he was a model of decorum. And at an election night party for Jim Folsom, Jr., Big Jim took great pains not to steal the limelight from his son. His entrance was carefully timed not to interfere with Little Jim's, and it was modestly executed. He and Jamelle sat near the back of the room and quietly greeted old friends and well-wishers, listened to their son's speech, and withdrew.

But he always loved to be the center of attention, and he derived strong emotional support from group settings. There he could sermonize or spin tales of political machinations, plot and counterplot aimed at him and his administration. Each diatribe against the evils of lawyers "stealing out of two pockets" (that is, serving in government while conducting an active legal practice) and each tale of conspiratorial action by the opposition allowed him to express his ideological positions and to mark out his central place in history. The role of others in these settings was that of chorus, singing agreement or occasionally adding a point which can serve as the beginning for a new message or anecdote. In early years the people around him were not so pliable, and he would routinely listen to others and often profit from what they had to say. But as those who could or would handle his willfulness fell away (due to death or exhaustion), he became ever more isolated in the midst of a comfortable group of hard-drinking, manipulative cronies, most of whom, it must be added, all but disappeared after 1962 when his power and political future vaporized.

An election or referendum campaign is the ultimate group setting and nowhere can a person be more completely assured of being the center of attention, even if the group is only a handful of farmers on the front porch of a Scant City general store. All too often when in office Folsom handled legislative defeats and administrative frustrations by generating a campaign complete with rallies, firebrand speeches, motorcades, and crowds of people who loved him, allowing for at least some temporary reassertion of control.

More than is commonly understood, his behavior often reflected a distrust of others and their motives. Very few people were allowed to become really close. The premium he placed on loyalty, especially early loyalty, can be seen as an aspect of his need for support and of the difficulty he had in establishing close interpersonal relationships. Many administrative mistakes in both terms can be attributed to Folsom's reluctance to remove people from key positions even when their actions began seriously to injure the public image of his administration and interfere with its dealings with the legislature. These individuals would be allowed to stay on for weeks or even months as their behavior intensified the administration's problems. On the other hand, he dismissed many on the basis of suspicion founded on nothing but gossip, and both terms were notorious for continuous backbiting among those close to him. Either way, they often reappeared in other posts and repeated in slightly different form what they had done before. The earlier their ties to Folsom, the more often they would reappear, but only those strong or venal enough to tolerate the strain of working with him. Bad as they were, Folsom needed the personal support of these people.

His tumultuous and flawed relations with subordinates could be traced to a fundamental inconsistency in what he demanded of key individuals. In most posts he wanted efficient professionals who were willing to release hardened criminals en masse, extort large sums of money from companies doing business with the state, aim government contracts to favored companies, or fix traffic citations. Few technically able administrators were capable of evading Folsom's more outrageous demands, and being unwilling to follow orders, they exited.

Folsom perhaps valued loyalty (or what he perceived as loyalty) so highly and was such a poor judge of people because of the manner in which his family looked after him in his early years. In this there is a similarity between Folsom and his younger sister Ruby. Ruby's uninhibited behavior (often amplified by heavy drinking) made her a legend in Montgomery, especially among the city's sedate upper crust which had to contend with her as one governor's first lady (1947–48) and another's mother-in-law. The span in ages in the Folsom family was such that Jim and Ruby were raised not only by their parents but also by the older children. While it was a caring and loving family, neither Jim nor Ruby ever lacked for adults to instruct them on proper behavior, nor were any of those adults shy about informing them when they failed to perform up to standard. Someone was always ready to step in and look after them. They may have come to expect that everyone would look after them and to have attributed the same caring motives to others that they had found within their family. Both combined almost childlike trust with sudden appearances of suspicion.

Another aspect of Folsom's character was his low tolerance for rules, regulations, and established procedures. He frequently interpreted waiting, temporary delays, and the like, as personal affronts or plots against him ("Nothing just happens, everything is arranged") and became frustrated and angry. Established procedures appeared as obstacles created especially to stop *him* and what *he* stood for. That he was sometimes correct in these dark suspicions reinforced them.

As governor, Folsom was responsible for many failures, but by most objective, expert testimony he was no worse than most governors who preceded and followed him. It is a mistake to attempt to absolve him, as many do, by blaming alcoholism and manipulative aides. Both were factors, but the mistakes can often be traced to a sober, ideological governor whose Jacksonian-spoils philosophy justified too much and allowed him to hope for too little by way of administrative reform.

The state's establishment, which so enjoyed looking down its azure nose at Folsom's spoils administration, must share a large part of the blame for not stopping his abuses. By assent and default, the legislature and the criminal justice system permitted and even encouraged Folsom's worst abuses and blunders. Indeed, the only time in his first term when the elite systematically attacked his administrative practices was when they were both efficient and just, that is, when Philip Hamm was equalizing property tax assessments.

Folsom's place in history hinges on his role as a civil rights advocate, and here his record is impressive. His brilliance is slightly tarnished by occasional compromises with the segregationist avalanche that threatened to overcome him in both terms and the 1962 election campaign, and it cannot be said that he was very effective. But the stands he took and the fights he fought required moral courage and political nerve not often found among politicians of any era. In Alabama Joe Langan, George Hawkins, and others stood with him or near him, but their numbers were few. Though he frequently sought escape by airplane, extended fishing trips, or binges, he returned to the fight again and again until he faded away. The words and actions of his opponents who represented the state's elite and a majority of its white citizens, including no small number of individuals capable of using deadly force, were light years removed from Folsom's. That he stood against these people at all is amazing. That he did it as bluntly as he did, applying a dark, sarcastic wit against his opponents, is incredible. What is more, his stand expanded the concept of civil rights beyond standard civil libertarian concerns of the 1950s. He focused not only on desegregation and voting rights but also on women's rights, freedom of speech, and malapportionment.

Although Folsom's measurable impact was minimal, he represented something important in Alabama history and politics that cannot be quantified. He was the leader who mobilized the forces of change already developing in the system due to the Depression and World War II. He gave hope and a sense of worth to average men and women who had been told that they were not fit for leadership, that their dreams were petty dreams, and that they were therefore rightly excluded from the democratic process. Folsom taught them that the Big Mules' myths of genetic superiority were false and corrupt. He instructed them on the dignity of the common man and woman and the important part they had to play if democracy was to work and on the fundamental changes in the political system that had to occur before they could participate fully in their own governance. He helped an entire generation gain self-respect. Vestiges of his impact remain today. We sense it in the thrill that ripples through a crowd and in the love it projects when the blind, aged giant enters the room and excited voices whisper, "It's Big Jim, it's Big Jim!"

APPENDIX

The Distribution of Power in a Political Community

At first glance, the question "Who governs?" may appear to be a rather easy one to answer. Anyone interested in the distribution of power in a state or community could simply determine which persons held high positions and conclude that they governed. This is the "positional approach," and, unfortunately, it can be as misleading as it is quick and simple.[1] It tells the observer nothing about the working relationships between the occupants of high positions, nor does it distinguish between competents and incompetents holding these positions. Furthermore, it completely misses the possibility that people "behind the scenes" may be influencing officials, and it ignores the fact that even dictators are to some degree responsive to public opinion.

A second technique, the "reputational approach," is able to deal with some of these problems.[2] Essentially, an observer using this method asks knowledgeable persons to identify who is powerful. This approach often detects the existence of behind-the-scenes power brokers, and it may even reveal some information about relationships between influentials (although this information is usually quite vague), but it is nearly useless in evaluating the importance of public opinion. In addition, to identify those knowledgeable individuals, the observer must already understand a great deal about power in the community—a clear problem of circularity. Finally, it assumes that those reputed to be powerful are in fact powerful, and this is often not the case.

An approach designed to deal with the problems raised above reconstructs in detail every possible element in the decision-making process on important and controversial issues.[3] The theoretical basis of this approach is the notion that power can only be evaluated when it is exercised and that it is exercised most clearly in the course of decision making. In the reconstruction of decisions those whose will prevailed can be clearly identified, whether they occupied formal positions of power, operated behind the scenes, or were temporary leaders of public opinion. This "decision-making approach" seemed for a while to resolve the difficulties of the positional and reputational techniques, but it in turn was found to contain serious flaws. Critics argued that researchers oriented to decision making had neglected to develop objective criteria for selecting cases for analysis.[4] Another criticism raised by Peter Bachrach and Morton S. Baratz and others was even more serious. They attacked the "assumption that power is totally embodied and fully reflected in 'concrete decisions' or in activity bearing directly on their making."[5] Drawing from E. E. Schattschneider's "mobilization of bias" idea,[6] they wrote:

> To the extent that a person or group—consciously or unconsciously—creates or reinforces barriers to the public airing of policy conflicts, that person or group has power. . . . Can [the researcher] safely ignore the possibility, for instance, that an individual or group in a community participates more vigorously in supporting the *nondecision-making* process than in participating in actual decisions within the process? Stated differently, can the researcher overlook the chance that some person or association could limit decision-making to relatively non-controversial matters, by influencing community values and political procedures and rituals, notwithstanding that there are in the community serious but latent power conflicts?[7]

Thus we are faced with the possibility that an elite could exercise power statically and almost invisibly simply by existing. For example, an elected public official might entertain thoughts of increasing taxes on property owned by an extremely wealthy member of the community, perhaps a member of the ruling elite. But, after some consideration, he decides that if he attempted it, this wealthy individual would lavishly finance the campaign of an opponent in the next election. As a result he does nothing. The wealthy individual has been completely inactive (he is not even aware that anything has occurred) and yet he has had his way. This occurrence would not have been observed by anyone attempting to reconstruct political decisions in the community. Decision-making theorists are drawn almost inevitably to situations in which *decisions are made,* where there is conflict, and the existence of conflict suggests that at least two groups are disagreeing and that power is in some sense fragmented. The theories and procedures used by these researchers would permit the nondecision-making process and the people involved in it to slip through their net.

The community power literature, before and after Bachrach and Baratz, has featured almost unending acrimony with few successful attempts at synthesis, but it may be possible to draw from this debate a comprehensive strategy for a researcher engaged in mapping a community power structure.[8] The components of this strategy, presented below, are points on which there is broad agreement among major community power writers.

Bachrach and Baratz, among others, advise the researcher to begin by examining a community's "mobilization of bias" including "the dominant values, the myths and the established political procedures and rules of the game."[9] In Alabama a rich combination of sources provides a fairly clear picture of the mobilization of bias for much of the state's post–Civil War history.

Moving from the general to the specific, many writers recommend an analysis of those who gain and those who lose from the mobilization of bias.[10] Today's sophisticated techniques for the analysis of governmental policies make this a practical recommendation, but the reader is cautioned not to equate "Who governs?" with "Who benefits?"[11] An unequal distribution of values in a community may be caused by a mobilization of bias and/or many other factors. The data from this "winners-losers" analysis could be checked against a reputational study, which should be able to locate potentially powerful groups and individuals and determine the scope of their influence.[12]

Continuing to move from the general to the specific, Bachrach and Baratz advise us to "examine the extent to which the manner in which the status quo oriented persons and groups influence those community values and those political institutions . . . which tend to limit the scope of actual decision-making to 'safe' issues."[13] This step should feature the sort of historical analysis with which Robert Dahl opens his book *Who Governs?*[14] The origins of community values and political institutions should be explored as deeply as possible. This information, combined with interviews, participant observation, and the data provided by the preceding steps, should make it possible thoroughly to explore this aspect of community power. The problem of covert activities will not be important here because the preservation of community values and political institutions tends to be fairly open. In Alabama the creation and defense of key values and institutions have been highly visible processes about which a great deal is known.

At this point, if the study has been successful, the observer will possess a great deal of "circumstantial evidence" about the community power structure, including the content of the mobilization of bias together with the manner in which it was created and is maintained; which individuals and groups possess reputations for power in particular areas of community life; and how these groups and individuals profit from the mobilization of bias. This is a considerable body of knowledge, but in order thoroughly to understand community power we must learn how to detect nondecision making. The literature is not very helpful on this point. This is not surprising, for normally the researcher is an outsider trying to delve into the innermost secrets of persons who very much want the secrets to remain unknown and who usually possess the ability to enforce their desires. The researcher is almost certainly going to be denied important information and deceived in any number of ways.

In their efforts to guide the researcher who is trying to delve into actual cases of nondecision making, Bachrach and Baratz, Matthew Crenson, and others place great emphasis on the distinction between "routine" and "key" decisions.[15] Bachrach and Baratz define a key issue as one that involves "any challenge to the predominant values or to the established 'rules of the game.'"[16] Everything else, they add, is "unimportant."[17] That is, everything else is the sort of "routine" decision making studied by Dahl in *Who Governs?* So, according to Bachrach and Baratz, the researcher should use "his knowledge of the restrictive face of power [gained from preceding analyses] as a foundation for analysis and as a standard for distinguishing between 'key' and 'routine' political decisions, the researcher would, after the manner of pluralists, analyze participation in decision-making of concrete issues."[18] There is little guidance beyond this general recommendation. One difficulty with this advice is that most communities experience challenges to predominant values with such rarity that key decisions might never occur. However, Alabama political history has been rich in key decisions.

Alabama historians do not address themselves to these methodological questions, but an important approach (hinted at by Dahl, Frey, and Aiken and Mott) is revealed in their work.[19] *An elite is visible and available for observation by social scientists using decision-making techniques under at least two conditions: when the elite is first taking power and when its existence is threatened.* If there are records of the elite's formation and if the elite's existence is periodically threatened, the investigator may be able to take a series of "snapshots" of the elite's membership, bases of power, methods of exercising power, internal conflict problems, interests, and almost anything else of importance. Changes in these characteristics may be observed over time.

The methodological conundrums described above are not the end of the problems with which scholars interested in power are obliged to wrestle. The three classic approaches to the study of power (positional, reputational, and decision-making) and the definitions that support them are biased in favor of particular conclusions. Many critics have observed that the use of reputational and positional techniques usually leads to the conclusion that an elite exists, whereas use of the decision-making approach typically generates a description of power as fragmented among a variety of conflicting groups.[20] Scholars relying on reputation and position tend to have a static conception of power, so that if someone possesses great wealth or a reputation for being powerful, he is powerful by definition.[21] Decision-making scholars reject this notion, relying instead on an image of power as a dynamic process. Since they focus on decision making and ignore nondecision making, and since decision making tends to concern controversy, they must usually conclude that power is fragmented.[22]

While problems of bias can ruin a research effort, it is possible to take advantage of them. If scholars using reputational or positional approaches find that power is fragmented or if decision-making scholars discover the existence of an elite, we may feel more confident of their conclusions than if their conclusions are the usual ones. The conclusions concerning power in chapter 3 and later chapters of this volume are based entirely on detailed descriptions of decision making. This strengthens our argument that Alabama state government was dominated by an elite before and during Folsom's career.

Notes

Chapter 1

1. James E. Folsom, Cullman, Jan. 1978; Miriam Hicks (Moses Folsom's great-great-granddaughter), by telephone, Montgomery, Jan. 1978.
2. James E. Folsom, Elba, Nov. 1980.
3. James E. Folsom, Cullman, June 1973.
4. Ibid.
5. Ibid., and Thelma Clark, Elba, July 1973. Family members believe that Folsom's sister Thelma became a determined Women's Christian Temperance Union member because of the nature of her father's death.
6. James E. Folsom, by telephone, Aug. 1982.
7. The Alabama census of 1850 (no. 139) shows that James H. Dunnavant was 51 years of age. Living with him were Mary B., 59, Samual A., 25, Thomas R., 20, Mary E., 20, George (no age), and a John H. Bransford. In the 1870 census Samual, Thomas, George, and John H. Bransford were not recorded. Folsom, without prompting, remembered one of these names (Samual), and he also remembered that a relative of some sort (Bransford) had been killed in addition to the three Dunnavants. Of course, this information does not constitute proof that they were killed in the Civil War, but Folsom's (and Uncle John's) story is plausible.
8. James E. Folsom, Cullman, June 1973; Thelma Clark, Elba, July 1973; Ruby Austin, Montgomery, June 1973.
9. E.g., Jack, Paul, and Daisy Windham, Elba, July 1973; Eris J. Paul, Elba, July 1974.
10. James E. Folsom, Cullman, June 1973.
11. Ibid.
12. Numerous interviews with Folsom family members and Elba residents, 1973–80.
13. James E. Folsom, Cullman, June 1973.
14. Numerous interviews with Folsom family members and Elba residents, 1973–80.
15. Eris J. Paul, Elba, July 1974.
16. This series of events is described in various letters in the Boyen collection. All letters referred to below are from this collection.
17. Lehman Farris, Elba, July 1974.
18. Philip J. Hamm, Dothan, June 1974.
19. Albert Boutwell, Birmingham, July 1974; James E. Folsom, Cullman, June 1973.
20. James E. Folsom, Cullman, June 1973, and Elba, Nov. 1980.
21. Letters in Boyen collection.
22. Many interviews with James E. Folsom, 1973–82.

23. Ibid., and Bob Folsom, Elba, July 1974 and Oct. 1980.
24. Ibid.
25. Merchant Marine record book in James E. Folsom's possession.
26. S. Fleetwood Carnley, Elba, July 1973 and Oct. 1980.
27. S. Fleetwood Carnley, Elba, July 1973.
28. See Carnley's letter to the editor in the *Mobile Register*, Oct. 10, 1929, analyzing Alabama Power Company's sales of hydroelectric power outside the state, sales which, he argued, caused high instate rates. See also the debate between Carnley and the editor of the *Hartselle Enterprise*, Jan. 2, 1930, with Carnley advocating taxation on the basis of ability to pay. Also, *Montgomery Advertiser*, Oct. 8, 1930.

Chapter 2

1. Some of the legislators in the Folsom camp were far from pure Folsomites, but they could be persuaded to vote for his bills except where civil rights matters were concerned.
2. James E. Folsom, Montgomery, Aug. 1978.
3. James E. Folsom, Cullman, June 1973.
4. Confidential interview, June 1974.
5. James E. Folsom, Cullman, July 1973; *Elba Clipper*, June 14, 15, 1933.
6. *Elba Clipper*, June 8, 1933.
7. Undated *Elba Clipper* article in J. A. Carnley files.
8. O. H. Finney, Albertville, June 1974; Cecil Noel, Folsom's CWA chief highway engineer, Boaz, Apr. 1974; and another CWA staff member who chose not to be identified, Guntersville, Apr. 1974.
9. Ibid., and countless people in Marshall County, Apr. 1974.
10. Ibid., and *Sand Mountain Banner*, Dec. 14, 1933; *Guntersville Advertiser*, Mar. 14, 1934.
11. Cecil Noel, Boaz, Apr. 1974.
12. See "Marshall Rehabilitation Farmers Insist on Mules Instead of Steers," *Guntersville Advertiser*, June 27, 1934.
13. Cecil Noel and other CWA staff members, Boaz and Guntersville, Apr. 1974.
14. Folsom probably did not seize the oxen or steers as his staff remembers, because this program was run by a different agency. See *Guntersville Advertiser*, June 27, 1934. As the division of labor between the CWA and the other relief agencies is characterized in Marshall County newspapers, Folsom should not have been involved in any agricultural aid activities, but his staff recalls that he was, and on a fairly substantial scale.
15. The nature of this change is described in *Guntersville Advertiser*, Sept. 26 and Oct. 24, 1934.
16. Oct. 25, 1934.
17. James E. Folsom, Elba, Nov. 1980.
18. *Elba Clipper*, Mar. 5, 1936.
19. Confidential interview, June 1974.
20. James E. Folsom, Cullman, July 1973.
21. Ibid.; confidential interviews, July 1973.
22. Confidential interview, July 1973.
23. James E. Folsom, Montgomery, May 1978.
24. Undated, handwritten draft in 1936 campaign files, Elba. Attached note reads, "Thelma. Send above out

as a form letter to county and city campaign mgrs. Carbon copies will be O.K."

25. *Elba Clipper,* Mar. 12, 1936.
26. 1936 campaign files.
27. Ibid.
28. Ibid.
29. Release, "To the Voters of the Third Congressional District," late Feb. or early Mar. 1936.
30. See letters to editor in *Mobile Register,* Oct. 10, 1929, and *Hartsell Enterprise,* Jan. 2, 1930. Also see *Montgomery Advertiser,* Oct. 8, 1930.
31. Letter to "Dear Friend" from O. L. West, Apr. 7, 1936.
32. Telegram to James E. Folsom from Frank W. Boykin, Feb. 28, 1936, in 1936 campaign files. Also James E. Folsom, Elba, Nov. 1980.
33. Letter to James E. Folsom from Ernie W. Wagner, March 1936, in 1936 campaign files.
34. *Alabama Magazine,* Aug. 9, 1937, p. 3.
35. Undated press release which quotes a telegram addressed to "Hon. Gaston Scott, President—State Highway Commission" and two telegrams attached to the release. In 1936 campaign files.
36. In 1936 campaign files.
37. 1936 campaign files.
38. Ibid.
39. Undated *Elba Clipper* articles in J. A. Carnley files.
40. Ibid., and James E. Folsom, Montgomery, Aug. 1978.
41. In 1936 campaign files.
42. Hamilton, *Alabama,* 7.
43. Murray, "Folsom Gubernatorial Campaign," 18, and Folsom interviews, 1973–80.
44. Key, *Southern Politics,* 37–41.
45. Cullman, June 1973.
46. Cullman, May 1978.
47. Ibid.
48. Kenneth Griffith, Cullman, June 1973.
49. "Little-Un," 53–55.
50. William Bradford Huie, Hartselle, July 1973.
51. Barnard, "Old Order Changes," 173.
52. April 3, 1942.
53. Barnard, "Old Order Changes," 173.
54. Ibid., 178.
55. John Steifelmeyer, Cullman, July 1974.
56. Confidential interview, Cullman, July 1974.
57. James E. Folsom, Montgomery, May 1978, and Elba, Nov. 1980.
58. McGill, *South and the Southerner,* 119–20.
59. Ibid. and Flynt, *Cracker Messiah,* 43–44.
60. Williams, *Huey Long,* 272.
61. In Huie, "Little-Un," 55.
62. *Birmingham News,* Apr. 19, 1942.
63. *Montgomery Advertiser,* May 1, 1942.
64. Kenneth Griffith, Cullman, July 1974.
65. *Cullman Tribune,* May 30, 1942.
66. *Montgomery Advertiser,* Feb. 27, 1942.
67. Atticus Mullin reported that top Graves lieutenants were being given major leadership positions in the Sparks organization in exchange for their efforts on his behalf. *Montgomery Advertiser,* Mar. 30, 1942.
68. Confidential interview, May 1976.
69. Confidential interview, June 1974.

Chapter 3

1. Key, *Southern Politics*, 37–57; Barnard, *Dixiecrats and Democrats*.
2. Key, *Southern Politics*, 37, 56.
3. Dahl, *Who Governs?*
4. Grafton, "Community Power Methodology and Alabama Politics," 272–75.
5. E.g., Ezell, *South since 1865*, 270–72; Woodward, *Origins of the New South*, 1–22, 179.
6. Woodward, *Origins of the New South*, 176–85.
7. Ezell, *South since 1865*, 220.
8. Wiener, "Planter-Merchant Conflict," 73–94; Wiener, "Planter Persistence," 235–60.
9. Wiener, "Planter Persistence," 238.
10. Ibid., 240–41; Huffman, "Old South, New South," 76, 148, 152.
11. Wiener, "Planter Persistence," 251–52.
12. Goodwyn, *Democratic Promise*, 27.
13. Ibid., 26–27.
14. Ibid., 27–28; Woodward, *Origins of the New South*, 180.
15. Wiener, "Planter-Merchant Conflict," 83.
16. Goodwyn, *Democratic Promise*, 29.
17. Wiener, "Planter-Merchant Conflict," 84; DuBose, *Forty Years in Alabama*, chap. 38.
18. *Acts of Alabama*, 1865–66.
19. *Columbus Enquirer*, quoted in *Montgomery Daily Advertiser*, July 11, 1868; *Montgomery Advertiser*, July 26, 1868; *Mobile Daily Register*, Feb. 26, 1871.
20. Wiener, "Planter-Merchant Conflict," 88, 90–91. Stories in the Mar. 5 and 30, 1879, *Montgomery Advertiser*s indicate that, based on mortgage figures, Black Belt farmers were getting out from under antebellum debt.
21. *Montgomery Daily Advertiser*, Aug. 1, 1874; Woodward, *Origins of the New South*, 9–10.
22. *Montgomery Daily Advertiser*, July 24, 1874.
23. Ibid., Sept. 11, 1874.
24. Ibid., Oct. 31, 1874.
25. *Montgomery Daily Advertiser*, Nov. 1, 1874, quoted in McMillan, *Constitutional Development*, 175. Also see Gross, "Alabama Politics," 22–25.
26. McMillan, *Constitutional Development*, 175–76; Gross, "Alabama Politics," 69–77.
27. The *Birmingham Independent*, quoted in the Aug. 3, 1875, issue of the *Montgomery Daily Advertiser*, after noting that blacks voted solidly against the constitutional convention, proclaimed: "The negroes, by their actions, avow themselves the enemies of the Southern whites; they take pleasure in voting for our slanderers and relentless persecutors. They lie, steal, and vote illegally for the Radicals. . . . The Samboes vote to crush and rob us." The *Advertiser* was saturated with commentary of this sort.
28. McMillan, *Constitutional Development*, 13–14.
29. Gross, "Alabama Politics," 80–81; DuBose, *Forty Years in Alabama*, chap. 36.
30. Convention chairman L. P. Walker stressed the need to maintain "perfect political and civil equity of all men of whatever race, color, or previous condition" (*Montgomery Daily Advertiser*, Sept. 11, 1875).
31. Gross, "Alabama Politics," 84–85.
32. McMillan, *Constitutional Development*, 210.
33. Going, *Bourbon Democracy*, 29.

Fraud was not the exclusive means of garnering black votes. Straightforward appeals for their support were common in the Black Belt. See DuBose, *Forty Years in Alabama*, chap. 37; *Montgomery Daily Advertiser*, Sept. 18, 1874; Williams, *Romance and Realism*, 49–50.

34. *Acts of Alabama* (1878–79), 72 and (1880–81), 29.

35. *Huntsville Advocate*, Dec. 8, 1880, quoted in Gross, "Alabama Politics," 88.

36. Ibid., 89.

37. Ibid., 89–90.

38. Apr. 6, 1879.

39. *Official Proceedings*, 2788.

40. DuBose, *Forty Years in Alabama*, chap. 39.

41. Ibid.; Goodwyn, *Democratic Promise*, 33.

42. Goodwyn, *Democratic Promise*, 34.

43. Ibid., 26–34, 87–91.

44. DuBose, *Forty Years in Alabama*, chap. 39; Goodwyn, *Democratic Promise*, 92–93; Hackney, *Populism to Progressivism*, 5–6. See the Jan. 1, 1890, *Montgomery Advertiser* for a bitter anti-Alliance editorial blasting the speeches of Alliance lecturer-organizer Ben Terrell. The *Advertiser* was especially critical of hints in Terrell's speeches that agrarians might split with the Democratic party.

45. Rogers, "One-Gallused Rebellion," 152–53; DuBose, *Forty Years in Alabama*, chap. 40.

46. Going, *Bourbon Democracy*, 59; *Montgomery Advertiser*, Mar. 27, 28, 1879; DuBose, *Forty Years in Alabama*, chap. 40.

47. The *Montgomery Advertiser* was not shy about its early opposition to the Alliance's political strategy: "The *Advertiser*, the faithful sentinel of the party for a quarter century, stood on the watch tower, saw the impending danger and disgrace [the Alliance and Kolb], and in clarion tones awakened the camp of the old guard which slept in security and peace beneath the battlements" (May 28, 1890).

48. Hackney, *Populism to Progressivism*, 12–13. See 23 reprinted Black Belt newspaper editorials on Kolb, *Montgomery Advertiser*, Jan. 5, 1890; also see *Montgomery Advertiser*, Jan. 12, 14, 18–19, Mar. 13, 19, 29, Apr. 5, 1890; DuBose, *Forty Years in Alabama*, chap. 40. The *Advertiser* showed a positive attitude toward Birmingham industrialization even earlier. See Mar. 19, 26, 1879.

49. Hackney, *Populism to Progressivism*, 14.

50. Ibid., 15–16; Gross, "Alabama Politics," 152–53.

51. Gross, "Alabama Politics," 155; DuBose, *Forty Years in Alabama*, chap. 40.

52. Gross, "Alabama Politics," 154–60; *Montgomery Advertiser*, Apr. 7, May 24, June 10, 1892; Johnson, *Oscar W. Underwood*, 24–25; DuBose, *Forty Years in Alabama*, chap. 41.

53. Hackney, *Populism to Progressivism*, 20–21; Hicks, *Populist Revolt*, 238–39.

54. Gross, "Alabama Politics," 163–64.

55. McMillan, *Constitutional Development*, 218–21. Populists were also guilty of vote fraud, but the consensus among historians is that they were far behind Black Belt conservatives in volumn and imaginativeness. See DuBose, *Forty Years in Alabama*, chap. 41, and Williams, *Romance and Realism*, 541.

56. McMillan, *Constitutional Development*, 226; Williams, *Romance and Realism*, 57.

57. *Montgomery Advertiser*, June 9, 1892, Sept. 25, 1901.
58. McMillan, *Constitutional Development*, 249–50; Alabama, House of Representatives, *Journal* (1892–93), 851, 1042, 1095, 1138; *Montgomery Advertiser*, Jan. 9, 1893; *Acts of Alabama* (1892–93), 837; Kousser, *Shaping of Southern Politics*, 48, 65.
59. McMillan, *Constitutional Development*, 224–26.
60. *Montgomery Advertiser*, Aug. 19, 1894.
61. Hackney, *Populism to Progressivism*, 70–76; Sparkman, "The Kolb-Oates Campaign," 18–43.
62. Goodwyn, *Democratic Promise*, 389; Youngdale, *Populism*, 9–10, 19.
63. Key, *Southern Politics*, 540–50.
64. Harris, *Political Power in Birmingham*, 12.
65. McMillan, *Constitutional Development*, 233–38.
66. The 1875 constitution was relatively easy to amend, requiring a two-thirds vote in each legislative chamber and then a simple majority of voters in a statewide referendum, but this process was little used, for reasons which are unclear. McMillan, *Constitutional Development*, 250–51. Also see Hackney, *Populism to Progressivism*, 157–70, and the discussion of the need to disfranchise "purchaseable votes" of both races to put politics on a "higher plane" in the *Montgomery Advertiser*, May 25, 1901. Of course, the "purity in elections" theme referred to the Black Belt's own use of election fraud.
67. McMillan, *Constitutional Development*, 259.
68. Hackney, *Populism to Progressivism*, 212. Also see McMillan, *Constitutional Development*, 269.
69. McMillan, *Constitutional Development*, 266–67; Hackney, *Populism to Progressivism*, 210–11; Gross, "Alabama Politics," 238–39.
70. Hackney, *Populism to Progressivism*, 212.
71. Ibid., 211–12.
72. Ibid., 212.
73. DuBose, *Forty Years in Alabama*, chaps. 43–44.
74. Farmer, *Legislative Process*, chap. 1, maps 1–4.
75. Kousser, *Shaping of Southern Politics*, 169.
76. Ibid., 238–65.
77. Jones, "Political Reforms," 173–94.
78. Thornton, "Alabama Politics," 87.
79. Ibid., 87–88.
80. Ibid., 89–91.
81. The July 13, 1927, *Montgomery Advertiser*, reflecting its planter-industrialist perspective, commented that "the most radical legislature since 1907 has fallen upon the industries and business of Alabama" and concluded that much of the money generated by the new taxes would go "to make the mothers of countless office hungry politicians exclaim: 'I'm glad I raised my boy to be a Klansman'" (quoted in Thornton, "Alabama Politics," 92).
82. Ibid.
83. Ibid., 95, 97.
84. *Montgomery Advertiser, Mobile Register, Selma Times-Journal,* and *Dothan Eagle*, Jan. 19, 1928, cited in Thornton, "Alabama Politics," 98.
85. Ibid., 99–101. Thornton's documentation is the *New York Times* and "Minutes of the Meeting of the Alabama Democratic Executive Committee, September 22, 1928."
86. Ibid., 101.
87. Ibid., 101–12. Using many news-

papers and letters in the J. Thomas Heflin papers, Thornton reconstructed the decision making on Heflin.

88. This is not to suggest that Grover Hall's attack on the Klan was hypocritical. In a letter dated Nov. 29, 1936, written to someone associated with the *Atlanta Constitution* whose name is obscured, Hall wrote: "You know as well as I do that Southerners with all their charm are worm-eaten with unreasonable prejudices. The law and order Southerners, one of the most bestial human beings ever born of woman, has been flattered continuously by politicians for more than a hundred years, so that today he has all the vanity of an authentic aristocrat. He is the active enemy of every civilizing force in Southern life, and all leaders must recognize the fact, for what it is worth, that he made the Ku Klux Klan a ruling power. He does all the lynching. He is for Sunday closing. He is for making it against the law for professors to 'teach' the principal of organic evolution" (Grover Hall papers, Alabama Department of Archives and History [hereafter cited as ADAH]). Many of his private letters have the same tone.

89. Gilbert, "Bibb Graves," 15–30; Jones, "Political Reforms," 173–94. Graves's campaign speeches and literature reveal him to be an aggressive and articulate but otherwise ordinary New Deal liberal.

90. Handy Ellis is viewed by some as a progressive. One scholar, objecting to our placing Ellis in the same category as Poole, wrote: "Ellis had labored long in the progressive vineyard as a Graves' lieutenant and had the support of the organized interest groups who stood to benefit from an expansion of state services." We believe that as Ellis aged, he moved rightward. Interview subjects could see little difference between Ellis and Poole in 1946. The following quotes come from interviews with a state senator and lieutenant governor, a judge, and two North Alabama journalists, respectively: "[Ellis] was controlled by industrial interests." "[Ellis was] a hip pocket politician who was devoid of principles like George Wallace." "[Ellis] was a member of the Big Mule class. He was a trained lawyer—suave—read personalities better than Poole—more adjustable than Poole."

91. Cash, *Mind of the South*, 4–29.

92. Ibid., 153. Also see 33–34, 154.

93. *Official Proceedings*, 9.

94. DuBose, *Forty Years in Alabama*, chap. 38.

95. *Official Proceedings*, 12.

96. July 29, 1874.

97. *Official Proceedings*, 9. See also T. W. Coleman's speech, 2709–14, and the *Montgomery Advertiser*, Sept. 18, 1874.

98. May 28, 1890.

99. Undated manuscript, J. Bruce Henderson file, ADAH.

100. Jan. 22, 1958, letter in the Henderson file, ADAH.

101. Mar. 28, 1947, letter in Henderson file, ADAH.

102. May 10, 1945, letter in Henderson file, ADAH.

103. Untitled Camden Presbyterian Church resolutions concerning church integration, 1959, in Henderson file, ADAH. In the same file were letters from Henderson to various law enforcement and public health officials in which he sought these data.

104. Letter to Grover Hall, Jr., Nov. 11, 1944, quoted in Barnard, *Dixiecrats and Democrats*, 98–99.

Chapter 4

1. James E. Folsom, Cullman, May 1974, and confidential interview, Sept. 1973.
2. S. Fleetwood Carnley, Elba, Oct. 1980.
3. See Wallace, *C'nelia,* 124–25.
4. Confidential interviews, July 1973.
5. Aug. 8, 1944.
6. Murray, "Folsom Gubernatorial Campaign," 29–30.
7. E. D. Nixon, Montgomery, July 1974.
8. James E. Folsom, telephone interview, July 1981.
9. Ibid.
10. Hobart Key and Roland Johnson, Cullman, Apr. 1974.
11. Cullman, Apr. 1974.
12. Cullman, Apr. 1974.
13. James E. Folsom, Cullman, June 1973.
14. Ibid.
15. James E. Folsom, Montgomery, May 1978.
16. Ibid.
17. James E. Folsom, Cullman, June 1974.
18. James E. Folsom, Montgomery, May 1978.
19. Cullman, June 1974.
20. Frady, *Wallace,* 106; Confidential interview, Montgomery, July 1974.
21. Confidential interview, July 1974.
22. Numerous interviews and Murray, "Folsom Gubernatorial Campaign," 63, 72–75.
23. Barnard, *Dixiecrats and Democrats,* 25.
24. Ibid., 26.
25. *Mobile Register,* May 1, 1946.
26. *Montgomery Advertiser,* May 1, 1946; *Birmingham Post-Herald,* Apr. 29 and May 4, 1946; *Huntsville Times,* Apr. 2, 1946.
27. *Montgomery Advertiser,* Feb. 26, 1946.
28. *Dixiecrats and Democrats,* 36.
29. Unlabeled newspaper clipping, Folsom file, ADAH.
30. Confidential interview, Sept. 1973.
31. James E. Folsom, Cullman, June 1973; *Florence Times,* Mar. 6, 1946.
32. Confidential interviews, Apr. and June 1974.
33. Confidential interviews, June 1974.
34. James E. Folsom, Cullman, June 1973.
35. Ibid.
36. Cullman, Apr. 1974.
37. *Montgomery Advertiser,* June 2, 1946.
38. James E. Folsom, Montgomery, May 1978.
39. Undated *Tuscaloosa News* clipping, Folsom file, ADAH.
40. Roland Johnson and Hobart Key, Cullman, Apr. 1974.
41. *Montgomery Advertiser,* Apr. 26, 1946.
42. James E. Folsom, Cullman, June 1976.
43. Ibid. and confidential interviews, June 1973.
44. Confidential interview, June 1973.
45. Confidential interview, July 1978.
46. Bill Lyerly, Montgomery, July 1973.
47. James E. Folsom, Cullman, June 1974.
48. Jamelle Folsom, Cullman, June 1973.
49. Ibid.
50. Ibid.
51. Confidential interview, July 1974.
52. *Montgomery Advertiser,* May 26, 1946.
53. Barnard, *Dixiecrats and Demo-*

crats, 49; John Temple Graves, *Birmingham Post,* June 18, Aug. 19, 1946; Grover Hall, Jr., *Montgomery Advertiser,* Aug. 18, 1946.

54. Ibid.; also *Montgomery Advertiser,* May 21, June 1, 1946.

55. See *Montgomery Advertiser,* May 26, 1946; *Birmingham News,* May 13, 21, 1946. Ellis was not the first to use racial slurs in the campaign. This "honor" rests with the Alabama Temperance Alliance, which had worked on Joe Poole's behalf. *Montgomery Advertiser,* Apr. 14, 1946.

56. *Huntsville Times,* May 13, 19, 1946.

57. *Montgomery Advertiser,* May 22, 1946.

58. James E. Folsom, Cullman, June 1973.

59. Confidential interviews, Decatur, July 1974.

60. *Birmingham Post,* May 28, 1946.

61. *Montgomery Advertiser* and *Huntsville Times,* May 26, 1946.

62. Twitty, *Y'All Come,* 86–87; *Huntsville Times,* May 26, 1946.

63. Milo Howard, Jr., Montgomery, July 1973.

64. *Huntsville Times,* June 5, 1946.

65. Letter to B. B. Gossett [date obscured], Dixion file, ADAH.

66. *Birmingham Post,* June 5, 1946; *Huntsville Times,* June 5, 1946.

67. *New York Times,* Aug. 11, 12, 30, 1946; *U.S. News and World Report,* May 31, 1946.

68. Cullman, June 1973. See also *Montgomery Advertiser,* Mar. 5, 1946.

Chapter 5

1. Ransone, *Office of Governor,* 139–40; see also Farmer, *Legislative Process,* chap. 8.

2. Barnard, *Dixiecrats and Democrats,* 56.

3. James E. Folsom, Cullman, June 1974.

4. Barnard, *Dixiecrats and Democrats,* 56–58.

5. See Bartley and Graham, *Southern Politics and the Second Reconstruction,* 24–25, 38–41.

6. *Smith* v. *Allwright* (321 U.S. 649, 1944); Barker and Barker, *Civil Liberties,* 396–97.

7. Barnard, *Dixiecrats and Democrats,* 61–63.

8. Dixon files, ADAH. See Lawson's *Black Ballots* for a detailed account of the many maneuvers employed against black voting, including the Boswell Amendment.

9. Letters to W. L. Hatcher (Enterprise), undated, and to James E. Folsom, Sept. 18, 1946, from J. A. Carnley, both in Folsom personal files, ADAH.

10. *Dixiecrats and Democrats,* 67.

11. *Birmingham News,* Jan. 21, 1947.

12. Twitty, *Y'All Come,* 97–100.

13. Confidential interviews, Jan. 1976.

14. Confidential interviews, 1977; letter to J. Bruce Henderson from John L. Ryan, president, Federal Land Bank of Louisiana, Dec. 18, 1956, in Henderson papers, ADAH.

15. Confidential interview, Jan. 1976.

16. Cullman, June 1973.

17. Confidential interviews, July 1974. Even the *Montgomery Advertiser*'s Grover Hall, Jr., by no means a Folsomite, warned the governor-elect against Henderson.

18. Confidential interviews, June 1973.

19. Huie, *New Life to Live,* 27–33.

20. *Huey Long,* 294.

21. James E. Folsom, Cullman, June 1973; Barnard, *Dixiecrats and Democrats*, 79; Vaughan, *Administrative Responsibility*, 36–38.
22. James V. Martindale and Edward J. Nofer, *Martindale-Hubell Law Directory* (Summit: Martindale-Hubbell, 1948), vol. 1., part 2, pp. 3, 16, 22.
23. Statement dated 1937 sworn and notarized by the Marengo County Extension Agent, Folsom personal files, ADAH.
24. Unsigned memorandum to Folsom, Folsom personal files, ADAH.
25. Draft of telegrams in Folsom personal files, ADAH.
26. Compilation in Folsom personal files, ADAH.
27. *Montgomery Advertiser*, Feb. 22, 1946.
28. Folsom, *Speeches*, 8–14.
29. Ibid., 15.
30. Feb. 27, 1946.
31. Mar. 3, 1947.
32. *Birmingham News*, Mar. 4, 1947.
33. Ibid.
34. *Birmingham News*, Mar. 5, 1947.
35. *Montgomery Advertiser*, Mar. 7, 1947.
36. Grafton and Permaloff, "Politics of Highway Construction."
37. Confidential interview, Aug. 1976.
38. Ibid.
39. Ward McFarland, Tuscaloosa, July 1973.
40. Report of the untitled committee to investigate irregularities of the Highway Department, Aug. 18, 1948, p. 9, in Folsom official files, ADAH.
41. James E. Folsom, Cullman, June 1974.
42. *Alabama Journal*, May 16, 1950.
43. Confidential interview with a newspaper reporter, Sept. 1978.
44. Confidential interview, Jan. 1976; *Birmingham News*, Mar. 27, 1955.
45. Ibid.
46. Farmer, *Legislative Process*, 23–29.
47. Ibid.
48. Ibid., 33.
49. Ibid., 36.
50. Albert Boutwell, Montgomery, July 1973; confidential interview, June 1973; Vaughan, *Administrative Responsibility*, 27; Bartley, *Rise of Massive Resistance*, 18.
51. Farmer, *Legislative Process*, 23–29.
52. Many interviews with legislators from these areas, 1973–80.
53. *Birmingham News*, May 7, 1947.
54. *Montgomery Advertiser*, May 17, 1947.
55. *Birmingham News*, Apr. 22, 1947.
56. *Mobile Press-Register*, July 8, 1949.
57. Confidential interview, Sept. 1978.
58. Confidential interview, July 1973.
59. Quoted in a confidential interview, Sept. 1978.
60. Confidential interview, May 1974.
61. Montgomery, July 1973.
62. *Dothan Eagle*, June 17, 1947.
63. *Birmingham News*, Feb. 7, Mar. 7, 1947; *Birmingham Post*, June 18, 1947; undated collection of editorials in Folsom personal files, ADAH.
64. *Birmingham News*, June 22, 1947.
65. Ibid., Aug. 18, 23, 1947; *Birmingham Post*, Aug. 19, 20, 1947.
66. *Birmingham News*, Aug. 28, 1947.

67. Ibid., Sept. 6, 1947.
68. Ibid., Sept. 12, 1947.
69. Ibid.
70. *Montgomery Advertiser,* July 24, Sept. 14, 19, 1947.
71. James E. Folsom, Montgomery, Sept. 1978; *Montgomery Advertiser, Birmingham Post,* and *Anniston Star,* Aug. 7, 1947. For Folsom's use of this issue in the self-starter campaign see *Birmingham Post,* Nov. 13, 1947.
72. Barnard, *Dixiecrats and Democrats,* 120.
73. *Montgomery Advertiser,* Oct. 28, 1947.
74. Ibid.
75. Ibid.
76. *Birmingham Age-Herald,* Oct. 29, 1947.
77. Ibid.
78. *Dothan Eagle,* Oct. 31, 1947.
79. *Birmingham Age-Herald,* Oct. 29, 1947.
80. *Birmingham Post,* Nov. 13, 1947.
81. Ibid.
82. *Birmingham News,* Nov. 4, 1947.
83. *Birmingham Post,* Nov. 13, 1947.
84. *Dothan Eagle,* Nov. 17, 1947.
85. *Birmingham Post,* Nov. 13, 1947.
86. *Montgomery Advertiser,* Nov. 21, 1947.
87. *Alabama Journal,* Nov. 3, 1947.
88. *Birmingham News,* Jan. 4, 1948.
89. Mid-December radio address reprinted in *Folsom's Forum,* Dec. 24, 1947, in Alabama Room, University of Alabama library.
90. *Montgomery Advertiser,* Jan. 1, 3, 4, 1948.
91. Ibid., Jan. 4, 1948.
92. Ibid., Jan. 8, 1948.

Chapter 6

1. Barnard, *Dixiecrats and Democrats,* 9, 12–16, 144–46.
2. Bartley, *Rise of Massive Resistance,* 280–81.
3. E. Black, *Southern Governors,* 189; Wilhoit, *Politics of Massive Resistance,* 91–92.
4. See Gilliam, "Second Folsom Administration," 338–48.
5. S. Fleetwood Carnley, Elba, July 1973 and July 1974, J. A. Carnley papers.
6. Barnard, *Dixiecrats and Democrats,* 96.
7. Ibid.
8. Folsom, *Speeches,* 100–104.
9. Jan. 30, 1948.
10. *Montgomery Advertiser,* Jan. 27, 1948.
11. Key, *Southern Politics,* 330.
12. *Birmingham News,* Jan. 30, 1948.
13. Ibid.
14. Folsom, *Speeches,* 108.
15. *Montgomery Advertiser,* Feb. 4, 1948.
16. *Dixiecrats and Democrats,* 106.
17. Feb. 28, 1948.
18. *Montgomery Advertiser,* Mar. 3, 1948; Huie, "Little Un" and *New Life to Live,* 22–31.
19. *Montgomery Advertiser,* Mar. 4, 7, 1948; James E. Folsom, Cullman, July 1974.
20. Huie, "Little Un," 66–72.
21. *Birmingham News,* June 30, 1948. Huie, Hartselle, July 1973.
22. *Montgomery Advertiser,* Mar. 12, 13, 1948; *Alabama Journal,* Mar. 11, 1948.
23. Ibid.
24. INS News Service, Mar. 12, 1948.

25. *Montgomery Advertiser*, Mar. 12, 1948.
26. Ibid., Apr. 14, 1948.
27. Ibid., Mar. 2, 1948.
28. Ibid., Mar. 20, 21, 29, Apr. 18, 1948.
29. Ibid., Apr. 6, 1948.
30. Ibid., Mar. 23, 1948; *Birmingham News*, Jan. 12, 1947.
31. Cullman, Apr. 1974.
32. Letter to Gessner T. McCorvey, Apr. 6, 1948, in Sparks file, ADAH. See also *Montgomery Advertiser*, Apr. 28, 1948.
33. Folsom-endorsed candidates for delegate-at-large included A. A. Carmichael, James E. Folsom, C. C. Horton, Dan J. Baker, John D. Morris, A. L. Patterson, and John C. Walters. The complete list of Folsom's presidential elector candidates included Forest Castleberry, Roy Mayhall, Robert B. Albritton, Bart J. Cowart, Tully A. Goodwin, Elvin C. McCary, J. E. Bains, J. A. Carnley, Verdo Elmore, Guy W. Hanna, and Thomas H. Maxwell.
34. *Montgomery Advertiser*, July 5, 1948; see also Barnard, *Dixiecrats and Democrats*, 111; *Baltimore Sun* account in *Montgomery Advertiser*, Aug. 2, 1948.
35. Key, *Southern Politics*, 335.
36. *Montgomery Advertiser*, July 15, 1948.
37. July 20, 1948.
38. *Montgomery Advertiser*, July 25, 1948.
39. Ibid., Sept. 7, 1948.
40. Ibid., Aug. 15, 1948.
41. Ibid., Aug. 17, 1948.
42. Ibid., July 21, 1948.
43. Ibid., Nov. 6, 1948.
44. Ibid. and Dec. 7, 1948.
45. Barnard, *Dixiecrats and Democrats*, 121.
46. The idea that Folsom was attempting to build an expanded future poor white and black constituency was commonly expressed in both of his terms. Gilliam, "Second Folsom Administration," 30, 41; interview with Sam Engelhardt, Montgomery, July 1974; citizen letters to Folsom in 1948, e.g., letter to Folsom from V. G. Appleby, July 30, 1948, Folsom official file, ADAH; *Montgomery Advertiser* editorial, Oct. 1, 1957; Luther Clantan, letter to the editor, *Montgomery Advertiser*, Jan. 22, 1958.
47. Folsom, *Speeches*, 114.
48. Strong, *Registration of Voters*, 22–23; Lawson, *Black Ballots*, 96–97.
49. Letter to Gessner T. McCorvey, with a copy to Frank Dixon from Wilkinson, Jan. 31, 1949, in Dixon files, ADAH.
50. Jan. 28, 1949, letter in Dixon files, ADAH.
51. Ibid.; for a similar perspective see John Temple Graves's column, *Birmingham Post*, July 27, 1949.
52. *Birmingham News*, Mar. 28, 1949.
53. *Montgomery Advertiser*, May 12, 1948.
54. Ibid., Mar. 4, 1949.
55. Ibid.
56. Ibid., Sept. 7, 1949.
57. Ibid.
58. *Birmingham News*, Jan. 12, 1950.
59. *Montgomery Advertiser* and *Mobile Register*, Feb. 12, 1949.
60. *Birmingham Post*, Mar. 24, 1949; see also *Montgomery Advertiser*, Jan. 2, 5, 1949.
61. *Montgomery Advertiser*, April 8, 1949.
62. Ibid., Mar. 9, 1949. The economy bloc members were R. J. Lowe (Madison); Albert Boutwell (Jefferson); Forrest Bridges (Macon); Albert Hughes (Geneva); J. Bruce Henderson (Wilcox); Preston Clayton (Barbour);

John E. Gaither (Cleburne); Graham Wright (Talladega); G. Robin Swift (Escambia); James B. Allen (Etowah); George Quarles (Dallas); Silas Cater (Montgomery); David U. Patton (Limestone); James S. Coleman, Jr. (Greene); W. A. Gulledge (Chilton); A. L. Patterson (Russell); and T. F. Burnside (DeKalb).

63. *Montgomery Advertiser*, Apr. 2, 1949.

64. Ibid., May 4, 1949; James E. Folsom, Cullman, July 1974.

65. *Birmingham Post*, May 21, 1949.

66. *Montgomery Advertiser*, May 7, 1949.

67. May 15, 1949.

68. *Montgomery Advertiser*, May 26, June 1, 8, 15, 1949.

69. Ibid., June 8, 1949.

70. Ibid., Feb. 23, June 20, 21, 1949; *Birmingham Post*, Feb. 21, 24, 26, June 20, 1949. The KKK cooperated by perpetrating a series of vicious beatings just before and during the legislative session. The unmasking bill was supported by many organized groups, including the Veterans of Foreign Wars and the American Legion, and Folsom, who, in one of his many comments on the matter, referred to the KKK as "a renegade bunch of hooded criminals" (*Montgomery Advertiser*, June 19, July 28, 1949).

71. *Montgomery Advertiser*, Aug. 14, 1949.

72. Ibid., July 17, 1949.

73. Folsom, *Speeches*, 165.

74. Ibid., 177.

75. Ibid., 183–84.

76. June 23, 1950.

77. In addition to examining the source materials documented throughout this and the previous chapter, an extensive quantitative analysis was conducted to determine the basis of support for the Folsom legislative program. This analysis focused on the demographic and electoral characteristics that the interview and other data sources suggested were associated with support for the Folsom program.

The interviews, official Folsom files, and newspaper coverage of the legislative sessions were used to identify the key elements of the Folsom program. Since the Alabama legislature pioneered the use of electronic voting machines, all floor votes relative to the programs were recorded roll-call votes, listed in the House and Senate *Journals*. Using these journals, support scores representing the percentage of votes for the governor's program on those program aspects that came to the floor for a vote of any kind (including procedural votes) were calculated for each county. These scores, therefore, represent public support for the program and are average scores if more than one individual represented a county. Separate scores were calculated for the House and Senate during each session of the legislature.

A regional breakdown of the support scores is totally consistent with the narrative presentation. North Alabama representatives and senators supported approximately one-half of the Folsom program in both sessions. The Black Belt counties had an average support score in the Senate of 35 and 27 percent in the 1947 and 1949 sessions, respectively, and House scores of 32 and 23 percent. Jefferson County Senate support was 45 and 0 percent and Jefferson County House support was 21 and 25 percent.

As one would expect from these figures, legislative support for the program was negatively correlated with percent nonwhite population (1947 House = −.38; 1949 House = −.56; 1947 Senate = −.32; 1949 Senate = −.45). As these correlations suggest, multiple regression analysis highlighted percent nonwhite as accounting for the most variance explained when demographic characteristics of the counties were used in an attempt to explain legislative support at the county level. The key electoral variable proved to be Folsom's support in the runoff primary. Runoff support was itself negatively correlated to percent nonwhite (−.72).

The overall evidence, both qualitative and quantitative, consistently supports the position that delegations with large nonwhite populations in their home counties were less supportive of the Folsom program than delegations from the predominantly white counties.

78. *Birmingham News,* Nov. 19, 20, 1949, Jan. 15, 22, 29, 1950.

79. Matthews and Prothro, *Negroes,* 148–52.

80. James E. Folsom, Montgomery, Feb. 1977; A. W. Todd (former commissioner of agriculture and industries), by telephone in Russellville, Jan. 1978. Agnes Baggett (former auditor) was interviewed in Montgomery, Feb. 1977, but she was unable to remember any pattern to Folsom's appointments. For indirect support of Folsom's and Todd's recollections see *Montgomery Advertiser* editorial, Nov. 23, 1955.

81. *Mobile Press-Register,* Mar. 17, 1950.

82. Confidential interview, Oct. 1980.

Chapter 7

1. Folsom mentioned this belief during several interviews.

2. Confidential interview, July 1973.
3. Confidential interview, July 1974.
4. Confidential intervieiw, Sept. 1974.
5. Confidential interview, July 1973.
6. Confidential interview, Apr. 1974.
7. Ward McFarland, Tuscaloosa, July 1973.
8. Confidential interview, June 1974.
9. *Dothan Eagle,* Mar. 16, 1947.
10. Letter [signature obscured], Jan. 6, 1947, Folsom official files, ADAH.
11. Jan. 21, 1947.
12. *Montgomery Advertiser,* July 13, 1947.
13. Ibid.; *Birmingham Post,* July 12, 1947.
14. Confidential interview with a reporter, Montgomery, July 1973.
15. *Birmingham News,* Apr. 10, July 13, 20, 1947.
16. Ibid., Apr. 10, 1947.
17. James E. Folsom, Cullman, July 1973. It is an illuminating commentary on Folsom's self-confidence that, upon hearing that one of the authors was about to make his first visit to the Alabama Department of Archives and History, Folsom's first response, after recommending that his personal files be examined, was to insist that the author review Hugh Sparrow scrapbooks that his office maintained.
18. Confidential interview, July 1974.
19. James E. Folsom, Cullman, July 1973.
20. Undated newspaper clipping in "Governor's Personal Book #1," scrapbook, Folsom personal files, ADAH.
21. *Birmingham News,* Nov. 15, 1946.
22. Ibid., Nov. 16, 1946.
23. James E. Folsom, Cullman, June 1973.
24. Ibid.
25. *Birmingham News,* Sept. 27, 1947.

26. *Alabama Journal*, Dec. 5, 1947, Jan. 7, 1948.
27. Ibid., Mar. 17, 1948.
28. Riordon, *Plunkitt of Tammany*, 3.
29. *Montgomery Advertiser*, Mar. 3, 1948.
30. Ibid., Aug. 21, 1948.
31. Confidential interview, Apr. 1980.
32. *Montgomery Advertiser*, Aug. 20, 1948.
33. Ibid.
34. Ibid.
35. Confidential interview, July 1974.
36. Ibid.
37. Act No. 1056, S. 1 Regular Session 1973 (*Acts of Alabama* 1973). Act No. 130, H. 24 Regular Session 1975 (*Acts of Alabama* 1975).
38. Confidential interview, Jan. 1974; *Birmingham News*, Mar. 7, June 12, 1947.
39. Confidential interview, Apr. 1974.
40. Confidential interview, Sept. 1973.
41. Confidential interview, July 1974.
42. *Birmingham News*, Feb. 22, 1947.
43. Confidential interview, July 1973.
44. Ibid.
45. Confidential interview, June 1974.
46. *Code of Alabama*, 1940, Title 55, Sections 85 and 179.
47. *Birmingham News*, Jan. 14, 1950.
48. Ibid.
49. A transcript of one such seminar, dated Apr. 17, can be found in Folsom personal files, ADAH.
50. Philip Hamm, Dothan, July 1974.
51. *Montgomery Advertiser*, Jan. 28, 1947; *Alabama Journal*, Nov. 1947.
52. *Birmingham News*, Sept. 7, 1947.
53. Revenue Survey Committee, "Alabama Revenue System," 14 in Folsom official files, ADAH.
54. *Montgomery Advertiser*, Aug. 7, 1947.
55. *Mobile Press-Register*, Oct. 10, 1947; *Montgomery Advertiser*, Oct. 28, 1947.
56. Oct. 24, 1947, letter in Folsom personal files, ADAH.
57. Philip Hamm, Dothan, July 1974.
58. *Montgomery Advertiser*, Aug. 4, 1949.
59. Ibid.
60. *Brewton Standard*, May 22, 1947; *Birmingham Post*, Feb. 11, 1947; *Birmingham Age-Herald*, May 5, 1947; and S. Fleetwood Carnley, Elba, Oct. 1980.
61. *Montgomery Advertiser*, May 5, 1947.
62. Confidential interview, July 1973.
63. Ransone, *Alabama Government Manual*, 266–67.
64. Alabama, Legislature, Special Legislative Committee Investigating Pardons and Paroles, "Report," 3.
65. Ibid.
66. *Montgomery Advertiser*, Mar. 19, 1951.
67. *Alabama Journal*, Jan. 14, 1951.
68. Alabama, Legislature, Special Legislative Committee Investigating Pardons and Paroles, "Report," 4, 19.
69. Ibid.
70. *Montgomery Advertiser*, Feb. 1, Mar. 7, 13, 1951.
71. The person who arranged these transactions was a former bank robber and honorary colonel in Folsom's state militia. *Montgomery Advertiser*, Mar. 7, 1951.
72. Alabama, Legislature, Special Legislative Committee Investigating Pardons and Paroles, "Report," 54.
73. Ibid., 34.
74. Ibid., 35.

75. Ibid., 38.
76. Ibid.
77. Ibid., 60, and *Montgomery Advertiser,* Feb. 20, 1951.
78. *Montgomery Advertiser,* Mar. 19, 1951.
79. Cullman, July 1973.
80. Confidential interview, July 1974.
81. July 30, 1951. Also *Montgomery Advertiser,* July 19, 1951.
82. *Montgomery Advertiser,* July 28, 1951.
83. Ibid., July 23, 1951.
84. Confidential interview in Montgomery, Sept. 1977.

Chapter 8

1. *Birmingham News,* Mar. 3, 22, 1950; *Montgomery Advertiser,* Mar. 5, 1950; *Dothan Eagle,* Mar. 19, 1950.
2. Edward deGraffenreid, Tuscaloosa, June 1973, and Carl Elliott, Jasper, Nov. 1979; *Birmingham Age-Herald* and *Montgomery Advertiser,* Mar. 23, 1950; *Birmingham News,* Mar. 22, 1950; *Alabama Journal,* Mar. 27, 1950.
3. Barnard, *Dixiecrats and Democrats,* 140; *Montgomery Advertiser,* Apr. 5, 1950.
4. *Birmingham News,* Mar. 22, 1950.
5. *Montgomery Advertiser,* Mar. 7, 1950.
6. Ibid., Mar. 24, 1950. See also Horace Wilkinson's comments in the Mar. 22, 1950, *Advertiser.*
7. Mar. 14, 1950, letter in Henderson papers, ADAH.
8. Letter to Henderson from Poole, Mar. 11, 1950, in Henderson papers, ADAH.
9. Ibid.
10. Ibid.
11. Folsom file, ADAH.
12. *Montgomery Advertiser,* July 29, 1951.
13. Letter to Gessner T. McCorvey from Walter J. Merrill, June 20, 1951, in Henderson papers. Merrill, an Anniston attorney, wrote that Pelham Merrill had "been one of the leaders in the fight to fairly apportion the representation in the Legislature, and neither he nor I can get up much steam over a proposition which is approached from the standpoint of pulling the Black Belt's chestnuts out of the fire on voter qualification, when the Black Belt is solidly behind the move to prevent the fair and honest thing with respect to reapportionment. For this reason, I have considerable doubt that Pelham will give any assistance to the voter qualification amendment until further avenues to secure some sort of just representation in the Legislature are explored." See also letter to Walter C. Givhan from Gessner T. McCorvey, June 22, 1951, in Henderson papers, ADAH.
14. *Montgomery Advertiser,* Sept. 14, 1951.
15. Ibid., June 21, 1951.
16. Confidential interview, July 1978.
17. Albert Boutwell, Birmingham, July 1974.
18. Alabama, Legislature, Interim Committee on Segregation, "Report." The committee membership also included J. Miller Bonner, Herbert Byars, Robert Randall, Jr., Ira Pruitt, and Jack Gallalee.
19. Ibid., 5.
20. Ibid., 3.
21. *Montgomery Advertiser,* Feb. 10, 19, 1952.
22. Ibid., May 10, 1952.
23. James E. Folsom, telephone interview, Cullman, Jan. 1982.

24. Jamelle Folsom, telephone interview, Cullman, Jan. 1982.
25. *Montgomery Advertiser*, Mar. 23, 1954.
26. Ibid.
27. Ibid., Apr. 23, 1954.
28. *Birmingham News*, Mar. 16, 1954; *Mobile Register*, Mar. 16, 1954.
29. *Montgomery Advertiser*, Apr. 30, 1954.
30. *Mobile Register*, Nov. 13, 1954.
31. Confidential interview, Sept. 1973.
32. *Mobile Register*, Feb. 13, 1954.
33. Ibid.
34. Twitty, *Y'All Come*, 167–69.
35. *Montgomery Advertiser*, Feb. 14, 1954.
36. Frady, *Wallace*, 103, and countless interviews.
37. Confidential interview, Montgomery, June 1974.
38. *Montgomery Advertiser*, Feb. 14, 1954.
39. Harrell Hammonds, Hayneville, Oct. 1982.
40. *Montgomery Advertiser*, Feb. 14, 1954.
41. Twitty, *Y'All Come*, 166–67.
42. Confidential interview, Sept. 1977.
43. Confidential interview, Aug. 1973.
44. Buster Hogan, Talladega, Oct. 1980.
45. Key, *Southern Politics*, 42–52.
46. *Montgomery Advertiser*, Feb. 14, 1954.
47. Ibid., May 7, 1954.

Chapter 9

1. James E. Folsom, Decatur, June 1974.
2. Wilhoit, *Politics of Massive Resistance*, 44.
3. *Montgomery Examiner*, Sept. 29, 1954.
4. *Montgomery Advertiser*, Jan. 18, 19, 1955.
5. James E. Folsom, Cullman, July 1974, and numerous other interviews.
6. Confidential interview, July 1974.
7. Hugh Sparrow, *Birmingham News*, Feb. 4, 8, 1955.
8. Albert Boutwell, Birmingham, July 1974; Sam Englehardt, Montgomery, Sept. 1976.
9. Sam Englehardt, Montgomery, Sept. 1976.
10. *Montgomery Advertiser*, Feb. 13, 1955.
11. *Birmingham News*, Feb. 18, 1955.
12. *Birmingham News*, Feb. 22, 1955.
13. *Montgomery Advertiser*, Feb. 25, 1955; *Alabama Journal*, Feb. 24, 1955.
14. Confidential interview, July 1974.
15. Ibid.
16. Ibid.
17. Albert Boutwell, Birmingham, July 1974.
18. Hamilton, July 1974.
19. Confidential interview, July 1973.
20. Confidential interview, Oct. 1975.
21. *Montgomery Advertiser*, Mar. 2, 1955.
22. Confidential interview, July 1974.
23. *Montgomery Advertiser*, Mar. 6, 1955.
24. Ibid., Mar. 25, 1955.
25. *Birmingham News*, Apr. 17, 1955.
26. *Birmingham Post*, Mar. 15, 1955.
27. *Montgomery Advertiser*, Mar. 13, 1955.
28. *Birmingham News*, Mar. 11, 12, 1955.

29. *Alabama Journal*, Apr. 1, 1955.
30. *Montgomery Advertiser*, Apr. 6, 1955.
31. *Alabama Journal*, Apr. 7, 1955.
32. *Montgomery Advertiser*, Apr. 13, 20, 1955.
33. Gilliam, "Second Folsom Administration," 164–65.
34. Quoted in ibid., 167.
35. James E. Folsom, Montgomery, Sept. 1977.
36. *Birmingham News*, June 2, 1955.
37. Ibid., June 1, 29, 1955; *Montgomery Advertiser*, June 2, 1955; *Alabama Journal*, June 7, July 29, 1955.
38. *Montgomery Advertiser*, June 1, 1955.
39. See Gilliam, "Second Folsom Administration," 219, and *Montgomery Advertiser*, June 25, July 2, 1955.
40. Gilliam, "Second Folsom Administration," 175.
41. *Montgomery Advertiser*, July 7 and 10, 1955.
42. Ibid.
43. For the maneuvering, see *Birmingham News*, Aug. 12, 1955, and *Montgomery Advertiser*, Aug. 14, 1955. The referendum campaign is covered in *Birmingham News*, Oct. 26, 27, 1955; *Huntsville Times*, Nov. 21, 1955.
44. Gilliam, "Second Folsom Administration," 182.
45. *Montgomery Advertiser*, June 22, 29, 1955.
46. Ibid., June 10, 25, July 7, 9, 1955.
47. Ibid., July 7, 8, 9, 1955.
48. Ibid., July 22, 1955.
49. Ibid., Sept. 4, 1951.
50. Ibid.
51. Ibid.
52. Gilliam, "Second Folsom Administration," 189–90.
53. Confidential interview, May 1974.
54. James E. Folsom, Cullman, June 1973.
55. Confidential interview, Montgomery, July 1973.
56. E. D. Nixon, Montgomery, July 1973.
57. Mrs. Parks had worked with various civil rights groups and with Nixon for several years. She must have known what he was trying to arrange, and what he would ask her to do after her release from jail (assuming that it had not been arranged in advance).
58. E. D. Nixon, Montgomery, July 1973.
59. *Montgomery Advertiser*, Dec. 7, 1955.
60. Thornton, "Montgomery Bus Boycott," 233.
61. *Montgomery Advertiser* and *Alabama Journal*, Jan. 10, 1956.
62. *Montgomery Advertiser*, Jan. 27, 1956.
63. *Dixiecrats and Democrats*, 53.
64. James E. Folsom by telephone, Jan. 1974; see Lewis, *King*, 29, 34, 36–37.
65. See also Gilliam, "Second Folsom Administration," 253–54. E. D. Nixon also denies that Folsom encouraged King to broaden his demands. E. D. Nixon, Montgomery, June 1974.
66. Harrell Hammonds, Hayneville, Oct. 1982.
67. E. D. Nixon, Montgomery, July 1973.
68. For example, *Alabama Journal*, June 4, 1960.
69. E.g., Frady, *Wallace*, 108–10.
70. Confidential interview, July 1974; James E. Folsom, Cullman, July 1974. House records show that Wallace voted not only for the self-starter (Sept. 18,

vote was 69–14) but on the same day against a constitutional convention as well.
71. *Birmingham News*, Jan. 18, 1956.
72. Ibid., Jan. 19, 1956.
73. *Montgomery Advertiser*, Jan. 26, 1956.
74. June 22, 1956.
75. *Montgomery Advertiser*, Feb. 4, 11, 1956.
76. *Birmingham News*, Feb. 4, 1956.
77. Ibid., Jan. 31, Feb. 2, 1956.
78. *New York Times*, Feb. 9, 12, 1956; *Birmingham News*, Feb. 1, 1956.
79. Folsom probably borrowed this remark from a Grover Hall, Jr., editorial.
80. James E. Folsom, Cullman, Apr. 1974.
81. *Montgomery Advertiser*, Feb. 11, 1956.
82. Henderson papers, ADAH.
83. *Montgomery Advertiser*, Mar. 1, 2, 1956; *Birmingham Post-Herald*, Mar. 2, 1956.
84. Wilhoit, *Politics of Massive Resistance*, 46–47; Gilliam, "Second Folsom Administration," 309; Bartley, *Rise of Massive Resistance*, 146.
85. Confidential interview, Mar. 1978.
86. Henderson papers, ADAH.
87. Gilliam, "Second Folsom Administration," 388.
88. Martin, *Deep South*, 21.
89. *Montgomery Advertiser*, Feb. 11, 1956.
90. *Birmingham News*, Feb. 11, 1956.
91. *Montgomery Advertiser*, Mar. 16, 1956.
92. James E. Folsom, Cullman, June 1973; *Montgomery Advertiser*, Mar. 25, 1956.
93. *Montgomery Advertiser*, Mar. 22, 1956.
94. Ibid., Mar. 29, 1956.
95. Ibid., Apr. 15, 1956.
96. Ibid., May 3, 1956.
97. Ibid., May 11, 1956.
98. Martin, *Deep South*, 109; *Birmingham Post-Herald*, Apr. 24, 1956.
99. *Montgomery Advertiser*, June 8, 1956; *Birmingham Post-Herald*, Mar. 6, 1956.
100. Confidential interview, Birmingham, Apr. 1974.
101. Quoted in Frady, *Wallace*, 107–8.
102. Confidential interview, July 1974.
103. Ibid.
104. Confidential interview, July 1973.
105. Ibid.
106. Confidential interview, July 1974.
107. *Montgomery Advertiser*, May 8, 1957.
108. Ibid., June 30, Oct. 1, 1957.
109. Oct. 1, 1957. See also Oct. 13, 1957.
110. Gilliam, "Second Folsom Administration," 537–38.
111. *Montgomery Advertiser*, Jan. 3, 1958.
112. Ibid., Dec. 8, 14, 18, 1957.
113. Ibid., Nov. 7, 1957.
114. Ibid., May 5, 1957.
115. Ibid., Sept. 15, 1957.
116. Ibid., June 23, 1957.
117. Ibid., July 27, 1957.
118. Ibid., Aug. 3, 1957.
119. Ibid., Aug. 15, 1957.
120. Ibid., Sept. 5, 1957.
121. Ibid., Sept. 7, 1957.
122. Ibid., Sept. 15, 1957.
123. Regional analysis of legislative

support scores for Folsom's second-term programs showed the same North Alabama–Black Belt support patterns that existed in the first term. The major difference was higher support for Folsom programs in both areas due to the larger number of bread-and-butter issues and the fact that many issues involving civil rights and civil liberties never got to the House and Senate floor for a vote. The Black Belt Senate figures were 42 percent (1955), 36 percent (1956), and 34 percent (1957 special sessions), and the House figures were 45, 21, and 46 percent during those same periods. North Alabama Senate figures were 81, 65, and 47 percent; North Alabama House figures were 72, 49, and 52 percent. The special session votes included several civil rights issues. Jefferson County figures fell between these regional levels. As in the previous term, legislative support for Folsom was negatively correlated with percent nonwhite population (1955 Senate = $-.63$; 1956 Senate = $-.54$; 1955 Senate = $-.39$; 1955 House = $-.61$; 1956 House = $-.69$; 1957 House = $-.17$). The lower negative correlations in 1957 and the lower support scores in both houses in that year again reflect the presence of civil rights and civil liberties issues and the growing intensity of racial issues within the state. Multiple regression analysis of demographic factors related to legislative support showed that the nonwhite variable explained more of the variance in support than any other variable. In the 1954 primary victory itself there had been a low to moderate positive correlation between percent nonwhite and county support for Folsom.

124. Confidential interview, Mar. 1979.

125. Confidential interview, July 1973.
126. Confidential interview, May 1974.
127. Confidential interview, July 1973.
128. Jan. 23, 1955.
129. James E. Folsom, Cullman, June 1973.
130. Ibid.

Chapter 10

1. *Montgomery Advertiser*, Jan. 29, 1955; James E. Folsom, Cullman, July 1974.
2. *Montgomery Advertiser*, Jan. 28, 1955.
3. Memoranda to Sam Engelhardt from Walter H. Craig, Mar. 4 and Sept. 29, 1959, in Engelhardt papers, ADAH; *Birmingham News*, June 24, July 1, 1956.
4. *Birmingham News*, July 1, Sept. 12, 1956.
5. Confidential personal interviews, July 1973 and July 1974.
6. *Montgomery Advertiser*, Feb. 12, 1956.
7. Confidential interview, July 1974.
8. Ibid.
9. Ibid.
10. *Birmingham News*, Aug. 10, 1955.
11. *Montgomery Advertiser*, Jan. 25, 1956; *Birmingham News*, Jan. 7, 8, 10, 15, 16, 19, 25, and 26, 1956.
12. *Birmingham News*, Jan. 29, 31, Feb. 1, 2, 3, 5, 10, 25, 1956; *Montgomery Advertiser*, Jan. 25, 1956.
13. Confidential interview, July 1974.

14. *Montgomery Advertiser,* Jan. 12, 13, 1956; *Birmingham News,* Jan. 12, 1956.
15. Ibid.
16. Confidential interview, July 1973.
17. Confidential interview, July 1974.
18. Folsom personal files, ADAH.
19. Henderson files, ADAH.
20. General Contractors Board File, Oct. 1, 1955–Sept. 30, 1956, Folsom official files, ADAH.
21. *Birmingham News,* June 24, 1956.
22. Confidential interviews, July 1973 and July 1974.
23. *Birmingham News,* Oct. 11, 1956.
24. Ibid., Oct. 11, 21, 1956.
25. Memoranda to Jake Jordon from James E. Folsom in "Governor's Emergency Fund File, Jan. 1955–Sept. 30, 1955," Folsom personal files, ADAH.
26. *Birmingham News,* Dec. 2, 1955.
27. Confidential interview, Apr. 1974. Folsom's brother Fred came out of his government service in considerably better condition than his famous brother. In 1960 he was ordered to pay $26,146.90 plus interest on taxes owed for the years 1948 and 1949. Virtually all of his income in this period came from such sources as "commissions" on goods sold to the state. See the *Montgomery Advertiser,* June 21, 1960.
28. Confidential interview, June 1974.
29. Confidential interview, July 1974.
30. Confidential interview, July 1973.
31. Confidential interview, Aug. 1973.
32. Rankin Fite, Hamilton, July 1974, and confidential interview, July 1974.
33. Confidential interview, July 1974.
34. Ibid.
35. Ibid.
36. Confidential interview, July 1973.
37. Confidential interview, Sept. 1977.
38. Frady, *Wallace,* 105, and James E. Folsom, Nov. 1980.
39. Frady, *Wallace,* 105.
40. Confidential interview, July 1974.
41. Ibid.
42. Confidential interview, June 1973.
43. Confidential interview, July 1974. There is some disagreement over Folsom's ability to remember names. Many believe that at his peak his memory was phenomenal, while others maintain that it was little better than average but that he could bluff people into believing he remembered their names.
44. Confidential interview, Aug. 1973 and July 1974.
45. *Mobile Press-Register,* Aug. 13, 1972; Stewart, *Tennessee-Tombigbee,* 1–2.
46. *New York Times,* Nov. 26, 1978; Morgan, *Dams and Other Disasters.*
47. Stewart, *Tennessee-Tombigbee,* 53.
48. *New York Times,* Nov. 26, 1978.
49. James E. Folsom, Cullman, July 1973.
50. See Stewart, *Tennessee-Tombigbee,* 11.
51. James E. Folsom, July 1973.
52. Austill and Baker, "Economic Feasibility Survey," Folsom official files, ADAH.
53. Construction of the docks was accomplished with the usual failure to select contractors through low-bid procedures and some overspending, but nothing on the scale of earlier scandals. See *Mobile Press-Register* stories for

Dec. 1958 and the *Birmingham News*, Dec. 11, 14, 16, 1958.

Chapter 11

1. *Montgomery Advertiser*, Mar. 23, 1958.
2. Ibid., Mar. 8, 1958.
3. Frady, *Wallace*, 121–22.
4. Bartley, *Rise of Massive Resistance*, 201.
5. *Montgomery Advertiser*, Dec. 6, 1958.
6. Quoted in Dorman, *George Wallace Myth*, 23–24; also see Yarbrough, *Judge Frank Johnson*, 62–72.
7. *Montgomery Advertiser*, Mar. 18, 1961.
8. Ibid.
9. This point was made forcefully in a *Montgomery Advertiser* editorial, May 19, 1961.
10. *Montgomery Advertiser*, May 21, 1961.
11. Ibid.
12. Ibid., May 22, 1961.
13. Ibid.
14. Ibid., May 24, 28, 1961.
15. Ibid., Apr. 16, 1961.
16. Folsom personal files, ADAH.
17. Newspaper reporter's notes, Montgomery.
18. Folsom personal files, ADAH.
19. *Birmingham Post-Herald*, Apr. 25, 1962.
20. *Montgomery Advertiser*, Mar. 4, 1962.
21. *Birmingham Post-Herald*, Apr. 12, 1962.
22. *Montgomery Advertiser*, Mar. 10, 1962.
23. Ibid., Mar. 9, 1962.
24. Ibid., Apr. 15, 1961.
25. Ibid.
26. Ibid.
27. Clipping in Folsom personal file scrapbook, ADAH.
28. Morris, "Clinical Notes," 41. "When he was told that he had been having Jacksonian seizures, he replied, 'That figures, I've always been a Jacksonian Democrat'" (40).
29. Confidential interview, Nov. 1978.
30. *Tuscaloosa News*, Mar. 16, 1974.
31. Morris, "Clinical Notes," 40–41.
32. Ibid., 41.

Chapter 12

1. Dye, *Politics, Economics, and the Public;* Dawson and Robinson, "Interparty Competition"; Sharkansky and Hofferbert, "Dimensions of State Politics"; Anton, *Politics of State Expenditures*.
2. Lederle, "Governors and Higher Education"; Jewell, "Governor as a Legislative Leader"; Kolesar, "Governor and the Urban Areas"; Alhberg and Moynihan, "Changing Governors"; Wood, "Metropolitan Governor."
3. Dye, "Executive Power."
4. Greenstein, *Personality and Politics*, 40–57; Easton, *Political System*, 1953.
5. In this chapter references to the South refer to the definition of the South found in Luttbeg, "Classifying the American States." All figures are based on calculations made from data found in the *Statistical Abstract of the United States*.
6. See Strong, *Registration of Voters*, 86–87.
7. Here and below we also compared Folsom to other Alabama governors using least squares trend analysis. Basi-

cally, this technique generates a trend line that best represents spending figures and then calculates the degree to which a particular year falls above or below the line. With few exceptions this approach highlights the same years as does the technique featured in the text.

8. *Montgomery Advertiser,* Feb. 8, 1959.

9. Permaloff and Grafton, "Road to Complexity."

10. *Montgomery Advertiser,* Feb. 12, Apr. 13, June 27, July 18, Aug. 2, 7, 1947; *Birmingham News,* Feb. 13, 1947; *Birmingham Post,* Mar. 15, Apr. 12, 1947; Reports of the Alabama Legislature's Interim Committee on Education and the Interim Committee on Finance and Taxation, 1947.

11. Dr. Austin Meadows, Montgomery, July 1978.

Appendix

1. Ricci, "Methodological Disputes," 162–69; Hunter, *Community Power Structure.*

2. Ricci, "Methodological Disputes," 152–62; Ehrlich, "Social Psychology of Reputations," 415–530; Hunter, *Community Power Structure,* 255–63.

3. Ricci, "Methodological Disputes," 170–72; Dahl, *Who Governs?* 89–103; Polsby, *Community Power.*

4. Frey, "Comment," 1081–1101; McFarland, *Power and Leadership.*

5. Bachrach and Baratz, "Two Faces of Power," 190.

6. Schattschneider, *Semi-Sovereign People,* 71.

7. Bachrach and Baratz, "Two Faces of Power," 191.

8. Wolfinger, "Nondecisions," 195.

9. Bachrach and Baratz, "Two Faces of Power," 195. See also Vidich and Bensman, *Small Town in Mass Society.*

10. Bachrach and Baratz, "Two Faces of Power," 195; Wolfinger, "Nondecisions," 1076; Frey, "Comment," 1096–97; Harris, *Political Power in Birmingham,* 40–56, 272–79.

11. Wolfinger, "Nondecisions," 1076; Frey, "Comment," 1097.

12. D'Antonio and Erikson, "Reputational Technique as a Measure of Community Power," 362–76; Presthus, *Men at the Top;* Domhoff, *Who Really Rules?* 14–36.

13. Bachrach and Baratz, "Two Faces of Power," 195.

14. Dahl, *Who Governs?* 11–86.

15. Bachrach and Baratz, "Two Faces of Power," 192–95; Crenson, *Un-Politics of Air Pollution,* 20–26; Barth and Johnson, "Community Power and a Typology of Social Issues," 269–70.

16. Bachrach and Baratz, "Two Faces of Power," 192.

17. Ibid.

18. Ibid., 195.

19. Ibid., 196; Dahl, *Who Governs?* 11–86; Aiken and Mott, *Structure of Community Power,* 19; Frey, "Comment," 1090–92.

20. Walton, "Systematic Survey of Community Power Research," 443–64; Freeman, et al., "Locating Leaders in Local Communities," 791–99; Presthus, *Men at the Top,* 50–63, 405–33; Ricci, "Methodological Disputes," 155–78.

21. Ricci, "Methodological Disputes," 155–78.

22. Domhoff, *Who Really Rules?* 125–27.

Bibliography

Primary Sources

Personal Interviews

Harlan G. Allen; Mabel Amos; Ruby Folsom Austin; Agnes Baggett; William Dean Barnard; Gould Beech; J. J. Benford; Jake Bonneau; Albert Boutwell; Melissa Folsom Boyen; Albert P. Brewer; A. K. "Temo" Callahan; S. Fleetwood Carnley; Thelma Folsom Clark; James S. Coleman; George Collier; Sam Collier; Edward deGraffenreid; Donald B. Dodd; Wynelle S. Dodd; Smith C. Dyar; Carl Elliott; Sam B. Engelhardt; J. Oscar English; Thomas Espy, Jr.; Lehman Farris; O. H. Finney; Robert Finney; Arthur Fite; Rankin Fite; Andrew Jackson "Jack" Folsom; Cecil Folsom; Jamelle Moore Folsom; James E. "Big Jim" Folsom; James E. "Little Jim" Folsom, Jr.; Robert "Bob" Folsom; Louis Friedman; A. G. Gaston; Wallace Gibson; Lowell Gregory; Kenneth J. Griffith; John J. Guthrie; Ralph Hammond; Harrell Hammonds; W. Guy Hardwick; George C. Hawkins; James Henderson; Miriam Hicks; Buster Hogan; Milo B. Howard, Jr.; William Bradford Huie; Ray Jenkins; Roland Johnson; James V. "Jake" Jordon; Hobart Key; Fuller Kimbrell; Robert "Bob" Kyle; Maynard Layman; McDowell Lee; Rachael Folsom Lichenstein; William "Bill" Lyerly; Ward McFarland; Knox McRae; Robert Matthews; Austin Meadows; J. Paul Meeks; E. D. Nixon; Cecil Noel; Eris J. Paul; W. G. "Gerry" Pruett; Noble J. Russell; Barrett Shelton; Barrett Shelton, Jr.; Kate Simmons; John Steifelmeyer; William Stewart, Jr.; Donald S. Strong; Rex Thomas; A. W. Todd; George C. Wallace; Ed Watkins; Daisy Windham; Jack Windham; Katherine Windham; Paul Windham; and others who prefer to remain anonymous

Alabama State Department of Archives and History: Papers and Files

Sam Engelhardt; Frank Dixon; James E. Folsom; Grover Hall; J. Bruce Henderson; Gordon Persons; Chauncey Sparks; George Wallace; Lurleen Wallace

Private Documents Collections

Judge J. A. Carnley Papers, held by Judge S. Fleetwood Carnley, Elba, Ala.; Folsom Family Papers and Letters, held by Melissa Folsom Boyen, Talladega, Ala.; Folsom 1936 and 1938 Congressional Campaign Files, held by Thelma Folsom

Clark, Elba, Ala.; Folsom Newspaper Clippings File, held by James E. Folsom, Jr., Montgomery, Ala.; Fuller Kimbrell Papers, Fayette, Ala.; Knox McRae Papers, Decatur, Ala.

Public Documents

Alabama. *Acts of Alabama.*
⎯⎯⎯. *Code of Alabama.*
⎯⎯⎯. House of Representatives. *Journal.*
⎯⎯⎯. Legislature. Interim Committee on Education. "Report." 1947.
⎯⎯⎯. Legislature. Interim Committee on Finance and Taxation. "Report." 1947.
⎯⎯⎯. Legislature. Interim Committee on Highways. "Report." 1947.
⎯⎯⎯. Legislature. Interim Legislative Committee on Segregation in the Public Schools. "Report." 1955.
⎯⎯⎯. Legislature. Legislative Interim Committee on Finance and Taxation. "Report." 1951.
⎯⎯⎯. Legislature. Prison Investigating Committee. "Report and Recommendations." Mar. 22, 1949.
⎯⎯⎯. Legislature. Revenue Survey Committee. "The Alabama Revenue System." January, 1947.
⎯⎯⎯. Legislature. Special Legislative Committee Investigating Pardons and Paroles. "Report." 1951.
⎯⎯⎯. Senate. Senate *Journal.*
"Economic Feasibility Survey of Proposed Inland Waterway Dock Facilities at Columbia, Decatur, Florence, Huntsville, and Walker County." Hurieosco Austill and Michael Baker, Jr. In Folsom Official Files, Alabama State Department of Archives and History.
Official Proceedings of the Constitutional Convention of the State of Alabama (May 21, 1901 to September 3, 1901). Wetumpka: Wetumpka Printing, 1940.

Newspapers

Alabama Journal; Alabama Magazine; Birmingham Age-Herald; Birmingham News; Birmingham Post; Brewton Standard; Dothan Eagle; Elba Clipper; Florence Times; Gadsden Times; Huntsville Times; Mobile Register; Montgomery Advertiser; Montgomery Daily Register; Montgomery Journal; Opp News; Tuscaloosa News

Secondary Sources

Articles

Ahlberg, Clark D., and Moynihan, Daniel P. "Changing Governors—and Policies." *Public Administration Review* 20 (1960):195–204.

Bachrach, Peter, and Baratz, Morton S. "Two Faces of Power." In *Political Power, Community and Democracy*, edited by Edward Keynes and David M. Ricci. Chicago: Rand McNally, 1970, 188–98.

Barnard, William. "The Old Order Changes: Graves, Sparks, Folsom and the Gubernatorial Election of 1942." *Alabama Review* 28 (July 1975):163–84.

Barth, Ernest A. T., and Johnson, Stuart D. "Community Power and a Typology of Social Issues." In *The Search for Community Power*, edited by Willis D. Hawley and Frederick M. Wirt. Englewood Cliffs: Prentice-Hall, 1974, 269–70.

Brownell, Blaine A. "Birmingham, Alabama: New South City in the 1920's." *Journal of Southern History* 38 (February 1972):21–48.

D'Antonio, William V., and Erikson, Eugene C. "The Reputational Technique as a Measure of Community Power: An Evaluation Based on Comparative and Longitudinal Studies." *American Sociological Review* 27 (June 1962):362–76.

Dawson, Richard E., and Robinson, James A. "Interparty Competition, Economic Variables, and Welfare Policies in the American States." *Journal of Politics* 25 (May 1963):265–89.

Dye, Thomas R. "Executive Power and Public Policy in the United States." In *The American Governor in Behavioral Perspective*, edited by Thad Beyle and J. Williams. New York: Harper and Row, 1972, 245–55.

Ehrlich, Howard J. "The Social Psychology of Reputations for Community Leadership." *Sociology Quarterly* 8 (Summer 1967):415–530.

Freeman, Linton C.; Fararo, Thomas J.; Bloomberg, Warner; and Sunshine, Morris H. "Locating Leaders in Local Communities." *American Sociological Review* 28 (October 1963):791–99.

Frey, Frederick W. "Comment: On Issues and Nonissues in the Study of Power." *American Political Science Review* 65 (December 1971):1081–101.

Gilbert, William E. "Bibb Graves as a Progressive, 1927–1930." *Alabama Review* 10 (January 1957):15–30.

Grafton, Carl. "Community Power Methodology and Alabama Politics." *Alabama Historical Quarterly* (Winter 1976):271–90.

―――. "James E. Folsom and Civil Liberties in Alabama." *Alabama Review* 32 (January 1979):3–27.

―――. "James E. Folsom's First Four Election Campaigns." *Alabama Review* 34 (July 1981):163–83.

―――. "James E. Folsom's 1946 Campaign." *Alabama Review* 35 (July 1982):170–99.

Grafton, Carl, and Permaloff, Anne. "Legislative Support for the Alabama Executive: Recurring Patterns and Changing Forces." Paper read at Midwest Political Science Association Meetings, Chicago, April 1981.

―――. "The Politics of Highway Construction: Testing the Conventional Wisdom." *Southeastern Political Review* 12 (Spring 1985).

Harris, Carl V. "Reforms in Government Control of Negroes in Birmingham, Alabama, 1890–1920." *Journal of Southern History* 38 (November 1972):567–600.

Hollis, Daniel W. III. "The Hall Family and Twentieth-Century Journalism in Alabama." *Alabama Review* 32 (April 1979):119–40.

Huie, William Bradford. "Little-Un—The Story of a Bastard." In *Wolf Whistle and Other Stories*, edited by William Bradford Huie. New York: Signet, 1956–59.

Jewell, Malcolm E. "The Governor as a Legislative Leader." In *The American Governor in Behavioral Perspective,* edited by Thad Beyle and J. Williams. New York: Harper and Row, 1972, 127–41.

Johnson, Evans C. "Oscar W. Underwood: A Fledgling Politician." *Alabama Review* 13 (April 1960):109–25.

———. "Oscar W. Underwood and the Senatorial Campaign of 1920." *Alabama Review* 21 (January 1968):3–20.

Jones, Allen W. "Political Reforms of the Progressive Era." *Alabama Review* 21 (July 1968):173–94.

Kolesar, John N. "The Governor and the Urban Areas." In *The American Governor in Behavioral Perspective,* edited by Thad Beyle and J. Williams. New York: Harper and Row, 1972, 240–45.

Lederle, John W. "Governors and Higher Education." In *The American Governor in Behavioral Perspective,* edited by Thad Beyle and J. Williams. New York: Harper and Row, 1972, 232–40.

Luttbeg, Norman R. "Classifying the American States: An Empirical Attempt to Identify Variations." *Midwest Journal of Political Science* 25 (November 1971):703–21.

Morris, John T., M.D. "Clinical Notes on His Excellency, James Elisha 'Big Jim' Folsom—Governor of Alabama (1947–1951 and 1955–1959)." *Journal of the Medical Association of the State of Alabama* 51 (January 1982):36, 39–41, 46.

Permaloff, Anne, and Grafton, Carl. "The Birmingham–Black Belt Coalition in Alabama Politics." Paper read at Southwestern Political Science Association Meetings, Dallas, March 1981.

———. "Road to Complexity: Understanding Alabama Highway Construction Politics, 1947–1975." Paper read at Southwestern Political Science Association Meetings, Fort Worth, April 1979.

Ricci, David M. "Methodological Disputes in the Study of Power." In *Political Power, Community and Democracy,* edited by Edward Keynes and David M. Ricci. Chicago: Rand McNally, 1970, 155–78.

Ruark, Robert C. "Big Kissin' Jim." *True,* September 1948.

Sharkansky, Ira, and Hofferbert, Richard I. "Dimensions of State Politics, Economics, and Public Policy." *American Political Science Review* 53 (September 1969):867–79.

Thornton, J. Mills III. "Alabama Politics, J. Thomas Heflin, and the Expulsion of 1929." *Alabama Review* 21 (April 1968):83–112.

———. "Challenge and Response in the Montgomery Bus Boycott of 1955–1956." *Alabama Review* 33 (July 1980):163–235.

Vaughan, Donald S. "Administrative Responsibility in Alabama." Unpublished monograph, University of Alabama, 1967.

Walton, John. "A Systematic Survey of Community Power Research." In *The Structure of Community Power,* edited by Michael Aiken and Paul E. Mott. New York: Random House, 1970, 443–64.

Wiener, Jonathan N. "Class Structure and Economic Development in the American South." *American Historical Review* 84 (October 1979):970–1006.

———. "Planter-Merchant Conflict in Reconstruction Alabama." *Past and Present* 68 (August 1975):73–94.

———. "Planter Persistence and Social Change: Alabama, 1850–1870." *Journal of Interdisciplinary History* 7 (Autumn, 1976):235–60.
Wolfinger, Raymond E. "Nondecisions and the Study of Local Politics." *American Political Science Review* 65 (December 1971):1063–80.

Books

Aiken, Michael, and Mott, Paul E., eds. *The Structure of Community Power*. New York: Random House, 1970.
Anton, Thomas J. *The Politics of State Expenditures in Illinois*. Urbana: University of Illinois Press, 1966.
Azbell, Joe. *The Riot Makers*. Montgomery: Oak Tree Books, 1968.
Barker, Lucius J., and Barker, Twiley W., Jr. *Civil Liberties and the Constitution*. Englewood Cliffs: Prentice-Hall, 1970.
Barnard, William D. *Dixiecrats and Democrats*. University: University of Alabama Press, 1974.
Bartley, Numan V. *The Rise of Massive Resistance*. Baton Rouge: Louisiana State University Press, 1969.
Bartley, Numan V. and Graham, Hugh D. *Southern Politics and the Second Reconstruction*. Baltimore: Johns Hopkins University Press, 1975.
Bass, Jack. *Unlikely Heroes*. New York: Simon and Schuster, 1981.
Bass, Jack, and DeVries, Walter. *The Transformation of Southern Politics*. New York: New American Library, Meridian Books, 1976, 1977.
Billington, Monroe Lee. *The Political South in the Twentieth Century*. New York: Scribner's, 1975.
Black, Earl. *Southern Governors and Civil Rights*. Cambridge: Harvard University Press, 1976.
Black, Hugo, Jr. *My Father: A Remembrance*. New York: Random House, 1975.
Cash, W. J. *The Mind of the South*. New York: Vintage, 1941.
Chester, Lewis; Hodgson, Godfrey; and Page, Bruce. *An American Melodrama*. New York: Viking Press, 1969.
Clark, Thomas D. *The Emerging South*. New York: Oxford University Press, 1961.
Cole, Taylor, and Hallowell, J. H., eds. *The Southern Political Scene 1938–1948*. Gainesville: Journal of Politics, 1948.
Crenson, Matthew A. *The Un-Politics of Air Pollution*. Baltimore: Johns Hopkins University Press, 1971.
Dahl, Robert. *Who Governs?* New Haven: Yale University Press, 1961.
Davenport, F. Garvin, Jr. *The Myth of Southern History*. Nashville: Vanderbilt University Press, 1967.
Dodd, Donald B. *Historical Atlas of Alabama*. University: University of Alabama Press, 1974.
Dodd, Donald B., and Dodd, Wynelle S. *Winston: An Antebellum and Civil War History of a Hill County of North Alabama*. Annals of Northwest Alabama, vol. 4. Edited by Carl Elliott. Birmingham: Oxmoor Press, 1972.
Domhoff, G. William. *Who Really Rules?* New Brunswick, N.J.: Transaction Books, 1978.

Dorman, Michael. *The George Wallace Myth*. New York: Bantam, 1976.
DuBose, John W. *Forty Years in Alabama, 1861–1901*. Montgomery: Alabama State Department of Archives and History, undated handwritten.
Dye, Thomas R. *Politics, Economics, and the Public*. Chicago: Rand McNally, 1966.
Easton, David. *The Political System*. New York: Knopf, 1953.
Ezell, John Samuel. *The South since 1865*. New York: Macmillan, 1975.
Farmer, Hallie. *The Legislative Process in Alabama*. University: University of Alabama Press, 1949.
Ferejohn, John. *Pork Barrel Politics*. Stanford: Stanford University Press, 1974.
Flynt, Wayne. *Cracker Messiah*. Baton Rouge: Louisiana State University Press, 1977.
Folsom, James E. *The Speeches of Governor James E. Folsom, 1947–1950*. Wetumpka, Ill.: Wetumpka Printing Co., undated.
Frady, Marshall. *Wallace*. New York: World Publishing, 1968.
Going, Allen J. *Bourbon Democracy in Alabama, 1874–1890*. Tuscaloosa: University of Alabama Press, 1951.
Goodwyn, Lawrence. *Democratic Promise: The Populist Movement in America*. New York: Oxford University Press, 1976.
Greenstein, Fred I. *Personality and Politics*. New York: Norton, 1975.
Hackney, Sheldon. *Populism to Progressivism in Alabama*. Princeton: Princeton University Press, 1969.
Hamilton, Virginia Van der Veer. *Alabama: A Bicentennial History*. New York: Norton, 1977.
Harris, Carl V. *Political Power in Birmingham, 1871–1921*. Knoxville: University of Tennessee Press, 1977.
Hawley, Willis D., and Wirt, Frederick M. *The Search for Community Power*. Englewood Cliffs: Prentice-Hall, 1974.
Hicks, John D. *The Populist Revolt*. Lincoln: University of Nebraska Press, 1961.
Huie, William Bradford. *A New Life to Live*. Nashville: Thomas Nelson, 1977.
Hunter, Floyd. *Community Power Structure*. New York: Doubleday-Anchor, 1953, 1963.
Ienman, Clarence P. *The Secession Movement in Alabama*. Montgomery: Alabama State Department of Archives and History, 1933.
Johnson, Evans C. *Oscar W. Underwood: A Political Biography*. Baton Rouge: Louisiana State University Press, 1980.
Key, V. O., Jr. *Southern Politics in State and Nation*. New York: Vintage, 1949.
Keynes, Edward, and Ricci, David M., eds. *Political Power, Community and Democracy*. Chicago: Rand McNally, 1970.
Kousser, J. Morgan. *The Shaping of Southern Politics: Suffrage Restriction and the Establishment of the One-Party South, 1880–1910*. New Haven: Yale University Press, 1974.
Lawson, Steven F. *Black Ballots: Voting Rights in the South, 1944–1969*. New York: Columbia University Press, 1976.
Lee, McDowell; Sterkx, H. E.; and Williams, Benjamin B. *The Role of the Senate in Alabama History*. Troy, Ala.: Troy State University Press, 1978.
Lewis, David L. *King: A Critical Biography*. Baltimore: Penguin Books, 1970.

Lineback, Neal G., and Traylor, Charles T. *Atlas of Alabama*. University: University of Alabama Press, 1973.
Link, Arthur, and Patrick, Rembert W., eds. *Writing Southern History*. Baton Rouge: Louisiana State University Press, 1965.
Long, Huey P. *Every Man a King*. Chicago: Quadrangle Books, 1964.
McFarland, Andrew S. *Power and Leadership in Pluralist Systems*. Stanford: Stanford University Press, 1969.
McGill, Ralph. *The South and the Southerner*. Boston: Little, Brown, 1959.
McMillan, Malcolm C. *Constitutional Development in Alabama, 1798–1901*. Chapel Hill: University of North Carolina Press, 1955.
Martin, John Bartlow. *The Deep South Says "Never."* New York: Ballantine, 1957.
Matthews, Donald R., and Prothro, James W. *Negroes and the New Southern Politics*. New York: Harcourt, Brace and World, 1966.
Mills, C. Wright. *The Power Elite*. New York: Oxford University Press, 1956.
Morgan, Arthur E. *Dams and Other Disasters*. Boston: Porter Sargent, 1971.
Newby, I. A. *Jim Crow's Defense*. Baton Rouge: Louisiana State University Press, 1965.
Polsby, Nelson. *Community Power and Political Theory*. New Haven: Yale University Press, 1961.
Presthus, Robert. *Men at the Top*. New York: Oxford University Press, 1964.
Ransone, Coleman B., Jr. *Alabama Government Manual*. University: Bureau of Public Administration, 1970.
―――. *The Office of Governor in the South*. University: Bureau of Public Administration, 1951.
Riordon, William. *Plunkitt of Tammany Hall*. New York: Dutton, 1963.
Rogers, William Warren. *The One-Gallused Rebellion: Agrarianism in Alabama, 1865–1896*. Baton Rouge: Louisiana State University Press, 1970.
Schattschneider, E. E. *The Semi-Sovereign People*. New York: Holt, Rinehart and Winston, 1960.
Sitkoff, Harvard. *The Struggle for Black Equality, 1954–1980*. New York: Hill and Wang, 1981.
Sosna, Michael. *In Search of the Silent South*. New York: Columbia University Press, 1977.
Stewart, William, Jr. *The Tennessee-Tombigbee Waterway*. University: Bureau of Public Administration, 1971.
Strong, Donald S. *Registration of Voters in Alabama*. University: Bureau of Public Administration, 1956.
Tindall, George Brown. *The Emergence of the New South, 1913–1945*. Baton Rouge: Louisiana State University Press, 1967.
―――. *The Persistent Tradition in New South Politics*. Baton Rouge: Louisiana State University Press, 1975.
Twitty, W. Bradley. *Y'All Come*. Nashville: Hermitage Press, 1962.
Vidich, Arthur J., and Bensman, Joseph. *Small Town in Mass Society*. Garden City: Doubleday, Anchor, 1958, 1960.
Wallace, Cornelia. *C'nelia*. Philadelphia: Holman, 1976.
Watson, Fred S. *Coffee Grounds*. Anniston: Higginbotham, 1970.

Wilhoit, Francis M. *The Politics of Massive Resistance*. New York: Braziller, 1973.
Williams, T. Harry. *Huey Long*. New York: Knopf, Bantam, 1969, 1970.
──────. *Romance and Realism in Southern Politics*. Athens: University of Georgia Press, 1961.
Woodward, C. Vann. *Origins of the New South*. Baton Rouge: Louisiana State University Press, 1951.
──────. *The Strange Career of Jim Crow*. New York: Oxford University Press, 1966.
Yarbrough, Tinsley E. *Judge Frank Johnson and Human Rights in Alabama*. University: University of Alabama Press, 1981.
Youngdale, James M. *Populism: A Psychohistorical Perspective*. Port Washington: Kennikat Press, 1975.

Dissertations and Theses

Gaither, Gerald Henderson. "Blacks and the Populist Revolt: Ballots and Bigotry in the New South." Ph.D. dissertation, University of Tennessee, 1972.
Gilliam, Thomas J., Jr. "The Second Folsom Administration: The Destruction of Alabama Liberalism, 1954–1958." Ph.D. dissertation, Auburn University, 1975.
Gross, Jimmie Frank. "Alabama Politics and the Negro, 1874–1901." Ph.D. dissertation, University of Georgia, 1969.
Huffman, Frank J. "Old South, New South: Continuity and Change in a Georgia County, 1850–1880." Ph.D. dissertation, Yale University, 1974.
Murray, William D. "The Folsom Gubernatorial Campaign of 1946." Ph.D. dissertation, University of Alabama, 1949.
Reed, Homer D. "The Government and Politics of Coffee County, Alabama." Master's thesis, University of Alabama, 1949.
Sparkman, John. "The Kolb-Oates Campaign of 1894." Master's thesis, University of Alabama, 1924.
Wagon, Judy Means. "Grover C. Hall, Jr.: Profile of a Writing Editor." Master's thesis, University of Alabama, 1975.
Wood, Robert C. "The Metropolitan Governor: Three Cases Inquiring into the Substance of State Executive Management." Ph.D. dissertation, Harvard University, 1950.

Index

Abernathy, Tom, 162
Agrarians, 48, 49
Agricultural Extension Service: Folsom's attempts to reform, 87–89; political role of, 63, 87, 90
Alabama: elite politics in, 38–55, 95–98
Alabama Constitution of 1868, 41
Alabama Constitution of 1875, 42, 47, 272 (n. 27), 274 (n. 66)
Alabama Constitution of 1901: 78, 95; as political control device, 49, 55, 78, 95; constitutional convention, 47–49
Alabama Farm Bureau Federation: opposition to Folsom's Auburn Board appointees, 88, 90; political role of, 63, 87, 90
Alabama governor: legislative role of, 77–78, 102
Alabama House of Representatives: composition of, 78; leadership of (1947–50), 82; leadership of (1955–58), 84–86; malapportionment of, 178, 284 (n. 13); organization of, 82, 178; speaker selection (1947), 84–85; speaker selection (1955), 178
Alabama Interim Committee on Segregation in the Public Schools, 166–67
Alabama Polytechnic Institute. *See* Auburn University
Alabama Senate: composition of, 78; leadership of (1947–50), 81–82, 86–87; leadership of (1955–59), 178; malapportionment of, 78, 95–99, 284 (n. 13); organization of, 81–82, 178; president pro tempore selection (1947), 82–83; president pro tempore selection (1955), 178
Alabama, localism in. *See* Localism: in Alabama
Alcoholic Beverage Control Board: composition of, 140; first term investigations of, 141–42; as source of funding, 93–94, 141, 217
Allen, James B., 102, 169
Antis: definition of, 180
Auburn University Board of Trustees, 87–88; blockage of Folsom appointees to, 88–90; Folsom appointments to, 88, 89–90, 100–101

Bankhead, John, 78
Barnard, William, 64, 80, 113, 121
Battles, Murray, 184, 212
Beck, Bill, 145; and the self-starter, 108; election to House speakership, 84–85; opposition to Folsom programs, 86, 99, 103
Beech, Gould: appointment to Auburn Board of Trustees, 88–90; background, 66; role in 1946 Folsom campaign, 64, 66, 103, 113, 137
Big Jim: development of nickname, 32
Big Mules, definition of, 22
Birmingham, Alabama: founding of, 46
Birmingham–Black Belt coalition. *See* Black Belt–Jefferson County coalition
Birmingham–Black Belt–Mobile coalition. *See* Black Belt–Jefferson County Coalition
Birt, Geoffery, 143

Black Belt: definition of, 1; furnishing merchants, 40–41; land ownership in, 39–40; overrepresentation of in Alabama government, 78, 95–99, 178, 284 (n. 13); reconstruction politics, 41–42; use of election fraud, 42–43, 45

Black Belt–Jefferson County coalition: basis of, 96–97, 180; causes of division, 165–66, 199; legislative activity, 85–86, 97–98, 195, 281–82 (n. 77), 288 (n. 123)

Black, Hugo, 50

Blake, Tom, 129

Bonner, J. Miller, 80, 118, 164

Boozer, Elbert, 64, 169

Bosses, 47–48, 49–50, 51

Boswell Amendment: declared unconstitutional, 123, 124; content of, 79–80; Folsom's opposition to, 68, 80; passage of, 80–81

Boswell, Frank, 137, 158

"Boswell, Jr.," 125, 128; and passage of, 164

Boutwell, Albert, 8; as Folsom program opponent, 180; freedom of choice plan, 189–90; as legislative leader, 190; political views of, 165, 180; as segregationist leader, 165, 166, 205; and the self-starter, 108

Boyen, Melissa Folsom, 169, 228, 234

Boykin, Frank, 18, 58; role in Folsom's 1936 campaign, 23–24; 1946 Senate campaign, 79

Brassell, J. W., 101

Brown v. Board of Education, 166, 177, 185, 187

Buck's Pocket, 168

Callahan, A. K., 184, 185

Calvin, Joe, 206

Campaign style: Alabama tradition, 31; Folsom innovations, 31–32, 36–37, 75–76; southern traditions, 31–32. *See also* Folsom, James E.: campaign techniques

Carmichael, Albert, 118, 132

Carnley, J. A.: as Folsom family political opponent, 12–13; in Folsom's 1936 congressional campaign, 21–22; influence on Folsom, 21–22; opposition to Boswell Amendment, 80; political views of, 13, 21, 270 (n. 28)

Carnley, S. Fleetwood, 137, 153

Carnley, Sarah. *See* Folsom, Sarah Carnley

Carwile, Henry J., 29

Catts, Sidney J., 31

Clark, J. Ross, 7, 23; death of, 182; in Folsom administrations, 94, 113, 139, 170

Clark, Thelma Folsom, 3, 7

Comer, Braxton Bragg, 50

Competitive bid bills, 206–7, 215, 216

Congress of Industrial Organizations (CIO), 58, 71

Connor, Eugene (Bull), 112, 230

Cooper, Roland, 181, 185

Corn shuck mop, 60. *See also* Folsom, James E.: use of symbols

Crop lien system, 40–41

Davis, Bryce, 214–15; as ABC Board head, 137, 140–41

Dawkins, Joe: as pro-Folsom legislator, 179, 184, 189, 195

Dawkins, Melvin, 141

DeGraffenreid, Edward, 161

DeGraffenreid, Ryan, 184, 185, 230, 232

Disfranchisement, 49, 79–80. *See also* Alabama Constitution of 1901, as political control device; Boswell Amendment; "Boswell, Jr."; Sayre election law

Dixiecrat Movement: 112, 126; Alabama's 1948 election ballot, 122; and bolters, 118; and delegate selection to 1948 Democratic National Convention, 112, 117, 118–19; and divisions between Folsom, Hill, and Sparkman, 119; and Folsom

loyalists, 118; and states rights, 121; at 1948 Democratic National Convention, 119–20; court actions against, 122–23; Folsom reactions to, 112–13, 130; segregationist loyalists, 118; southern Democratic convention, 120; voter reactions to in 1950, 161–63
Dixon, Frank, 28, 74, 155; and Boswell Amendment, 80; political beliefs of, 53, 54, 55; racial views of, 55
Drinkard, Roy, 158
Drinkard, William, 212; as finance director, 136; background of, 65, 136; role in finance department investigations, 143–44; role in Folsom elections, 65, 175; role in pardon and parole investigations, 155–58; role in state parks investigation, 214–15
Dunn, Loula, 137
Dunnavant, John, 4–5
Dyar, Smith, 106, 206

Eagerton, Ralph, 142–43, 144, 145
Educational funding, 98–99, 186, 187, 188, 206
Economy block, 127, 128, 129, 280–81 (n. 62)
Elite myths, 52–55, 121
Elites, political: development of in Alabama, 39–46; disintegration of, 256–59; 1901–46, 47–51; study of, 265–68
Elliott, Carl, 133, 220
Ellis, Handy, 121, 275 (n. 90); as 1946 gubernatorial candidate, 63, 71, 73
Ellis, Ruby Folsom, 57, 262
Emergency Aid Insurance Company, 24
Engelhardt, Sam: and School Placement Bill, 186; as Black Belt leader, 165; as opponent of Folsom programs, 180–81; political views of, 165, 180; as state Democratic Party chair, 235–36; and White Citizens' Councils, 199, 201–2

Farmer, Hallie, 77, 96
Faulkner, James, 169, 226
Field, Marshall, 88
Finney, O. H., 184; in Civil Works Administration, 16; in 1936 congressional campaign, 20–21; in Folsom administrations, 137, 212; in gubernatorial election (1946), 64, 66
Fite, Rankin, 129, 184, 195; elected House speaker, 178; as Folsom legislative leader, 181, 189
Folsom, Andrew Jackson (Jack), 237, 241
Folsom, Carl, 20, 58
Folsom, Cecil, 182
Folsom, Eulala Cornelia Dunnavant, 5–6, 66
Folsom, Fred, 4, 7, 23; in Folsom administrations, 139; income tax investigations of, 182, 289 (n. 27)
Folsom, Jamelle Moore, 139; as campaigner, 169, 241; marries Folsom, 119; meeting Folsom, 69–70
Folsom, James E.: administrative style, 16, 20–21, 133–36, 146, 150, 154, 158, 159, 160, 213, 216; and alcohol, 57, 58, 100, 105, 198, 202, 204, 218–19, 221, 228; arrest of, 167–68; attitude toward campaigns, 105, 114–15; attitude toward the press, 144; attraction to voters, 75, 105–6, 173; behavioral excesses and eccentric behavior, 83–84, 104–5, 114–15, 147, 203–4, 217, 218–19; campaign techniques, 22–23, 30–32, 36–37, 59–62, 64–65, 67–68, 103, 174–76, 232–33; in Civil Works Administration, 15–17, 270 (n. 14); college years, 6–10; congressional campaign (1936), 18–24; congressional campaign (1938), 24–25; criteria for personnel choices, 133–36; and death of Ross Clark, 182, 203; and death of Sarah Carnley Folsom, 56–57; as delegate to 1944 Democratic National Convention, 57–

Folsom, James E. (*continued*)
58; and desegregation of the University of Alabama, 197–98; and Dixiecrat Movement, 112–13, 116, 118–19, 120, 122–23, 129–30; drifting, 10–11; early years, 1, 3–6; first campaign, 14–15; gubernatorial campaign (1942), 27–37; gubernatorial campaign (1946), 59–76; gubernatorial campaign (1954), 168–76; gubernatorial campaign (1962), 230–36; gubernatorial campaign (1974), 237–40; honesty of, 136, 145–146, 149, 158, 170, 218; impact as governor, 100, 244–54, 259, 263, 290–91 (n. 7); inaugural speech (1946), 81; illnesses of, 235, 236, 240–41; and John Sparkman, 79; legislative program of (1947–50), 87–90, 97–98, 98–99, 101, 102, 127, 128; legislative program of (1955–58), 178–91 *passim;* legislative slate (1954), 174–75; legislative tactics of (1947–50), 81–85, 99, 125–27; legislative tactics of (1955–59), 177–78, 179–182, 191, 208–9; and Lister Hill, 79; mansion and other funds, 149–50, 217; marries Jamelle Moore, 119; marries Sarah Carnley, 24; meets Jamelle Moore, 69–70; in Merchant Marine, 10–11, 56; move to North Alabama, 25–27; opposition to President Truman, 57–58, 110–11, 116; opposition to racism, 227–28; out of office (1958–62), 167–68; paternity suit against, 114; platform (1942), 33; platform (1946), 62; political views, development of, 4, 5, 8, 13, 16–17; presidential campaign, 110–12, 115–16; racial views, 62, 68, 73, 109, 209, 230-32, 241; relationship with children, 169, 203, 228, 237; rhetoric of, 171–72, 174; television appearance (1962), 234–35; use of humor, 68, 72, 106, 170, 171, 173, 174, 201, 232; use of radio and television, 107–8; use of symbols, 60–62, 67, 72–73, 170–71, 174; views on civil rights, 110–11, 130, 157, 160, 210, 229–30; views on criminal justice system, 130, 157, 159–60; views on democracy, 81, 210; views on economic structure, 16, 19, 127; views on loyalty, 134–35; views on loyalty oaths, 128–29; views on voting rights, 130–31, 132, 163, 200, 205, 209–11; views on women's rights, 132, 210; and voter registration, 131; voter support base (1942), 33–34, 36; voter support base (1946), 70, 74–75; voter support base (1954), 173, 176; working with, 16, 147, 218–19; in Works Progress Administration, 17–18. *See also* Patronage
Folsom, James E., Jr. (Little Jim), 234, 236–37, 241, 255
Folsom, Joshua Marion, 3–4
Folsom, Melissa. *See* Boyen, Melissa Folsom
Folsom, Robert (Bob), 11
Folsom, Sarah Carnley: courtship of, 12–13, 15; death of, 56–57; marries Folsom, 24
Folsom, Thelma. *See* Clark, Thelma Folsom
Freedom of choice plan, 189–90
Freedom riders, 229–30, 231
Friedman, Louis, 146, 228
Friends and neighbors politics. *See* Localism

Gallion, McDonald, 230
Gilliam, Thomas, 197, 199
Givhan, Walter, 102
Glass, Brooks, 138
Goodwyn, Joe, 187
Goodwyn Plan, 187–88
Got Rocks. *See* Big Mules
Grant, George, 161
Graves, Bibb: as 1942 gubernatorial

candidate, 27, 28; as Progressive leader, 50, 51
Graves, John Temple, 73, 126
Gray, Fred, 196
Griffith, Kenneth J., 28–29; in 1942 gubernatorial campaign, 27–28, 33; political beliefs of, 27–28
Grooms, Hobart, 197
Gullatte, Winston, 169

Hackney, Sheldon: analysis of 1901 constitutional convention, 47–49
Hall, Grover, Jr.: coverage of 1946 Folsom campaign, 64; views on Folsom, 64, 102, 103, 108, 113, 115, 149; view on 1948 National Democratic Convention action, 119–20
Hamilton, Virginia Van der Veer, 25
Hamm, Philip J., 133; background, 8, 102, 137, 151; as commissioner of revenue, 113, 118, 151–52; 1950 gubernatorial campaign, 162, 163; U.S. Senate campaign of, 113
Hammond, Ralph, 202, 221; in Folsom administration, 212–13
Hammonds, Harrell, 212
Hardwick, Guy, 127, 129, 145, 178
Hawkins, George, 178, 179, 195, 215
Heflin, J. Thomas, 50, 51
Henderson, J. Bruce, 129, 162–63, 169, 198, 199, 217; and Boswell Amendment, 80; family history, 82; in opposition to Folsom programs, 86, 90, 99, 101, 163; political beliefs of, 53–55, 82–83; as president pro tempore, 82–83; racial views, 82–83, 86–87; selection as president pro tempore of Senate, 82, 83; and self-starter campaign, 108
Hill, Lister, 163; anti–civil rights role, 122; and Dixiecrat Movement, 116, 117, 118, 119, 122, 161; opposition to Boswell Amendment, 80; role in Sparkman's 1946 election, 79; voter support for, 79

Hogan, R. E. ("Buster"), 175
Horn, W. LaRue, 99, 212
Hudson, R. F., 162
Huie, William Bradford, 29, 114

Ingram, Bob, 230
Inland docks, 224, 225, 289–90 (n. 53)
Internal Revenue Service investigations, 170, 182
Inzer, Clarence, 85

Johnson, Judge Frank M., 227
Johnson, Roland, 60, 67
Johnston, Christine, 114
Johnston, Joe, 49
Jones, Bob, 161
Jones, Thomas Goode, 44–45
Jordan, Jake, 191

Key, Hobart, 59, 75
Key, V. O., Jr., 26
Kilby, Thomas E., 50
Kimbrell, Fuller, 171, 181; as finance director, 212, 215
King, Martin Luther, Jr.: and Montgomery Bus Boycott, 193–94
Kissin' Jim: development of nickname, 32, 105, 114–15, 147–48
Knox, John B., 52
Kolb, Reuben, 44–45
Ku Klux Klan, 50–51, 275 (n. 88), 280 (n. 70)

Lamberth, Broughton, 118, 126, 129; as Senate president pro tempore (1955–58), 178, 184
Langon, Joe, 122, 129
Legislative support for Folsom: first term, 281–82 (n. 77); second term, 228 (n. 123)
Liquor companies: as funding source, 94–95
Localism: in Alabama politics, 25–26; in Folsom campaigns, 33–36
Long, Henry S., 125
Long, Huey, 32, 61

Lucy, Autherine, 196–97, 198
Lyerly, Bill, 148, 221; background, 75, 136–37; in Folsom administrations, 136, 150, 170, 212; meeting Folsom, 65–66; role in Folsom campaigns, 65, 68–69

McCorvey, Gessner, 53, 118; as chair, Democratic party, 117; Folsom's support of, 117; political views of, 53, 54, 124; reaction to Boswell Amendment overturn, 124; views on race, 124
McFarland, Ward: as highway director, 92, 137, 138; background, 65, 137; in Folsom administration, 212; in 1946 gubernatorial election, 65
McKay, Charles, 200
McMillan, Malcolm C., 42
McRae, Knox, 212
Malone, Wallace, 101, 126
Manor, Pitt Tyson, 191, 226
Meadows, Austin: and educational funding, 183, 186, 188, 206; evaluation of Folsom's impact, 252
Metcalf, Neil, 220–21
Mitchell, J. B. (Jake), 138
Montgomery Advertiser, 33, 52, 128, 185, 233
Montgomery bus boycott, 192–93, 196; Folsom's role in, 193–94
Moore, Jamelle. *See* Folsom, Jamelle Moore
Mullin, Atticus, 33, 59
Murray, William D., 57
Myers, Polly Ann, 196

NAACP: court cases against, 206; legislation against, 185–89
Nelson, Herman, 138, 212
Nixon, E.D., 58, 196; and Montgomery bus boycott, 192
North Alabama: definition of, 1; disfranchisement of, 54
Nullification resolution, 195, 200

O'Daniel, W. Lee, 32, 61
Old age pensions: Folsom's attempt at reform, 181–83; Townsend Plan, 19
Owen, C. C. (Jack), 169

Pardon and Parole Board, 154–60
Patronage, 90–91, 126, 135, 136, 139–40, 145, 148–49, 214; and cash payments, 93–94; and legislative activity, 90–95, 102, 214, 215–16; and patronage jobs, 92, 139–40, 213; and purchases, 143, 213–14, 215, 216, 289–90 (n. 53); and roads, 91–92, 125–26
Patterson, Albert, 118, 126, 227
Patterson, John: background, 226–27; as governor, 229–30; 1958 gubernatorial campaign, 226
Persons, Gordon: as governor, 163–64; 1946 gubernatorial campaign, 64; 1950 gubernatorial campaign, 141
Pick, General Lewis, 222
Pinkston, Charles, 171
Planters, 48
Plunkitt, George Washington, 143
Political elite. *See* Elites, political
Poole, Joe, 80; as 1946 gubernatorial candidate, 63, 71; as Black Belt leader, 51; ties to J. Bruce Henderson, 83, 162–63
Populism: birth of, 43; history in Alabama, 43–46
Powell, Adam Clayton: visit to governor's mansion, 194, 197, 200–201
Price, Annie Lola, 132
Progressives, 48–50
Property tax reform, 102, 151–53, 186–87

Rains, Albert, 161
Ransone, Coleman, 77–78
Reapportionment: Folsom's attempts at, 97–98, 102, 196; sixty-seven senator bill, 97–98, 131, 164

Relative's Responsibility Act, 183
Right-to-work law, 184–85
Rives, Richard, 80
Road construction: Folsom's programs, 101, 178–79; politics of, 91–92, 179–80, 207–8. See also Patronage: and roads
Roberts, Escar, 184
Robison, Vaughan Hill, 208
Rodgers, Ed, 145

Sayre election law, 45–46
School Placement Bill, 186, 188–89
Segregationist legislation, 186, 188–90, 195, 205–6; Folsom's reaction to, 210, 211
Self-starter: advocates of campaign for, 106–8; explanation of, 102; Folsom's campaign against, 103–6, 107–8; Folsom's view of, 103
Shelton, Barrett, Sr., 152
Sherlock, Chris, 30, 33, 145
Sixty-seven senator bill. See Reapportionment
Skidmore, E. W., 184, 208
Social Darwinism. See Elite myths
Southern Farmer, 88
Sparkman, John: background of, 79; and Dixiecrat Movement, 116–17, 118, 119, 161; opposition to Boswell Amendment, 80; Senate campaigns of, 79, 113; voter support for, 79
Sparks, Chauncey, 76, 80, 117, 162; as 1942 gubernatorial candidate, 27, 33, 35, 51
Sparrow, Hugh, 126, 141, 195
Spies, Thomas, 146
States rights, 121
Steagall, Henry B., 18–19, 23–25
Steifelmeyer, John, 30, 59
Strawberry Pickers, 59, 103, 169
Suds bucket, 59. See also Folsom, James E.: use of symbols
Sweet, Henry, 169–70
Swift, Robin, 145

Tax reform, 102, 151, 183–84, 207–8. See also Goodwyn Plan
Tennessee-Tombigbee Waterway, 222–23; Folsom's role in, 222–23, 225
Thomas, Rex, 107, 173
Thompson, Ira, 66
Truman, Harry S.: civil rights actions of, 110, 112–13
Turner, Howell, 155

University of Alabama: desegregation of, 196–98

VanAntwerp, Garet III, 184, 187
Vardaman, James K., 31
Vinson, Glen D., 155–58
Voter Qualification Amendment. See "Boswell, Jr."
Voter registration: Folsom's actions on, 131, 244–45; restrictions on, 45–46

Wade, R. R., 138
Wallace, George C., 84, 121, 126, 171, 230; as Barbour County judge, 227; break with Folsom, 194; gubernatorial campaign (1958), 226; gubernatorial campaign (1962), 230, 232, 233; role in 1948 Democratic National Convention, 120; gubernatorial campaign (1974), 237
Welfare administration, 147
Welfare funding, 98–99
Wells, Eugene, 212
White Citizens' Councils, 200, 201; birth of, 199; use of violence, 201–2. See also Sam Engelhardt
Wilkinson, Horace, 80, 124
Williams, Aubrey, 88, 103
Williams, T. Harry, 84
Wiregrass: definition of, 1; political tradition of, 1
Wood, J. Emmet, 158

Young Democrats: Metcalf campaign, 220–21

www.ingramcontent.com/pod-product-compliance
Lightning Source LLC
Chambersburg PA
CBHW030128240426
43672CB00005B/61